Growing up, Jim McConkey was enthralled by his parents' tales of the Depression, WWII, and McCarthyism. In 1967, he graduated from the George Washington University with a degree in journalism, and cut his authorial teeth staff writing for Disabled Sports USA, which does sports and recreation for people with physical disabilities. After his parents' deaths, he resolved to write their story, basing it on hundreds of saved letters and extensive reading into the history of their time. Jim lives in Pennsylvania with his wife, Diana.

In loving memory of my parents, Anna and Darel, and my departed siblings, Pat, Helen and Mary.

To my wife, Diana, for her patience and support.

Jim McConkey

Anna and Darel

AUSTIN MACAULEY PUBLISHERS®

LONDON • CAMBRIDGE • NEW YORK • SHARJAH

Ordering Information
Quantity sales: Special discounts are available on quantity purchases by corporations, associations, and others. For details, contact the publisher at the address below.

Publisher's Cataloging-in-Publication data
McConkey, Jim
Anna and Darel

ISBN 9798886938982 (Paperback)
ISBN 9798886938999 (ePub e-book)

Library of Congress Control Number: 2024900716

www.austinmacauley.com/us

First Published 2024
Austin Macauley Publishers LLC
40 Wall Street, 33rd Floor, Suite 3302
New York, NY 10005
USA

mail-usa@austinmacauley.com
+1 (646) 5125767

20241119

I want to thank Will Slater for his proofreading, copyediting, and numerous pointed comments on my manuscript. I thank Richard Saunders for allowing me to see the manuscript of his now-published biography of Dale Morgan, with its many vital details on the man who was possibly my father's best friend in life. I thank the staff of the University of California's Bancroft Library at Berkeley, California, for arranging the loan of microfilm of my father's letters to Dale Morgan. I am also grateful to Reverend Nathaniel Gadsden for his patient counsel on the lives and aspirations of African Americans during the nineteen-teens, twenties, thirties, and forties.

Chapter One

I Remember Ma(ma)
Pop(pa) Too

"We need to demythologize our parents."
—John Bradshaw, Pop Psychologist

MY PARENTS WERE JUST ABOUT the wisest people I knew. Had the nation erected a marble statue to my father, I would not have been surprised. I wasn't surprised either by the small, closed-casket funeral to which fortune had brought us on that freezing, snowy, Groundhog Day in 1961, in the "almost visible" town of Lovettsville, Virginia, six miles by air, fifteen by ground, from Harper's Ferry, West Virginia. He'd always worn a bemused expression, as if the world was more to be chuckled at than railed against. Grown men were unembarrassed to say they loved him. He was fifty-five. I was seventeen, called to bear pall without having had an adult conversation with him.

Recollections welled up randomly. In the earliest, I'd wet the bed. *Oh, no, I thought, not again,* or the nearest equivalent a two- or three-year-old was capable of. Now I had to get a parent out of bed. Why that should have mattered to a two- or three-year-old I don't know, but it did. My father answered the call. He was patient, helpful, nonjudgmental. After changing the bed, he asked if I wanted anything else. I wanted "a half and a quarter of a glass of milk"— the proportion had been going through my head. "Oh," said my father, "three quarters?" Yes! Three quarters! He brought me the milk and returned to sleep.

He had his family's high, broad brow. He had dark, wavy hair combed straight back with a handsome widow's peak. Never having attained his six feet, I would ever have looked up to him.

The minister read Pop's favorite literary passage from *The Crock of Gold*, by Irish writer James Stephens. "Justice is the maintaining of equilibrium," it began. It was a childhood refrain I found impossible to understand. It had become his favorite while he was in his twenties. Maybe I'd understand it in mine; but, having gotten off on the wrong foot, took fifty years to see the scales of justice in "the maintaining of equilibrium." Justice, Stephens said, is not human but natural law. The concept would have been highly satisfying to my father.

The bright red coat my mother wore at the funeral was the only coat she had, and there wasn't supposed to be a funeral anyway. He'd loathed the mortuary industry and wanted to be cremated, but a family friend had dissuaded her. She would continue living in that narrow community, he said. Cremation would have turned it against her. The general-store owner refused to attend anyway, because of her compromise solution—a closed-casket service.

My mother was smart and humorous, too, though less obviously than my father. She prospered from his glow. "If it hadn't been for your father," she confessed, "I'd have been a wallflower for..." but didn't finish the thought.

"Wallflower?" I hadn't realized we dignified the concept.

The only makeup I ever saw her use was lipstick. There was a powder puff on her bureau. She wore nylons and a bra when we went out, but cared more about what was in her head than what was on her face. My parents' default was ever to solve the affairs of the universe.

We weren't huggy-kissy. Affection showed through playful, "gotcha" barbs, "I've been thinking…." "Uh, oh, *thinking* again." Sympathy cards and valentines were second-hand sentiments. You didn't let strangers express them for you.

Patriotism had to be approached with care. Being born American might make you luckier than some, but it didn't make you better. That was up to you. The country didn't make the people great; the people made the country great. The founding fathers gave us a great framework, but it was what we did with it that counted. Patriotism is not worshipping the flag; it's honorable conduct in our daily lives.

They waxed nostalgic over the "Kilgore Committee," (which investigated

An arresting studio portrait

"cartels," whatever those were); over "WPA" and the "Writer's Project" (two different names for the same thing?), the "Depression," "The War;" and "Roosevelt." An arresting studio photo of my father, Scotch-taped to walls in our various homes, was part and parcel of the larger whole.

We went to the movies a couple of times a year. I don't remember ever going to an amusement park, though we did go to the circus once. We didn't get a television until 1960, and even then, it was for something more important than entertainment. But we never seemed to get bored.

The job well done was its own reward. No task was too small for total commitment—even changing a light bulb—with one exception: in my mother's world, housekeeping was no match for the affairs of the universe. *Sanitation* was important—she was crazy for disease prevention. But tidiness? With five miniature hominids running riot, housekeeping was a complete waste of time. Messiness ruled. Unfortunately, it masked the sanitation, and some judged us for it.

Pop had a mission to ensure that no dinner fork suffer bent tines. Whether at home or dining out, if his fork's tines were misaligned, his butter knife would be levering them true. He would turn the implement this way and that, making adjustments as needed till it was back in fighting trim.

They were hounds for grammar. "Where's it at?" always fetched, "Between the 'a' and the 't' on preposition street."

A family friend once expressed amazement that Pop could hold adult conversation with children crawling over, under, and around him.

Our various houses groaned under cases rife with books. Pop read bedtime stories to my younger brother and me—*Winnie the Pooh* (my teddy bears were all named "Pooh.") My younger brother was Jerry, nicknamed "Buster," but I don't remember his bears' names. Our older brother, Pat's, was named Boolisser after our Aunt Margaret's bear, which had survived her childhood and now sat slumped atop a highboy in her grownup house. Margaret was our mother's younger sister.

Don't think our parents never had to apply counterinsurgency measures while transforming us from miniature anarchists into modestly civilized human beings. I don't remember being all that rebellious myself—pretty much happy to go along with the program—but then, one tends to think well of oneself, doesn't one? Some of my siblings were less compliant, but on the whole, we were among those fortunates who *liked* their parents, while many of our contemporaries bridled at parental conservatism, lack of imagination, and irredeemable materialism. We actually had fun growing up.

Pop was the youngest of eight kids, born May 9, 1905, and reared on a West Virginia farm. It would have been nine kids, but his twin brother died in infancy. There was never a question but that West Virginia was the best place on Earth to be from. This may sound strange to people who think West Virginia is where your house is on wheels and your car is on blocks, but Pop had his reasons that we'll get to.

His parents named him Darel. In 1962, at the movie *The Longest Day*, an alternative spelling penetrated my awareness. What point, I asked, was Mr. Zanuck, the movie's producer, trying to make with that D-A-R-R-Y-L nonsense?

"McConkey" was in its own class, rhyming with donkey and looking like monkey. From us kids' earliest school days, it was worth great mirth to our classmates. Still, for our mother, Anna, it must have been a vast improvement over her own hilarious "Schuddeboom."

She was born in Holland, March 14, 1908. Holland is why our Aunt Margaret's bear was named "Boolisser." Ma wasn't the people person my father was, but she was a rock. No, she was a boulder. In fact, the way she held the family together during my father's final illness and our dive into poverty, she might be called a megalith.

Pat, my older brother, said that Ma's father, "Gramps," was in the Dutch reserves completing his army stint when World War I broke out. By then, married with two daughters, he said to hell with war and legged it to America. I was in my fifties before learning that wasn't true. When Archduke Franz Ferdinand was assassinated in June 1914, touching off the war, Gramps had been in America nine months, and our grandmother, with Ma and Margaret, for eight.

Pat also said that Gramps went to work for Du Pont making explosives for the war he'd just fled, and that part has basis in fact. When Gramps registered for America's military draft, he gave his occupation as "carpenter" with E. I. Du Pont De Nemours and Co., Hopewell, Virginia. The plant made gun cotton; an explosive six times more powerful than black powder.

He was built like a boxer, and once bet he could load something—what is unclear—weighing three hundred pounds into a wheelbarrow single-handedly. He won the bet but ruptured himself doing it, and for the rest of his days wore a cumbersome leather truss, which in his heavy Dutch accent he insisted on calling a "trussell."

That's *my* mother?

He joked about his days as a "damned furriner" and laughed at a cow pie's being called a "Dutchman's razor." He had a poor sense of smell, and said, "I don't smell good."

There's probably not a kid alive who thinks his or her parents are anything but impossibly old. Old people were old because they *wanted* to be, not because they *had* to be. But in some early pictures, my mother is positively stunning. "That's *my* mother?" I gasped.

Ma and Pop lived in sin for three years before he made an "honest woman" of her—or rather she made an honest man of him. He was married and separated when they met, and his divorce wasn't final till three years later. She once hid him in a closet when Gramps showed up unexpectedly. Another time, she told me, Gramps tried to run him down with his car. The story diminished neither man in my jejune vision.

My father relished being Irish, with the bit o' devilment the heritage implied. His humor was barbed velvet, and showed among other things in some essays he titled *McAesop's Fables*. He spoke of going into business selling "ten-foot poles not to touch things with." When we pestered our parents to "buy me this" and "give me that," he hung the moniker, "the gimme gang," on us. Once, when the "gimmies" got too much, he curtly stated, "In two words, *no*."

I learned later in life that our ancestor came not from Ireland but Scotland. Scotland? Who wanted to be from dour old Scotland, after Ireland with its fairies and leprechauns? Pop preferred Ireland and cooked our ancestry. If a place gets your fancy, be from it. Where's the harm?

Legendary among my parents' exploits were their summers on an island in the Potomac, living in an army-surplus tent. Among their papers was a blueprint, white line on a blue field, of a ten-foot sailing dingy. I understood Pop had always meant to build it but never did. In my fifties, I found a photo of him actually making it—on the island with the tent behind him.

We didn't believe in the Tooth Fairy and we didn't believe in Santa Claus, but every Christmas Eve Pop read us *The Night Before Christmas*, and we could not have been more enchanted had we believed it true. Pop's family had perpetrated Santa Claus on him, and he had wondered how that fat man could get into the house through the stove pipe. When he realized his parents had *lied*, he was hurt and disillusioned, and swore that no child of his would suffer that indignity. The magic of Christmas was not a whit diminished by knowing Santa's pedigree. We loved the story *and* knew the truth, while others groped in darkness.

Ma and Pop decorated the tree and wrapped our presents Christmas Eve after we had gone to bed, so everything was new and cozy and cheery when we descended in the darkness before dawn to the glow of tree lights. Even with little sleep, they delighted in our delight. They took the tree down New Year's Day. It always seemed strange that other people had trees up long before they were supposed to, and didn't take them down until long after they should have.

As axiomatic as our disbelief in Santa Claus was Pop's spontaneous conversion to agnosticism at age thirteen. They kept telling him that if he confessed, he would feel better. So he confessed, and kept waiting to feel better, and never did. So, he gave up on religion and started studying ants. Some things just aren't knowable. We never went to church with one glaring exception. At Easter, 1948, in the sleepy little town of Burke, Virginia, nestled in the Fairfax, Annandale, Springfield triangle (stand-alone towns then, with farms between), we dressed up and went to church.

That was it. We never went again as a family, though playmates occasionally hijacked one or another of us into going with them. Years later, a friend of Pat's told him, "You grew up with an anti-religious bias," and I think that is true. Our parents claimed their bias was against *organized* religion, but I think it extended to religion generally.

Pop loved a fireplace. I don't remember a house without one. Ah, the grownups sitting after dinner by the hearth, lighting pipes or cigarettes, coffee at the elbow, talking of strange and wonderful things. I loved sitting on the floor listening to them. What marvels inhabited the grownup mind. Pop's father, who besides being a farmer had been a cabinet maker, had built the rocker Pop now used. His father had made it for his bride, Pop's mother, to "rock her babies in." I still have that rocker.

Gramps and Pop were polar opposites politically. Gramps became a Republican when Roosevelt "made" Henry Ford fly the Blue Eagle; Pop became a Democrat when the New Deal gave him a job. They never reconciled. Gramps was always citing some "very inter-resting ark-tickle" in the conservative *Saturday Evening Post*. He loved telling of the WPA telegram requesting "MORE SHOVELS."

"OUT OF SHOVELS," came the reply. "TELL MEN TO LEAN ON EACH OTHER." When Gramps visited, Pop hauled out the dominoes, and the two interacted without having to interact. Gramps would tally the scores in his head, aloud. It was always impressive.

He was slightly under average height with a café au lait complexion, and would have been built like a fireplug except fireplugs aren't square. Gramps was very square, starting with broad, square shoulders. Even at seventy years, his biceps bulged, his abs rippled, and his pecs were firm and full. When Ma and Margaret were kids, he would hold his arms out straight and let Ma swing on one and Margaret on the other. Though I resemble my mother's side of the family, genetics declined to favor me with that physique. And Gramps wasn't complete without a cigar in his mouth.

He was always good to us kids, and my parents never said a word against him. Contrary hints emerged over time, but in memory, Gramps remains swathed in a protective shroud that persists only slightly thread-worn.

Chapter Two

Awakening

B UT LOOK AT ME, running on about things that happened years along without telling how it all started. Well, how it *all* started would be indelicate, but Ma broke her ankle just before delivering me, September 15, 1943. We were living in Lincolnia, Virginia, just west of Alexandria.

All I remember of Lincolnia is the bed-wetting. Pat is reported to have "walked out" of a second story window, though how you "walk out" of a window was never explained. He survived. In 1945, we moved to Alexandria—509 Fontaine Street—where I began learning valuable life lessons. Sitting in the front yard with Pat and Helen (my older sister). Pat said, "You can eat dirt," with a *whoever said you couldn't?* tone of voice.

Sure, I thought, *whoever said you couldn't?* and ate some, proving the postulate. I declined seconds, however. It didn't taste all that good and was impossible to chew. I don't know whether Pat ate any. I assumed he did, but maybe he didn't.

We had a white cat named Bambi who produced endless litters of kittens. Bambi, Pop quipped, was "a girl who can't say no." I didn't know what he meant, but knew it was supposed to be funny. A neighbor gave a pet show, and I took Bambi with a blue bow that Ma had tied around her neck. I got stung by a bee on the way and went back home.

Pop's book—*Out of Your Pocket: the story of cartels*—came out while we were on Fontaine Street. "You were three and I was forty-one when this book came out," he wrote in my copy. "There are no cartels in the world of three years old. They are *one* of the hard things you find out later." I later wondered why my copy's back cover was sliced several ways and Scotch-taped back together. It took me sixty years to realize that the slasher was probably my own, three-year-old self armed with scissors.

Ma and Pop's fourth child was born on Fontaine Street the year we moved. They named him Tommy, which is what Pop's family had called him. Why they called Darel Tommy I don't know. It figures nowhere in the three proper nouns they labeled him with, but call him Tommy they did.

Unfortunately, this Tommy arrived with a heart defect and survived only nine months. Helen found him dead in his crib. Ma bore a grudge against the medical profession ever afterward. The day before Tommy died, the pediatrician had told her she needed to get a quantity of fluid into him over twenty-four hours. "Do you know how impossible it is to get fluid into a fussy baby that doesn't want it?" she said. Maybe she felt that the medical professional had dumped the problem on her. Maybe she felt she had been held accountable for the outcome. The episode seared her deeply. Maybe that's why she subscribed to *Prevention* magazine, which went into print four years after Tommy's death. We've made a lot of strides in nutrition; *Prevention* was a trailblazer.

Health food—in spirit if not always in practice—was present for as long as I can remember. "Do you good and help you, too," Pop liked to say. If you peeled an apple, you threw away the best part. Ma cooked salt-free, and I never missed it till I left home and started using it myself. "Eat to live, don't live to eat," she said, and was one of those rarities who could do it. Later, I loved telling people that my mother was into health food: she thought food, like medicine, in order to be good for you, had to taste bad. It wasn't entirely fair, but I liked the joke.

The health-food mindset didn't stop our parents from smoking. In addition to cigarettes, Pop smoked a pipe—most men did. I always looked forward to the end of the evening meal, when Pop took out his pipe, filled it, and lit it with his chrome-plated Zippo that closed with a distinctive clink. I loved the smell. Maybe I was pre-addicted, living in that cloud. Ma had smoked right through her pregnancies.

Today it's hard to imagine a time when people *didn't* see anything wrong with smoking, but such a time there was. Even the medical profession had no clear idea how bad it was. Some doctors encouraged expectant mothers to smoke to settle their nerves. Whatever else smoking may or may not do, it does settle the nerves.

My first driving lessons came at a tender age in our 1934 Plymouth. I was between Pop and Ma, mesmerized by the keys dancing in the ignition switch. The dashboard dropped straight down from the windshield and the key stuck straight out. I reached and pulled it free, shutting the engine off. "Never do that," Pop said, firmly but without reproof. Another time, it was the gearshift knob, a shiny, black ball atop a plain rod sticking straight up from the floor and vibrating most enthrallingly. I reached for it and shifted the car into neutral. "Never do that," Pop repeated. Those were my first driving lessons.

Some neighbors were visiting, and a kid and I were playing in, over, and around that Plymouth like a big, flop-eared dog. The car's door hinges stuck out from the body, opening and closing like the jaws of a vice. I closed one on my playmate's finger. He screamed hideously. I tried opening the door, but that particular handle was balky. I ran for help.

Dale Morgan and Jimmy, summer 1947

Pop popped the door in a trice. The next time I saw the kid, his finger was encased in a huge bandage. The memory still gives me the willies.

Then there was the time we were driving home along Russell Road, Dale Morgan, a highly congenial family friend who was stone deaf, at the wheel. You "talked" to him by writing notes. I was in the back seat by the passenger-side door. My best reconstruction has me dozing and dreaming we'd stopped at a store. I started to open the door, heard Helen yell, "Jimmy, no!" my replying, "I want to get out, too," and stepping onto the pavement racing below me.

The car's "suicide" door—hinged at the rear so the rush of air yanked it open—expedited my exit. I don't remember the impact, rolling, skidding, pain, or any of that. I gave chase while Ma tried frantically signaling Dale to stop. Next, Pop was carrying me into the house, and Helen was crying, "Is he going to die? Is he going to die?" Obviously, by the "friction burns" down the length of my forearms, I'd skidded. The scabs were awesome.

Chapter Three

Burke

IN 1948, we moved to Burke, Virginia. The house sat on an acre of ground, a broad lawn separating it from the barely paved street serving our five-house neighborhood—three handsome residences, bookended by the Lintons' tarpaper shack as you entered, and "Uncle Bill's" tarpaper shack up at the dead end. Southern Railroad tracks ran parallel on the other side of the street, and beyond them was an open field, over which lay the town center consisting of a church, a general store, and a post office. Envelopes with, "McConkey, Burke, VA.," were fully addressed. I was four years old.

Our house was a turn-of-the-century frame with shiplap siding, white with green trim and shutters, colors all but universal to the style, which architecture unhelpfully calls "Eclectic." A porch ran across the front and around one side. Two gables crowned the second floor. Back of the house was a lily pond with goldfish and frogs, and a faux-log playhouse which we never used. The garage was corrugated-metal painted green. Behind it was a duplex chicken house.

At the property's rear, a vegetable garden covered the lot's entire width. Each spring, a rawboned local named "Lick" Cameron turned the soil with his bay Percheron and single-bottom plow, and Ma and Pop worked the plot all summer. Garden-fresh vegetables were significant staples of those years.

We were eighteen miles out of D.C. Tree frogs sang us to sleep. In the spring, tortoises migrated én masse. The life cycle of the frog—egg to tadpole to adult—played out in the lily pond. The Milky Way was clearly visible at night.

We peopled the chicken house with many hens and two roosters. The roosters fought and it wasn't pretty. Lord Plushbottom—named for a faded plutocrat in the *Gasoline Alley* comic strip—was the hands-down alpha male. We separated them—one to each side of the duplex—but they continued drawing blood through the fence. So, Pop dispatched the omega to the stewpot, and the harem devolved to Lord Plushbottom.

Lord Plushbottom

When a hen showed signs of "setting," she would find herself ensconced in a "brooder box"—a sort of doghouse affair with a small, enclosed, outside run—incubating a selection of eggs. After three-weeks, out would pip a half dozen or so of the cutest, yellow-down peepers you ever saw.

Unfinished portrait

The Burke house had a sun room where Pop staked out his study, though flotsam from the rest of the house threatened to overwhelm his claim. A desk with a crippled roll-top stood heaped with papers. A spindly, government-surplus typing stand managed to support a magnificent, shiny black, standard, manual typewriter with "Royal" emblazoned in gold letters, solid as the Rock of Gibraltar and heavy as a ship's anchor. Such a mechanical marvel! The clack of typewriter keys was ever music to my ears. Thirty years after replacing my manual with the word processor, I still miss the sound.

In the study hung a signed and numbered print of Elizabeth Shumateoff's unfinished portrait of FDR. I had no idea who he was, but he looked very judgmental and I wondered why my parents had it.

Witnessing a catastrophe

Another print was even worse—a group of fashionable people in auditorium seats witnessing a catastrophic event. Supposedly, it was an audience being moved by a symphony, but I'll never shake that first impression.

Our neighbors stage left, the McKennas, had the first television we ever saw. They also had a wind-up Victrola. We had neither. We sampled "Howdy Doody" and "Hopalong Cassidy," and even then found "Howdy Doody" pretty dumb. We didn't miss TV; there was plenty else to do. Still, sometimes at school kids would burst out laughing at the mere mention of Milton Berle or Red Skelton, and we'd feel a bit left out.

Our neighbors stage right, the Lymans, had a lawn party. "Want a hot dog?" Pop asked.

"A what?"

"A hot dog."

"What's a hot dog?" Sort of a long Vienna sausage, which we sometimes ate, but it didn't taste like one. What we really had a lot was creamed tuna fish, which, when made with peas, became "peed" tuna. The canned broccoli, which Ma boiled twenty minutes to murder any lingering trace of the botulism to which canned goods could be heir, did little to enhance the plate. In fairness, the garden furnished significant nourishment, and she canned much of its produce. Her occasional shad-roe cakes were a treat.

Pat and Helen had their tonsils out. There was talk of getting mine out, but it never happened, so I regularly got tonsillitis—strep throat which Ma soothed with fresh-squeezed orange juice in ice which she wrapped in a dish towel and crushed with Pop's mallet—high fevers, complete bed rest, and penicillin. I *liked* penicillin pills and chewed them before swallowing. Thomas Lucas, M.D.—"Dr. Luke"—with his bow tie and pencil mustache, checked in from time to time.

Mothers could treat anything. Puncture wounds—I stepped on nails with sickening regularity. Behind the playhouse was the scrap lumber pile, with materials for any imaginable project. Unfortunately, nobody bothered to remove nails, they just tossed the scraps back there and I stepped on them. The cure was soaking the foot in Epsom salts water as hot as you could take it.

Punctures could heal first on the outside, sealing in the lockjaw. Soaking helped keep the outside open while the inside healed. Soaking and tetanus shots. Mothers just knew these things. There were daily doses of foul cod-liver oil. Sometimes it took Ma and Pop together to get the stuff into us. Surrender, eventually, proved the lesser of two evils. *Prevention* magazine probably gets credit for that bit of unpleasantness.

We lived by the railroad tracks, and nothing could have been more thrilling. From 1948 to 1951, when we left for Mexico, we had a front-row seat on the steam era's grand finale. No spectacle could beat a steam locomotive at the highball, whistle screaming for the grade crossing. The ground shook, smoke billowed, and cinders flew, getting in our hair and sometimes our eyes, inflicting tiny burns on tiny arms. We would race to the front fence, or at night bolt from our beds to see the sparks and the firebox glow. We learned the boxcars, gondolas, coal cars, flatcars, tank cars, the tender and caboose. C&O, B&O, Santa Fe, Norfolk Southern logos were as familiar as Safeway and Woolworths. Pat became a certified train freak and never recovered.

Our parents loved classical music. We kids could never understand why. One Saturday they tried listening to the opera. Our howls of protest fixed that, and they never tried it again. Another time, they took us to an open-air concert. I fidgeted through the whole ordeal and could not have been more relieved when it was over. They never took us to another one of those either.

It was Pat, under the spell of a disreputable pal named Eddie Thurman, who brought home country music, and that was what stuck, even more than rock 'n' roll, which was just taking shape. Our parents once indulged Pat's predilection for the bumpkin genre, and took us to the Saturday "Lawn Party" of radio station WARL in Arlington, Virginia, with up-and-coming Jimmy Dean and his Texas Wildcats.

I later learned to appreciate classical music, along with folk, rock, jazz (which our parents couldn't stand), blues, Indian classical, but there remains in my heart a special place for country. I'm sorry. I am not responsible. My bruther done it.

Somewhere along the line, we acquired our very own "Man Who Came to Dinner." His name was Phil. He came to dinner and stayed two years, until we left for Mexico. He was easygoing and friendly. He built a cabinet for dishes at one end of the kitchen. He'd be working on it when we came home from school. On mature reflection, with fifteen years of carpentry under my belt, I'd say it was expertly done, even though I was only six or so at the time. But we kids learned very little of him.

Exactly one week before I started school, on August 29, 1949, the Soviet Union exploded its first atomic bomb.

Pop loved to drive. Thousands do, but we didn't know that; his pleasure seemed special, and some drives qualified as real adventures—twisty little two-lane roads with no guard rails, hairpin turns just inches from fathomless precipices, in his beloved West Virginia. To a child, whose eye-level barely overtopped the bottom of the car window, the road's edge would be climbing the mountainside one minute, only to disappear when curving the other way, leaving a ravenous, open void from which Pop rescued us time after flawless time.

He instilled respect for the craft of driving. If someone went roaring by, out would come his homespun, "A man in a hurry has nowhere to go." It seemed a wise thing to say, and I always thought I'd understand it when I grew up, but the older I get, the less sense it makes. But the lesson took. He modeled driving, like so much else, as a craft, and none of us, even in our teens, was ever tempted by speed. If his love of driving was not unusual, that last fact may well be.

They told us that the roadside signs exhorting, "Don't be a Litterbug," were there for good reason. "We're *inside* litterbugs," Pop would proudly announce as candy wrappers and peanut bags swirled around our feet.

Four-lane roads were almost nonexistent. Sometimes you'd get behind a tractor trailer going five miles an hour on an endless upgrade. If the way ahead was clear, the driver would wave you by. Or you'd get stuck in single-lane traffic while negotiating road repairs. Flagmen didn't have walkie-talkies. The last car in line simply took the flag and delivered it to the flagman at the other end. Pop discharged that responsibility many times.

The best adventure was driving an old logging road up Spruce Knob, West Virginia's highest peak. "Hang onto your uppers," Pop would call as we skirted boulders and bounced through streambeds. Now *that* was an *adventure.* In 1966, I took my future wife up Spruce Knob. The road was paved and the summit had a parking lot! I felt cheated. Also light-headed. Spruce Knob is 93 percent the altitude of Denver, Colorado.

Ma was terrified of cars and never learned to drive. To her, the automobile was a deadly projectile with a two-ton throw weight.

We'd traded the fourteen-year-old Plymouth for a nine-year-old Studebaker while still on Fontaine Street. In July 1948, a month after moving to Burke, we drove it to Wisconsin where Pop taught a two-week summer course at the University of Wisconsin, Madison, based on his book, *Out of Your Pocket.*

We picked up Pop's sister, Gladys, in West Milford, West Virginia, and took her with us, settling into a tourist cabin off the university campus. Pop taught his class, though we kids weren't paying much attention. We took a tour of the Wisconsin Dells's glacier-carved rock formations in a solid, varnished, wooden tourist launch. The cabin was enclosed, and I thought, *If this thing sinks, there'll be no way out.* The rocks *were* unique.

There were lots of things for sale at the Dells. Pat and I tried on Indian regalia and Pop took our pictures, but we didn't buy them.

On the way home, we drove down Lake Michigan's west shore and stopped to browse the beach of a body of water we couldn't see across. Pop said something about the curvature of the earth, and I saw, or imagined I saw, just the upper part of a ship way out on the horizon.

We drove *under* the Detroit River into Canada, and then crossed back into the United States at Niagara Falls. The roar of the falls was discombobulating, and the rush of water made me feel I was racing upstream while standing still. Helen remembered going on the *Maid of the Mist*, but I don't. Pop said, "The falls made the small fry so excited that we had to take them away."

Then we were home.

Pop was a member of the Burke Volunteer Fire Department, even its president one year. Off would go the siren, and the volunteers dropped what they were doing, like Minutemen, jumped in their cars, and flew to L&M Grocery and "Old Red." The fire department, when we arrived, consisted of a

1930s-era pumper, "Old-Red," parked next to L&M Grocery in the town's center.

That was it. It filled its tank in Pohick Creek, a hundred yards up the road toward Simpson's Hill (over which stood the elementary school). One day in school, we watched Old Red fly by, siren

Old Red leads the firehouse parade

wailing. Soon it came back for a refill, then back to the fire. Three or four times it returned. That may have been when the department upgraded—a real fire house with two new engines and paid staff—the Curtis brothers. Each summer they held a homemade carnival—sack races, ring toss, no Ferris wheel or other rides—that included an auction with a wonderful toothless old auctioneer. "Come on, folks….Them engines cain't run on water!" We bought a radio/record player at that auction. AM only and 78 rpm records. A record "album" really was an album, a book. Each leaf was a sleeve that held one record—about two and a half minutes per side.

A Thanksgiving turkey shoot—with targets standing in for turkeys—raised yet more money.

Not only was Pop a fireman, he was also a lumberjack. He felled trees for neighbors in return for the firewood for his beloved fireplace. The first tree I remember was a tall, dead oak in our own front yard.

Pop's ax was an old, hand-forged, "double-bitted" job from his family, visibly ground down from its original dimensions. When Mr. Linton, in our street's first tarpaper shack, sharpened it, he said the ax was so hard it took more off the grindstone than the grindstone took off the ax. Mr. Linton also sharpened our two-man crosscut saw.

That was our father, a firefighter, our very own Paul Bunyan, our master of the steering wheel, author of literate tomes, and man of great good humor.

On June 25, 1950, North Korea sent 135,000 troops into South Korea. At age six, I managed not to hear about it.

Ma played piano and sang most sweetly. I once drew a musical staff on a piece of paper, added a random assortment of notes, and she played it for me!

She would sit on the front porch of a summer's eve, fireflies winking over the lawn, and sing Brahms' "Lullaby" a cappella in Dutch to our new baby sister, Mary, whom we came to call "Bunny."

Bunny was born on George Washington's birthday, February 22, 1951. Ma's round belly was familiar, Buster having arrived within my living memory. Sometime later, Buster said he'd asked Pop where babies came from. "Where?" I asked. Pop had told him, "I planted a seed inside your mother." Visions of a garden trowel, flower pots, and potting soil—than which few things could have been less sanitary—leaped instantly to mind, and I shot back, "He did not!" What could be more ridiculous?

"He did, too," by which Buster probably meant, "did too '*say* it.'"

"Did not," by which I meant, "did not '*do* it.'"

"Did too [say it]."

"Did not [do it]."

Pop and family friend Joe Colgan pulled a prank on Buster that could have come straight from the vaudeville stage. It was on a farm near Burke that was owned by a family named Shultz, who sold us raw milk. They had an electric fence that we kids dared each other to touch. One time, Joe and Pop grabbed the wire and held it. When satisfied that they could tolerate it, Joe took the wire, Pop took Joe's hand and motioned Buster over. Buster grabbed Pop's hand and the jolt sent him about two feet in the air. It wasn't a nice thing to do to a four-year-old, but it was comical, and I still can't help laughing about it.

The Shultzes had a television. One day they were watching a grade-B shoot-'em-up with a cowboy named Jim. The bad guys were going to kill him, and that I could not watch. How could they show such a thing? I fled the room. When I returned, the good guys were poking around the crime scene. Only ashes remained. They knew it was Jim, though, because they found his belt buckle.

For three quarters of a century, cowboys had been the American avatar. Joe Colgan had been one in Arizona and New Mexico in the nineteen-teens and -twenties. Looking at him, the last thing you'd think of was a cowboy. Cowboys should be lean and rawboned. Joe was thin and dapper, distinguished-looking, slightly effeminate with long, artistic fingers, wearing a bow tie and pencil mustache. His graying, wavy, hair, worn in what, until the sixties, would have been considered the "long-hair" or "artistic" style, combed straight back with a respectable widow's peak.

But the tales both true and tall with which he regaled us left no doubt that a cowboy he had been. He would bring a few Ram's Head Ales, in steel cans with cone-shaped tops, and he and Pop would sit in canvas chairs on the front porch at sunset and drink them.

"Tell us a story, Joe. Tell us a story," we would plead, and he rarely failed to oblige. He always had time to play with us at our secret spot by a stream in the woods behind the McKennas'. Even though extremely old, around fifty, he'd let out a war whoop and go galloping through the trees. He often shared Thanksgiving and Christmas with us. He'd been to Korea in the late forties. He did research for the Navajo Tribe's lawyer, Norman Littell, and went to cool places like Window Rock, Arizona, and Gallup, New Mexico. He also did research for Dale Morgan.

Chapter Four

Mexico

IT PENETRATED MY AWARENESS that FAO—the UN's Food and Agriculture Organization that Pop worked for—was sending us to Italy after my second grade, in 1951. I told all the kids. My Italian name was Giacomo (ZHA-ko-mo). Jimmy McConkey was funny enough, but *Giacomo* McConkey? Look out.

Later, we weren't going to Italy but Mexico, and not with FAO but the Department of Agriculture. Italy was a fifteen-year assignment, but Pop wanted his kids growing up American. Mexico would only be six months. Mexico had foot-and-mouth disease, and the Department of Agriculture wanted Pop to write its book about it. My Mexican name was Jaime. Predictably, Pat's was Patricio, Helen's was Elena, and Bunny's—Mary's— was Maria. But Buster's—Jerry's—his was *Geronimo! ¡Ai, caramba!* (Heh-

RAW-nee-mo, not Je-RA-na-mo.) "Do you want to go to Mexico?" I'm said to have exclaimed to him. "*Cowboy* country!"

Naturally, we drove. Pop traded the Studebaker for a sleek, black 1950 Ford sedan—two-door (no kids stepping out the back door of this one). It was lower-slung than the Studebaker, and lacked a running board. Pop said, "You have to leave your head behind when you get into one of these things." You used to step in, turn, and sit down. Now you had to insert a leg and begin sitting while you were still half outside, duck and drag your head in last.

We sold our house to a Colonel Glore and pulled out on August 7—two parents, four kids, and one five-month-old nursing infant. Our neighbors, the McKennas, waved good-bye. Paddy, my playmate, was crying.

We left Lord Plushbottom and our dog, Jack, with Ma's sister Margaret, who had just bought a farm on the Shenandoah River near Woodstock, Virginia, to raise chickens and homilies. Gathering eggs was "picking the cackle-berries;" a housefly in your baking dough was an "ambulatory raisin;" if presented with a large plate of food, Margaret would ask, "How am I going to get on the outside of all that food?" And there was always, "Don't look at me in that tone of voice." Margaret never married. Gramps and "Mom" moved with her.

We slept in tourist cabins, navigating by a map from AAA, the route highlighted in green grease pencil. We made Bristol, Tennessee, in the rain the first night. After that, the stops are a blur. It was 2,500 miles to Mexico City and took ten days. Most highways were still two-lane and didn't go around towns but through them. We wanted to swing through the Great Smoky Mountains, but time was short and we only viewed them from afar. Farther

At the Alamo

south were palm trees and Spanish moss. When we crossed into Texas, Helen called out, "Hello, Texas-aire!" A photo shows us in front of the Alamo. We stopped in a bar, I don't remember why, but do remember a pair of longhorn horns mounted over the mirror.

At the Mexican border, an official slapped a starburst sticker emblazoned with the word, "Turista," on our windshield. We weren't tourists! My father had a *job* in Mexico. I didn't know Spanish but could see what a "turista" was, and we weren't one.

Another photo shows us by a "Tropic of Cancer" sign, peering into the Torrid Zone. Somewhere in the desert, we had to change a tire. A bumping sound kept getting worse. A silver-dollar-sized spot had worn completely through the tire, and the inner tube was blistering outward. While Pop changed the tire, Pat ran over to some prickly pear cactus, confident his "leather gauntlets" (kid-sized, Boss work gloves) would protect him from getting prickled. They didn't.

At the Tropic of Cancer

We drove through a butterfly migration. They stuck to the windshield and we had to keep stopping and cleaning it. They got plastered on the radiator. A gas-station man blew them off with an air hose to keep the engine from overheating. They got on the rest of the car too, but those didn't slow us down.

Kids along the road played chicken with the cars—waiting, then darting across just ahead of them.

We approached Mexico City in the dark. We all had to pee, and Ma exhorted us to hold it, it was only twenty more miles. Somehow we did, and checked in at the brand-new Hotel Monte Cassino.

We dined at a nearby restaurant. I was extremely fidgety, and Pop walked me back to the hotel, where I tested positive for a fever.

A man named Carlos Bosch brought us sample tortillas. He said many Americans thought they tasted like wet cardboard. Ma said we didn't have to eat them if we didn't like them. I liked them, but then I also liked penicillin pills. *And* brussels sprouts.

As for the Hotel Monte Cassino, Ma noted that the "small-fry dubbed it the 'city dump.'" The characterization probably originated with Pat. He was good at keeping us amused, much to Ma's relief, I hope. One day, we made clothes for our teddy bears. On another, we "counterfeited" money, drawing dollars on bill-sized pieces of paper. They looked amazingly real. We had to crumple them and flatten them back out, so their newness wouldn't arouse suspicion. Pat knew everything.

Our next stop was a house, 521 Avenida Pirineos, a squarish, two-story, white stucco structure with a low-pitched, terra-cotta roof. An ample wrought-iron gate brokered the entrance, and a high evergreen hedge marched across the front and around the sides. A sagging wire fence marked the rear border. That fence did not long survive the eruption of a clangorous playground on our neighbors' rear flank. In time, a stuccoed fortification, with broken glass set in cement along the top, was rising in the fence's stead.

The Swedish ambassador lived across the street. Their kids were Wendy and Peter. Wendy was the first girl I got naked with—her idea, not mine, the Swedish, don't you know? Here's what happened. Ma and Pop were watching Peter, Wendy and the rest of us at the ambassador's home while the ambassador and his wife went somewhere. Wendy suggested getting naked and into bed. "Which part do you like to look at?" she asked. I pointed to her chest. She was puzzled, there being nothing remarkable in the eight-year-old female chest.

"Which part do you like to look at?" I asked. She indicated the obvious.

Ma marched into the room. "Put on your clothes."

"But, *you* do it," I pointed out.

"That's for grownups."

It helps to know that 521 Avenida Pirineos came furnished, down to the art on the walls, and that Mexico, if memory serves, was in love with classical Greek art. In Ma and Pop's bedroom hung a picture of a Greek goddess, probably Athena, seated on a throne wearing a warrior's helmet and holding a spear, fetchingly draped from the waist down. Pat gestured toward the picture, said, "milk bags." I was transfixed on the spot. The fact that Ma had breastfed me was no help. We're all boob men. We're wired that way.

Naturally, the house had a fireplace. Mexico City sits in a dry lakebed a mile and a half above sea level. Being tropical, the city is hot during the day, but at night the clear air surrenders its heat, making the fireplace a welcome refuge. Before long, vendors and their burros laden with neatly split faggots were regular visitors.

There were other vendors, too. You heard their cries as they plied those manicured byways. My favorite was the tortilla lady, a buxom woman with a frilly apron and a large basket of warm, aromatic, freshly made tortillas. There was a tortilla "factory" within walking distance of our neighborhood, a vacant lot commandeered by tortilla-makers.

There they would be every morning, patting out *masa* by hand and toasting the flat rounds on charcoal braziers, turning them out by the thousands, the early sunlight refracted in the braziers' smoke.

One of our maids, Fidencia, had us buy a *metate* so she could make her own *masa*, and from that our own tortillas. The *masa* was hard corn soaked in water mixed with lime, washed, and ground to a dough on the *metate*. The *metate* was carved from porous, volcanic rock to a shape that somewhat smacked of a

Tortilla lady

washboard on three stubby legs. The surface was not ribbed but slightly dished. The grinder, or pestle, somewhat smacking of a rolling pin, was tapered at each end so its contour matched the *metate*'s dish shape. Packaged supermarket copies can't hold the skirt hems of those tortillas.

At *El Super (SOO-pare) Mercado*, where we did much of our shopping, there was an appealing street urchin about my age who always ran up calling "O, Patrón, O, Patrón," offering to guard our car for a few *centavos*. We always indulged him, though you never knew how much guarding

"Patrón"

he actually did. I called him "Patrón" right back, not realizing that all "Patrón" meant was "patron." We never learned his real name, but I gave him some of my toys and clothing.

We also met a policeman named Enriques. Bunny fell in love with him. She called him "Ites," and once in her sleep repeated, "Ites, Ites, Ites…."

Pop was to blame for our love of *paisanos*. If people lived near the earth, they were by definition good.

Hardly had we settled at Pirineos than school loomed up. I don't know where Helen went, but Pat and I went to an all-boys' Catholic school, *La Escuela de la Iglesia*, The School of the Church.

"Ites" and Mariqauita

I had genuinely liked my first two years in Burke. *La Escuela* fixed that. I sat in the middle of a dim, cavernous room whose ceilings disappeared in the gloom above. One side was illuminated by a bank of tall, arched windows. A menacing brother approached and unleashed a torrent of unintelligible Spanish. I finally gleaned that he was trying to determine what grade to put me in, but I didn't get the drift quite right and answered, "*Dos*," the best I could manage for the grade I'd just finished. *La Escuela* put me in second grade again. I have absolutely no memory of anything to do with lessons.

There are only three things I do remember—four counting the so-called playground where two of the things took place. Unlike Burke's expansive greensward, *La Escuela* had a crowded, inner-city, asphalt surface enclosed by a chain-link fence. My first memory of that exercise yard is a species of insurrection masquerading as soccer.

The second memory was only a threat. Pat sought me out one day and said with breathless relish, "There's going to be rumble at recess."

"What's a rumble?"

"A fight," he could barely contain himself.

About what?

It's *fun*!

Fun? I emerged onto the playground greatly trepidatious, but the promised riot never materialized.

The third thing was Pat's inviting me to play hooky. He said that when the bell rang, we would go hide at the base of the *Angel de la Independencia*. That famed monument, just across the street, was a Winged Victory—slimmed down, head and arms restored, burnished in gold leaf—atop a lofty column in a traffic circle in *El Paseo de la Reforma*, Mexico City's most famous thoroughfare. From the *Angel*, we caught a bus to the apartment of an American classmate of Pat's. An apartment struck me as a strange way to live.

Years later, Helen told me she and Pat played hooky nearly every day. For some reason, Ma and Pop took us out of school after just two months.

Ma, who'd been a teacher, would school us at home, which must have been like presiding over the sack of Rome. Even though we had maids—who could need supervising of their own—Ma was riding herd on five midget hooligans, one crawling, one still pre-school, and three at different grade levels. And she'd been out of the classroom for nineteen years. I later liked saying I missed—didn't skip but *missed*—the whole third grade and most of the fourth. In memory, she was an easy task master.

I recall just two snippets of my home schooling. She had me write about *burros*. I looked them up in our *World Book Encyclopedia*. And somewhere in my lesson plan there figured a book called something like *Earth Peoples*. A photo showed a white bwana in a pith helmet standing between two pygmies, his outstretched arms just brushing the tops of their heads. Readin' yes, some, but of writin' and 'rithmetic I have no memory. Helen liked home schooling.

All this time, Pop was chronicling the battle against deadly foot-and-mouth—*aftosa* in Spanish—an ancient scourge of cloven-hoofed animals, causing high fever, blistrous eruptions on lips and tongue and on the tissues between and above the claws of the hooves. In rare cases, skin can lift away from the tongue and hooves can drop off. Recovery can also be quick, but recovered animals can still spread the disease, "with the speed of burning gunpowder," one newspaper said.

Countermeasures were drastic, and required by a law—driving herds into excavated pits and shooting them, quarantining healthy herds, disinfecting personnel and vehicles moving between ranches or exiting the quarantine area. Owners were indemnified at fair-market rates, but resistance could still be fierce, even lethal. In the worst single incident, a mob beat and stabbed a veterinarian and his seven-soldier escort to death.

Aftosa had first shown up in 1946, probably in September, but it took a change of administrations, December 1, for the government to act. Because the disease might cross the border, the United States joined Mexico in the "Mexico-United States Commission for the Eradication of Foot-and-Mouth Disease." Some American cattlemen even clamored for a border fence. Fencing off healthy herds from infected ones was, in fact, an effective preventive. It also created a barbed-wire shortage. The Commission authorized two fences, one north and one south of the quarantine zone (which included

Mexico City). Ultimately, only about 120 miles of the east end of the northern fence seem to have been built, but they performed yeoman service.

A year into the campaign, the slaughter was causing economic dislocation. Because nine to ten million more animals needed to be slaughtered to control the outbreak, the Commission added vaccination to its arsenal, which Mexicans had favored all along. The newspaper *El Universal* applauded suppression of the "sanitary rifle," while far-off Washington cried "failure in Mexico."

But it was through massive vaccination—killing only infected animals—that *aftosa* was finally beaten. The last three infected animals were destroyed January 11, 1951. On the 16th, the epidemic was declared over. It took another year to demobilize.

Sometimes Pop went to his downtown office, at others hit the road for destinations around the country. One time, his secretary, Polly, came for lunch. A photo in our album shows her with hair pulled back. "She was wearing ears that day," Pop said. For another gathering, the maids prepared *flores de calabasa*—batter-fried squash blossoms, which were delicious—but the *mole Poblano*, chocolate chicken, a Mexican delicacy, was so *picante* you couldn't eat it, though the Mexican guests found it "*¡Muy sabroso!*" Very savory!

Humor came home from the office—"*La Noche* before Christmas" from the *Aftosa* newsletter:

'Twas *la noche* before Christmas
And all through *la casa*
Not a creature was stirring.
Caramba que pasa?

It went on for several stanzas, one of which included:

Santa *esta* at the corner saloon
Muy borracho[†] since mid-afternoon.

What excellent people our father worked with.

[†] Very drunk

We went to polo matches, a professional sport in Mexico, played in stadiums. We took pony rides at Chapultepec Park, and managed not to learn that one of the last battles between the Aztecs and the conquistadores had been fought right there.

They played polo in stadiums

We went to Teotihuacan, the Aztec metropolis outside Mexico City. We didn't climb the Pyramid of the Sun, but Pat made sure we knew that the Aztecs had sacrificed humans up there. The Pyramid of the Moon wasn't excavated yet. A quarter of a century later I chuckled at before–and-after pictures. *Why, I knew that pyramid when it was just a pile of dirt!* Teotihuacan had been the Americas' biggest city, rivaling European settlements.

"Pyramid of the Sun"

The absolute best thing we did in Mexico, however, was learn rope tricks. One day, there we were at Rancho la Tapatia, under the tutelage of a *charro* named Pépe Ortega. For each of us—Pat, Helen, myself, and Buster—he patiently spliced an eye into one end of a length of tightly wound cotton rope, of a stiffness appropriate to the use for which it was intended. He sewed a scrap of leather into the outer edge of the eye to protect it from wear.

Our first lesson was simple: toss out the rope to its full length then coil it back up, giving a flip with each turn so the coils would lie flat. Repeat. This gave a feel for the rope. Next, you laid a loop on the ground, four or five feet in diameter, holding up one edge in your outstretched hands, flipped it up and over your head with a little flourish to impart angular momentum, let go the loop but held the stem with a twirling motion to keep the loop spinning. At first, only comic tangles resulted. But you kept trying until the loop stayed open, and from there advanced to stepping into the loop instead of putting it over your head, and further variations.

On Sundays, the *charros* gathered at Rancho la Tapatia to bull and bronc ride, spin ropes, and dance in the rancho's arena. There was an event called *coliando* ("tailing" in gringo-ese), Mexico's version of bulldogging. Instead of grabbing the bull by the horns, a *charro* grabbed it by the tail, wrapped the tail around his leg, and veered off causing the animal to lose its footing.

Paso de la Muerte, the "step of death," was downright dangerous. Two *charros* galloped around the arena with a bronc between them. One would get to his knees in the saddle, and leap onto the bronc. Pépe Ortega once fell between the horses doing that. The dislocated hip paled beside the torn sombrero another *charro* had favored him with for the feat. I once played *paso de la muerte* on two burros, though no amount of tugging and tail-twisting by the other kids could goad those flop-eared equidae into more than one step every minute or so. On Sundays, we participated in the kids' festivities—rope tricks, etc.—before the grandstand.

A *mariachi* orchestra played in the grandstand, and we came to love the lilting rhythms of guitar, fiddle, and cornet. The *mariachi* costume was like that of the *charro*: tight, boot-cut pants with flares down the outsides of the legs like vestigial chaps; boots; an embroidered blouse; vest; a large floppy bow tie; and the broad-brimmed sombrero, upturned slightly at the front and more in back.

The costume was similar, but *mariachis* favored extra embroidery and appliqué. Pat's blouse and mine had Mexico's national symbol, an eagle on a prickly pear devouring a snake, embroidered on their backs. The Aztecs had arrived at the lake in the Valley of Mexico, saw the eagle devouring a snake, thought it a good omen, and established Teotihuacan on the shore.

Helen got a full skirt and a lusciously embroidered blouse. She and Pat took dance lessons, and in addition to rope tricks, danced Mexico's national dance, the *Jarabe Tapatio*, in the arena. Pop served as the rancho's unofficial photographer.

Pépe Ortega was one of only nine *charros completos* in all Mexico. He could do everything—roping, bronc- and bull-riding, *paso de la meuerte*, dancing, *coliando*, rope tricks. He told what expert thieves Mexicans could be: "They'll steal the socks off your feet without removing your shoes."

Once on a bus, a thief stole his hat. Pépe was on the rear seat. The windows were glassless, and the thief—clinging to the outside as many people did— lifted Pépe's hat without his even feeling it.

Pat was always reading far above his age level. I sometimes tried to emulate him but was hopeless. I'll never forget the day he gleefully inflicted words I can only think came from *Revelation* on Helen and me:

> If any man worships the beast and his image, and receive *his* mark in his forehead or in his hand, the same shall drink of the wine of the wrath of God, which is poured out without mixture into the cup of his indignation; and he shall be tormented with fire and brimstone in the presence of the holy angels, and in the presence of the Lamb: and the smoke of their torment ascendeth up: and they have no rest day nor night for ever and ever, who worship the beast and his image, and whosoever receiveth the mark of his name.

I can't swear that's the exact passage, but words like those haunted me for years. What business did a twelve-year-old brother have exhuming such antiquarian horrors?

On US Election Day, Pat said, "We're going to listen to the election returns" (Dwight Eisenhower versus Adlai Stevenson). I may have had a vague idea what an election was. Pat tried tuning the radio. "We'll stay up all night if we have to," but reception was poor and the project fizzled.

If you told Pat not to do something, he was duty-bound to do it. I was the opposite. If you told me not to do something, it was OK. I was and still am perfectly at peace working within the rules. There's plenty of latitude. People who went around violating rules were wasting their time on superficialities. But tell me I *had* to do something? That was my cue *not* to do it.

"You *will* go on vacation during the hot season," they said, much later in the Peace Corps. "*Nobody* stays in the village during the hot season." Nobody? Just watch me. You had to have at least one hot season in the village or you hadn't experienced India. So, when Ma told Pat and me not to go to the *barranca*, it was fine with me, but for Pat it was the only place we couldn't *not* go.

A *barranca* is a ravine. The *barranca* itself wasn't objectionable but the packing-crate slum it contained was. This was no piddling gully. It housed an entire subpopulation. A slum, obviously, held no good for *chico* gringos. Therefore, we were forbidden to go. Therefore, we had to go, I merely by being the little brother.

The *barranca* must have been within walking distance of the house. Why there should have been *barrancas* and tortilla factories so near our manicured neighborhood is lost to memory, but we didn't seem to have any trouble reaching them. I only remember going to the *barranca* once, and what we did there was innocence itself. We spent the whole time jumping off a rock promontory into pure warm sand a few feet below. We never set foot in the slum.

Ma had no idea where we'd gone, so there was no reprimand, but I chugged a glass of water, my stomach cramped, my vision tunneled, I headed for the floor, and woke up on the couch. For the rest of the day, I felt like something I only learned of later—hung over. Do not drink fast when you're parched. I'd have rather been in school.

Then there were the slingshots. Pat took them and me out into the neighborhood to demonstrate a game he'd invented: shooting pebbles underneath cars, leaving the drivers blissfully unaware they'd been shot at. We fired away for how long I know not until one pebble struck the car instead of the space beneath it. The driver screeched to a halt, read us out in some very impressive Spanish we didn't understand, said, "Police!" and sped away. Pat and I scrammed home and confessed. Ma confiscated our ordnance. That driver is probably still laughing…on his cloud in the great beyond.

Pop did his part in the child-rearing. In Lincolnia, there had been the bed-wetting. Later, in Burke, he gave Buster and me our nightly sponge baths. In Mexico, he took us to the movies. *The Wizard of Oz* was completely unnecessary—that wretched green witch with her flying monkeys. He meant well, Pop did. He just didn't know any better.

Another movie, *The Kon-Tiki Expedition,* was something else. By today's standards, it was astonishingly primitive—black-and-white shot with a hand-held 16-mm camera—yet it won the Oscar for best documentary in 1951. It told of Thor Heyerdahl's 1947 voyage across the Pacific on a balsa raft, and was the most galvanizing thing I'd ever seen. With sticks scrounged from the massive shade tree overhanging our backyard, and strands stripped from the leaves of a yucca plant, I lashed together the best model of the *Kon-Tiki* raft I could. I'm sure we went to that movie because Pop wanted to, but it inspired me to join the Peace Corps fifteen years later.

Carlos Bosch and Helen

Mexico City sits in a basin that once was a lake. All roads out take you to higher ground. Even in the early fifties, you could look down on a brownish-yellow haze over the city. An *aftosa* coworker joked that the cloud was dust from all the maids sweeping gringos' homes, but of course it wasn't. It was smog.

Pop took Helen and Pat on a tour of some Mexican points of interest. A picture shows Helen and Carlos Bosch in the crater of an extinct volcano. Later he and Carlos took Buster and me on our own trip.

Carlos had brought us our first tortillas at the Hotel Monte Cassino. He cut a dashing figure and had the most beautiful wife I thought I had ever seen, Conchita. He came from Spain, and Pat said if he went back, he'd be stood against a wall and shot. Mature reflection suggested participation in the Spanish Civil War on the Loyalist side. In actuality, Conchita's father was the

head of Spain's Republican government in exile, and if anybody was going to be shot, it was doubtless he.

Mexico was volcanic and earth-quake prone, though I managed not to notice the one earthquake of our stay. Everybody else was

Popcatepetl

suddenly talking about it, while I only heard of it from them.

We often drove in view of Mexico's most famous volcano, Popocatepetl, standing vigil over his dead love, Iztaccíhuatl. Popo and Iztac were Mexico's Romeo and Juliet. Iztac's father had promised her in marriage to Popo, provided Popo took up arms in Oaxaca (we'd *been* there!). Convinced he'd sent Popo to his doom, Iztac's father told her he'd been killed, whereupon she expired from grief. But Popo returned, and, learning of the father's treachery, committed suicide.

God changed the lovers into mountains. Iztaccihuatl's was *"La Mujer Dormida"* (the "Sleeping Woman") because it looks like a woman lying on her back. Popo became a volcano, raining fire in rage over the loss of his love. Sometimes he still billows impressively.

La Mujer Dormida

"My volcano," Paricutín, was our trip's destination. Paricutín (Pa ree coo TEEN) was "my" volcano because it erupted the year I was born, 1943. I never felt right claiming the thing because it erupted in February when "I" was still just an embryo. But the book, *All About Volcanoes and Earthquakes*, had a chapter on Paricutín, so I knew of and was glad to visit it. Pop said we would climb to the top and pee it out, but we arrived too late in the day. We did see miles of volcanic ash that looked like the surface of the moon.

Walking back to the hotel after breakfast next day, Pop and Carlos dawdling in conversation, I asked if Buster and I could go ahead. "Do you know the way?" Pop asked.

"Yep," I assured him, but at the first intersection, my confidence dropped like a stone. Was this really right? Pop and Carlos were still visible, but the car wasn't. Buster and I could duck down that way, and if the next corner didn't bring the car, race back. I'd made my boast, but my heart was in my throat as we sallied forth. Pop and Carlos were out of sight and the car wasn't in sight. What if we'd gone the wrong way and didn't get back in time? We'd be lost. And it would be my fault. We came to the last turn and there in all its glory was our no-longer-shiny black Ford sedan with the *turista* sticker on the windshield. We climbed onto the hood and sat glued there until Pop and Carlos arrived.

Who lets an eight-year-old run off in the streets of a strange Mexican town? It strikes me as odd even now, but both of our parents seemed to have a weird faith in us. Ma would give us bus fare and turn us loose in Mexico City. She'd make sure we had fare for the red buses, which you couldn't cling to the outsides of. We, of course, took the cheaper green buses you *could* cling to the sides of, and spent the excess on forbidden foods from street vendors. (I've never tasted finer tamales.)

At twelve and thirteen, Pat was apparently deemed old enough to lead these expeditions, which seemed to penetrate the city's more questionable precincts. In one such locale, a

Glued to the hood

drunk insisted on retarding our progress with a monologue that couldn't find its end. I hadn't noticed until that moment, but Pat was holding the stone pestle to our *metate* at the ready. That piece of ordnance hadn't materialized from nowhere. It was premeditated. I'm still amazed our parents let us do those things.

The *aftosa* manuscript entered its final phases. The original assignment of six-months had been extended twice. After a year, the owner sold Pireneos out from under us, and we spent our last six months in a bungalow at 171 Monte Parnasso, with a spectacular view of the mountains.

My parents were not above ignoring the law on suitable occasions. They smuggled out some forbidden Aztec pottery. You couldn't legally take it, but Pop had visited museum basements where shards littered the floors and people trampled them underfoot. Some artifacts, he reasoned, would be better off in sticky gringo fingers.

We crammed something else Mexican into the Ford going home. Our maid, Fidencia Rodriguez. She had been a jewel, and we brought her back with us.

Chapter Five

Burke Again

W̲E WERE HOME at the end of January, 1953, and rented a place in Arlington, Virginia, while shopping for a house.

On our first day back in school, it snowed. It was Fidencia's introduction to snow, our reintroduction to it, and my introduction by Ma to Newtonian relativity. Going to school, I stopped to make a snow angel, without gloves. The cold stung so badly that I went home crying. Ma ran a basin of cold water. "Cold?" I gasped. I wanted my hands warm, not cold.

"Yes," Ma said, "put your hands in." I did, and, my hands being colder than the water, the water felt warm! My mother was a genius. "Don't let Fidencia hear you crying," she whispered.

We bought the Burke house back from Colonel Glore. Mrs. Robinson, a sturdy neighbor up Lee Street, other side of Burke Lake Road, welcomed us home, dragging a finger over the china cabinet we'd brought from Mexico and inspecting the result. Bunny, two years old and completely bilingual, told Ma, "*Esta mujer es muy feyo* (That woman is very bad)." Ma continued talking to Bunny in Spanish until the day Bunny said, "Don't talk to me like that anymore."

The train tracks were still there, but after Mexico, we never saw another steam engine.

My old playmates were there—Paddy McKenna next door, Carl and Teddy Jenson across the lane behind our property—and a new one, Ronny Smith, who lived in the house where the lane joined Burke Lake Road. I'll never forget Paddy's teaching me the word, "turd." He omitted explaining what it meant, but it was one of the funniest-sounding words I'd ever heard. I went home and called Pop one. He didn't find it as funny as I did, and registered his disapproval with a knuckle-rap to my head.

Helen and I were back in Burke Elementary, Pat had moved on to secondary school, Buster had yet to begin. I had missed the entire third grade and most of the fourth. Surely, Pat and Helen bore similar scholastic embarrassments, but the schools spared us the indignity of repeating grades. I only learned multiplication tables as punishment for failing to hear the bell after recess one day.

But there was something worse: I'd hardly been back a day when a kid named Danny Slader, who hadn't been there when we left, threw me down, gripped my head between his knees, and gave my scalp a knuckle burn. What was that for? He didn't know me!

I must have been an easy mark. Thanks to the school's having let me start two weeks before my sixth birthday, I was generally the youngest and smallest kid in class. Our Mexican sabbatical had eroded my social status. I was a year and a half down academically, and a deer-in-the-headlights look, that some pictures show, couldn't have helped. I did know, however—automatically, without being told—that you don't snitch. That would make you teacher's pet, which was even worse. I thought fighting was something you either knew or didn't know, and not knowing was a character flaw. All I knew was the movie technique. It never occurred to me that you could *learn* to fight. To our parents, fighting was irredeemably low, and no kid of theirs would go there if they could help it.

There was a bright side. The school bus stopped at our street—Lee Street—before making a giant loop and coming back by L&M Grocery at the town center, farther from home but still an easy walk. Sometimes I stayed for the whole loop just for something to do, and aboard was the prettiest little third-grader you ever saw, Jenny Parkman, who lived a little past my stop, across from the tree that changed its mind. We talked more and more over time, until one day a kid asked, "Is she your girlfriend?"

I'd never thought about it, but said, "Yes."

"Would you kiss her?"

"Sure," I said, and kissed Jenny Parkman on the lips. She didn't object, and that was that. We were hitched, and stayed hitched for two years, until I pulled an asshole stunt that ended it, which we'll tell of in its allotted time.

The "tree that changed its mind" had begun normally, but something had bent it sideways. Somebody had cut the horizontal section partway back. From that part, two vertical shoots had sprouted and flourished. The tree had started up, gone sideways, then went up again. Pop called it "the tree that changed its mind."

August 12, 1953; I was waiting in the car with my mother at a shopping center. A newspaper headline said the Soviets had exploded a hydrogen bomb. My mother's silent sense of foreboding telegraphed itself. The possibility that all could end in one massive flash was a tightening knot in the collective gut. I only remember doing "duck-and-cover" in school once. Duck-and-cover and the mushroom cloud seem quaintly amusing today, but in 1953 they came shrouded in dread.

Soviet dictator Josef Stalin had died five months short of that portentous blast.

One day in 1954, we went to another movie which, like *Kon-Tiki*, Pop must have waited eagerly to see. Mount Everest had been topped in May 1953 by Edmund Hillary and Tenzing Norgay, and the movie, *The Conquest of Everest*, was released in December. After seeing it, Paddy, Buster, and I played Hillary and Tenzing every chance we got, on the bank between Uncle Bill's house and the railroad track. His house was our end of Lee Street's high point, and offered a much grander "mountain" than could be found in our "lowland."

Willie "Uncle Bill" Harlow was Paddy's uncle. The McKennas called him Uncle Bill, so we did, too. He was the ne'er-do-well jack-of-all-trades who had helped roof our house before we went to Mexico, and played fiddle up there as darkness fell. Refrigerators, bicycles, washing machines, car tires, bits of reinforcing rod, weeds surrounded his tarpaper shack. Probably in the summer of '53, the shack caught fire. We rushed out to see. Paddy was jumping up and down, crying and screaming, "Uncle Bill! Uncle Bill!"

From inside came the sound of cartridges going off as fire consumed the structure. Joe Quirk, town drunk, school janitor, and volunteer fireman, crawled in on his belly and determined that Uncle Bill wasn't home. The town got together and built him a new house. Pop had been at work in Washington during the fire and hadn't joined the brigade but did join the carpenters in the rebuild.

Before construction began, a bulldozer leveled the site, pushing raw dirt over the edge of the precipice above the railroad track, creating a perfect, bare crag, our Mt. Everest, on which we substituted imaginary ice axes and crampons for real ones.

We rarely saw the fires the volunteers responded to. We would hear the station's siren, see the cars racing there, hear the engines' sirens fade toward the emergency, and that would be it. But the forest fire on Hearst's Hill, down the tracks to the west of our house, lives on vividly. Flames pirouetted above the treetops and burned for two or three days. Pop hurt his back climbing a fence with a water pack, but the damage wasn't permanent.

Pop took Paddy and me to a 3-D "Bowery Boys" movie that had its moments—a hypodermic needle protruding menacingly into the audience. Paddy clenched his fists to the sides of his head, shut his eyes, kicked his feet, and screamed. Pop, on my other side, seemed bemused. I tried copying him.

Paddy's mother, Helen McKenna, was heavy-set and wore panties on her head, I kid you not. I supposed the panties were in lieu of a hairnet. It didn't strike me as hilarious until much later. She could tolerate just so much playtime in her jurisdiction, then out she would stomp with a butcher knife in her teeth, threatening, "I'm gonna cut your ears off!" We couldn't get alarmed, but knew it was time to go.

Mrs. McKenna could eat no lean, her husband could eat no fat. "Daddy Pat" was a slight, wiry Irishman with a brogue you could hang a wet towel on. He may have been a World War I veteran, for he owned a steel helmet of the kind worn then. It made Paddy the envy of the regiment when we played war. At the height of one of our battles, however, Daddy Pat growled, "Did you ever kill somebody?" Paddy shook his head. Daddy Pat said no more, but the implication was clear—he had.

Pépe

Not long after we reoccupied Burke, Pépe joined our family. Pépe was a fine-looking three-quarters Border Collie, one-quarter German Shepherd, as congenial a littermate as ever lived. He was black with a white ruff, white socks, and a white flag on his tail. The Shepherd showed in his tan cheeks and eyebrows, and soothed the Border Collie in him. He came from a place called "The Pound."

Tom Sawyer inspired me to try out mischief. My mind didn't run to mischief. Almost everybody else—starting with Pat—came to mischief naturally. Could its absence in me be a character flaw? With *Tom Sawyer*, I resolved to correct the flaw. The book started with Aunt Polly calling, "'TOM!' No answer…'Now what's gone with that boy?'"

So, I sat under the elm tree at the far corner of our acre reading *Tom Sawyer*. When Ma called, "Jim-m-my! Jim-m-my!" I ignored her. The tree's base was carpeted in an uncomfortable species of gravel, however, so I sauntered back to the house where Ma had the gall not even to ask where I'd been.

Another time, Tom inspired me to announce that I was running away.

"OK," Ma said.

OK? What do you mean, *OK?*

After absorbing that shock, I said, "OK, I'll go pack."

"Oh, no," she said. "You have to go the way you are."

"Oh….O…K." But already, she'd defused me.

Like the time I said I was sick and couldn't go to school. "OK," she said, "but you'll have to stay in bed." Figuring the worst day in bed was better than the best day at school, I agreed, but after two increasingly boring hours, I declared myself cured and walked the mile to school.

There was nothing to do but admit it. I lacked the aptitude for mischief. Trying to do it was more trouble than it was worth.

Our parents once tried sending us to a summer day camp at Burke Elementary. It was one of the most boring days of our lives—programmed activities, no surprises, no fun. We never went back.

An alternative, however, emerged with a woman named Nell Hatcher who had a place outside Burke with riding horses and a half-acre pond, and we went there often. My maiden solo horseback-ride was unpromising. The horse and I were turned into the paddock, and the horse went straight for a low-hanging branch. It could have scraped me right off but politely stopped and stood there till help arrived.

Beyond the paddock was a pond. A float was moored near the middle where you could cavort, dive, sunbathe. I couldn't swim yet and had to watch from the kiddie enclosure, whose enticements quickly paled. One day, I slipped out, waded into the depths, and was quickly in water up to my chin. I nearly panicked and almost called for help, but, literally on tiptoe, worked my way back to the shallows, emerging unembarrassed, chastened, and smarter.

Back home, Buster fared less well, even under parental eyes. They were visiting the same Mrs. Robinson who had given our china cabinet the white-glove test. Buster was petting her dog. Without warning, it jumped and bit his face—lower tooth marks on one side of his mouth, upper tooth marks on the other. We were shocked coming home to news that Buster was in the hospital getting sewn back together. The attack left him impressively scarred. Scars don't grow while you do, however, and today his are proportionally so small as hardly to be visible.

All this took place against a backdrop of a polio epidemic. In 1952, while we were in Mexico, the United States had 58,000 cases. The following year, when we returned, there were 35,000. By 1954, the outbreak had mostly subsided, but Ma never stopped warning us not to overheat while playing.

Ours wasn't the only health she fretted over. It was also Pop's, but his had to do with cooking oil. We'd always cooked with lard or Crisco. Now, conspicuously, we were using corn oil, because it had less "saturated fat." And she had him taking vitamin E because it was good for the heart. In fact, we all found ourselves popping vitamins, which she laid out next to our dinner plates. "Natural" vitamins advertised in *Prevention* magazine.

Ma also made butter. Before milk started being homogenized, the cream rose to the top, and many milk bottles had bulbs at the top where the cream collected. That's what Ma made butter from. Early on, she just put the cream in a Mason jar and shook it till it turned to butter. That was hard work, and eventually, we got a proper churn.

We returned to buying raw milk from the Shultzes, possibly in response to the arrival of homogenized milk, which seems in memory to have coincided roughly with the arrival of cardboard milk containers. There'd been half-pint cardboard sizes in our lunches for some time, but quart and half-gallon sizes seemed preposterous. They worked, though, and one evening Joe Colgan, our cowboy "playmate," trying to set Ma a good example, threw an armload of empties into the fireplace. The waxed surfaces went up like a flame-thrower, setting the chimney on fire and fetching the Burke Volunteer Fire Department.

Of the trees Pop felled, the one I best remember was in our neighbors, the Lymans', backyard, which Pop may not actually have felled but merely cut up. Memory puts a hole in the ground at the tree's base, suggesting it came down by itself or was helped down by the elements. That was the tree where Pop initiated me, aged ten, into the mysteries of the two-man crosscut saw. It was also where Gramps nearly scalped Pat with an ax.

The trunk was being reduced to manageable lengths—six feet or so. Gramps was splitting those lengths into smaller-diameter pieces with a sledge hammer and wedges. Rarely, when you split a log, do the sections fall cleanly apart. Strands connecting the sides, called "cords," need to be cut with an ax. The wedges were lying between the log's halves, and Gramps was cutting the cords and had already begun his swing when Pat bent down to retrieve a wedge. It was a glancing blow that opened a red geyser on Pat's dome. The first I knew was a towel bunched on Pat's head and the car speeding off to the hospital. I didn't see the geyser, but those who did said it sprayed most excellently.

Pat came home with a shaved spot on his scalp and an awesome row of black stitches. The doctor wished our grandfather, "Better luck next time."

That was the second time Pat had escaped with his head. Some years earlier, a playmate had rendered similar service with a mattock. An exploding light bulb had cost the playmate an eye, and that deficit may have thrown off his aim.

My first book report came in fifth or sixth grade. "Check a book out of the library and write about it," the teacher had said. My eye fell on a volume titled *American Conservation*.

"Conservation," I reflected. "That's a good subject." Why a fifth or sixth grader should think conservation is a "good subject" I don't know. Leafing through the book, a strange-looking picture, representing a gravitational tug pulling the planetary disc from the sun, leaped at me. That picture hung in our house! I showed it to Ma.

"Your father wrote part of that book," she said.

Really? The illustrator had given him the original. Somehow, I must have absorbed conservation's "goodness" from my parents. Unfortunately, the book was beyond my powers of comprehension and went back to the shelf unmolested.

Chapter Six

The Farm

I' M NOT SURE when we started looking for another place, or why, but we did. What was wrong with Burke? We liked Burke, didn't we? It was 1955.

Of course, moving every couple of years was something we just seemed to do. And escaping a soured relationship is a time-honored reason to leave town. It was the first time I left that way. I wish it hadn't been I who soured it, but that last scene with Jenny Parkman, my girlfriend…I was eleven—nuff said?

Either I asked or told Ma I was riding my bike to Jenny's. What I did there I don't remember…until I started riding up and down Burke Lake Road. Traffic in those days was no issue, but Susan's mother called me to come back. I ignored her. She called again. Jenny joined in. "She's not my boss!" I yelled back, and sped home. Nobody was there, but all houses were unlocked in those days, and there I stayed until family returned.

That was my infraction. It must have been agreed that I would be under Trumbull eyes for the duration, but I don't remember anybody sharing the secret with me. Maybe they did, but…

Next day, Ma told me to apologize to Mrs. Trumbull, so I went to their house. A note on the door, written by Jenny, said, "No, no, no. I not want be your girlfriend!"

Not long afterward, we moved to the farm. I've always regretted that incident. Jenny, if you see this, I'm sorry.

If anybody epitomized, "You can take the boy out of the country but you can't take the country out of the boy," Pop did. Dale Morgan once said, "Your father would have farmed in a window box if there'd been nothing else." Getting back to the land had surely sparked the move from 509 Fontaine Street to Burke. But it had long been Pop's dream to retire on a farm, raise Black Angus cattle, and write. The place he chose, near the "almost visible" town of Lovettsville, Virginia, population 250, fifty miles from D.C., answered magnificently.

The way from Burke to the farm went through Tyson's Corner, Virginia, at the intersection of Rt 7 (Leesburg Pike) and Chain Bridge Road. Today, Tyson's Corner is a massive commercial nightmare. In 1955, it was a meat packing plant and a radar tower. From Tyson's Corner to Leesburg and beyond, Route 7 was a two-lane road traversing farmland and little else. There was no Reston, no Sterling Park, no Broad Run Farms. Herndon Junction was a wide spot in the road.

You entered Leesburg past a hamburger stand called "Mighty Midget," at the apex of the "V" where Loudoun Street goes left and Route 7 becomes Market, the main drag. The town boasted 2000 inhabitants. US 15, the major north-south artery, crosses Rt.7 at the town center, pranked up by the red brick courthouse on a spacious lawn.

Westward out of town, a lengthy upgrade lugged the engine—Catoctin Mountain, which people just called "The Mountain." Broadcast personality Arthur Godfrey had a farm where the summit leveled out. As you started back down, Route 9 branched off to the right, taking you through the town of Peonian Springs. A few miles on, a right on county road 287 took you past Wheatland (so small that both signs were on the same post) to Lovettsville.

Three miles after Lovettsville, over two different dirt roads, was the farm. A stone fence bordered its last quarter mile to the head of the lane, an unprepossessing opening in a wood that led another quarter mile along the edge of a deep ravine to a ford in a stream before opening out into the barnyard.

It is a privilege to have lived on those 132 acres in Virginia's Blue Ridge Mountain foothills. The Potomac River swept a quarter of a mile along the farm's back pasture, below a high bluff. It flowed through

View from the back pasture

a gap in the mountain ridge five miles away, seen from the pasture's eminence. The stone farmhouse, its walls two feet thick, dated to around 1750. In the kitchen, a six-burner cook stove stood before a massive fireplace, whose culinary function the stove had replaced. Fireplaces in the dining and living rooms rounded out the home's original heat sources. A coal furnace (which we fueled with wood) had been added beneath a large register in the dining room floor.

A 40- by 60-foot bank barn was set into a slope near the pasture's low end. A two-foot-thick, stone foundation walled the barn's lower level on three sides. That south-facing level, with horse stalls and a milking stall, walked out into the barnyard. Above was the hayloft—or hay "mow" (rhyming with "cow"). The barn had burned and been rebuilt twenty-five years earlier. Eight-by-eight chestnut timbers, mortise-and-tenoned together, formed the timber-frame. It was sheathed with vertical siding whose barn-red paint and whitewash trim were fading with dignity when we arrived.

Lesser outbuildings included a hog pen, a corn crib, a carriage house, a machine shed, a log smokehouse and a log workshop in which we housed calves, two chicken houses, a springhouse, and an outhouse (still very common on farms).

A spring, enclosed in a stone-lined grotto, supplied water. Its crystal pool hosted a variety of small freshwater creatures, the most numerous being tiny crayfish. A galvanized pipe, inserted into the pool, drew water to the house.

Going in the other direction, the spring's outflow passed through a flagstone-covered channel into the springhouse a few steps away, then exited to join a weak stream originating in what remained of the orchard—two or three apple trees, a lone black cherry, and an apricot tree, widely dispersed over a couple acres of scrub grass. You haven't tasted apricots until you've tasted tree-ripened apricots.

Here and there were remnants of ancient split-rail fences.

The farmstead was seated in an open vale with fields rising all around. To the west, through a depression in the horizon, where the lane left the road, was a small slice of Blue Ridge. Everything else visible from the house was ours. My parents paid $17,000 for the whole caboodle in 1955.

The farm came with a cow, an old, bony, golden mongrel with a crooked horn named Lucky, who had more milk in her than her appearance advertised. There was a pair of draft horses: a Percheron mare named Pearl, for her color, and a bay Belgian gelding named Bounce. They didn't convey with the farm, but we were free to use them. A third horse did convey, Beauty, solid black, all-purpose—she knew the harness but for us was always a pleasure horse. At fourteen hands, she was just barely not a pony.

We moved the last day of March and slept the first night on the dining-room floor.

The farm's location was critical. Across the river in Brunswick, Maryland, Pop could catch the B&O commuter train to D.C., fifty-some miles downriver. The express was OK, he said, "but that local…it stops at every doghouse. And if it's a double doghouse, it stops twice." He rose at 4:30 every morning and got home at 7:30 at night.

The commute was an hour and a half each way, and Pop used the time for writing. Parallels between foot-and-mouth eradication and his current job at Agriculture—screwworm eradication—started him on a novel about the former. The main character was a World War II veteran named Ward who was raising Black Angus cattle in West Virginia. Ward hired a refugee from the Hungarian revolution who inadvertently brought something—never named—contaminated with the foot-and-mouth virus. The outbreak and abatement, which Pop knew so well, fleshed out the story.

The Hungarian revolution had begun with a student demonstration in October 1956, and was quashed by the Soviet army eighteen days later. Pop invited a Hungarian of his acquaintance to the farm for details.

Ma served Hungarian goulash, which required paprika. Little Lovettsville would not stock so useless a condiment, but procured somewhere it was. I don't know that there were compliments to the chef, but Ma proved her culinary chops that time.

A week after crushing the revolution, Soviet Premier Nikita Khrushchev threatened, "We will bury you." Today, you cannot recapture the anticommunist paranoia that reigned in our land.

During the time of our move, a Japanese publisher, Iwanami Shoten, began negotiating for a Japanese edition of *Out of Your Pocket*.

The farm had no phone. We made do without until walking the half-mile to our neighbors, the Greens, to use theirs, proved unsustainable. Theirs was the last phone on the line. The phone company needed more poles to serve us, and wanted to charge us for them. Pop wouldn't have it. People on down the road, he said, would be getting phones, and "our" poles would serve them too. The company yielded.

We shared a party line with four other houses. Each had its own ring—two shorts, three shorts, a long and a short—but neighbors could and sometimes did pick up and listen in on you.

Around mid-summer, I said something to Ma about somebody being an Albert Einstein…or not being an Albert Einstein…something about Albert Einstein. "He just died a couple of months ago," Ma said. Died? You mean he was a real person?

Ma became the farm manager. The way she strode into the role made me think she just naturally knew it, that our Agriculture Department *Yearbooks of Agriculture* were just part of the furniture. They were dense texts on every subject from grass to livestock to trees to vegetables and, being government publications, free for the asking. Surely, they loomed large in Ma's education—livestock's dietary needs, crop rotation, when and what to plant—but I thought she just naturally knew it.

Ma overseeing livestock

What she refused was chemical agriculture. From the first, our farm was going to be organic. It had been chemically farmed, but we would restore it. Synthetics, she told us, destroyed the soil's ability to nourish plants. I never got a fix on Pop's attitude toward organics, but they mattered to Ma. The fields averaged ten to fifteen acres, so organics there were diluted, but we heavily composted, manured, and mulched the vegetable garden until, by our sixth year, potato bugs could not survive on our potato plants.

If Ma was the outfit's brains, Pat became its brawn. At fifteen, he was a big guy and strong. How to load hay, cut corn, thresh grains, came from hiring out to local farmers, at the men's wage of four dollars a day. Pop taught him how to milk cows.

Because we lived on a farm, school put him on the vocational agriculture track. "Live on a farm? You're Vo Ag." That was the criterion. Being Vo Ag automatically enrolled him in Future Farmers of America. Future Farmers of America had an initiation ritual, but nobody was going to put Pat through any hocus pocus. On initiation day, he pocketed a pair of "cow kickers"—a hobble for cows' hocks to prevent kicking—to defend himself from marauding initiators. I never learned the story's denouement, but the cow kickers apparently remained holstered.

Pop's job at Agriculture had swung from *aftosa* to the screwworm, the larval stage of a flesh-eating blowfly. Females laid eggs around open wounds or a host's nasal, oral, or anal areas. The larvae hatched within a day and dove into living tissue, creating painful lesions and decimating cattle herds.

Attempts at control had been futile until some genius hit on the "sterile insect technique." The female reproduced just once. If you flooded the environment with sterile males, females would lay sterile eggs. Sterile eggs, no larvae; no larvae, no screw worms. Radiation could sterilize the males without killing them. Airplanes could release them into the environment. The practice was first tested successfully on 2000 square miles near Orlando, Florida. Pop's job, as public information specialist, was to convince people that the mutant blowflies wouldn't make them radioactive.

Once again, work had him traveling. He was forever flying off to Florida or Nebraska or someplace. One frigid day in winter 1955–56, post cards arrived for each of us kids from Nebraska. Mine showed some American bison, even then still recovering from the great nineteenth-century slaughters. "I haven't seen any of these critters, yet," he wrote. The rest of the message is lost to memory, but he closed with, "So long, old wood chopper." At twelve, helping heat the house was one of my chores.

Buster and I fed the calves, Helen fed the chickens, Pat milked the cows. Bunny was too young for chores.

After Mexico, Pop had hoped he wouldn't have to travel any more, but things hadn't worked out that way. To me, his absences testified to his work's importance. I never particularly wondered what he did, but that somebody would fly him around and pay his hotel bills meant that what he was doing was

You know damn well that thing can't fly

worth the bother. Screwworm eradication was most of what I knew, with little clue to the details. Except, maybe those four-engine DC-7's or Lockheed Constellations. "You walk out on the runway," he'd say, "and see that great big thing and know damned well it can't fly!" He was a presence even in his absences.

He was very present on the first day at our new school. Buster and I were sentenced to Lovettsville Elementary. The previous year, that school had been Lovettsville High, but on our arrival, a county-wide, thousand-inmate high school had opened in Leesburg. Pat and Helen went there—Pat to tenth grade, Helen to eighth (Loudoun County had yet to institute junior high).

Buster and I rebelled. We'd only been there one day, and had to start school already? What a cheat! Our 132-acre playground needed exploring. Straw bales in the barn needed converting into forts. A haystack needed summiting. Buster hid in a closet. We pleaded for one more day. For a sixth-grader like me, and worse for a second-grader like Buster, the loss of one lousy day was out of all proportion to the benefit. Pop didn't have to work, so why did we have to go to school? But a good example our parents would make of us, and to school we went.

Its double entry door opened right onto the gym, which had a stage and doubled as the auditorium. As we walked in, some kid straight from *Rebel without a Cause*, upturned collar, hair in a D.A., made a highly audible basket that banged off the backboard and sproinged around the rim before sinking.

His few paces slowing down looked like nothing so much as a victory lap. His name was Willy Roberts obviously one of the school's "most popular."

In that gym, a few days later, I got my first and only polio shot. At Lovettsville Elementary, that was inoculation number two. Thanks to our move, I had missed Burke's inoculation number one, but luckily it has lasted sixty-nine years.

Maybe Pop took Buster to his room. Ma led me to mine. Classes must have started while we did paperwork. By the time we reached my room, it was full of bridling sixth graders giving me the eye. Mexico had left us wanting academically, but the teacher agreed to let me read among the bright ones before deciding where to place me. *Reading*, I thought. *Great*. I'd loved reading in second grade.

The bright ones sat by the windows; the dummies sat toward the dimmer, inside wall. Initially they put me there, but I would reclaim my birthright any day. In reality, it was more like two weeks, and I'd begun wondering if they'd forgotten their promise. My chance came, however. I joined the bright ones who were taking turns reading a story in the advanced reader. I gave it my best shot, was sent back to the dark side, and there remained for the rest of the year. Nobody ever explained why.

In Burke, there'd been bullies, but Lovettsville's Wayne "Possum" George, so named because pinched features made him resemble a possum, was the absolute worst. In two months, Possum dealt my self-esteem a blow that took a lifetime to outgrow. Then he dropped out of school and I never saw him again. Years later, while traveling to an army pre-induction physical after LBJ's troop call-up following the Tonkin Gulf incident, I learned that Possum had been shot in the elbow in Vietnam and had the joint fused.

"That poor, dumb bastard," was all I could think. I actually felt sorry for him. But sixty-nine years later, a glass of wine still helps get me going conversationally, even among friends.

As an antidote to my new school's perils, I requested a basketball for Christmas so I could become popular like Willy Roberts. Pop mounted the hoop on the corn crib, but the ruse didn't work. I could make set shots surprisingly well but, dribbling invariably meant tripping on either the ball or my own feet.

Kids still played hardball at Lovettsville Elementary. One day, Neddy Ayres was having fun lobbing pitches straight at me, but I still hit a grounder between second and third. Possum fielded the ball as I ran for first. The next thing, I was on the ground with a buzzing sensation in my head. It took me a moment to realize I'd been knocked out. Surely, Possum claimed it was an accident, but I've no doubt he did it on purpose.

The rest of the day was a blur. Back in class, we were standing singing a rousing tune with stamping of feet. The input was too much. I asked the teacher if I could sit down. She let me. My head felt nauseated. I put it on the desk feeling very weepy. There was a visit to the nurse. Then Ma and Pop were at the school collecting me. We stopped at McLain's Grocery. They asked if I wanted anything. I said a fireball.

An old family friend, Earl Hyde, was visiting, and I heard him say, "Don't let him go to sleep. I knew a boy once who fell off a wagon. They let him go to sleep and he never woke up." That scared me enough to keep me awake. The fireball probably helped, at least until it dissolved. I don't think we went to the doctor. I don't remember hearing the word "concussion," but surely there was one.

The school used softballs afterwards.

Bullying confronts a kid with an impossible situation. Do you go tell the teacher and admit to everybody that you can't handle it yourself? Or do you stuff it, throwing up to the bully that his efforts mean nothing? Stuffing it saves face. Unfortunately, it also becomes a habit that's almost impossible to break.

Why didn't I just fight back? Because nobody ever taught me how! Nobody ever told me it didn't matter if you got hit. That by itself would have helped. Sometimes I fought back anyway, but my methods came from the movies, not the Marquis of Queensbury, and were magnificently ineffective.

Like every victim of bullies, I wondered why people didn't like me. Everybody liked my father. What was wrong with me? Only decades of hindsight have offered an answer. Pop went through school with the same group of kids. His place was secure. Ours wasn't. The kid who keeps changing schools is ever an outsider. Every time we moved, we were outsiders all over again. And of course, there was "McConkey"—"Conk," "Monkey," "Donkey." I can laugh about it now, but back then it was no joke.

There were moments of hope. A different student would read a poem each day, and I asked the teacher to let me read Dr. Seuss's "Scrambled Eggs Super," which had appeared in *Children's Digest*. The class howled and begged the teacher to let me read the next time, too. Popularity! But the family library revealed a hard truth: most poetry isn't funny. Tiring of the search, I settled on Kipling's "Fuzzy Wuzzy" because the title sounded funny. Unfortunately, the poem wasn't, and I wasn't asked to read again.

Nor was everyone cruel. Two brothers, Leo and Johnny Gates, sort of adopted me. They weren't twins but were in the same grade because one had been held back. But, like Possum and Neddy Ayres, they dropped out after sixth grade. A couple of others, Wade Henry and Owen Charles, also from the dim side of the room, stayed pals into high school, until one and then the other—and Willy Roberts—dropped out. The Bright Ones weren't actively hostile, but never invited me into their circle. I didn't reach out to them either. There's more to penetrating a circle than being born into one.

In seventh grade, another tack dawned on me. If I couldn't do it with basketball, maybe I could with rope tricks. I brought my rope and *charro* outfit for show-and-tell. "Oh," said the teacher. "We're having an assembly. You can do it there." So, I costumed up and walked out before the whole school. Suddenly aware that my presence needed explaining, I rattled off the story of my father's job in Mexico and how we'd learned to spin ropes. I ran through my repertoire of tricks and retired satisfied that I'd made my place.

Wrong. No one said a thing. Nothing changed. Maybe they thought I was trying to show them up. At the time, however, their lack of response merely confirmed that something about me wasn't likable.

I volunteered to help write a play about Christopher Columbus. A committee of us occupied a corner of the auditorium/gym. While the other three or four discussed things endlessly, I sat apart writing. Every once in a while, they would say, "Don't write such a long play." I wasn't. In a pattern that has been with me all my life, I was boring in on a small opening scene, and wrote and rewrote the same few lines. When we returned to class, everyone was astonished at how little I'd done. They used the scene, but didn't use me in the play. All parts went to The Bright Ones. I didn't even know they'd used the scene until I saw the play.

The school itself was part of the problem. I'd shown some aptitude with art, and in seventh grade fell in love with oil pastels. I duplicated a scene from a western movie—cavalry riding through desert terrain—submitted it to an art show and won first prize…for one day. Then the judges decided no seventh grader could have created the picture and took the prize back. It was a backhanded compliment, but their assumption was clear: I'd cheated. They acted without a single word to me. My mother's inability to drive, and my father's schedule, doubtless played a part in their not pursuing the matter.

The mayor's son *always* won the village talent show.

It was among our parents' friends, Joe Colgan, Dale Morgan, and Earl Hyde that we felt welcome. Pop called Earl Hyde the "last universal genius." He knew everything. He'd graduated high school at age fifteen, worked his way around the world on steam freighters, and ended up back in the States at eighteen teaching school. Among his pupils, according to family lore, was American opera singer Grace Moore. He spoke an indeterminate number of languages, read and wrote more, and the Library of Congress certified him to catalog books in two hundred. He made money speculating in currencies during the Depression. He'd also led a Civilian Conservation Corps crew that built farm-style stone fences along both sides of the thirty miles of US Route 50 between Middleburg and Winchester, Virginia.

Unlike Dale Morgan or Joe Colgan, Earl Hyde came to us kids after we moved to the farm. One day, we got home from school, and there he was. We couldn't wait to show him our barn. "Come and see the barn, Mr. Hyde," we chimed. "Call me Earl," he said. "My name's not 'Mister.'" He seemed ancient, so it surprised us that he gripped the ladder to the barn's hay mow and climbed right up. "I love old barns," he said. "I love the way they smell."

How or why my parents should have known this personage wasn't explained, but the history was palpable. He was now living in a converted jail in Moorfield, West Virginia. Once when we visited there, he pulled a book from a shelf and asked Pop, "Have you read this?" Pop tried to open it, but it was not a book, it was an exquisitely crafted hip flask from Prohibition days that looked exactly like a book. The two exchanged knowing chuckles.

School was the nightmare, but there were compensations. We had arrived on the farm just as spring was ready to burst. A song in class contained the line, "sweet is the air with new-mown hay," and I associate that smell with a green, sunrise countryside suffused in golden mist. Green, gold, and new-mown hay. These weren't things you "got away to" at widely spaced intervals, they were yours, every day.

I'll never forget the first time the chickens got out. We all raced around in mad pursuit. Pépe, our three-fourths Border Collie/one-fourth German Shepherd, joined the frolic. "Catch Pépe! Don't let him get the chickens!" I caught up with him just as he caught up with a chicken…and held it down for me! He was a shepherd, and a better chicken-catcher than we were!

There are those who can't grasp the appeal of farm life, but you can't grasp the appeal by thinking about it. It's like the three bricklayers. A passer-by asks the first, "What are you doing?"

"Laying bricks," replies the worker.

The passer-by asks the second, "What are you doing?"

"Building a wall."

But the third mason tells the passer-by, "I am working on a magnificent cathedral." Those who see farming only as an endless procession of unrewarding chores are like the first bricklayer. A person I once knew was like the second. "All they do is spend the summer getting ready for winter!" Then there are those like the third bricklayer, to whom each task fits a magnificent whole.

Farming demands lots of time outdoors. It has lots of hard edges: the elements, long hours, tasks that have to be done rain or shine, freeze or thaw, seven days a week, 365 days a year. Each season, new tasks rub new blisters that turn to calluses, then fade back to tender skin that needs toughening up again the next year. Livestock generates massive quantities of manure. That's why they invented manure spreaders. Operating farm machinery is a jolting, jerking, juddering occupation. "Milk from contented cows?" Ha! Cows are contrary, obstinate, recalcitrant, and pig-headed.

What compensates for these aggravations? The absence of civilization's hum—you can hear silence. You can take long walks and never leave your own piece of Earth. You can view acres of undisturbed snow from your kitchen window. You're a piece with the owls and buzzards and rabbits and deer. You own the mornings, the sunrise, the mist, and the dew. You own the overcast and the rainfall, the sunsets, rainbows, clouds, the moon, the stars, the Milky Way. In cities, these are communal property, their view sliced and diced by buildings and electric wires, dimmed by air and light pollution.

Farming keeps you fit. Exercise releases endorphins. Endorphins give pleasure. Thanks to endorphins, farming makes you feel good. When Pat joined the Army, he gained weight in basic training.

Yet, we may have been presumptuous to call ourselves farmers, despite our 132 acres, our horses, cows, pigs, and chickens. Pop was a farmer—once in the blood, farming is there to stay. Things had changed in the years since he'd left—tractors were ubiquitous, along with combines, milking machines, hybrid seeds, synthetic fertilizers, insecticides, antibiotics, but he knew his stuff. Tethered to his desk, his part for now was relegated to weekends, but one day his farm would be a going concern.

Ma and Pop had taken us aside. On a farm, they said, there would be chores. We had to promise to do them or there would be no farm. We promised, and kept our word.

At first—except for the chores—the farm was one giant playground. Behind the house spread the pasture, eighty acres (including twenty acres of woods) with the area's highest hill giving a sweeping view of the countryside. Woods crowned the hill and tumbled down its western flank. Over on Mr. Wells's place, forest may have blanketed a hundred acres more, all the way down to Dutchman's Creek and up the other side. The hill rose abruptly, and for Buster and me became the new Mt. Everest. We would make the "first-ever" wintertime "attempt," with Pop along as team photographer. One of the best things about mountain-climbing was the chocolate bars for emergency energy.

By winter, however, attempts to sled *down* the mountain had replaced attempts to climb *up* it. Our sleds hadn't come with us from Burke, so we made our own, more like toboggans. Staves from an old nail keg, nailed to flat boards, served for the curved front ends. The staves didn't rise as high as real toboggan fronts, but up the hill we'd hike and down it would launch ourselves.

I never made it to the bottom. Not that the craft wouldn't go, but when it attained a certain speed, something—maybe the low front end—caused it to raise great clouds of powder from the inside of which one felt he was suffocating. I invariably baled about two thirds of the way down. Buster may have had better luck.

That first year at Lovettsville Elementary, a fifth grader named Eric Johnson introduced himself, and I have always been grateful for his friendship. We had just about everything in common. He had a marvelous book called *The Boy Mechanic* with 200 projects making everything from your own gramophone to an image projector. How many, if any, of those projects we ever finished I don't know, but it was plenty just to wish-book them. He had an 8mm movie camera. His family had a "portable" reel-to-reel tape recorder. We tried recording an audio scene from Walt Disney's *The Great Locomotive Chase*, using BBs on a cookie sheet to simulate the sound of rain. We tried to build an airplane—a real one. Eric and his younger brother, Carl, and Buster and I, swam in Dutchman's Creek and built rafts. We took up guitar-playing. His mother took us to Braddock Heights amusement park out past Frederick, Maryland, and to the occasional church social having specimens of food we never saw at home. In the summer of 1956, Pop drove Buster and me, Eric and Carl, twelve miles to Purcellville four weekends in a row for Red Cross swimming lessons. Eric and Carl's father was a newspaperman who commuted to D.C. on the same train as Pop.

In summer, 1957, an appealing, slightly built, gray-haired man bootlegged himself a shanty on our river bottom. Buster and I discovered him. Pop said he could stay, but insisted he pay a dollar every six months to avoid establishing squatter's rights. No real estate broker could have resisted that location, fronting on the Potomac's broad sweep.

Buster and I, Eric and Carl, saw him more than anybody else. He taught us how to pole a boat, assured us we could just borrow the wooden jon boats that fishermen kept beached at the water's edge. We sometimes poled across to Brunswick to buy him groceries, and he would make us something to eat. His story emerged slowly and incompletely. He'd been a railway dining-car chef, but was on the lam from something in Maryland and couldn't go back, something to do with somebody getting murdered with a shotgun, a thing we found impossible to connect with this unprepossessing soul we called "The Old Man." That's about all we ever heard.

In the summertime, the horses gathered under the wooded canopy atop the hill,

Pat seeding wheat by horsepower

where the ground leveled out. One day early in our stay, they burst out of that lair, running, whinnying, kicking. An outburst like that didn't happen for no reason. I walked up and found the bay Belgian work horse, Bounce, flat on his side, dead as a doornail, leaving us with one, Pearl.

Bounce had helped with Pat's Future Farmers of America project. Every FFA member did a project. This was Pat's big chance to experience life as it once was. He raised three acres of corn the old-fashioned way. First, he fenced the plot. Then, using Pearl and Bounce and a set of "gears" (harness) from Raymond Smith (we'd bought the farm from the widow of Raymond Smith's brother), and a single-bottom walking plow, he worked evenings and weekends plowing, planting, hoeing weeds. In the fall he harvested the crop by hand, cutting the stalks with a corn knife and standing them in shocks to ripen.

Over the summer, probably with money earned helping local farmers, he bought a one-ton, 1929, Model-A Ford, stake-body truck for fifty dollars from Kingfish Everhart, Lovettsville's junk man. As a farm vehicle, it didn't need to be registered or inspected, and Pat, at fifteen, didn't need a license to drive it.

Who in his right mind would endure all that sweat and toil when there were easier ways to do it? For one thing, we didn't own a tractor but we did have horses, but that was just pretext. The toil and sweat went back to our desire to be pioneers. Pioneers endured the extremes, but reading about them was nothing like experiencing them. We wanted to experience them.

Also, the farm isolated us. We had one car, which Pop drove to the train every day. Ma never learned to drive. Pat's junkyard-fugitive—his Model-A truck—wasn't road certified even when it ran. With mobility impaired, sports were beyond our reach. So, we substituted horseback riding and farm work. Those were more novel to us than baseball or football anyway. Nobody watched, nobody cheered, but they proved our mettle to ourselves if to no one else. Nobody watched, that is, except local farmers. As we grew, Pat and I came in demand as farm hands. Buster was just reaching employable age when we left the farm.

We edged toward the cowboy end of the scale when we started boarding horses—one of the simplest ways of making your land pay. The owners wanted their horses ridden so they didn't forget the rules, so every weekend a-riding we would go. A man from across the river referred boarders to us and also someone to shoe them, for as surely as you have horses you need to keep them shod.

If Joe Colgan made a questionable cowboy, our

A-riding we would go

horse shoe-er, John Haws, was the type's spittin' image. He'd probably never been west of Maryland, but where Joe was not even rawboned, John Haws was rawboned and wiry to boot. His face was wind-worn and sun-browned. He rolled his own smokes. "How old do you think I am?" he asked on our first meeting. We all guessed around sixty.

"If I live to the end of next month," he said with a twinkle, "I'll be forty-nine." "Phorty-nine," rather, as he wasn't wearing his teeth. Phorty-nine looking sixty. What a life *he'd* had!

My first time horseback on the farm was no more promising than it had been under Nell Hatcher's low-hanging branch back in Burke. I got on gentle old Beauty—bareback—and headed up the lane at a walk. Close to the top, Beauty decided to turn around and go back home. Failing to read her intention, I slid slightly to one side. Once she got me going, I did the rest myself, landing with a thud on the ground.

Improvement was rapid, however. We had three saddles: two rugged, used, forty-pound westerns and a brand-new Mexican—with its signature "dinner-plate" saddle horn—that we'd brought from Mexico. Pat and Helen got the westerns and I, being third in line, got the Mexican which, unfortunately, was more show than substance and didn't last long. That left me mostly bareback, but if bareback does nothing else, it teaches you to stick to your horse.

Pat and I rode down to Mr. Wells's place, I on Junior and Pat on Hairless Joe, a worn-out racehorse. Somewhere in the woods near Dutchman's Creek, Junior easily went over a downed tree, but Hairless tripped, fell, and lay on his side with all four feet up on the log. We needed to roll him over, but the western saddle impeded that plan. We had to get it off him, but how? Tie a rope through the fork of Pat's saddle, the other end to the horn of mine, and pull? Couldn't hurt to try.

We uncinched Pat's saddle and hove to. The saddle came free, though the stirrup and its strap stayed behind. We rolled Hairless over, he got up, we repaired the stirrup, resaddled Hairless, and stopped in on Mr. Wells, who was living in his corncrib.

Hairless was sick. His real name was Joe, but we added "Hairless" because he literally lost his hair. "Hairless Joe" was a character in the "Lil' Abner" comic strip. Hairless also lost his appetite. He wouldn't come in when we put out hay. We tried taking it to him, but he still wouldn't eat. One day he was down and couldn't get up, and Pat put a .22 slug in his head.

Desirous of insinuating improved agriculture on the locals, Pop bought two hybrid, Beltsville #1 hogs, a strain developed at the Agriculture Department's research station in Beltsville, Maryland, outside D.C. They were longer and leaner than the Belted Hampshires most common to American farms. Being longer, with less fat, there was more meat per pound. A local farmer, Mr. Hughes, said they looked like they needed roller skates under their bellies, but he bought a sow for breeding. Not only did Pop bring home the latest thing in bacon, he also brought home Agriculture Department plans for the latest thing in hog feeders, and built one.

The most classical plan he brought home, however, was for the latest thing in outhouses. In the summer of '55, we replaced the old two-holer that came with the farm. The two-holer made it possible to share bowel functions with another family member, if so moved, but it didn't have a pit under it. You'd use it until the waste rose close to your bottom, then move it.

The new and the old

Pop set about building an up-to-date facility with a commodious pit which, though only eleven, I helped excavate. Earl Hyde, helping supervise, remarked, "I could tell he's husky by the way he shoveled dirt out of there." "Husky" had not yet become a euphemism for "fat," so Earl must have meant energetic, because "scrawny" would more aptly have described my physique.

At a point, Pop asked me to hand him a "straight edge." I hadn't a clue what a "straight edge" was and cast about hoping to see something that might announce itself as being one. Mr. Wells, also supervising, picked up Pop's handsaw and sighted along its back edge judging straightness. "There," said Pop. "Mr. Wells knows what one is."

Pat's ascension to farmer-in-chief came at a cost both to his education and, as I saw it, to his honor. Pat was headstrong and rebellious. Genetics had grafted Gramps's strength to Pop's height. As a ten- or eleven-year-old, he'd established country music as the house brand. At age thirteen, when we got back from Mexico, he'd resolved to take up smoking, and no extremes of parental opposition would change his mind. He'd threatened Future Farmers of America with a cow-kicker tattoo. Now, at the end of his tenth year of school, he was talking of dropping out.

That was the cost to his education. The cost to his honor came in the form of a big, handsome, sorrel gelding named Dusty who came to us as a boarder. He was as hard-headed as Pat, and Pat fell absolutely in love with him. Pat said he'd finish school if Ma and Pop would buy Dusty for him. They agreed. The price was $600, no minor investment in 1955. Then Pat dropped out anyway. The issue stayed between him and our parents.

Pat's favorite picture of himself on Dusty, summer 1956

He dove into farming literally with horsepower. Pearl could never have pulled the weight alone, and a bay mare named Queen replaced the departed Bounce. Various horse-drawn implements appeared—a mower with a five-foot cutter bar, a side-delivery hay rake, a double-bottom riding plow, a two-row corn planter. These machines were easily come by. As farmers upgraded their operations, they were glad to let you have their cast-offs at fire-sale prices.

But even when it's idle, you have to feed a horse—it continues breathing, stamping, snorting, pooping, and peeing with unabashed gusto. Tractors, when you turn them off, are off. While awake, they generally do what you tell them to. Getting cooperation from horses is a two-way street. I ingested that principle in the spring of 1958, when country singer Don Gibson's "Oh, Lonesome Me," hit the charts. I sang that while harrowing the field above the orchard. Every time I got to "Ohhhhhhhh, lonesome me," Pearl and Queen would stop. "Come up, here, god damnit!" I'd yell.

The more often that happened, the more confused they got and the madder I got. I finally gave up, brought them in, and went to the house complaining I couldn't do anything with those goddamned horses. Within minutes, Pat and Ma deduced that the horses had confused "Ohhhhhhhhh" with "Whoooooa." No tractor would have made that mistake, but we didn't have one.

Lacking a hay baler, we put our hay up loose. Pat mowed it with the horse-drawn mower and raked it into windrows with the horse-drawn rake. Then, after a day curing in the sun (praying it wouldn't rain), pitchforked great piles onto Pat's Model-A stake-bed and brought them to the barn. That's where that menacing-looking hay fork, dangling from a track under the roof's ridge, came into play.

You actually had to pull it down (no, it wouldn't fall and impale you), jab it into the hay, set its barbs, hook a hoist line behind the horses, holler, "Git up!" and watch a mass of hay whoosh to the ridge and whir sideways over the mow. A trip rope released the fork's barbs, and down would fall the hay, where you arranged it with a pitchfork.

For all its hitches, horse farming was a trip I would never give back, but we could indulge it only to a point. We shared out our first full corn crop to a guy named Rob Ulrich. For plowing, planting, and harvesting, he got sixty percent. For use of our land, we got forty. At season's end, he picked his sixty percent and left ours in the field. Nothing would persuade him to come back. Our only choice was to pick it by hand—six acres—and it took a whole, very frigid winter to do it.

Buster and I each picked a half bushel per evening after school, and a full bushel on each weekend day. It kept us in corn, but it was hard to see progress on the field. At sixty bushels an acre, our six acres held 360 bushels. We were picking nine a week. One cold, windy day, Pat and I tackled the field with horse and wagon. "Ain't nothing between here and the North Pole but a bob wire fence," Pat quoted from a cowboy book.

"On a day like this," I expanded, "you need a two-foot thermometer with the zero at the top!" There was another frigid, gusty, snowy Saturday when I resolved to pick my whole two bushels at one go, wearing a pair of unlined work gloves with holes in the fingers, just like the pioneers, and was rewarded with a suitably pioneer case of frostbite, mild, but quite painful.

Another weekend, toward spring, Buster, Pat, Pop, and I invaded the field. Buster and I had cleared about half the corn by then, but at that rate it would have taken well into the next growing season to finish. Doubling manpower for one day helped, but not much. The highlight was my spying what looked like an ear of corn, finding it empty, saying, "Aw, shucks," and Pop's retorting, "That's right!"

Finally, one Saturday, while we went to Leesburg, our horse shoe-er, John Haws, nearly finished the job. "How'd you manage to get so much done?" I asked. "Oh," he said slowly, "y' just keep mopin' along." That byword has served me well in life.

Movies have portrayed farm work as a frenetic attack on hay bales, cows, and garden hoes, but you'd be useless in half an hour going at it that way. You don't charge the work, you walk along with it. You don't *push* the plow; the horse *pulls* it. Strike up a rhythm, pace yourself, and you'll pitch hay bales ten hours to the stretch, just mopin' along. At a day's end, there can be fifteen acres of corn shocks to look at and say, "I did that," then walk to the house. You're already home.

Farming can be dangerous, but much can still be done on autopilot while your mind wanders Elysian Fields. I've done some of my best daydreaming just mopin' along. But let your attention lapse, and danger lurks. I once dropped a pitchfork into the mouth of a threshing machine and almost stepped in after it. I got kicked by a cow and spent five weeks in a cast. Mr. Hughes, who bought that Beltsville #1 sow, had lost a forearm to an ensilage chopper. "I once knew a boy who fell into an ensilage chopper," Pop said.

"Did it kill him?" I asked.

"No. He picked himself up, put himself back together, and went inside and said, 'I'm hungry.'"

A high-school classmate had a tractor turn over on him. It slid sideways on a wet slope and flipped. His father lifted the tractor off him with his bare hands.

Only years of hindsight have taught me to appreciate how much Pat did to keep that farm going. Clipping weeds in the pasture was like mowing a 60-acre lawn. His presence was vital to keeping the place from falling to ruin, let alone keeping it moving.

We, in school, rarely saw him in that role. Our impressions came more from what we did see—Ma trying to get him up in the morning. She finally gave up and dumped the responsibility on him. It worked.

On the gray, overcast morning of Sunday, September 15, 1957, I got up, went downstairs, made a pot of coffee, and poured myself a cup. I was fourteen, the age in our family when you got to drink coffee. Pop made much of his love for the brew. My introduction was a step toward those gatherings of friends for conversation at the hearth about strange and wonderful things, coffee at the elbow.

That fall, we made apple butter in the McConkey-family copper apple-butter kettle. It took all day. The kettle was kept at a low simmer with a wood fire in the backyard. It had to be stirred slowly but constantly during the entire process. We all took turns, including Bunny who was only six. The apples came from the one producing apple tree in the orchard.

We sent a Beltsville #1 hog to a local slaughterhouse, and it returned in neat, frozen chops and roasts bearing no resemblance to the animal we had known. Also included was scrapple and five gallons of lard. "They use everything but the squeal," Pop said.

Few people had a clue to how bad lard was for you. The ham and bacon were unfrozen, ready for smoking. We cut down a non-bearing apple tree for its green, smoky wood with flavoring properties, rubbed the meat with Grandmother McConkey's seasoning mix, and hung them in the smokehouse.

That same fall, the Soviet Union orbited humanity's first artificial satellite, "Sputnik." How could this have happened? *We* were supposed to be first. Our mortal enemies had beaten us to the punch! It galvanized the nation and suddenly everybody was a rocket scientist. "For every action, there is an equal and opposite reaction."

"Escape velocity?"

"17,000 mph."

"Expert," Pop chortled. "An 'ex' is a has-been, and a 'spurt' is a drip under pressure."

Infatuation with rocketry exploded. You could wrap a match in a scrap of foil, slip it over a partly straightened paper clip, hold a lit match to the nose, and watch it shoot up three or four feet. Buster resolved to raise the stakes and patiently filled a toilet-paper tube with matchheads. He fashioned a nose cone and created a nozzle from a thread spool which fit snugly into the rear of the tube. A length of old house gutter, leaned against the hay rake, served as the gantry. Pop decided he'd better light the thing himself. The fuel blew the thread spool out of the back without generating a whisper of forward thrust.

"Sputnik" scared us, echoing "Bolshevik," but it introduced a cultural artifact. The "nik" fell humorously on American ears. When the Soviets orbited a dog, we dubbed it "Muttnik." A *San Francisco Chronicle* columnist thought it would be funny to add "nik" to "Beat"—a class of people a bewildered public was chortling at. (The Beats considered themselves both "beaten down" and "beatific.")

The *Chronicle* turned them into "Beat*niks*," who played bongos, contemplated their navels, and asked nonsense riddles—"Why is a mouse when it's flying?"

"The higher it goes, the faster it spins."—that had to do with something called "Zen." Even Pop brought home a nonsense riddle.

We thought those riddles were oh so new, but that mouse had some miles on it. In Sinclair Lewis's 1922 novel, *Babbitt,* when Babbitt's wife drags him to a Theosophical and Pantheistic Oriental Reading Circle, he remarks, "It sounds like 'Why is a mouse when it spins?'"

Pop sawing, Bunny observing, Pat...?

We were making progress on a "beaten-down" conceit of our own—heating a two-hundred-year-old house with the firewood we gathered in our own woods and sawed and split with raw muscle. Snow sifted around those antique window sashes and collected on the two-foot-wide sills.

I entered ninth grade in 1957, determined to follow Pat's lead and drop out of school. I was sick of cliques and bullies, and attributed disinterest in uninspiring curricula to my academic backwardness thanks to Mexico. To deflect the parental opposition Pat had had to deal with, I would first prove my unsuitability for school by failing ninth grade.

Given that I'd decided to be a writer when I grew up, it may seem strange that I chose to fail English, but the choice targeted the teacher, not the subject. The students regarded Mr. Naylor as the faculty's biggest joke, and I still find it hard not to agree. His very jowls sagged in assent. I became a cutup, once sailing a paper airplane right under his nose. He made no effort to trace the missile's origin.

It wasn't strange that I chose English, but it was strange that, having missed the entire third grade and most of fourth, I still had to work at failing. Even without study, I had to give answers I knew were wrong. If ever a teacher deserved to have a pupil flunk, it was Mr. Naylor. At year's end, I flashed my F and declared I wasn't going back to school. But Pat was made of sterner stuff than I. All my parents had to say was, "Oh, yes you are," and I was sunk.

I went back, and was shocked to find myself in tenth grade after all. Vocational Agriculture was so important that it earned a credit and a half instead of just one. Two years of Vo Ag had earned back the credit lost in English.

That year, another outsider, Michael Phillips, and I formed an intellectual clique of two, and I began emerging from the redneck circle I'd been in—not entirely objectionably—since our arrival. Having failed at failing, buoyed by Mike's friendship, I began applying myself.

I asked to be switched to college-prep, but the advisor said my grades weren't good enough. So, I began taking college-prep courses as electives— Latin, chemistry, the second years of both algebra and geometry. I still had to make up the lost year of English, however, and graduated a year late despite Vo Ag.

Mike and I did a biology project together. It consisted of a brief description and a drawing of an instance of each biological phylum. Mike was quite artistic, and I had some ability, too. I suggested including something about where each specimen fit on the evolutionary tree. His reply took me by surprise. "I don't see how anybody can believe in evolution." I'd never given it much thought but assumed evolution to be settled doctrine. The next day, however, Mike showed me a Jehovah's Witness pamphlet quoting Darwin himself to "prove" the evolutionary fallacy.

I took the pamphlet home. Ma produced a gorgeous, leather-bound, early edition of *The Origin of Species*. Such books once showed up in used book stores at prices even Depression-era bibliophiles could manage. The pamphlet had quoted Darwin saying that any instance of the spontaneous generation of life would cause his theory to fail. The quote failed to include Darwin's "but I have found none." Loudoun County schools didn't teach evolution. They did teach that the gulf between humans and animals was great enough to justify treating humans separately.

I never confronted Mike, and we stayed friends. He took up the mandolin and with Eric Johnson and me tried forming a musical trio that suffered from too many chiefs. Our *Santa Lucia* made it to the school's talent show but didn't win anything.

Chapter Seven

Heart Attack

MARCH 30, 1958, was exactly three years since our last day at Burke. It was bedtime, and Pop was having chest pains. There was no 911. Phone books didn't even have special pages for emergency numbers. Ma had to thumb through the small print to find an ambulance in Brunswick. Two firemen eased Pop down the steep, narrow, winding, colonial-era staircase in the ladder-backed chair Pop's father had made. The chair was a legend. Seasoned rungs had been hafted into green legs. As the legs dried, they shrank and held the rungs with a grip no glue could equal. Pop had helped weave the split-hickory seat. At the bottom of the stairs, he turned to Bunny, just seven, and said, "Always be good to people."

The scene was dead sober. There was concern, but we didn't know what to do with it. The rescue workers laid Pop on a stretcher, took him to the ambulance, and drove away. I don't remember whether Ma went with them. Maybe Pat drove her.

A week later, Dale wrote to Pop:

It seems to be the fate of my friends in recent months to get knocked down with heart attacks, and maybe what this shows is a relationship with me is a perilous thing to sustain…

It is a crisis for your family at the moment…but the truth is, you have been carrying too big a burden for too long, and it was high time that the others [began] to carry their full share. What has happened to you may easily be the making of your family, by giving them the sobering challenge of real responsibility, and the opportunity to show what is in them.

If I can help a bit in one way or another, please let me know. Meanwhile, relax, fellow, relax, read a good book if you can find one before I publish another (joke), and don't try to solve all the world's problems in the next twenty minutes.

In the interest of full disclosure, I must include what Pop wrote to Dale July 19:

During my illness, I have gradually learned, you were getting some pretty one-sided information about this family [from Joe Colgan]. I don't really think that our children are worse than anybody else's, though admittedly they have put me in the humor for mayhem, upon occasion. One of these occasions was on the day I got sick, when I cut wood all day in a drizzle and three able-bodied boys sat inside keeping themselves warm. I can only add, in all honesty that it is probable that my own feelings, pretty well sustained through the day, caused an artery to kink up that night, so I am surely as much to blame as anybody. At my age, a man ought to control his bile better than that. Along the same general line, any advices you got that reflect on Anna had better be taken with a 50-pound block of salt.

That was six and a half decades ago. I have no recollection either of Pop cutting wood all day by himself, or of anybody's making a deal of it. I recall vividly another instance where my mother made a deal of not asking him to take me to a high school function after he arrived home weary at 7:30 p.m., and so think I'd have remembered a wood-cutting injunction too.

I feel bad about the wood-cutting. That day, of course, there was no clue that a heart-attack was lurking, or that Pop was out there stewing. Maybe we boys felt we'd done our share keeping the house warm during the week and were entitled to some relief on the weekend. It took a lot of wood to heat that house. In six and a half years, we cleared the deadfall from twenty acres of woods and started cutting down live trees.

The next time I saw Pop, he was in an oxygen tent, doped up on pain killers. In those days, health insurance was optional. You had to go down to the payroll window on payday and pay your premiums in person. Pop had let his lapse. Now his income was slashed by sixty percent, and we became poster children for universal healthcare.

There were no bypass surgeries, stents, or clot-busters in 1958. Blood-thinning was in its infancy. You took morphine and waited to see how much of your heart survived. Today they get you up as soon as possible, to keep the heart muscle toned. Back then, they feared increased demand on a crippled organ would make things worse. Pop was in bed for three weeks. They sent him home with orders to rest, exercise lightly, and regulate his heartbeat with digitalis. Dietary changes may or may not have been advised. There wasn't a whisper about cholesterol, except in *Prevention* magazine.

Pop followed doctor's orders with one exception—he would not quit smoking. "Well," said the doctor, "it's your gut."

"And that," said Pop, "was putting the responsibility exactly where it belongs." Smoking's effect on the ulcer the doctor worried about—not its effect on the heart. That was then, this is now.

He had to avoid stairs, so we installed a bed in a first-floor room. We rented a sander and Pat redid the floors. Joe Colgan painted the room and refinished Pop's desk.

At age fourteen, you're apt to believe things will be OK, but inside a knot wouldn't untie itself. Pop was uncharacteristically quieter. Ma, too, was quieter, but she'd always been quiet.

Farms don't pause for heart attacks. Chickens don't stop laying eggs. With Pop's income at forty percent of his regular pay, the farm had to start making up deficits. That's when I joined the milking team. I wasn't really paying attention, but if we needed more milkers, we must have gotten more cows.

Milking isn't very interesting. Until I got kicked in the knee and spent five weeks in a cast, the biggest thing about joining the milking team was trying to make a fist in the morning. It felt like a knitting needle was embedded in my forearm, jabbing the heel of my hand. The sensation disappeared with the milking motion, but persisted for my first few weeks. We lacked milking machines and the money to buy them. Or the inclination. We were pioneers and liked it that way. The milking stall had a dirt floor and wood stanchions. Grade-A improvements were beyond us. So we sold grade B, the stuff of Cheese Whiz and Elmer's glue. It shipped in ten-gallon cans instead of stainless-steel tank trucks.

Getting ourselves out of bed was far more entertaining than milking. Depending on how many cows we were milking at the time, Pat and I rose at 3:30, 4:00, or 4:30. We had a loud Big Ben alarm clock, so placed that you had to get up to turn it off. Eventually, however, you sleep through anything, and when one of us started sleeping through Ben, we'd pass him off to the other. Once I tried being funny, tiptoeing into Pat's room, holding the clock to his ear, and detonating the alarm. Out swept an arm that sent the clangor and its mechanism into a corner. The clock took it better than Pat did—it never missed a tick.

One night, Big Ben shredded the darkness and as fine a stream of profanity as I've ever heard issued from Pat's room. Our top floor was a finished attic, four rooms with sloped ceilings. There was no hall. Access to each room was through the last. The stairs rose into Pat's room, and his bed sat against the railing at the edge of the stairwell. It was an old four-poster with pegs for stringing ropes.

Bypassing the ropes, a box spring and mattress brought it level with the top of the railing. The foot of the bed was under the low edge of the ceiling. He'd gotten turned around in bed, and was only saved from launching into the stairwell by sitting up and hitting his head on the ceiling.

Under maternal oversight, we cleaned our milk buckets, milk cans, and milking stall fastidiously, netting below average bacteria counts on which price largely depended. Price also depended on butterfat content. Except for a large Holstein named Midge, whose low butterfat she made up for with four gallons of milk twice daily, our herd was mostly Jerseys and Guernseys, who boosted our butterfat as much above average as our bacteria count was below. We averaged 25¢ a gallon. Grade-A dairymen poured Lysol into their bulk tanks to suppress bacteria. We never did that.

The Farmall, Pat, Buster and Jim in 1960

It became obvious that one brother couldn't run a 132-acre farm with one pair of horses, and one day there stood a handsome, faded-red, '40s-era, Farmall-H tractor. It had five forward speeds and could start from a dead stop in any of them. It had to. Tractors knew nothing of synchronized transmissions. If you wanted to shift gears, you had to stop to do it. Our Farmall did fifteen miles an hour wide open in high gear, and you wouldn't risk it anywhere but, on the road, where the chance of tipping over was minimized. Most farm work was done in second and third.

Threshing Crew   By the author

From our first summer, Pat had hired out as a farm hand. I first hired in 1958, if you forget the two days the previous summer I'd worked the bagger on a threshing machine, at kids' wages, two dollars a day. Now, at age 14, I got men's wages—four dollars, no benefits (farmers didn't have to give them). It was hot, dusty, sweaty, itchy work, whether getting in hay or shocking wheat. We still threshed in our neck of the woods—wheat, oats, barley, orchard grass. Combines (n. COM-bine) were making inroads, but you couldn't combine (v. COM-bine) orchard grass, a good cash crop for growing horse hay. If you let the seeds ripen on the stalk, they would fall off before you could harvest them. So, you cut it slightly under-ripe and set it in shocks to mature. Old horse-drawn binders—the crowning elaboration of McCormick's reaper—tongues sawn off so tractors could pull them—cut the grains and bound them into sheaves. Wheat was waist high back then. Today, it has been bred down to knee-height, leaving more energy for the seed heads.

The typical workday was ten hours, but that included midday "dinner." And boy did they feed you. You washed in one of an array of wash basins, then tucked in to all you could eat of pork chops, green beans in bacon fat, mashed potatoes, buttered biscuits, apple pie, all washed down with gallons of iced tea. Gastronomically, I had died, gone to heaven, and did my best to make up for fifteen years of what passed for food in my mother's universe. Ma told Dale that the vegetable garden suffered by my absence, but I do remember donating a fair part of my earnings to the family coffer.

All the while, Pop was anticipating returning to work in the fall. He walked the fields, resting as needed. In the pasture behind the house, the cows had worn a path to the back acres (which overlooked the river). That path was now a rut, and the cows started a new path beside it. Pop dropped stones in the rut lest it wash to a gully.

He told Dale of picking blackberries. "The sky has never been bluer, the grass never greener, the beasties artfully arranging themselves on the hillsides never a more beautiful sight. I have thrilled again to fireflies, moonlight on the landscape, stars coursing in the sky—things I came near to never seeing again. Altogether, I couldn't have had a more perfect time or place in which to convalesce. By December, I should be well back into the routine at the Department."

Convalescence gave him time to move on his own writings. Old friend Millen Brand, poet, novelist, man of the publishing world, took Pop to school on his novel about foot-and-mouth disease. A novel can't just be about an issue like foot-and-mouth; it "is preponderantly the vehicle of character." Pop took the lesson to heart and began working up a fix. Brand had read Pop's *Father April* in 1954, when he was with Crown Publishers. He'd loved the writing, he said, and the book truly deserved a home, but unfortunately it wasn't "popular" enough for his current employer.

Judson King, a veteran New Dealer and advocate for public power, was coming out with a book, *The Conservation Fight, from Theodore Roosevelt to the Tennessee Valley Authority*, and asked Pop to do the index. He dove into the task with gusto, scouring the book for indexable items, noting each and the pages where it appeared, on a 3x5 card, and filing the cards alphabetically in a cigar box. King died before the book appeared, but his widow gave Pop an antique musket for his efforts. We never tested if the gun could be fired without exploding.

Ma and Pop seemed to be enjoying each other in a way they may not have since the Depression. Ma told me, much later, that if it hadn't been for Pop, her isolation on the farm would have been intolerable.

He went briefly back to work but in early November had a "setback" and returned to the hospital. He had driven the tractor one day, remarking, "That was the first time I ever drove a tractor," but the exertion was apparently too much. Lacking power steering, the tractor could be a beast to manage. I never learned exactly what "setback" meant, but suspect it was another, if minor, heart attack requiring more convalescence. He was home for Thanksgiving.

Still recovering a month later, Pop wrote to Dale, "Christmas history was made in our household. The children did all the shopping, wrapping, bringing in, setting up, decorating, and taking down the tree. I had a separate Christmas—slept very late and received my presents after all others had been passed out." Ma and Pop scrounged gifts from what they had in the house. I got *The Romance of Leonardo DaVinci* by Dimitri Merejkowski, a wonderful book which I finally read ten years later in an Indian village.

"Ain't no disgrace bein' poor; it's just so damned unhandy." We still had music, books, conversation, horseback riding, swimming in Dutchman's Creek, sunrises, sunsets, untrammeled snow, the gold-green haze of a spring morning, the smell of wood fires and new-mown hay. Ma shouldered her husband's illness and the avalanche of debt uncomplainingly. Helen took off her junior year to help out at home.

On January 8, 1959, Fidel Castro entered Havana, Cuba, installing himself in place of Fulgencio Batista, whom he'd ousted after two years of guerilla warfare. Pat had been pulling for Castro and was glad he'd won. Me, I'd heard of neither Fidel Castro nor his rebellion, but if they made Pat glad, they must have been OK.

That same day, Pop's sister Gladys wrote: "Am sorry your family has had such a time with broken bones, but as sure as there is a big family, a lot of things can happen."

It wasn't a broken bone; it was a torn ligament. We'd bought a skittish young cow from Mr. Flook (our horse-shoer, John Haws, was Flook's tenant farmer) and named her Flookie. Flookie didn't want to be touched, much less milked. Pat had tried installing hock chains—"cow kickers"—without success. He'd lost his temper, spooking Flookie even more. Ma asked me to try.

I tried my best, but suddenly found myself against the back wall of the milking stall moaning, "O-oh. O-oh." My knee wouldn't support me. There was no pain, but I kept moaning, "O-oh, o-oh." Pat, using his Boy Scout training, lifted me onto his back with my arms around his neck, crossed over his chest, and carried me moaning to the house.

Ma told me, "Don't let your father hear you," but I couldn't control it.

I couldn't get upstairs so slept on a rollaway cot in the living room. The next morning, I tried walking again, uselessly. The knee was two or three times its normal size and still wouldn't support me. Better yet, we were snowed in and it was four days before we could get to the doctor in Leesburg. Pop had an appointment of his own, and while he saw his doctor, mine unsheathed a massive 200cc syringe and drew great quantities of fluid from the knee, then put me in a cast from my hip to my ankle, added a pair of crutches, which he told me to stop using as soon as possible. A torn ligament takes longer to heal than a broken bone.

Buster, eleven years old, took my place on the milking stool till I healed.

A few weeks later, Ma dished up something else. She wanted an orchard grass-lespedeza mix in the field above the orchard, and appointed me to sow it. I was still in the cast but walking, and Carl Sandburg's *Abraham Lincoln, the Prairie Years,* had me enthralled. To prove my pioneer bona fides, I tried swinging the bag of seed over my shoulder despite the cast. It whirled me like a top and landed me on the ground—three times before I gave up in disgust. Surely I was a better pioneer than *that!* I sowed the field with a horn seeder, and that restored my yeoman sensibilities.

Few implements could have been more pioneer than the horn seeder. It must have been as old as agriculture itself, yet even with Sputniks and Boeing 707s buzzing overhead, you could still buy a horn seeder at the hardware store. The seed pouch had a shoulder strap, a little sleeve off the pouch's lower corner, and a tapered metal tube—the "horn"—extending a foot beyond the sleeve. Swing the horn one way on one pace, the other way on the next, and in less than a day you've seeded ten acres, even with a cast on your leg. Simon and Schuster's logo immortalizes the process, sans horn.

Iwanami Shoten of Japan had published *Out of Your Pocket* in Japanese, starting during the time of our 1955 move to the farm, and that edition was still drawing royalties. The book had sold 17,000 copies in English. The Japanese ultimately bought 25,000, but the currency exchange rate made for a meager royalty. On May 29, Pop wrote to Dale: "Well, I'm still in business in a small way. Today the mail brought me a draft from Japan for 'dollars 55 cents 12,' my 6 percent on an additional 3,000 copies of *Out of Your Pocket* in Nippon. (It sounds better when you realize it comes to 19,890 yen.)" At that rate, the entire 25,000 copies would have netted $457.50 over the years.

Since February, Pop and Dale had exchanged lively correspondence about Pop's long-term project, *West by God Virginia.* In 1963, West Virginia would be celebrating its centennial, offering a golden marketing opportunity. Dale's letters brimmed with advice on seeking backing for the project, and possible marketing strategies, including starting small with magazine articles on various of the book's aspects.

Pop's optimism about restarting his writing career spilled into his accounts of smaller matters. "Our poppy bed was a glorious sight today," he wrote on May 19. "Then it came on to blow and rain very hard, and the blossoms, which faced up before the rain, simply turned themselves into umbrellas and turned upside down. Clever people, these poppies. They'll bloom out in a day or two—and another year goes by in which I do nothing about opium extraction. They don't seem to put out do-it-yourself kits on the subject." Our entire poppy crop consisted of one 10-foot row.

Chapter Eight

Aphasia

ON JUNE 6, I'd just finished clipping fields for the neighbor who had bought Mr. Wells's place and was driving the tractor home when I spied Pat walking toward me. Only one thing could not have waited till I got home. "Father's back in the hospital."

He'd had a stroke. It affected his speech. He couldn't find words, they told me. When we visited him in the hospital a couple of days later, he didn't seem as incomprehensible as I'd thought. But, as we prepared to leave, he said, "It's getting far." He meant "late" and tried again, but it came out the same. "It's getting far."

He was home in four days. We hadn't lost him—his life hadn't been threatened—but a part was missing. He understood us, but struggled to reply. The condition was called "aphasia." So ironic; his life's calling, built on language, stricken by the one thing needed to sustain it.

His physical skills remained. He continued making house repairs, replacing cracked windowpanes, re-puttying and painting the sashes, remarking how much warmer the house would be. "On work at the house, the 'wiring' system works as ever before," he wrote in November. With his father's nifty old, wooden, tongue-and-groove plane, he prepared a match board to replace a missing one from the door between the kitchen and the summer kitchen. You'd never have guessed anything was wrong.

He engaged Buster in the task, and glowed teaching his twelve-year-old son. Those tools were a presence in our house. Why Buster and not Pat or me wasn't clear, but retrospect suggests he was reprising his own childhood. Pop was the youngest himself, and was the only son his father had taught the use of tools. Now he was passing the skills to his own youngest son.

Among the things we missed was Pop's humor. He still saw humor—still laughed—but aphasia made it hard for him to generate it.

There was a moment when talk turned to skunks, and Pop, trying to clarify, asked, "a stunk?"

Buster and I stifled laughter, but in that same conversational round, Dale's name came up, and Pop, again trying to clarify, asked, "Jail?"

Buster and I couldn't contain ourselves. Ma scowled and ordered, "Don't laugh."

"They can laugh," Pop said, "…it's funny." ("If it's funny.")

Another time, however, I had to agree with Ma. Pop was at the kitchen sink washing milk buckets in a violent thunderstorm.

"Don't use the sink in a thunderstorm," Ma warned.

Pop kept washing. She repeated the admonition. He kept washing. Suddenly there was a deafening BANG and a huge spark jumped from his calf to the cook stove, inches behind him. Pop burst out laughing. *Laughing*! What could *possibly* be funny about getting struck by lightning?

Pat, sitting on the porch, saw a fireball strike the pipe that fed water from the spring to the house. Running along the surface, the pipe made a backward lightning rod. Apparently, the cook stove, stove pipe, and stone chimney took the current harmlessly back to ground after passing through my father.

Closets in colonial houses were scarce to nonexistent, and ours was in full period fashion. Instead of closets, pegs were arrayed head-high along the walls, though after two hundred years, just one lone peg remained in the whole place. It would have been easy to cut lengths of dowel and drive them into the holes, but that one remaining original had a diamond-shaped enlargement at its end to help keep articles from slipping off. That was the design Pop set patiently about recreating, one by one.

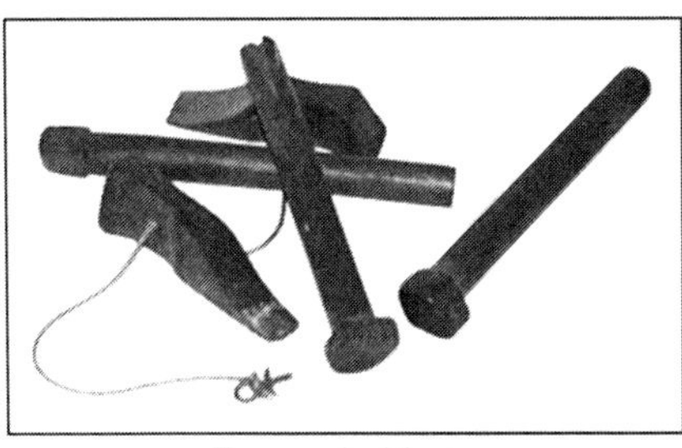
Pegs and widgets

Then there were the window sashes, which fit so loosely that snow filtered in and collected on the sills. To tighten the sashes, he designed wedges to insert at the edges. He called them "widgets," and briefly considered them as an income-generating alternative to writing.

Furniture repair, however, emerged victorious. As a boy, he'd helped his father put the split-hickory bottom in the old ladder-back chair. A neighboring farmwife taught him to replace the caning in cane-bottom chairs. Soon he was doing it at home, starting with our own but moving to neighbors' chairs, re-gluing loose rungs as needed, with the dining-room table as his workbench. By March 1960, he'd done seventeen.

Meanwhile, his doctor suggested that television might help his speech recovery, and for a time, he walked the half mile to the Greens, our nearest neighbors, to watch baseball. Mastering the name, "Harmon Killebrew," who had his breakout season with the Washington Senators that year, gave him special satisfaction.

From watching baseball with Fenton Green, the idea grew of getting a home set. It was something we could never have done on our own, but Dale Morgan got one for us—a 21" black-and-white console. The farmhouse sat in a hollow, and the antenna had to be raised thirty feet to get a signal. The TV's effect on Pop was hard to gauge, but we kids could suddenly talk to classmates about "Alfred Hitchcock Presents," "The Twilight Zone," "Maverick."

A more professional form of therapy had also begun taking shape. After a September, 1959, doctor's appointment, Pop had written aphasically to Dale, "Anna phoned to Dr. Hawes that he expects to hear his talk with us in two weeks to see us at Leesburg on October 6." Dr. Hawse was an evaluator at the

Woodrow Wilson Rehabilitation Center in Fishersville near Staunton, Virginia, Woodrow Wilson's birthplace.

We waited. Whether or not an interview took place on October 6, we find this November 19 note by Pop: "Any plans for my 'school' at Fishersville may not expect before February." In a February 15 letter to his sister, Gladys, he wrote, "We hope to hear by Feb. 24 when I may go to Fishersville to 'school.'" And in a letter to Dale dated March 2, 1960: "No report there Feb. 24 as we had a thought, but Mr. Hawse gave us a call on March 8. I want to keep my 'school' through for October."

"This letter started," he added in pencil, "before a 11-inch snow through 3 days of wind and mornings at 5° A.M. Drifts fell over the road and we may see hope to get the March 8 for the Hawse. Meantime I worked 3 chairs on fixing canings, making 15 chairs all together."

On the 23rd, he wrote, "The snow of March 8 kept out of the farm and Mr. Hawse on my Woodrow Wilson 'school' at Fishersville. We saw him instead on March 22. He got things going, and may see in April when I go south."

Our poverty deepened. There are those for whom one and one make six, or ten, or a hundred, but they are few. For us, one and one never made more than two…and often considerably less. Ma fielded phone calls from bill collectors. She told the Sears guy he'd get his money as soon as we had it. Apparently, that satisfied him. McLain's Grocery in Lovettsville let us run a tab, ultimately to the tune of four hundred 1960 dollars. Virts's Sinclair took stacks of rubber checks so we'd have gas for the tractor. The bank repeatedly accepted interest-only on the loans. Perhaps the Depression had fitted Ma for the role, but back then there had just been the two of them. Now, with bill collectors ringing the phone off the hook and her husband's health precarious, she had five kids to raise and a farm to run.

Pop's illness aside, it was the perfect rags-to-riches scenario—living our forebears' hardships, hand-sawing wood to heat a leaky stone house. The cobbler in Brunswick, his shop smelling of leather and rubber cement, cat dozing on his work bench, re-soled and re-heeled our shoes till the tops wouldn't hold stitches. We got snowed in every winter. Power outages could last two weeks. Life was giving us skills we'd never get any other way.

"Things have to get better," we'd joke. "They can't get any worse."

Card-carrying ne'er-do-well Joe Colgan chimed, "Why weren't we born rich instead of so god-damned good looking?" The riches part of rags-to-riches, naturally, would be along in time.

The '50 Ford that took us to Mexico had long since expired, and economics had thrown us on the mercies of Gene "The Walking Man's Friend" Ridgeway, who sold used cars for fifty dollars each. Ridgeway looked more like a frat boy than a used-car dealer, but the archetype still lurked beneath the crewneck and penny loafers. On Pat's 21st birthday, September 1, 1960, we bought a classy 1948 DeSoto—solid body, wood dashboard, rolled and pleated seats—and the same mechanical wreck as the others.

We had a drought that summer, that tried crops and livestock alike. Six hot, dusty, sweat-caked weeks hardly raise an eyebrow in some regions, but on the rain-fed Eastern Seaboard, six weeks of sparsely scattered showers is long. Corn leaves curl up like drinking straws. Trees shed foliage. A ruined stone springhouse stood below our barnyard. Ma and Pat enlarged its pool to give the animals an alternative to the dried-up pools elsewhere. Pop made notes—language exercises. In late September: "Pat and Anna have seen more water by the old stony house near the spring. Good water from the animals have no water in some spring. This is dry a long time."

Drought generates dust, dust swirls up to the stratosphere refracting sunrays into mind boggling sunsets, and Pop noted: "Anna and I went that evening to see the sky. We both the time these good things to see." And: "Wonderful skies from the evening, Anna and Helen came to see it too."

Drought painted the sunrise sky as well: "At 6 a.m., the sun had already risen, and the morning was just beginning. One star stood in the East to sun sky. A crow was flying across the farm. Two bats were giving in the early time."

As he wrote to Dale on November 12, "I have enough from loss of language to write poorly little, speak some better as improved somewhat, and reading again with a slow process." His assessment agrees with memory. His speech seemed more comprehensible than these writings. Remarkably, the aphasia had had no effect on his spelling, punctuation, or penmanship.

The Charleston (West Virginia) *Gazette* serialized E. B. White's *Charlotte's Web*, and Pop read it to us segment by segment as therapy. "I have been reading with difficulty *Charlotte's Web* by E. B. White; and had lots of fun to read the story," he wrote to Dale. Dale had given him a subscription to the paper in May, just before his stroke, to keep his *West by God Virginia* material current.

Helen graduated and joined Pop's old division at Agriculture for the summer. She rose in the dark and Pat drove her to the train. On July 9, four of Pop's former co-workers came to the farm for his sendoff, at last, to Fishersville the following day.

"I think that I will have a business after this is done," he wrote from there on July 11. The shop worked from eight to four, and at first it was just more chair-caning.

Pop, second from left, with some co-workers from Ag, in front of the smokehouse, July 9, 1960

He had a half-hour of speech therapy, an hour for lunch, and two fifteen-minute coffee breaks. "This shop will make things one can do by being in pride in the work." From caning, he moved to structural repairs—turning rungs on the lathe—to blending lacquer and other finishes, and finally to upholstery.

The Center had a lake where residents could fish. Ma fretted over his health, mailed him vitamins and reminders to take them. The whole place had one television. Pop liked the westerns—*Rawhide, Wagon Train, Laramie*— plus baseball when he could, but "the kids" often monopolized the set, so his viewing was catch as catch can. He enjoyed outings to Natural Bridge and Skyline Drive, and to football games at the University of Virginia and Washington and Lee.

The Democratic convention was getting underway. Ma and Pop supported Adlai Stevenson, but the nomination went to John F. Kennedy. When the Republicans met two weeks later, Ma and Pop exchanged gibes. "I listened a little while yesterday to Nixon's pious mouthings," Ma wrote, "and then turned it off in disgust."

"I look in on Hoover's speech at the convention," Pop responded, "and that was enough for all of them." Herbert Hoover, defeated by Roosevelt in 1932, yet lived.

They missed each other terribly. "Anna, Sweet, I had to be lonesome when you went away in a taxi.…It was wonderful for you to be here for whatever you can."

"Darel, my darling—sometimes it just seems impossible to be without you. I miss you so much."

But most of their exchange was nuts-and-bolts, Ma's about horses escaping their enclosures; cows coming fresh; crops needing rain; hay needing sun; "the boys" off working for this farmer or that. "Am making peach jam right now." "The Japanese Beetles are pretty bad. I'm going to talk to the county agent about getting some of that Spore Dust that we used in Burke."

"Anna, Sweetie," he wrote on August 23, "Thank you for sending me a buck. I was at 12 cents by the time you send this money, and half of it was for two cigarettes."

As if Ma didn't have enough on her plate, the children of Annie Smith chose now to try getting the farm's purchase price out of us in one lump. Mrs. Smith, evidently, held the mortgage herself. "Mrs. Annie Smith came yesterday," she wrote Pop on July 26. "She is going to try to persuade her children to let us keep the place." Ma struggled with the issue through August, and on September 3 could write that local moneylender, Lytle Baker, "told me that Wilbur Hall thinks he has figured out the proper approach to intercede with the Smiths."

Sept 14: "I hope Lytle Baker is right about the Smiths so they won't trouble us for a while." Evidently, they didn't, for the subject drops. No details of the agreement survive.

By then, Pop was preparing for a month at home. On September 12, he wrote, "I suppose I will write one or two more times this week, then I'll disappoint you-all for me to come instead of a letter." His gut was bothering him again. He'd done a couple of rounds with ulcers before his heart attack.

The Center sent him for gall bladder tests. Finding nothing, they tried—successfully—for a duodenal ulcer. Because of the ulcer, the Center ordered a four- to six-week sabbatical. It hit Pop hard. "I was very unhappy about leaving the workshop."

The doctor told Pat, "He'd be better off if he didn't try to like everybody."

As if ulcers weren't enough, the De Soto was spending more time with Gene Ridgeway than with us, but it was ready to get Pop on the 16th.

He resumed home repairs, but on October 7 had a fainting spell. By the time he regained consciousness, an ambulance had arrived from Brunswick to take him to Leesburg. He was home on the 10th, less concerned about the fainting than that he'd had to listen to the World Series on a hospital radio. His doctor thought he'd had an Adam Stokes attack which, Pop told Dale, "didn't seem to be anything worthwhile." Maybe they didn't think so in 1960, but Adam Stokes is a serious marker which, left untreated, sees fifty percent mortality within a year.

A week later, he was back at the Center, where it emerged that neither the psychiatric nor the medical staff had ever felt Fishersville was right for him. Miss Johnston, the speech therapist, thought he had made much more progress at home than in his half-hours a day with her. Ma told her that at Fishersville he wrote many more letters, and she acknowledged that advantage.

After two hours talking, Miss Johnston agreed to another trial period. She would try to convince him that his need for perfection was stressing him, contributing to setbacks. She did think Pop could write again if he could achieve more tranquility.

Pop told Dale, "There was quite a business on whether I stop making tension, to make my ulcer or my heart cause trouble. So I'm trying to take it easy, a hard thing to do."

Ma had impressed Miss Johnston. "She says," Pop went on, "that Anna has done the best job of working up yet done by a person on aphasia. She would like for Anna to work at the Center." He added, "Pat and Anna drove me to Fishersville. The car was in bad shape, so they stayed overnight, and the car fixed in the Center."

Back home, Ma wrote him, "Please darling relax and don't worry so we can all be together again." And, "No more car trouble on the way home."

Because of the ulcer, Pop needed to watch his diet, but doing so seems to have been left to the patient. "Some steak last night was something I should not have eaten," he confessed, and later, "The hot dogs at lunch today was something I shouldn't eat."

He complained about "graveyard stew," which consisted of bread and milk in a bowl—pretty draconian, especially if a dietician thought it up. Milk, we now know, is bad for ulcers. Ma supplied Pop with Maalox.

Still, October 30 "was another beautiful day, so this afternoon the bus was full to go on Skyline Drive. The mountains and the colored trees were gorgeous. The drive went on up at alt. 1900, up and up on a mountain at 3000, and worked o.k., and gradually back down to 1300 at the Center. As it is, I am a little glad—maybe I could go over the mountains to West Virginia." He'd wondered if his heart would tolerate the altitude.

The home front had its own distractions. On November 2, Anna wrote, "we were in a whirl all day. Nothing serious, just a day of obstacles." Helen, home from work nursing a cold, found herself driving Pat to a dentist to get a couple of abscessed teeth pulled. Pat came home to sleep off the drugs, Helen to sleep off her cold. The rest of us being in school, Ma was left to get in firewood and feed the cows.

Buster came home early from school to show his vocational agriculture teacher the heifer he was rearing—his Vo-Ag project. The cows chose then to visit our neighbor, Mr. Kite's, alfalfa field. It took an hour to round them up, with Mr. Koffelt, the teacher, opening and closing gates.

That night, we had spaghetti for dinner. Spaghetti was a rare treat in our house. When we did spaghetti, Chef Boy-Ar-Dee's spaghetti kit—pasta, sauce, and Parmesan cheese in one brightly colored box—was it.

We didn't have a colander. When you could hold the saucepan lid a little off center and drain the water through the slit, why waste money on a colander? Maybe the Depression had taught our mother to do without. On this night, Buster wanted to drain the spaghetti himself, and when Buster wanted to do something, the easiest thing was just to let him.

Also, he was thirteen years old, and you didn't tell a thirteen-year-old *how* to do it. When Buster did something, he did it *all*…by himself. One piece of information could have helped: press lid firmly against pot. Without that pressure the spaghetti, inevitably, slid into the sink along with the water.

Today, I wouldn't think twice about scooping the mass back into the pot, rinsing it off, and using it. But to a mother who would boil canned broccoli for twenty minutes to ward off botulism,[‡] spaghetti in the sink was spaghetti polluted. So, Pat being in pain and Helen being sick, I drove to Lovettsville for a second Chef Boy-Ar-Dee. Buster's second try was no more successful than his first, and back I went for a third. I'm not the only one to remember that story.

[‡] She came of age in the time before penicillin, when such fears had a basis in reality.

Pop responded, "Your big day to whirl Wednesday, got near all of it. There is one more thing: what did Bunny whirl that day? Didn't she whirl?"

Bunny had whirled, but two weeks earlier. She'd discovered the cows on the lane while riding her bike up to get the mail. She climbed into the field above the lane and ran ahead of them. When they saw her, they entered the woods below the lane. Joe Colgan was visiting at the time. She fetched him, but by the time they caught up with the herd, it was on the road and nearly down to Dutchman's Creek. "Joe and I went to get them," she said. "When we got back we were bushed."

Pat fixed the fence between us and Mr. Kite's alfalfa. I sometimes cringe recalling the tumble-down barriers that had come with that farm. Good fences make good neighbors, and we ran new fence as time and money allowed. But our fixer-upper farm boasted four or five miles of fencing—nearly two just around the perimeter—so it was a tug-of-war between new fencing and plugging holes as they opened.

November 8 was Election Day. Ma sent Pop "A note and a little dinero....The car has been at the garage....We'll soon know who our next president will be."

It was John F. Kennedy by the narrowest popular-vote margin in US history.

About mid-November, it started snowing, a little or a lot, practically every day, and thus began a record-breaking winter. On the 19th, Ma wrote, "We're in the process of being snowed in again....This is really a heavy snow....Children were let out early and Government workers too."

Every winter, the county put up snow fencing on the Greens' property along the west side of the road, which would have kept our escape route free of drifts, except they always left a two-foot gap between the end of the fence and the Greens' barn. Snow blew through that gap a couple of times every winter and snowed us in with drifts eight and ten feet deep.

Luckily, the road was open for Thanksgiving, and Pop spent a quiet week at home, then back at the Center before month's end. On November 29, Ma wrote him:

Darel, my dearest—

How I hated to go away from you last Sunday night. To me, it's harder each time. But Xmas after all is not so far away. So maybe it won't be too bad to wait to see you.

We got back home at about 4:30 AM last Mon. morning. The boys started in on the milking and then took the milk out. After that they both went to bed and slept awhile. I did too. I do hope that trip wasn't too much for you. It was pretty cold, wasn't it?

Jimmy drove all the way home [130 miles] but none of us could sleep because of those oil fumes. We stopped at the truck stop and that was all. The boys got coffee but I got hot chocolate. Had too much coffee.
It's supposed to get cold tonight and maybe snow tomorrow. Oh well it's that season isn't it?

That was the only time I went to Fishersville. We'd all seen Ma and Pop show affection and respect for each other. But now, as Pop prepared to exit the car, I saw them embrace in the rear-view mirror, and the embrace was more than affection—it was passion. That I'd never seen. Twenty-nine years, they'd been together.

Many remarked on Pop's progress, and probably no remark was more welcome than Dale Morgan's. "You have made marvelous progress," Dale wrote on December 1. "It is truly remarkable to compare your more recent letters with even the first ones from Fishersville, for they now deal effectively with complex ideas and exhibit considerable variety in expression." His writings showed it, but he still questioned whether he'd ever be as he'd been before.

He was having dizziness, and Dramamine made "me into the shape of being a vegetable." The cold was making his stomach hurt, and a tooth "gave me the works during the night." The tooth "came out pretty quick" on the 6th, he said, and he went back to upholstering. He spent his afternoon coffee break sitting outside in a rare interval of sunshine, "but then it got quite chilly, and when I ran in the doors, the jaw gets a bit cold and achy." A week later, he had "another tooth out, and it feels better even now." We don't know which jaw, but angina can manifest in the lower left.

We had jumped from the frying pan of a failing-DeSoto into the fire of a round-back, 1950 Chevy-Fleetline. The Fleetline gave headaches that made the DeSoto look high-performance. Gas fumes made us drive with the windows cracked no matter the weather. The son of one of Helen's co-workers found a two-dollar water pump, which he and Pat installed, hoping among other things to reactivate the car's heater. A couple of days later, the car wouldn't start at all. A few days further on, Gene Ridgeway reported that he wasn't sure he could find the parts we needed, and Ma told Pop we were looking for another one.

Pop was "sorry that the old car is such a wreck, and that I can't do much about it."

On December 12, he supposed "that the snow has the road filled up," and Ma replied, "We've been snowed in since Sun morning. This is Tuesday."

Barnyard with Fleetline

On Friday the 16th, Helen wrote Pop from D.C., "Up at home they're still snowbound. On Monday I rode Cinnamon out to get two milk cans and about a mile from home he threw me and ran all the way back home, so I had to walk and drag a milk can."

The same day Helen wrote that letter, I rode Dusty to Lovettsville for the mail, some groceries, and two more milk cans, got him stuck in a six-foot drift, and shoveled him out in the dark in my sock feet. I tell that story elsewhere and won't repeat it here. The very next day we got plowed out.

"All kinds of excitement," Ma wrote. "We'll tell you about it next week when we see you."

He was scheduled to come home on the 22nd, but, "There was a big snow around Lovettsville on Dec 11," he wrote, in language markedly improved,

with the house was snowbound the whole week. There was more snow, about Dec 20, and the Center phoned, asking them to get me back home. Also, Jesus Salas, a brown boy from Guam, was to go home for Christmas with us. Pat and Anna got to the Center about 8:30, and the car had no lights, and no mechanic, so we went on a flashlight to Staunton to get help. The car was finished at 11:30 p.m. and we went on, with snow along the way.

We got home at 6:30 a.m. There were no chains to get home [down the lane], so I walked for about a quarter of a mile. God, was it cold! My stomach in the cold, made it hard for me to get to the house. I figured that

I might have gone another quarter of a mile, and that would be the end of me. Buster stayed awake all night and there was some warmth in the house. The next night, or the next, it was -10° zero.

Christmas was white and cold but good. The flow of letters, that might have preserved the details, didn't resume until Pop was back at Fishersville. Fires certainly burned warmly. We decorated a tree. Ma, whose cooking I've joked about, could put it on as occasion required, and surely this occasion was no exception. Jesus was a former policeman from Guam whose right side had been disabled by a stroke. We gave him a carton of cigarettes—Kents. Pop had bummed one from him to learn what kind he smoked.

Pop gave us each something he'd made in the woodworking shop—for me a picture frame of quarter-sawn oak. I remarked on the exceptional smoothness of its finish. "When I make it," he said, "it's soft as a girl's behind." It was the first time he shared such innuendo. Much raunchier had naturally passed between me and my contemporaries, but this was different. My father had welcomed me to adulthood. It was his last gift to me, and I treasure it to this day.

He finagled a few extra days on the pretext of watching season's-end football games on TV, something hard to do at Fishersville. Ma wrote that Darel, with "'a wonderful twinkling grin,' said, 'Thanks to Dale [the TV set] we had a little extra time.'"

In the upholstery shop, he was learning the sewing machine. Someone had neglected to order fabric, so upholstery slowed to a stop. In the interim, Pop started making a quilt from six- to eight-inch squares of cloth, and was pleased with his progress. "I have sewn quite a bit faster, and most of it is fairly straight."

Ma assured him, "Darling your writing is getting better all the time. Keep it up. You'll be writing the story of aphasia yet. Just wait and see. Also the 'West by God Virginia.'" Occasionally, he mentioned to Dale the possibility of collaborating on that.

On Inauguration Day, January 20, "The snow fell 8½ inches around Staunton, so apparently about the same around Washington for President Kennedy. We saw part of the Kennedy business on Friday."

Winter continued hard. "The boys carry shovels wherever they go in case they get stuck," Ma wrote. "Well its winter time with a vengeance isn't it?"

The Center was selling the students army surplus shoes at fifty cents a pair, and Pop wrote home for sizes. "Just think, the three boys could get shoes for $1.50." He also sent a newspaper clipping about a study showing Southern California's climate to be good for heart patients.

The hallways in the center were unheated, and he told how "my gut hurts when I'm cold. Last night I walked from the Canteen to Red Cross to see whether the movie was worth going. I had to stop about three times and wait for my tummy to feel better."

He resigned himself to quitting, or at least cutting down, his smoking. "I don't know how many times my stomach hurt my gut. I thought, there must be some way to stop an ulcer. I said, I'll stop smoking, right now. I knew that smoking was causing my tummy.

"I had no smoke all morning, no cigarettes and no lighter at the shop." But withdrawal "made me mean as I could get."

Ma joined him. "I love you dearest and miss you so much," she wrote on January 27th. "Please take real good care of yourself. I'm almost down to 3 smokes a day too."

He never got the message.

Ma wrote Dale, "On Sunday evening last [actually Monday], I had a call from Waynesboro Hospital. The Dr. told me that Darel had had another major coronary occlusion. Our car could no longer be trusted to make the trip so my sister took me down."

Darel was conscious once and I was there. Dale, he had so much to live for. He held out his arms and I couldn't reach him because of the equipment oxygen [illegible] etc. around his bed. The Dr. took off the oxygen mask. He smiled. I said, 'Hang on darling. We'll make it.' He smiled and said, 'I'm alright' and went to sleep again. There were more hours of sleep and then he was gone.

Late on the evening of the 30th, the phone rang at home. Helen answered it. Sensing that we had just minutes left of "normal" life, I grabbed my guitar, Buster grabbed his, and we launched into song. The phone call ended. Helen hung up and screamed, "Father's dead!"

Silence dropped like a bomb.

The next few days are a blur, with a few quick scenes flashing by in no particular order. Pop's glasses, dentures, and wristwatch sat the on the dining room table when I finished milking. "Why're those here? He needs… Oh… no….Not anymore."

A last letter, written the day of his heart attack, eerily brought his voice back from the dead. "What do you folks think—you youngsters—feel like going to California, some time? You all are thinking about your life, and I'd like to think if ever we think of going into a warmer place?"

Ma buried her face on my chest and sobbed. "He had so much to live for." I gave her a one-armed hug. She pulled away, and that was the only show of emotion I ever saw. Grief was there and it was deep. We all knew it, all had it. Helen heard Ma crying at night, but stiff upper lip was the order of the day. Emotion was weakness. Reason, the higher order, must prevail. And yet how cold and empty the world becomes in the presence of death. Even flipping a light switch can seem utterly without meaning.

Joe Colgan and Earl Hyde materialized. Lovettsville's young Lutheran minister came to the house. I was getting firewood and wasn't present for the discussion. Pop detested funerals, as he'd made clear in an essay written after his mother's death. He wanted to be cremated, a very fringe option in those days. Earl brought a different perspective.

Ma was going to be living in this community, he said. If she ordered cremation instead of burial, she was sure to be ostracized. It has to have been a horrible choice, but she settled on a closed-casket service with the Lutheran minister presiding. Bob McLain, at whose grocery store we had a $400 tab, declined to attend even that.

Ma had telegraphed Dale, "Darel died January 29." In her grief, she got the date wrong, as she did in her subsequent letter, quoted above. He died on the 30th.

Dale answered:

I came home last night to your telegram, and never opened a telegram with greater reluctance, for I knew what news it must convey. The past several years we have lived with the knowledge that such news might come at any time, and though Darel told us all that he was not afraid to die, that he too prepared for what might happen, the impact upon us is not any the less.

I have lain sleepless most of the night, remembering and grieving, but in a painful way sometimes smiling too, recalling Darel at his most characteristic, the earthy, even comic view he sometimes had of life, things he had said and done over the whole 21 years of our friendship. We have those memories now, all of us, and they are sustaining memories. But how hard that there shall be no more of them to come.

Please, when you can, write me some of the details beyond the stark fact of his passing on the 29th. And also tell me whether there is anything I can do. I shall write again when I am in a little better control of my feelings. For I loved Darel like a brother, more than a brother, for we choose our friends, and our blood relationships sometimes just happen to us. In all the time I have known him, the fact that Darel was in the same world made it a better, happier, and more warmhearted world to live in. At the moment, I am more grateful than I can say that I had the privilege of a last visit with him last spring.

Chapter Nine

We Leave the Farm

WE HAD $20,000 IN DEBT—$180,000 in 2020 dollars. Ma's sole source of income, aside from sixty twice-weekly gallons of grade-B milk at 25¢ a gallon, or the sale of an occasional pig or calf, was her Civil Service survivor's benefit, around $1,900 a year. On the farms, men's wages were now $5.00 a day, and Pat and I turned much of our earnings over to the family, though farm labor was very catch-as-catch-can.

If the financial picture was bleak, the emotional was worse. What had it all been for? "Thoughts on Darel's unfinished work were in my mind that night coming home from Waynesboro," Ma wrote to Dale. It all seemed so pointless. He would never see his work help others. "It's hard to grasp that he will no longer get pleasure from this world of ours. Every step forward on this farm was a part of his plan, and now these accomplishments seem futile, since he can't enjoy them."

Twenty-nine years earlier, she and Pop had met and begun the process of ceasing to be individuals and becoming a relationship. Becoming a relationship takes hundreds of adjustments large and small. The line between you and the other blurs. For over half your life, the relationship has identified you. Now that identity starts unraveling, and you're helpless to stop it. There's a great open void. No longer are you the comforting "we," but the utterly lonely "I," and you're left to relearn who that is, all by yourself, step by excruciating step.

Dale helped keep things in focus. Pop's papers. What was to become of his research and unfinished work? "Anna," he wrote, "you should consider the best disposition of Darel's papers. You might want to keep them in the family; but you might also find reason to have them permanently preserved. Darel's own work, his correspondence with writers, his West Virginia interests, all give his papers enduring value. I would seriously consider giving them either to the Library of Congress or to a West Virginia institution." Coming from Dale, a veteran sleuth of original sources, this was weighty advice.

"You are right," she answered, "that disposition of Darel's work must be given careful thought. This will take time. Neither Darel nor I was ever methodical about filing." But she started right in—surely in part to keep him alive to her—and was still at it four or five years later. Nine months after Pop's death, she still hadn't "arrived at the point where I can read these papers without re-living the life that produced them." She confided such things to Dale. To us, she was the same rock she'd been since our childhood.

Ma showed me a *Prevention* magazine article about something called "auto-conditioning." Basically, it was meditation, but they couldn't call it that in 1961. Meditation was given wide berth because Beatniks contemplating their navels was such a good joke. So, *Prevention* called it "auto-conditioning." The practice led to a state of total relaxation. I gave it a try, and surprisingly found myself in a state of peace I had never dreamed of.

Once in that state, the article said, you could plant suggestions in your mind about things like quitting smoking or losing weight. As I had no problem with either, my mother's reason for showing me the article was puzzling. That it might have had to do with helping me avoid my father's difficulties with stress didn't occur to me. Ma had good ideas, but sometimes ran short on explanation. But I liked the results and periodically revisited the practice.

She showed me another article, "Get Out of the Habit of Dying," which said people get it in their minds that they will live to a certain age, and then do. "I tried talking your father out of the idea, but…." He had told her in the first month of their relationship that he didn't expect to live much past fifty. And here he was gone at fifty-five.

Sometime that spring, a heifer we'd named Rocketship had her first heat. As a calf, she'd earned her name by giving new meaning to "hightailing" it wildly hither and yon. (Calves' tails stick straight up when they run.) Pat and I saddled Dusty and Grulla (pronounced Gruya) to play cowboy and drive Rocketship to the Greens' bull half a mile away. We opened the barnyard gate and she was gone like her namesake. All we could do was try catching up with her. She must have gotten up to the road, but somehow, we were then chasing her back down the lane.

The lane, as earlier described, was cut into the upper edge of a deep gorge which a small stream had patiently carved over countless millennia. The lane, at its low point, forded that stream, and a little past the ford, a trail followed the stream down to Dutchman's Creek. I was high up on the lane. Fearing Rocket Ship might head for Dutchman's, I urged Grulla down the precipitous face of the gorge to cut her off.

On our frothy mounts

The maneuver had its roots in a story that Joe Cogan had told from his cowboy days. He'd descended a similarly precipitous face, though possibly longer and steeper since it was, after all, way out West. When he rejoined his partner, the incredulous partner asked, "Did you ride down that?" Joe affirmed that he had.

"Well…you damned fool!"

I couldn't resist reprising the stunt, rendered extra foolish by Grulla's weak front knee, where another horse had kicked her, severing a tendon. The odds that Rocketship would bolt toward Dutchman's were real, though the odds that this crazy shortcut would get us there in time to cut her off weren't great. But the game was afoot. Off we launched down the incline and luckily gained the streambed intact.

There was no sign of Rocketship, but I had rightfully earned my own "damned fool" stunt to brag about. I caught up with Pat in the barnyard, and Ma snapped a picture of us on our frothy mounts. Pat and I retired to the kitchen for the obligatory cup of coffee and Rocketship, executing the perfect closed-box magic trick, appeared *inside* the house's fenced yard. We never bothered trying to figure out how she got in.

A little later, Ma had me plant some dwarf fruit trees in the orchard, so at least through the spring she seems to have meant to keep the farm.

My academic resurgence faltered. Among my college-prep electives was chemistry. I'd done well the first semester, but could not grasp the second and squeaked by barely ahead of failing. Three decades later, I finally realized the part my father's death must have played in that second-semester dive.

I did fail Government, but while doing so, on Fridays, read and listened to the class discuss the student news magazine, *Senior Scholastic*…if I could stay awake. Farm kids often have trouble in school because they don't get enough sleep, and I'm pretty sure that was one of my problems. On the first Friday in March, however, a story about a Kennedy initiative, queerly-named "Peace Corps," woke me up and changed my life.

Maybe I could drop out of school after all. Maybe I could go straight to something grander. You only had to be eighteen, which I would be in September. They didn't even require a high school diploma. I had to act fast. That program was going to fill up.

Ma said, "It's something your father would like to have done," and showed me an application he'd made to accompany Admiral Byrd to Antarctica in 1929, and the admiral's regrets.

I made up Government in summer school and stayed on to graduate the next year.

By then, Ma had decided to sell.

Helen had left the nest for her job at Agriculture, and fallen in love with Jack Collins, a biologist at the Food and Drug Administration. "This is Jack," she introduced him. "He injects mice." They married in June. Pat drove us to the wedding with Gramps navigating. Years earlier, Gramps had known that part of town intimately, but one's internal map deteriorates. With every wrong turn, Pat got more irritated and his epithets grew closer together.

Thanks to the delays, we missed picking up Joe Colgan, but the wedding managed without him. Helen's maid of honor was her best friend from high school, and Bunny, looking very grown up at age ten, was a bridesmaid. Earl Hyde gave Helen away. I took pictures with Pop's Mamiya 120 that Iwanami Shoten, the Japanese publisher of *Out of Your Pocket*, had given him as part of his royalties.

Pop had a $10,000 life insurance policy that left us kids $2,000 each. Pat took his share and became the second hatchling to fly the coop. At age twenty-two, with plaudits from Joe Colgan, and as Pop's oldest brother had done, Pat sought to cast his lot in the West and drove off in Gramps's 1951 Ford pickup, which had all but become ours. Along the way, he picked up another dharma bum named Jerry, who undertook to show Pat how to extract food from churches, and might have succeeded had he not, just as the door opened, passed some loud and highly aromatic gas—worthy no doubt of Pop's father's quote, "Something must've crope up inside you and died."

In Galveston, they got work clearing debris from Hurricane Carla. From there, Pat ended up at a feed lot near Wilcox, Arizona. He liked Wilcox but, discouraged by the dearth of cowboy work, and running low on money, headed back home. The truck threw a rod in Tennessee. He entrusted his shotgun to a Greyhound ticket agent in return for bus fare, and was back home before October was out. He sent the guy money, and the guy returned the gun.

Pat bought a '55 Ford station wagon, then joined the Army and left the car with us. He and Ma began an extensive correspondence—two and three letters a week. Pat gained weight in basic training. At Fort Belvoir, Uncle Sam taught him to repair generators, then sent him to a nuclear missile base in Germany where he spent two years driving a truck.

In November 1961, we sold the farm and moved to a wonderful, rambling, "Eclectic" house in Lovettsville proper, like the Burke house only bigger. Enough pasture adjoined the lot, though it didn't belong to it, that we could keep our few remaining horses—Dusty, Beauty, Cinnamon, Bunny's pony King—and store hay in a small barn.

Ma turned fifty-four in that house. She hadn't worked in thirty years and had a household to support and debt to pay off. Much debt had been liquidated with proceeds from the farm, but much remained. On April 30, she wrote to Pat, "Tomorrow I should be able to make the last payment on the cow note."

Well I remember driving her to Leesburg for that payment. When she emerged from the bank, she sank into the passenger seat and breathed, "We're legal again."

She had sold the cows while they were still serving as collateral for the loan. We kids understood the extremes under which she labored, and were never tempted to take up crime ourselves. Now, with an eye to going straight, she drew out a ragged typing manual and, on the old, indestructible, Royal standard typewriter, began teaching herself touch typing, clacking out "asdfgf…asdfgf…" over and over without looking at the keys.

In her letters to Pat, she spilled much ink on his '55 Ford. When it ran, it ran well. The problem was the medley of excuses it concocted for failing to do so. On January 22, Ma wrote, "We finally have some good news. The Ford people in Woodstock have found a rebuilt transmission." It looked promising until the mechanic at Virts's Sinclair, the service station where we dealt, found loose parts lying around inside. But she said on February 4, "I believe that at last your car is fixed. All but one thing, the overdrive doesn't work."

Two days later, it conked out on my way to school. The school's vice principal came and pushed me to a garage where I left it for the day. Another push got it started at noon (I only needed half a day of school to make up my lost credit), but it conked out again near the top of "The Mountain" going out of Leesburg. The manifold was red hot. I hitchhiked home. Virts towed the car.

Returning from Helen's baptism (a condition of her marriage to a Catholic) near the end of February, we started having trouble shifting into high. "This time it's probably the clutch," Ma said. "It got so it wouldn't go into high at all unless Jim jerked it. I was glad when we got on 70-S [I-270 today] on the way home where he wouldn't have to shift much more. Every time he went in low or second it was a gamble whether or not he'd get into high again. Virts is going to look at it tomorrow."

On April 25, "The car stopped in Leesburg when Jim was on the way home. Virts is going after it today. Jim hitchhiked home and I suppose he'll do the same this evening."

What dominated in these letters, however, was not cars but Ma's passion for world events. Heretofore, her political ideas had generally been spoken, and with other adults. Her letters to Pop in Fishersville had occasional references to the presidential campaign, but her big worry then was his health. Now her twenty-two-year-old son took the baton. Separated by geography, their discourse poured out in writing. There was much to talk about—John F. Kennedy, the most exciting public figure since Roosevelt.

"Did you see any of Kennedy's press conference?" she wrote on April 12. "The reaction to US Steel's price increase I mean. He really laid it on."

The steelworkers had agreed to freeze wages for a year, and industry agreed to freeze prices. Ten days later, US Steel announced a $6.00 per ton increase. Kennedy took to the airwaves. The increase was "a wholly unjustifiable and irresponsible defiance of the public interest….A tiny handful of steel executives whose pursuit of power and profit exceeds their sense of public responsibility" had "utter contempt" for the United States, he said. Steel retreated, Democrats cheered, Republicans rent their garments. Ma had "never seen Kennedy so obviously indignant."

"Mr. Kennedy certainly doesn't take his defeats lying down. He's going to take his medical care bill to the people in November." Conservatives in Congress and the American Medical Association shouted down this early draft of Medicare with dire predictions of *socialized medicine!*" and *creeping socialism!*" Kennedy didn't take it lying down, but it was his successor, Lyndon Johnson, much better at pulling congressional strings, who got the measure passed in 1966.

The clamor for civil rights had been growing since World War II. On September 30, 1962, African American student James Meredith integrated the University of Mississippi—"Ole Miss." What today wouldn't draw a yawn was then an historic step. On Oct 1, Ma wrote, "I suppose you've heard of the holocaust in Mississippi; I don't know whether to be glad or sorry that the government won at the expense of bloodshed. It constantly surprises me that these things can happen in a supposedly civilized country."

Mississippi governor Ross Barnett, defying Brown v Board of Education, swore, "No school will be integrated in Mississippi while I am your governor."

After legal maneuvers by Barnett and the White House (Mississippi tried passing a law prohibiting Meredith's admission), Barnett agreed to let Meredith register in return for a face-saving out. He would block the door and let US Marshals remove him at gunpoint. The administration refused to make him a martyr, instead spiriting Meredith in at night ahead of the deadline. Barnett had promised order, but state police mysteriously vanished and thugs from around the state began throwing bricks and burning cars. Before troops could arrive, two hundred people were injured and two had been killed.

Troops occupied Ole Miss for nearly ten months, and a contingent of Marshals protected Meredith until he graduated.

Along with the rest of the country, Ma was intoxicated by the space program. She hung on every launch. The Soviet Union's orbiting of Sputnik in 1957 had galvanized the world. Just six weeks earlier, they'd fired the world's first intercontinental ballistic missile, able to reach targets anywhere on Earth.

Not since Russia's first H-bomb in 1953 had the Cold War been so focused. The US had been first with the bomb, but the Soviets were only nine months behind. With Sputnik, they were clearly ahead, and gloated shamelessly. Four months later, after a dismaying series of misfires, we finally got a craft into orbit, but by then the Soviets had launched "Muttnik," a dog in orbit. The fact that the dog didn't survive was completely lost amid fears that we were losing the race entire.

Pop had not yet suffered his first heart attack when those events transpired. Two and a half months after he died, Soviet cosmonaut Yuri Gagarin became the first human in orbit, April 12, 1961. The space gap seemed to narrow when, a month after Gagarin, the US launched Alan Shepard on a "sub-orbital" flight, but the gap re-widened in August when a second Soviet cosmonaut circled the world *seventeen times*. It took until February, 1962, before John Glenn finally made America a member of the orbital club. His three-orbit, third-place finish, was a triumph. Suddenly, you'd have thought we'd won the race after all.

"Well, they did it!" Ma exulted. "I haven't any words to express my gratification and elation at the knowledge that man is really capable of these accomplishments. How Darel would have loved these displays of ever greater victory over our environment."

After eight years of Republican drift under Eisenhower, Kennedy put spring back in our step. We were sweating the space race, but it wasn't three months after his inauguration that he announced the goal of putting a man on the moon.

The space race was just one Cold War face. Today we tend to treat communism cavalierly, but then most saw it as a bare-knuckle existential threat. "We will bury you," Soviet Premiere Nikita Khrushchev had blustered in 1956. The statement was taken out of context, but "We will bury you" is what politicians and the media played like a broken record.

What was all that *peace* stuff about in the sixties? The Vietnam War and civil rights (which sometimes seemed like the same movement)? Those were effects, not causes. They grew out of the fear of nuclear annihilation. Warfare had discovered means to destroy life on the planet. It was time to explore peaceful ways of settling our differences. When Ma wrote, "We have arrived at that stage in our journey where all further progress can easily turn out to be useless if we don't learn how to live at peace with the rest of humanity," she spoke for a vast swath of humankind.

But discouragingly, Vietnam, a comparatively minor irritant for most of Kennedy's time, was already shaping the proxy-war alternative. America backed South Vietnam, the Soviets backed the North, and we superpowers let the Vietnamese do our fighting for us. But ultimately that *peace* stuff traced back to nuclear annihilation. It crumbled along with the Berlin Wall in 1989, and we've mostly forgotten it, but in its day, it was very real.

Occasionally the Cold War seemed to thaw. Russia's second orbital cosmonaut, Gherman Titov, visited Washington and met with fellow spaceman John Glenn. Ma remarked, "The Glenn-Titov program was excellent and full of good humor. I wish all our relations with other nations could be as cordial."

They weren't. The thaws never lasted. The issue wasn't the space race but the arms race. Only MAD, fear of "Mutual Assured Destruction," held annihilation at bay. Nuclear testing itself raised alarms. Atmospheric tests released strontium-90. Rain washed the isotope into pastures where cows grazed, and it wound up in the milk children drank, settling in their bones, marrow, and blood. A testing moratorium had been in effect since Eisenhower, but the U-2 spy-plane shoot-down, the Bay of Pigs invasion, and the Berlin Wall built pressure until, on September 1, 1961, the Soviets broke the moratorium. Two months later, they exploded the biggest bomb in human history, 3,800 times more powerful than Hiroshima's. Reluctantly, President

Kennedy resumed testing underground. When intelligence reports confirmed that Soviet tests were helping reduce the size of their warheads, he ordered atmospheric tests resumed in April 1962, but made clear that he did so with utmost reluctance.

"I understand that the nuclear tests are beginning again," Ma remarked, "and I still don't know in my own mind whether we should have done it. I'm going to listen to [ex-CIA chief] Allen Dulles this evening."

Confrontation went old-school on October 11. The Soviets blockaded and held for 48 hours a US convoy headed for Berlin. Ma wrote to Pat, "I sure hope there isn't any serious kind of trouble over Berlin. It's terrible to have you over there where the trouble might be, though it's always the same for whatever families are involved."

The area had been touchy since Hitler's defeat, when Germany was divided into Soviet, American, French, and British sectors. Soviet Premier Stalin, smarting from German treachery in both wars, wanted control of all Germany, and initially thought the Allies would lose interest and leave it to him. They didn't. Berlin, the German capital, lay a hundred miles inside the Soviet Zone, and was itself divided into zones.

Stalin's gripe was the escape hatch Berlin gave people fleeing Soviet dominion. So long as a hundred-mile corridor was open to the Allied zones, a person had only to enter Berlin's Allied sector and catch a train. The corridor, however, had never been diplomatically agreed to, and as Allied interest failed to wane, Stalin imposed harsher travel limits on it.

The first Berlin crisis, in 1948, rose over currency. The Soviets had crippled German recovery by overprinting the Reichmark. Cigarettes were a better medium of exchange. The Allies introduced a new, strong Deutchmark to help rebuild the economy. Stalin refused to let it become legal in Berlin, but the Allies had already delivered a quarter billion, and they immediately became the currency of choice. Fearing a revitalized Germany, the Soviets closed he corridor.

Three diplomatically sanctioned alternatives remained—air corridors from the three Allied zones—and the Allies contrived the Berlin Airlift to keep the city's two million residents supplied, gambling that the Soviets wouldn't shoot down unarmed, civilian cargo planes. The Airlift began in June, 1948, and soon a plane was taking off or landing every five minutes around the clock. Soviet fighters harried the caravan, but no shots were fired. With winter, coal became more urgent, and the rate accelerated to two planes a minute. Finally, a year after the lift began, Stalin relented, and ground traffic resumed.

Every few years, there was another crisis—1953, 1958, 1961. The last one probably settled Pat's deployment to Germany. Nikita Khrushchev had succeeded Stalin, and Kennedy had succeeded Eisenhower. Khrushchev requested a summit for June, 1961, in Vienna. Reporters said Kennedy gave as good as he got, and that image long persisted. It would have been ruinous had they told how unprepared he'd really been. Khrushchev said he was going to sign a treaty letting East Germany (the Allied sectors had fused into "West Germany") decide for itself whether to continue allowing access to Berlin. Such a "treaty" with Khrushchev's East German puppet could only mean the end of access.

Kennedy could not tolerate losing Berlin, even if it meant war. "West Berlin has now become the great testing place of Western courage and will," he told the nation. "We cannot and will not permit the Communists to drive us out of Berlin.…For the fulfillment of our pledge to that city is essential to the morale and security of Western Germany, to the unity of Western Europe, and to the faith of the entire free world."

He hadn't said what he would do; he didn't know himself. The Allies had drastically cut their forces after the War. Short of nuclear war, they could never have countered a Soviet action. Nor could Kennedy get conventional forces up to strength by Khrushchev's year-end deadline. He asked Congress for more military spending and began moving such troops as we had to Western Europe. Pat went with them.

Meanwhile, Kennedy deployed the old Churchillean tactic: "jaw, jaw, jaw"—keep 'em talking. That policy contributed to one of Kennedy's best press-conference moments. He'd said that heads of state should never negotiate agreements, but only ratify agreements made at lower levels. As the stalemate dragged on, many began wondering if he wouldn't end up "eating his words."

At a press conference in March, 1962, a reporter asked him about that. Kennedy shot back, "I'm going to have a dinner for all the people who have written it, and we will see who eats what."

By then, the Berlin Wall had gone up. American and Soviet tanks had stared each other down through a gap in the Wall called "Checkpoint Charlie," but Khrushchev's deadline passed and Berlin remained open.

As things turned out, the real confrontation came not in Berlin but much closer to home, in Cuba, October 1962. As early as August, US intelligence had observed the Soviets moving equipment onto the island. Rumors claimed there were missiles able to reach most western-hemisphere cities. Polls showed growing public impatience with Communist influence there. As midterm elections approached, Republicans started fanning dissident flames. Kennedy, still smarting from the Bay of Pigs, moved cautiously.

On August 31, intelligence confirmed the presence of *defensive* surface-to-air missiles, though no *offensive* emplacements were found. Soviet Ambassador Dobrynin insisted that the buildup was just business as usual. Kennedy said that if it endangered American security, we would do what we had to do to protect ourselves. Moscow warned that any action against the bases would mean war.

All came to a head just three days later. Arthur Schlesinger, Jr., called it "the most dangerous moment in human history."

On October 22nd, Kennedy's press secretary announced that the president would address the nation at 7:00 p.m. on a matter of "highest national urgency."

By then, though it meant postponing the Peace Corps, I was giving college a try at The George Washington University in D.C., and while Ma sold the Lovettsville house, was staying with Coleman Rosenberger, whom Pop had worked with on the Kilgore Committee and who had bought 509 Fontaine Street when we moved to Burke. Coleman flipped on the TV.

"Good evening, my fellow citizens," the President began in measured tone. "This government, as promised, has maintained the closest surveillance of the Soviet military buildup on the island of Cuba. Within the past week, unmistakable evidence has established the fact that a series of offensive missile sites is now in preparation on that imprisoned island. The purpose of these bases can be none other than to provide a nuclear strike capability against the western hemisphere....

"This secret, swift and extraordinary build-up of Communist missiles, in an area well known to have a special and historical relationship with the United States and the nations of the western hemisphere, in violation of Soviet assurances, and in defiance of American hemispheric policy—this sudden, clandestine decision to station strategic weapons for the first time outside Soviet soil, is a deliberately provocative and unjustified change in the status quo which cannot be accepted by this country, if our commitments are ever to be trusted again by friend or foe....

"We will not prematurely or unnecessarily risk the costs of world-wide nuclear war in which even the fruits of victory would be ashes in our mouth, but neither will we shrink from that risk at any time it must be faced....Our goal is not the victory of might, but the vindication of right; not peace at the expense of freedom, but both peace *and* freedom, here in this hemisphere, and, we hope, around the world. God willing, that goal will be achieved."

Most tellingly, the President said, "It shall be the policy of this nation to regard any nuclear missile launched from Cuba against any nation in the western hemisphere as an attack by the Soviet Union on the United States, requiring a full retaliatory response upon the Soviet Union."

The Soviets equivocated, said our surveillance photos were fabricated. America's UN Ambassador, Adlai Stevenson, challenged Soviet Ambassador Valerian Zorin: "Do you, Ambassador Zorin, deny that the USSR has placed and is placing medium—and intermediate—range missiles and sites in Cuba? Yes or no. Don't wait for the translation. Yes or no."

"In due course, sir, you will get your reply," Zorin groused.

Stevenson said he was "prepared to wait until Hell freezes over."

Kennedy had made clear that "our unswerving objective" was to secure the withdrawal of offensive weapons from the western hemisphere. "To halt this offensive buildup a strict quarantine on all offensive military equipment under shipment to Cuba is being initiated. All ships of any kind bound for Cuba from whatever nation or port will, if found to contain cargoes of offensive weapons, be turned back."

Pfc Pat McConkey in Germany, October 1962

We didn't have long to wait. The very next day a Russian flotilla neared the quarantine line. In the lobby of Monroe Hall at GW, I waited both for class and for word. Would history end in a blinding flash before sunset? It wasn't anxiety, just an eerie limbo, a few hours devoid of content. Then we heard that the Soviet ships had stopped.

Khrushchev had taken Kennedy's measure in Vienna and thought he had his number. He'd failed to reckon on the president's growth since then.

Ma told Pat, "I write to you this evening with a very heavy heart. I can scarcely believe that we, as the top of the life scale, allowed our human affairs to come to such a pass. I am sick also because you may be in the thick of the fray, for this is bound to be linked to Berlin. But come what may we are all proud that you do have a part in the settlement....Let's all hope that the day isn't too far off when you and all of us will be able to do our bit for the improvement of man's lot on this miserable and glorious planet without the constant threat of nuclear annihilation.

"I feel almost glad that Darel doesn't have to witness the mess we humans have made of our affairs. But I can't quite feel that way because he misses the satisfaction of seeing how his children rise to the situation so magnificently."

In the next two days, all the Soviet ships turned around, and life seemed to regain a semblance of normalcy. "We'll hope that by the time you get this the news will be a great deal better than it is now," Ma wrote. "There seems to be some easing of tensions due to various things that have happened in the course of this day."

But the semblance was illusory. Work actually accelerated on the installations already in place. When the State Department's press officer called attention to the President's statement that "further action" would be "justified" if work continued on the missile sites, headlines shrieked that an attack on Cuba was imminent.

But Kennedy held firm against escalating the standoff. Following the shoot-down of a U-2 spy plane over Cuba, he declared only that fighter jets would begin escorting reconnaissance flights. Another Soviet ship was nearing the quarantine line. Both militaries were on high alert. In Florida, the US was massing the biggest invasion force since D-Day.

Diplomatic conduits throbbed. Personal exchanges passed between Khrushchev and Kennedy. Then, on Sunday morning, October 28, word came that Khrushchev had accepted Kennedy's conditions, and the confrontation was over.

Ma wrote, "We came home to turn on the news and found that Khrushchev had indeed sent his offer to President Kennedy to dismantle the bases in Cuba, etc. From where I sit, Kennedy steered a remarkably exact diplomatic course in this crisis. A do-nothing policy could easily have led to war and nuclear destruction. The course upon which Kennedy embarked was fraught with danger, but at least it had the advantage of being less hazardous than a war with a well-armed Cuba." He had pushed as far as he'd had to and no further, allowing Khrushchev as dignified a retreat as possible.

"It seems to me that our Mr. Kennedy executed one of the most masterful strokes of real statesmanship ever witnessed by mankind," she continued. "He's not going to have an easy time of it now, for the pressure to get rid of Castro in one fell swoop is on again, and the Republicans are saying that they were the ones who warned the president in the first place." Despite the Republicans, the president's stature rose exponentially.

Ma later added, "The thing that worries me now is that Khrushchev may be deposed in December or at least be restricted to such an extent by the Stalinists in Russia that he will be virtually powerless. This could result in a much more belligerent Russia than we now have to deal with." The opinion likely came from a media pundit, but it was prophetic. Much more hardline Leonid Brezhnev replaced Khrushchev in 1964.

The Cuban crisis was a high-point in a presidency that enjoyed the highest approval since FDR.

Ma told Pat, "It becomes daily more apparent that I need to move closer to town. Don't worry about Dusty, I'll take good care of him whatever move we make. We're just not wealthy enough to support much travel back and forth to D.C." More than economics was going on. D.C. was pulling her back. In Lovettsville, Pop had been her intellectual mainstay, while the failing farm, the lack of decent clothes and grooming, were barriers to even such society as Lovettsville offered.

She acknowledged Pat's regret over loss of the farm—we had all voiced the sentiment. She felt it, too. "I get a great longing for country living at times, but there is something very endearing about Washington. I have always looked upon it sort of possessively. Not in the sense of ownership but a kind of rapport with the city itself." So, "When the prospect of Jim's entrance into college bolstered my other practical reasons for moving to the city, I was not loath to do so."

Later, she wrote Dale, "I am sure you have heard of the fate of your old D.C. home, the Raleigh Hotel." It stood gutted and awaiting demolition.

"This city is gradually filling itself with bright new unimaginative square structures that serve, I suppose, the needs of government and industry, but it is still Washington and I still have a great affection for it."

In September, the Lovettsville house sold to a family named Mason. Ma had until the first of the year to find another place. A family named Bruzee offered to keep the horses, just to keep their pasture "mowed." All Ma had to do was supply hay.

Lovettsville's Shylock, Lytle J. Baker, to whose usurious lair our financial straits had sometimes driven Ma, tried to dissuade her from dealing with the Bruzees. "Lytle Baker has amassed a fortune in a manner on which I don't like to speculate. No one seems to like him though everyone respects the damage he can do if crossed. He was very put out when we sold the Lovettsville house, and has tried in numerous ways to take it out on the Masons. In his opinion, I had no business dealing with Mr. Bruzee, since he only came to Lovettsville to get what he could out of the community. This is what Baker would like to have the people of Lovettsville believe."

With Baker deprecating Lovettsville, she came to its defense. "Quite the opposite is true. Mr. Bruzee is a man with about the same talents as Joe Colgan. However, unlike Joe, he has enough sense to see that his ability as an actor or an artist will not make a living for his family. He does not try to disguise his interest in culture, nor does he pretend to know more about horses than he does. He is willing to learn where the need presents itself. He is directing the Loudoun Playmakers this season, but according to the blustering Baker, this sort of activity should not make him friends in 'backward' Lovettsville. Nevertheless, the Bruzees are well liked and have made many friends. These 'backward' people reach past the differences in newcomers and make a pretty good judgment on their real worth."

Chapter Ten

13 Russell Road

POP HAD LIKED SAYING 13 was his lucky number, and was glad we'd gotten P.O. Box 13 in Lovettsville. Thus, it was with no small sense of satisfaction that the house Ma bought in Alexandria, Virginia, was number 13 Russell Road.

She hired a moving company at considerable expense, and signed off on the delivery without taking inventory, only to discover that the ladderback chair Pop's father had made, the seat of which Pop had helped weave as a youngster, that the paramedics had carried him downstairs in when he had his first heart attack, was gone. It wouldn't have meant much to anybody else, but it had meaning for us, and now it was gone.

Ma dove into a job hunt, possibly part-time teaching or part-time research. She paid off a few more debts when she sold the Lovettsville house, but it was still hard to keep the family going on what she was getting. If professional work didn't materialize soon, she would try for Christmas sales. "It will take a little time to find something in my line because people don't want to hire someone over 50 years old. I have several leads."

At the end of November, she started a clerical position at the Bureau of National Affairs, which published technical bulletins. "I have to get up bright and early, and I guess I'd better start learning to go to bed earlier. It's a temporary job and doesn't pay much, but it will give me some experience to put down on future applications. I was really lucky to get anything since I have had no salaried experience since the thirties." By March, however, she confessed that "the 'lil' ole job gets more and more boring."

A threat possibly more insidious than the nuclear showed up with the publication of Rachel Carson's *Silent Spring*, which fired the environmental movement's opening salvo. In April, CBS aired a documentary on it. "We watched Rachel Carson's *Silent Spring* on T.V.," she wrote to Pat.

"You may know that this book told the story of how pesticides, etc., are poisoning much more than the pests they are designed to get rid of. It was very well done and documented. The next day I had lunch with Virginia Tatum from Darel's old office. You can imagine the repercussions in the Department of Agriculture. At least now they are openly admitting that there is room for improvement and I imagine that their biological control of pests program will be stepped up and that the products on the market will be somewhat controlled."

Luckily for the movement, pesticides threatened America's national symbol, the bald eagle, with extinction. Kennedy ordered an investigation, which verified Carson's claims. Over the ensuing decade, a number of pesticides—DDT most famously—were banned. Richard Nixon approved the Environmental Protection Agency and the Clean Air Act. If Ma's guiding light since the fifties had been *Prevention* magazine, *Silent Spring* was her vindication. It is a compelling read even today.

Ma had a special place in Hell for TV advertising, owing to its failure to live up to Christ's Sermon on the Mount. She was open to the question of whether Jesus had ever even existed, but didn't deny the truth of the words attributed to him. "Just think what a change could be wrought if people who have something to sell would use their commercial time for skits with good social messages," she wrote.

"Instead, we have appeals to all our primitive instincts. We have found the most refined ways of destroying ourselves, but we have also learned to produce all of man's needs with so much facility that no one really needs to be hungry, under-clothed, or without shelter. These are the truths that should be touted in commercials, with examples of how we can realize the lessons of the Sermon on the Mount. Our prestige should come from our tolerance of others' frailties, from our willingness to sacrifice for others, and from our good neighbor policy toward all people. But with their appeal to base instincts, the advertisers are helping perpetuate feelings which could undo the free enterprise system in which they advertise."

Fine words and true, but we McConkeys were naïve. TV advertising was still new to us. We'd only had it for a couple of years. But advertising is *for* selling brassieres, not preaching sermons on the mount. The baser the instinct you appeal to, the more brassieres you sell. Like mopping the floor or balancing the checkbook, advertising is here to stay. Ma meant well. She didn't do any harm. But throughout our childhood, there were few worse epithets than "Madison Avenue."

As spring approached, we found ourselves getting homesick for the country. I wrote Pat that we should be ankle-deep in mud and spreading manure, getting ready to plow and plant instead of pounding concrete sidewalks. The uniformity of our house's central heating was making my skin crawl. Back in the leaky old farmhouse, stoves and fireplaces had been islands of warmth you moved between. That constant change had been invigorating. Our dissatisfaction with city life had Ma feeling discouraged, and perhaps that discouragement carried over into her feelings about her job.

Not only had she told Pat that her "lil' ole job gets more and more boring," but also that "I sometimes think that nobody appreciates my efforts to increase our income." Sad to say, she was right. We take our parents for granted, and rarely comprehend their sacrifices until it's too late to thank them. "They all hanker after the country, as I do too," she said, "but I know that our situation there was impossible. The kids know it too but they don't want to accept it."

It may have been a blessing when she learned that her boring 'lil' ole job would end on April 12. "I hope it is not too long before I find another one, since we are not immediately in a position to lose the few shekels I earn." That was Friday. By Monday, she was working again—another clerical job—in the comptroller's office at The George Washington University. The lady whose place she had taken lay at death's door and wasn't expected to survive. She did, however, and within a month Ma was pounding the pavement again. But only for a few days. In mid-May, she was working at Acacia Insurance Company.

Acacia paid better than the jobs she had left, but the insurance culture brought new perspective on the business world. Any fraction of a penny, for example, that was in the company's favor—whether nine tenths or one tenth—was rounded *up* to the next whole cent. If the fraction was in the policyholder's favor, it was rounded *down*. The job lasted until August 27, when she was dismissed "mainly as a result of not keeping my big mouth shut." She didn't supply details.

Less than a month after Ma joined Acacia, three civil rights themes crammed a single day, June 11, 1963. Alabama Governor George Wallace, the "Banty Rooster," who had inaugurated his administration crowing "segregation now, segregation tomorrow, segregation forever," famously blocked a Deputy US Attorney General and three carloads of federal marshals from escorting two African American students into the University of Alabama. In response, President Kennedy nationalized the Alabama National Guard and ordered it to the campus, where the students succeeded in registering.

That same evening, we watched Kennedy's televised Civil Rights Address, which put the legal arguments for comprehensive civil rights legislation onto moral ground. "One hundred years…have passed since President Lincoln freed the slaves," Kennedy told the nation, "yet their heirs…are not fully free."

Seven hours after that speech, civil rights activist Medger Evers was assassinated outside his home in Jackson, Mississippi, for presuming to register black voters, to organize boycotts of businesses that discriminated against blacks, and to reopen the investigation into the 1955 lynching of 14-year-old Emmett Till. George Wallace's segregation speech, Kennedy's Civil Rights speech, and Medger Evers's assassination, all in one day. Evers's murderer turned a low-profile Mississippi activist into a national rallying cry.

Two and a half years after Pop's death, Paramount Pictures released the Oscar-winning movie *Hud*, a drama starring Paul Newman that featured an outbreak of foot-and-mouth disease on a Texas ranch, cornering thereby the foot-and-mouth market. *Hud*'s treatment of the disease was superficial, but it would effectively have upstaged any hope for Pop's novel, *Let No Man Blame Us*.

The Bruzees were going to Florida for the winter, so the horses had to move. Hardly had Ma had a chance to research alternate digs than they escaped Bruzee's pasture into the neighbor's corn—neighbors we had known socially—the Weatherlys. "As you know," Ma wrote, "once horses have gotten out it takes a mighty good fence to keep them in.

"At that moment I could cheerfully have shot every one of them." She resisted the temptation, however, and, "after two days and seven dollars' worth of [long-distance] calls," found lodging with the Masons, who'd bought our Lovettsville house. It was a temporary measure. Water had to be hand-carried, and a horse can drink five to ten gallons a day. Ma had hoped to bring them closer to home so Bunny could ride, but the perfect world was elusive.

Kennedy, meanwhile, made the European trip that burnished his presidency to a high gloss. The Atlantic Alliance—led by the United States, Great Britain, France, and Germany—was faltering. It had pulled together during the Berlin and Cuban crises, but was now wavering before Soviet pugnacity. Some allies favored and some opposed closer ties with America. British Prime Minister MacMillan was in trouble at home because Kennedy stopped work on the Skybolt missile, which Eisenhower had promised to share with Britain. French President De Gaulle insisted on his own nuclear deterrent. Now, landing in Bonn, the West German capital, on June 23, Kennedy said, "I have crossed the Atlantic…at a crucial time in the life of the Grand Alliance. Our unity was forged in a time of danger; it must be maintained in a time of peace."

Three days later, windblown under a glaring sun, he delivered the speech that got the most rousing response of his presidency. Before 150,000 people massed outside Berlin's city hall, he began, "Two thousand years ago, the proudest boast was '*Civis Romanus sum* [I am a Roman citizen].' Today, in the world of freedom, the proudest boast is 'Ich bin ein Berliner [I am a Berliner].'

"Today there are many people in the world who really don't understand, or say they don't, the great issue between the free world and the Communist world. Let them come to Berlin." Nine minutes later he concluded, "All free men, wherever they may live, are citizens of Berlin, and, therefore, as a free man, I take pride in the words, 'Ich bin ein Berliner.'"

A hundred fifty thousand people exploded into chants of "Ken-ne-dy, Ken-ne-dy, Ken-ne-dy." Watching on a 21-inch black-and-white TV, it was impossible not to be swept up in the moment. A month later, the world's three nuclear powers—the United States, Britain, and the Soviet Union—sent delegates to Moscow to seek a way to end testing in the atmosphere, the oceans, and outer space. Since his Senate days, Kennedy had advocated a nuclear test ban. He had pressed the issue through his presidency.

A PLACE IN THE SUN
A 1963 Herblock Cartoon. © The Herb Block Foundation

Finally, as he flew home from Europe, word came that Khrushchev was ready to talk. Now, for ten days in July, negotiators stitched together an agreement, initialed in Moscow on the 25th. For the first time since nuclear weapons' birth, leaders were stepping back. It took two more months for the Senate to ratify the treaty. Kennedy signed it on October 5. Special Counsel Theodore Sorensen wrote, "No other single accomplishment in the White House ever gave him greater satisfaction." Ma hoped, "with the President, that this is indeed a first step toward a more stable world." The *Washington Post* ran Herblock's cartoon on its front page.

In August, a quarter million people converged for Martin Luther King Jr.'s March on Washington. Back in June, Ma had written: "It seems that the race problem in this country is rapidly coming to a head and I for one think it is about time. This is dirty linen that has long needed washing. I have some trepidations about the possible demonstrations in Washington this summer, and they are practically bound to come because there are still a few filibusterers in Congress, and several organizations have warned that they will sit in the galleries if Congress is too laggard in passing the civil rights legislation the president sent Congress this past week."

Now, "This week brings the big demonstration to Washington. Most everyone I know expects to stay home that day, whether employers give it off or not." She would greatly have liked to participate but doubted her joining the 140,000 predicted participants would help very much.

"My sympathies are all with them and I fervently hope that it comes off without any more trouble than could ordinarily be expected when that many people are gathered in one city."

As things turned out, 100,000 more than anticipated showed up. It was one of the biggest demonstrations in US history. If there was a defining moment in the civil rights movement, surely the March on Washington was it. Like most white Americans—the Kennedys included—our family was slow to wake to the realities of black life in America. True, Ma had written, "It is wonderful to realize that during most of my life with Darel all of this was getting ready to happen, and how I wish he could be here to see the fruition."

We knew segregation was a travesty, lynching evil, voting rights vital, education crucial, job discrimination abominable. We fretted over these things, but largely they were background noise to our daily lives. They affected few of us personally. Almost nobody had black friends. Even in the office, a black person was a rarity. Tortuously, public schools were being integrated, though nine years after Brown v Board of Education, Virginia had still graduated me from an all-white school.

Like Ma, I toyed with going to the march but didn't, for much the same reasons as hers and maybe even more out of abject laziness. There was also the aversion to fire hoses, attack dogs, and tear gas. But mainly, at bottom, there was no escaping my lack of the true believer's motivation. I was still too white, and stayed home.

Martin Luther King had just begun his "I Have a Dream" speech when I walked into the TV room. My jaw left a dent in the floor. This was *oratory*, that belonged to the Age of Pericles. You never dreamed in your own lifetime you'd see it. Kennedy was a moving *speaker*, but Martin Luther King was an *orator*. This was *historic*. It was taking place forty minutes from my doorstep, and what was I doing? *Watching it on television*!

My first impulse was to grab a bus and head into town, but it would all be over by the time I got there. I've kicked myself ever since. Two hundred fifty-thousand people, and the March went off as peacefully as a Labor Day parade.

"The demonstration in D.C. was a moving & wonderful thing to watch. Wish Darel could have witnessed it." A few days later, responding to a letter from Pat, she wrote, "As you say it would indeed be comfortable if we did not have to concern ourselves with integration. However, it is being forced upon us whether we like it or not. The problem might never have reached such proportions if we had been willing to give a little of our precious selves in times irrevocably gone. It will avail us nothing to point fingers at past generations and say the problem is not of our making. It has been left in our laps, and cope with it we must. If we take the same attitude that we bemoan in our ancestors, we will get a like unsatisfactory solution."

In October, she found another job—still clerical—with Nuclear Utilities Services, a group of consulting nuclear engineers.

On November 1, South Vietnam's president, Ngo Dinh Diem, was assassinated. A day earlier, I hadn't known South Vietnam had a president. Laos had been more in the news than Vietnam, and neither was much of a story. The American presence consisted of 11,000 advisors.

"I don't know what to think of the mess in Vietnam," Ma wrote. "I hope it doesn't get hot enough to cause shooting. I have an idea that Diem was not in fact a suicide, and I hope that Madam Nhu doesn't succeed in going back. I don't believe she is good for her country."

Three weeks later, Kennedy was assassinated. On that fatal November 22, I was at Joe Colgan's Dupont Circle apartment when the phone rang. "This is *not* People's Drug Store," Joe muttered, lifting the receiver. Callers had been dialing his number trying to reach People's, and he was tired of it. Joe was doing a map for one of Dale Morgan's books, *Overland in 1846*, and had asked if I'd like to help. *Like* to? Any place I could stick a finger into the publishing world, I would so stick.

"Hello? Yes, I have. It's lovely," I heard him say. "What! Who shot him? Oh, my God. We're going from bad to worse." He called me to the phone. It was Ma. I think she was crying. Kennedy had been shot. There was an unconfirmed report that he was dead. Joe poured himself a drink. I told him to pour me one, too. Dismay, fury, confusion, mixed in a cocktail shaker. I tried doing a little lettering, but my hand shook too badly. Ma called back and confirmed. Kennedy was dead.

I went out to see if I could get a paper, but none had come out yet. We decided to go find a radio, and walked to the Embassy Steak House, Connecticut Avenue just above the circle. Joe ordered a martini and asked if I wanted wine. I said I'd have a martini, too. The news reports came every five minutes. After a little while I got restless and told Joe I wanted to get to school. I walked back toward his place and turned up New Hampshire Avenue instead of out P Street and walked all the way to Q before realizing I wasn't where I was supposed to be. I ran back to Dupont Circle, walked rapidly to Joe's, picked up my books, and started toward school.

I had just crossed L Street when I saw a boy running with an armload of papers—the *Washington Daily News*. I bought one. "JFK IS SLAIN," blared the 2½-inch headline. I went to my Burmese friend, Binnya Maw's room. He'd been asleep and was shaving. His radio was on, softly, and I assumed he'd heard the news. After a barely audible newscast, I said, "What kind of barbarians are we?" He looked at me quizzically. He hadn't heard. "The president has been assassinated," I said. He didn't get it. I had to say it three more times and show him the headline. "Gee-e-

e..." he said. "What...? In America...? Those days are over. ...Here...? My... golly...Ken-ne-dy, Ken-ne-dy, Ken-ne-dy," he trailed off.

"Truly these are black days for all mankind," I wrote to Pat the next day. "Even Mother Nature seems to know, for her brow is gloomy and she has been weeping profoundly for her hero." It was gray, overcast, and raining.

Ma wrote, "I was sitting in a phone booth letting the phone ring at Edythe's apartment when I heard someone at the lunch counter say, 'Kennedy is shot in Texas.' I hung up the phone and dialed Helen. She'd been driving when the news came over the radio and wondered why she didn't go off the road. Back at the office, there was no radio, but were enough lines to government agencies, since we deal in atomic power, to keep us informed. But none of us little guys could get an outside line.

By the author

"I had no idea last week when I was mentally composing a letter to you, that the world would have such cause for grief. How is it possible that we as a great nation have been so blind to the kind of emotional illness that can prompt men to such violence? There seems a diabolical paradox that a victim of mental illness should have taken the life of the man who had set as one of his goals the alleviation of that malady.

"And no more than 48 hours later, more violence to destroy the man who was charged

with the murder of the President. In this manner one life taken for the life of a man who deplored violence as a means of settling anything."

She later told me, "This is one thing I'm glad Darel didn't live to see."

We moved through the days in a fog. The three national television networks did a remarkable thing. From the assassination through the funeral three days later, they didn't run a single commercial.

John F. Kennedy had burst on the scene like a skyrocket, and was gone.

The assassination put Lyndon Johnson in an awkward spot. After Kennedy's dash, humor, and erudition, Johnson's crudeness, his Texas drawl, were an affront to our delicate Liberal sensitivities. But Johnson understood his deficits, and, in the short run, could not have been a better man a heartbeat from the president. He was a voracious political animal who had put party over ego to play second fiddle to a man he had fought bitterly for first place and didn't particularly like.

Hardly had the gunfire died before people were sniping that Johnson was eager to take his "rightful" place. He wasn't. He struck a fine balance between looking too eager and not eager enough. Two days after the funeral, with a finesse worthy of Kennedy himself, Johnson addressed a televised joint session of Congress.

"All I have," he told us, "I would have given gladly not to be standing here today. The greatest leader of our time has been struck down by the foulest deed of our time." "No memorial oration or eulogy," he said, "could more eloquently honor President Kennedy's memory than the earliest possible passage of the Civil Rights Bill for which he fought so long."

Johnson moved quickly to make civil rights a signature crusade. Riding the tide of national grief, using his mastery of legislative process, he finessed Kennedy's bill through Congress and signed it on July 2, 1964. It was a great national victory. It had also come with a price. Southern Democrats—still smarting from the "War of Northern Aggression" a century before—were Democrats solely because Abraham Lincoln had been a Republican. Johnson's alleged statement, "We have lost the South for a generation" thanks to the Civil Rights Act, is not reliably documented, but Senator Richard Russell (D-Ga.) did warn LBJ that the act "will not only cost you the South, it will cost you the election."

Russell was wrong about the election but right about the "Solid South." It went solidly Republican in '64. Two months after the act took effect, Strom Thurmond, one of the Senate's most high-profile segregationists, switched parties, declaring that he was not abandoning the Democratic Party, the Democratic Party had abandoned him.

A month after the civil rights victory set LBJ's star soaring, came the event that started bringing it back down. Intelligence reported that on August 2, three North Vietnamese torpedo boats had fired on the US destroyer Maddox in the Gulf of Tonkin, off North Vietnam. Reports of a second attack two days later led Congress to pass the Gulf of Tonkin Resolution giving LBJ carte blanche in Vietnam, with consequences invisible at the time but known too well to history.

Family affairs diverted attention from world affairs. All the way back in February, Gramps had called from Woodstock barely coherent. "Mom," Ma's mother, had "had an attack of some kind" and was taken to the hospital, conscious but seemingly "out of her mind." She asked about Ma so, the following weekend, Ma went to Woodstock. Mom recognized her once but the rest of the time only knew she was somebody familiar. She asked Ma if she was from Holland, and if she had met Margaret.

The hospital couldn't see completely to Mom's comfort, so Ma hired a special nurse to stay during the day. By Ma's next visit, March 22nd, Mom seemed better. "It may not be kind to keep Mom alive," Ma reflected, "but no one would have allowed her to go on without trying to make her more comfortable."

She would "need constant care as it looks now for the rest of her life." It would be expensive, "but you can't let your mother suffer more than necessary just because she is dying by inches so to speak."

Ma told Pat she would try contacting him through the Red Cross if Mom died, so he could wire Gramps condolences. "He is very upset, and no matter what we think of his past actions, he is a human being in need of moral support." A three-minute call to Germany ran $12—almost $100 in today's money. Perhaps the Red Cross would pass the information for free.

Mom had always seemed frail and rarely seemed to talk, though she never seemed anything other than integral to the family unit. She wrote us more letters than Margaret and Gramps combined. She had a quirky, understated sense of humor. On arrival in America, she'd thought the telephone poles looked "drunk," and that America must be very constipated, given all the laxative ads. She died on March 28, 1964. "Now we go into the next world," she said, "and see which one we like the best."

Ma probably financed the nurse, and a share of the funeral, through Household Finance Corporation—a name that was practically a household word for us during this period. That type of credit had only become possible because of equity that the house had accumulated in the little more than a year since our move there.

The debt spurred Ma to take a Civil Service exam, as she told Dale in mid-April, "not because I dislike my work, but because I need to increase my income, and the government pays better for the work for which my 'advanced' experience qualifies me"—a respectable $4500 to $5500 per year, as much as half again her salary at Nuclear Utilities Services. Her NUS job was, in fact, "very challenging and interesting. We deal with the nuclear field and it is interesting to see how this form of energy is gradually coming into its own as a means of giving us the power we need."

She was entrusted with "reports to read and edit, in addition to organizing the files and records." However, "I passed the Civil Service exam and submitted a Form 57. Now I wait to see if the government will allow me to find employment. My superiors keep saying they are going to increase my salary, but the scuttlebutt is that they try to keep you happy with promises as long as possible, so I don't expect any action there until I have another offer."

A week later, she had her raise. Nevertheless, she wrote to Pat, "We are going to have several months of relatively hard sledding, though not as hard as the years in Loudoun. Probably none of you realize just how hard those days were, for you did not know that on you depended the barest needs for several members of your family. I am at present supporting five people for food during the week."

Joe Colgan had been evicted from his apartment and was staying with us. "Jim," she continued, "has decided to go to summer school, so that means tuition. I am happy to do these things and happy that I am able to, but it does explain why, with the extra expenses for Mom's hospital and funeral, I will be pretty pinched." By January, with the nurse and funeral paid off, there'd be an extra $100.

She'd been scraping after dollars for six years, since Pop's first heart attack. My tuition had started at $13 an hour but was rising steeply, and on May 10, I wrote to Pat: "The cost of education is beginning to alarm. There is the question of how to pay for it. Ma has been paying for mine." I had loaned her my $2,000 of Pop's life insurance, and she was paying me back in tuition.

"I once felt as you do about not wanting to depend on someone else to pay for my education. I said to Ma that I never wanted to feel indebted to anyone. Her retort changed my view. She said, 'What you really mean is that you don't want the responsibility.' After all, none of us wants to feel indebted to anyone, do we? We only want them to be indebted to us. Let me tell you that I am proud of our mother. I owe her a lot—more than I can repay. Few people are lucky enough to owe their parents as much, and I think that's something to be proud of."

As our family did, I shared the letter with the house before mailing it. Ma was quiet momentarily, then asked, "Did you have a happy childhood?"

"Yes," I answered unequivocally.

"I'm glad to hear that," she said. "I sure didn't."

The presidential election was looming and the politics were impossible to ignore. Democrats crowed about the Civil Rights Act, but Barry Goldwater, the loose cannon on the political right, alarmed everybody by winning the Republican nomination, and with his claim that "extremism in the pursuit of liberty is no vice."

The scenario triggered one of Ma's finest tirades. "This is one election during which I will pass up no opportunity to do my bit against the 'extremists' who are trying to take over the country." She would "leave no stone unturned in exposing the dictator-type forces that put" Goldwater where he was.

"Every pocket of underprivilege is fertile soil for communist seeds. If you look at the way communists have seized power, usually it was in areas where the regime was doing nothing to alleviate grievances. Goldwater's claim that extremism in the defense of liberty was no vice came one day after the GOP platform committee refused to repudiate extremist groups. Asked why, the committee pled that they didn't condone extremism, but they hadn't wanted to risk naming some groups and leaving others out. Goldwater chimed that his own words referred to extreme actions, such as our 'freeing of the Panamanian republic,' Vietnam, and Cuba. The 'clarifications' sounded pretty weak following the platform committee's statement. Goldwater also seemed to think the federal government should police the streets to rid them of violence. What better way could there be to create the storm troopers needed to stage a coup? I hope these pessimistic prognostications are not true."

After trying to convince herself she was just seeing "ghosts under the bed," she heard many people expressing the same fears. Yet she worried about their apathy—just what a Hitler, a Lenin, a Stalin, or a Mussolini needed. They would give pat easy answers, and people would take the pat easy way and vote for them. During the thirties, people saw firsthand the tactics Communists used to get footholds. Those same people also saw the play, *It Can't Happen Here*. To an amazing degree, Goldwater's campaign was following the blueprint laid out in the play, which was written not as a how-to book but as a warning. "I hope it won't be necessary for us to experience such a regime to learn how to combat it."

As if Goldwater weren't enough, "Freedom Summer," from June through mid-August, saw 1000 white northern volunteers join thousands of mostly black southern organizers in a voter registration drive in Mississippi. Mississippi had some of the country's worst Jim Crow laws and the lowest proportion of black voters, denied rights by poll taxes, intimidation, and literacy tests that few whites could have passed.

Lawyers donated services for arrestees and victims of voter registration blocks. Clergy and divinity students demonstrated at courthouses. The project established 30 to 40 voluntary summer schools. Medical professionals taught health education classes. Doctors volunteered emergency care for activists, and they were needed. A thousand people were arrested, eighty were beaten, three were murdered. Seventy black-owned homes, businesses, and churches were bombed or burned.

On a Thursday in August, Ma came home to, "Mother, there's bad news. We have to move the horses."

Dixie Virginia Payne[§] had called and said there'd been two accidents. One resulted in seventeen stitches in the scalp and face of her new husband. The other had knocked her daughter, Bobbie, unconscious. The Ford being on sabbatical, Helen drove Bunny and me to Lovettsville, where we found that they were not so upset as had seemed. Both accidents had happened with Dusty, whom they acknowledged they had been warned not to ride. But Bobbie loved him and spent much time brushing and currying him.

Some horses will spook at a mirage, and Dusty was one of them. He had spooked at something and thrown Bobbie into a ditch, knocking her out. For the other accident, Mrs. Payne's husband had dismounted and was replacing bars in a gap in the fence. Dusty kicked up his heels striking the man in the head, and took off running. Seventeen sutures later, the man was back home. Dusty had once paid Pat a similar compliment.

Ma found a place in Herndon, Virginia, to keep them until she could sell Cinnamon. When Pat came home, it would fall to him to do something with Dusty. Ma gave the pony, King, to the Paynes' little boy. The two had become practically inseparable.

On September 15, my twenty-first birthday, I made the biggest mistake of my life. I started smoking. "I can't imagine how anybody could want to start smoking," said my mother, somewhere between cigarettes of her own. I didn't argue, but smoking was a rite of passage. She had told me, "Not until you are twenty-one," and I had waited patiently. Unlike Pat, who had usurped the right at approximately age fourteen, I had earned it and nothing was going to stop me. Three months later, I tried to quit, and was hopelessly addicted.

[§] It was the Masons who bought the Lovettsville house, where the horses were staying. My memory has not preserved the identity of Dixie Virginia Payne or why her husband and daughter were involved with the horses. I only find them here, mentioned in my mother's letter.

"Next Tuesday is Election Day," she wrote on November 1, "and I am going to vote for the first time in my life." The assertion surprised me when I learned it researching this book. "Before, I never got my poll tax paid. Now, thanks to the Civil Rights Act, it didn't need to be paid. Jim and I stood in line over an hour to get registered. I mean to vote and stay up Tuesday evening until the results are certain, then go to work at noon on Wednesday."

Republicans were crying that the Democrats would rig votes, and were placing poll watchers "to insure fair play." The real reason seemed to be that they hoped to challenge enough votes to hold up the process, leaving many unable to vote by closing time. Such a tactic should work in Republicans' favor, as low voter turnout generally helped conservatives. The Democrats planned to counter with legal counsel at the polls to settle disputes quickly.

"Dear Pat, I'm very happy, as I know you must be, that Goldwater was so resoundingly defeated." LBJ had beaten him by the biggest margin since FDR routed Hoover in 1932.

Pat's discharge was scheduled for January, 1965, but the Army showed its softer side and let him out for Christmas. Four months earlier, following the Tonkin Gulf incident, things had looked very different.

"The way things look in SE Asia," he'd written August 6, "I'm liable not to even see home again for the next few years. I'm inclined to believe we'll be in another war before Christmas. In a way, I'd rather have it happen while I'm *in* the Army than after I get out. If we get into a real war in Vietnam and I get sent there, the chances of my getting a leave on the way across the States should be pretty good.

"It would also resolve what to do when I get out, or put off the day when I'd have to face it. Then, too, were this to become another Korean-type conflict, there'd probably be another GI bill, so I'd not have to worry about how to pay for college." Pat had gotten his GED in the Army. "Red China could end up defeated, and we wouldn't have them disturbing world peace for a while. So, even if something *does* break in SE Asia, it may turn out that the world is better off for it after it's over. I might also be better off. This is admittedly an overoptimistic viewpoint, but if one isn't optimistic with the world in the shape it's in, he'd go nuts."

Now, with his discharge, those speculations were moot.

Ma replied, "I have my doubts about whether we should go in there [Vietnam] at all. It seems to me that we could do a great deal more for the people there by a Peace Corps type operation."

Despite her enthusiasm for NUS's science, the company was getting on her nerves. "I'm getting educated in the process of corporation-building. It's a rat race to grow and stay profitable. Excellence is not enough. A new company must take care not to threaten established organizations which could force it out of business. Our free-enterprise system is very complex and needs much guardianship. Even if I don't like the philosophy that pervades most of NUS, something is gained from working there, besides the two substantial raises I've gotten since October '63. Our outfit's social and political philosophy ranges from liberal Democratic to John Birch rightist."

When Kennedy was assassinated, Ma gave her immediate superior the news. He looked up from his desk, said, "I'm a Goldwater man myself," and went back to work.

When Pat left home, his mother was an unemployed widow who hadn't worked in thirty years, struggling with $20,000 in debt. In three years, she had gone from file clerk at a small publisher to file clerk at an organization of nuclear engineers, reading and editing technical papers.

By the time Pat got home, she'd landed as close to her dream job as possible, with the United Planning Organization (UPO), one of the Community Action Agencies of President Johnson's "Great Society" program. UPO was a private, nonprofit, community-action agency that had been set up in 1962 to implement human services for low-income D.C. residents. It was already a year and a half old when the anti-poverty program tapped its network.

It had established eight neighborhood development centers, inaugurated a Neighborhood Youth Corps, funded a Model School System, inaugurated a pilot Head Start program, launched the community credit union movement, and established a Neighborhood Legal Services Program and a Small Business Development Center. "It is the most gratifying work that I have had since coming back to the metropolitan area. There is the same enthusiasm that we all enjoyed so much during the early days of WPA."

Within two years, she was conducting field visits to neighborhood centers, producing reports, and assisting setting up a primary-source library. "We have daily confirmation that, given the means, a great many of life's outcasts will pull themselves out of their slough of despair."

She and the librarian became friends. The librarian was buying a house in D.C. to rent out rooms. By then, I was working full-time and going to school at night, and had been considering a move to town to cut commuting time. Barbara Bryan's rooming house just off the GW campus, seemed perfect. At the beginning of January, 1965, I moved. In the four years since Pop's death, Ma had ushered three of her brood out the door: Helen, Pat, and now me. Buster was graduating high school in the spring. Bunny was starting high school in the fall.

The civil rights movement was evolving. Competing with Martin Luther King's integrative Southern Christian Leadership Conference was a separatist group called The Nation of Islam, led by a fiery speaker named Elijah Muhammad, who preached black superiority and advocated social and economic independence. Its followers were called Black Muslims. Heavyweight boxing champion Cassius Clay became one, taking the name Muhammed Ali.

A disaffected acolyte named Malcolm X was assassinated on February 21. For me, those developments were part of a slow awakening. Ma may have known that the Nation of Islam had been in existence for thirty-five years, and Elijah Muhammad had been its leader for thirty-one, but we never talked about it.

Pat escaped Vietnam by finishing his service before the unpleasantness got rolling. I was ripe for the plucking, though for now my student deferment insulated me. On March 8, President Johnson, drawing on the powers vested in him by the Tonkin Gulf Resolution, ordered 3,500 Marines to Vietnam to protect US air bases.

That "escalation" (use of the word seemed almost comical at first) became 200,000 by year's end. People started talking about a "credibility gap" between what the White House said it was doing and what it really was doing. On April 17, 20,000 people marched down the National Mall in protest, the biggest to date. Pat and I went, as much out of curiosity as anything. We still hadn't made up our minds.

Within a year, a new directive came down. Any student not expecting to graduate "in the normal time" would no longer get a deferment—part-timers, like me, i.e. They assumed if you were going part-time, you were just foot-dragging to avoid service. The assumption was an insult. They ordered me to Richmond for a pre-induction physical, "in case" draft calls rose dramatically.

OK, I thought, *if that's the way you want it…*I moved back home, traded full-time for part-time employment, got a loan, and registered for summer school and full-time classes in the fall, to finish by spring 1967.

Barely had I moved back home than I met my future wife, Anya, and moved in with her, just off campus, instead. Buster was at the University of Virginia. With just Bunny left at home, Ma sold Russell Road and moved to a garden apartment on Duke Street, behind the George Washington Memorial Masonic Temple. Anya and I drove Gramps to Woodstock in the spring of '67, and admired the authority with which, at eighty-four, he lit into splitting firewood. Later that weekend, he had a stroke which robbed him, among other things, of his eyesight. He returned to Alexandria to Ma and Bunny's care.

In February, before Gramps's stroke, I had taken the most consequential step of my life. I applied to the Peace Corps. The Peace Corps came with a deferment similar to the educational, but that only partly explains my action. I'd planned to join ever since President Kennedy announced its formation six years earlier. In mid-July, I took leave of my family and distraught future wife, and flew to California for training. "See you when I get back," I told Gramps. "I won't be here," he said. "Oh, sure you will," I assured him. He wasn't, but he hung on for another year and a half.

A training hiatus took me to San Francisco where I visited Dale Morgan. He gave me a blank journal and told me to write my impressions at the end of every day. That germ grew, in four decades, into my self-published Peace Corps memoir.

I also gawked at hippies, still mostly regarded as a San Francisco phenomenon. Ma shared society's bewilderment with the species. "I wish I could fathom what the Hippies are aiming at. I see a protest against a society that has never come near solving all its problems. Is there more than this? I don't know whether your view of these people is extensive enough to tell me, but if it is I would appreciate some enlightenment." My view wasn't extensive enough. At some point, somebody flashed me a peace sign at close range, and I jumped back alarmed before realizing the gesture had come with the words, "Peace, brother."

Peace was in short supply that summer. While my fellow trainees and I ground through a grueling training regimen, race riots—some resulting in major injury and even death—dotted the national landscape. Detroit and Newark topped the charts. But bad as the summer of '67 was, it was a mere overture to 1968, a notorious year in US history.

Chapter Eleven

1968

ID BEEN IN THE PEACE CORPS in India for three months when, on Tet, the Vietnamese New Year, January 30, 1968, 80,000 Vietcong fighters launched simultaneous attacks on 100 targets in South Vietnam, including the US Embassy in Saigon. The Allies were taken completely by surprise. How had this happened? General Westmoreland had said we were winning, that the North Vietnamese were utterly "unable to mount a major offensive," that they were "certainly losing." He hoped, he told *Time* magazine, that they did try something, "because we are looking for a fight."

The Communists didn't keep a single position they attacked, but the offensive was a public relations disaster for the White House. How had those "underfed little people" mounted such a complicated offensive in total secrecy? The credibility gap widened to a chasm. Selective Service called for 48,000 more draftees. College campuses exploded in protest. For the first time, more Americans opposed the war than favored it. Some civilians vented their anger on the least blameworthy participants, returning draftees.

The war undid Johnson's presidency. On March 31, he announced: "I shall not seek, and I will not accept, the nomination of my party for another term as your president."

Four days later, Martin Luther King, Jr., fell to an assassin's bullet. The news, Ma said, "brought shock and grief throughout the land." Pat was completely undone. "Dr. King has been my major hero. He was my candidate for president. I hung the title, 'The greatest man produced by this country in this century,' on him. My reaction to his death was stunned disbelief. I didn't go to work Friday, simply because I couldn't. I was just walking around in a daze." By then, Pat was working at UPO, too. Though some did report for work, the staff was let out in respect for King.

That evening, crowds gathered in Capitol Heights around 14th and U, N.W., then a poor, solidly black neighborhood. Stokely Carmichael, former head of the Student Nonviolent Coordinating Committee, led SNCC members in exhorting neighborhood stores to close out of respect for the martyred leader.

DC Armed camp   by Burt G Inn

What began peacefully deteriorated. People started breaking windows, and by 11:00 p.m. looting was underway.

Morning dawned peacefully, but by noon buildings were ablaze; firefighters were pelted with rocks, bottles, and bricks. Not even tear gas could disperse the mobs. LBJ called in 13,600 federal troops, including 1,750 federalized DC National Guardsmen, many of whom had joined the Guard to avoid serving in Vietnam. Marines placed machine-guns on the Capitol steps. Soldiers took positions around the White House. Rioting got to within two blocks of the mansion before the mob turned back. A 5:30 p.m. curfew was ordered, later tightened to 4:00. Smoke and tear gas hung in the air. Fire sirens wailed. Troops patrolled the streets. Tanks and armored personnel carriers rumbled through the city.

The estranged wife of one of Pat's army buddies was trapped in the Hecht Company department store at 7th and G. A mob had surrounded the building, and even though the store was closed and the staff released, she couldn't get out. The buddy asked Pat to let him know she was OK. It was four hours before he could.

Ma's sister, Margaret, spent two hours getting ten blocks from her office at the US Information Agency to her parking lot below the 14th Street Bridge. It took two more hours to crawl across the bridge and into thinner traffic before she could proceed home to Woodstock. Hordes of people were walking home because the buses were barely moving.

Seven blocks from the White House, Anya, my future wife, was near the center of action. She described the noise of military vehicles keeping her awake at night. She removed to the house of some friends on Capitol Hill. Pat had been at her apartment when Ma called with the news. He ignored the curfew and brought Helen over from her own nearby apartment so they could all be together.

Living in Alexandria, Ma was somewhat removed from the trouble, but from the Masonic Temple grounds she could see smoke over the capital. Traces of tear gas persisted for days. She remarked on the fatigue in the faces and voices of news commentators. Yet the outpouring of volunteer assistance—food, clothing, and housing for displaced people—heartened her. "For me, it is there that faith in the human race is at least partially restored."

D.C. was the hardest hit of any American city, its military occupation the largest since the Civil War. In five days of rioting, 1,200 buildings went up in flames with damages totaling $27 million—nearly half a billion in 2020 money.

Students at historically black Howard University added a new wrinkle to protesting—the occupation of university buildings. Paradoxically, Howard offered no black history courses, no African American authors in literature classes, no jazz, blues, or gospel in the fine arts building, and the administration tried suppressing criticism by the student newspaper.

"Howard University," complained the freshman class president, "should serve a purpose other than preparing people to fill slots in white society." On March 20, the university threatened to expel 39 students involved in disrupting the March 1 "Charter Day" observance of the school's founding, and 1,200 students occupied the administration building, shutting operations down for four days. The demonstration ended peacefully with the students winning all their demands save resignation of the university president.

The following month, students occupied buildings at Columbia University, partly over its plan to build a segregated gymnasium—which black students dubbed "Gym Crow"—and partly to protest Columbia's affiliation with the Institute for Defense Analyses, a think-tank that worked with the Defense Department. At the insistence of the black students, the protests were segregated, but together they shut down the university for the duration. Because Ivy League Columbia got national coverage, where regional Howard didn't, many thought Columbia's occupation was first, but the home team was the original. Columbia's black demonstration, brokered by black lawyers and black New York policemen, ended peacefully while the white students were routed with tear gas and an assault on the seized building. Columbia nixed the segregated gym.

In May, just up the pike from D.C., the so-called Catonsville Nine broke into the Selective Service office in Catonsville, Maryland, outside Baltimore, removed dozens of draft records, and burned them with napalm in protest of the Vietnam War.

Just when things couldn't get any crazier, they did. On June 5, two months after Martin Luther King, Robert Kennedy was mortally wounded in Los Angeles minutes after speaking on his victory in the California presidential primary. Three Kennedys down. Originally, Joe, Jr., was to have been president, but died in World War II. Jack survived the War and succeeded to the position but was killed less than three years into his term. Now promise of another President Kennedy was buried. Teddy, ultimately, declined to run.

No civil disturbances attended Bobby's killing; the nation grieved and one might have thought we were weary of riots and done with them; but August's Democratic convention in Chicago gave that theory the lie.

Ten thousand demonstrators of varying stripes—radicals, hippies, Yuppies, and moderates—flowed into Chicago along with the convention's delegates. Their loosely shared objective was opposition to the Vietnam War, being fought on the thinnest pretext with forced American labor. Rennie Davis, project director for the National Mobilization Committee to End the War in Vietnam, said many members had given up on elections. "We think that the energies released are creating a new constituency for America." Yippie leader Jerry Rubin planned a six-day "Festival of Life," celebrating the counterculture. The Yippies thought it would be fun to dump LSD into Chicago's water supply.

Chicago mayor Richard Daley was not amused. He refused to grant permits for marches and gatherings. As a result, most of the name musicians—Joan Baez, Judy Collins, Country Joe and the Fish, pulled out. Disappointed, thousands of demonstrators pulled out too. Still, 10,000 came. The Festival was reduced to a somewhat disheveled affair. Abbie Hoffman and Jerry Rubin addressed the crowd. Folk singer Phil Ochs and a number of local singer-songwriters performed. Pete Seeger showed up but didn't perform.

Having criminalized the event by denying its permit, Mayor Daley unleashed 23,000 police and National Guardsmen on the 10,000 attendees. Abbie Hoffman told people to resist rioting. Tom Hayden told them to move into the streets, so the tear gas would spread throughout the city. Police and guardsmen attacked the protesters daily in full view of television cameras.

Defending his tactics, Mayor Daley stumbled over his tongue: "The policeman is not here to create disorder," he said, "the policeman is here to preserve disorder."

Violence wasn't confined to the streets. Journalists Dan Rather, Mike Wallace, and Edwin Newman were roughed up on the convention floor, leading Walter Cronkite, anchoring CBS, to remark, "I think we've got a bunch of thugs here." Abraham Ribicoff, nominating George McGovern, guaranteed that, "With George McGovern as President of the United States, we wouldn't have to have Gestapo tactics in the streets of Chicago!" Daley screamed, "Fuck you, you Jew son of a bitch."

Eight organizers were charged with conspiracy to incite riot and held for trial. Bobby Seale (co-founder of the Black Panther Party) was separated and sentenced to four years not for conspiracy but for contempt of court. No longer "The Chicago Eight" but "The Chicago Seven," the defendants were given varying sentences. The convictions of all eight were overturned on appeal. An official investigation called the disturbances a "police riot." Nevertheless, across the nation, most people *supported* Mayor Daley!

The convention nominated LBJ's vice president, Hubert Humphrey, by a landslide over George McGovern and Eugene McCarthy, both opposed to the Vietnam War. Richard Nixon rose Phoenix-like from the ashes of his career to win both the Republican nomination and the presidency. "You won't have Dick Nixon to kick around anymore," he'd told a news gathering after losing the California governorship in 1962, and the media had pronounced him politically dead. Now, like the Ghoul of Christmas past, he was back. Liberals were despondent. Democrats lost ground in Congress but held their majorities.

America has rarely seen a year like 1968. I missed it, being in India, but we were a changed country when I returned. Hippy anarchism had gone national. The suit and tie had fallen from grace. The beard was pejorative—I was thoroughly upbraided for mine, even though it had sprouted eleven thousand miles away in innocence and isolation. War hawks called the Buddhist peace sign "the footprint of the yellow American chicken." Girls were enchanting in their flower-child tresses.

There was also the "hooker look," with spike-heels, mini-skirts, and exaggerated eye makeup. The term "groovy" committed suicide through overuse. Youth was on the move. Ma, reminded of the twenties, reveled in the ferment. Yoga and marijuana, for her, were a bridge too far, but peers said what a cool mom we had.

Chapter Twelve

Last Years

Ma in Charlottesville

GRAMPS HAD GONE into the hospital at the beginning of January 1969 and died in mid-February. "He had become a pure vegetable," Ma wrote, "and so it was best this way." Pat was working in Fairmont, West Virginia. Helen was married, raising two kids in Hyattsville, Maryland. I was in the Peace Corps half a world away. Buster was in college in Charlottesville. Bunny was the only one at home, and on her 16-year-old shoulders had fallen much of the care of that incontinent, blind, deaf, dying old man. Taking a test in school, she broke down crying. The teacher asked what the trouble was. They called Ma, and Gramps went back to Woodstock to spend his remaining days with Margaret.

In June, Bunny married Buster's UVA college roommate, Clarence Crews, and settled in Charlottesville. The following month, Ma moved to a smaller apartment on D.C.'s Columbia Road, declaring herself free at last to pursue her own interests after thirty years of motherhood. She could walk to work from the address. A year later she downsized again, to a Dupont Circle apartment which she described to Dale: "I am living in an old walk-up. Darel and I lived in this building from 1937 thru August 1939. I hope I'm settled for a while."

Time, unfortunately, was not with her. She'd found a lump in her breast. She'd also turned 60, and UPO had only agreed to take her if she would waive benefits—vacation, sick leave, and health insurance. The tumor was mercifully slow-growing, but she had to wait to age sixty-five, when Medicare kicked in, before getting it looked at.

Cancer still carried a stigma, which, for all her intellectual proclivities, Ma couldn't seem to shake. It was Anya, my future wife, rather than her children to whom she'd confided, "There's something terribly wrong with me." Anya was a board-certified medical technologist. If ever anybody was born for medicine, it was she. Only fragile health had kept her from climbing higher on the totem pole. She had elevated her stock in the family eye the previous year by diagnosing Helen's *idiopathic thrombocytopenic purpura*—a blood condition treated by removal of the spleen—before Helen had even seen a doctor.

Perhaps it was less intimidating for Ma to confide in someone with medical bona fides than in her own children. Maybe she was embarrassed, as a lifelong health advocate, to have gotten cancer anyway, though the cigarettes—which she had smoked for thirty-five years—are always a good excuse for cancer.

And in fact, she didn't *not* get the cancer looked at. All the way back on the farm, she had acquired a book, *A Cancer Therapy,* by Max Gerson, MD, that it's reasonable to suppose she read about in *Prevention* magazine. She'd handed me the book and I'd read it. Its theory was that you cleanse the body of toxins by eating vegetables, drinking fruit juices, and taking coffee enemas—also by eating raw calf liver—and the body would cure itself.

The Gerson Institute was in upstate New York, and you needed a doctor's referral to get in. A doctor whom Anya had known when he was a medical student was in his residence at St. Elizabeth's Hospital. He signed the referral. The Institute also required $1,500. A friend, Ida Sharkey, sprang for that. Ma traveled to upstate New York in 1970 and returned visibly improved.

Her Medicare was still three years away, and a return visit to New York was out of reach. But by then, another alternative treatment was making news,

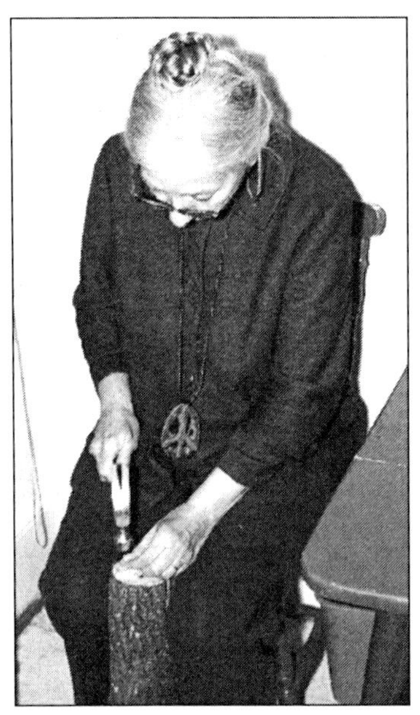

Cracking apricot pits

Laetrile, a synthetic version of the naturally occurring cyanogen, "amygdalin," found, among other places, in apricot pits. Laetrile was not sanctioned in the US. You could get it in Mexico, but Mexico was as out of reach as New York. The same could not be said of apricots. Ma began buying them in quantity. After eating one, she'd crack the pit with a hammer and lick the amygdalin.

She had told Dale she hoped she was "settled for a while," but she wasn't. Once a mother, it seems, always a mother. Bunny and Clarence begat Misha. Ma moved to Charlottesville to assist with the birth— which occurred on Ma's own birthday, March 14—and bestow some grandparental care.

Two weeks after Misha's birth, Dale Morgan died of liver cancer. He had clung to life just a year longer than Pop had himself.

D.C. was Ma's spiritual home, and it was calling her back. For many, "D.C." stands for everything wrong with America, but D.C. is more than a bunch of politicians conjuring ways to suck blood from their constituents. It has a symphony, art galleries, museums, libraries, universities, theater.

Its restaurant scene was still largely meat-and-potatoes but was starting to sophisticate. Run by Congress, by edict of the US Constitution, D.C. had a charming dysfunctionality that residents felt bemusedly possessive about. She moved first into a flat in the Clermont at 21st and F Streets, N.W. Anya had lived there when she and I met. It was a four-story walk-up that has long since been erased for newer/bigger/better.

From the Clermont, she moved to the Norwood on Columbia Road, in the very mixed, very activist Adams-Morgan neighborhood. It was hardly more than a block from "The Alley" where she and Pop had first met.

I had helped with every move since the farm—the farm to Lovettsville, Lovettsville to Russell Road, Russell Road to Duke Street, Duke Street to Columbia Road, from there to 19th and Q, to Charlottesville, to the Clermont, to the Norwood—nine moves in eleven years, five of them between 1969 and 1972. When we'd set the last box down, I looked at her and said, "The next time you move, hire somebody." I wasn't a nice thing to say to your mother. She looked at me without answering, and never moved again.

I may have visited her a few times after she settled in, but Anya and I were married and starting our own life in a Capitol Hill fixer-upper, both of us working. We stayed in touch with Ma by phone, but didn't see her for about a year. Then it was a shock. Her hair was a snowy halo and her body was three-quarters its original size. Pat, who had been living in Chicago, returned and became her primary caregiver. Anya and I took meals once a week; Helen changed the dressings on her cancerous lesion.

The country continued in turmoil. In May 1970, Ohio National Guardsmen killed four Kent State University students protesting Nixon's incursion into Cambodia, after promising to get us out of Vietnam. Five days later, 100,000 people descended on D.C., mostly peacefully protesting the same action.

While still in Charlottesville, Ma had seen Daniel Ellsburg leak the "Pentagon Papers," a secret Defense Department study which proved that administrations had for decades, "systematically lied, not only to the public but also to Congress" about the war.

With the rest of the country, she watched the Watergate scandal unfold stage by Byzantine stage until, on August 8, 1974 Richard Nixon got his comeuppance. For the first time in American history, a president left office prematurely for a reason other than death. It was the stuff of Greek tragedy, a rise to prominence undone by a character flaw. With his resignation, Gerald R. Ford became the nation's first, and so far only, appointed president.

In 1975, Raymond Moody published *Life after Life*. We had watched the moon walk at Raymond's apartment in Charlottesville, before he became *Raymond Moody*. He'd attended Bunny and Clarence's wedding. I found the book riveting and recommended it to Ma, but she wouldn't be enticed. "Oh," she said, "I think we all pretty much know what happens [when we die]." In typical family fashion, I let the matter drop.

The National Gallery of Art held an exhibit of artifacts from Tutankhamon's tomb, the original discovery of which must have enflamed Ma at age fourteen. She asked Anya and me to take her to it, but we putzed around and never did, to my everlasting regret.

Pat said she would sit in her chair with her feet up, hour by hour, generating and solving mathematical equations, "off in her own world."

She was in and out of the hospital getting chemo and radiation. The cancer had metastasized to her bones, which could have been excruciatingly painful as the tumor tried to expand in the bones' unyielding space. Mercifully, she was spared that agony, but her skeleton was dissolving and she was shrinking. She broke a bone in her wrist opening a mayonnaise jar.

During what turned out to be her last hospitalization, I suddenly realized we were about to lose a cache of family lore. I asked the first thing that came to mind: when had we moved to Burke? She couldn't remember and was too tired to try.

At one point, she remarked, "Well, I've had a good life." Anya found the statement surprising. From the outside, maybe it was. Her life had not been the envy of Wall Street, but Ma was a Depression-era bohemian. In the things she cared about, life had been a Renaissance tapestry.

A day or two later, her doctor called. She was succumbing to congestive heart failure and wasn't expected to survive the night. Helen came, Bunny came, Anya and I came, Pat came. Buster had moved to Venezuela and couldn't. In her room, she seemed stable, so after a couple of hours we said we'd be back in the morning. Anya and I left first. "See you," she said with a smile. Helen was the first to return in the morning, and found her dead, May 3, 1978. I turned thirty-five that year, the same age she'd been when I was born.

Those were the parents as their children knew them.

Chapter Thirteen

Who Did We Think We Were?

Darel McConkey's oldest brother, Clyde, at home on the family farm, Dixie, after World War I.

IN ANY GIVEN TIME, nobody feels "old-fashioned," no matter the era—Medieval Europe, Ancient Egypt, Bronze-Age Russia. Whoever is in it not only feels but is up-to-the-minute. Up-to-the-minute is like that first potato chip out of the bag. None that follow can compare. The Model-T Ford looks hopelessly outdated today, but in its time, it was that very first potato chip. For many it would better have been left in the bag, but for most it was just a milestone in the march of human progress. By 1905, when Pop was born at a farm near Good Hope West Virginia, they already had "filling stations" where you could buy gas without going to the hardware store. When he was two, "taximeter cabs arrived in New York City from Paris."

When Henry Ford doubled the prevailing wage to $5.00 a day so his workers could afford the cars they were making, he became a national hero. Ford's fellow industrialists howled that such outrageous pay was a disservice to labor itself!

The first "Tin Lizzy" rolled off Ford's assembly line the year Ma was born, 1908. A week before that signature event, an explosion over Siberia's Tunguska region leveled an area of forest two-thirds the size of Rhode Island. Fluctuations in atmospheric pressure were detected all the way to Britain, but no one investigated for ten years, owing to the site's remoteness. It has been blamed on a comet, a black hole, antimatter, and even Nikola Tesla. Most now believe it was an asteroid.

When Pop made his entrance, scarcely a year and a half had passed since that gray day when a bicycle mechanic from Dayton, Ohio, Wilbur Wright, rose from the earth in a powered, heavier-than-air contraption at Kitty Hawk, North Carolina. Few people credited the Wrights' claim until a demonstration near Le Mans, France, in 1908. Six years later, the airplane went to war.

Wright brothers' first flight

The U.S. was still three states short of 48 when Pop was born, and the movie industry was barely out of diapers. The first continuous-action film, *The Great Train Robbery*, all of twelve minutes long, had been released just two years earlier. The first "nickelodeon," built exclusively for films, opened in Pittsburgh when Pop was a month old. But like airplanes, movies grew up fast. The first multi-reel feature, lasting over an hour, came out in Australia in 1906. By the time Pop was ten, the industry had grown from *The Great Train Robbery* to D. W. Griffith's three-hour, technically sophisticated, deplorably racist, *Birth of a Nation*. At its best, film was true art. Lacking sound, stories advanced as much by mime as by dialogue cards. Some cinematography rivaled the old masters of oil and canvas.

At the risk of confusing things, I'm going to switch nomenclatures. Ma and Pop unarguably became our parents, but not in 1905 and not in 1908, so I'm going to call them what people called them then—Anna and Darel. Darel's family called him Tommy, and as a teen Anna went by Annie, but Anna and Darel are quite enough.

Of all that happened the year Darel was born, the most earth-shaking was publication of a theory by a Swiss patent office clerk named Albert Einstein, who yanked from under us the notion that there existed a solid platform from which to judge reality. For Anna and Darel's generation, however, that tectonic shift had less effect than the earth's palpable 1906 shaking in San Francisco. The world plunged ahead as if Albert Einstein had never existed. A century later, we're still coming to terms with the theory's psychological and philosophical implications.

In the world Anna and Darel were born to, you were more likely to hear the clop of horses' hooves than the guttural whir of automobile engines. In 1905, America had 8000 cars and 144 miles of paved roads. People knew their hames from their horse collars, their traces from their wagon tongues, and that a doubletree was not a chain of luxury hotels.

With Thomas Jefferson, we largely believed that virtue dwelled naturally in workers of the land. Over half of us still lived on farms or in small towns. The farm was the last bastion of pre-industrial freedom from the "job" as we know it today.

We thought we were mild-mannered and good-humored, sometimes a little clownish; slow to rile but when riled, watch out; short on book larnin' but long on horse sense. Many harbored a mistrust of education, a sense that books tended to fill our heads with a lot of tomfool nonsense. We were hard-working, god-fearing churchgoers, slow to take charity but quick to give it. We drank hard and played hard. We were made of rough, pioneering stuff, tough yet pliable as harness leather. Such inconveniences as racism troubled few of us.

Still, modernity was encroaching, and it wasn't just Albert Einstein or Sigmund Freud. On May 29, 1913, women in Good Hope, West Virginia, Darel's birthplace, still wore split bonnets when Igor Stravinsky's *Rite of Spring* sparked a riot in the Théâtre des Champs-Elysées in Paris. Maybe such things quickened spirits in New York, Philadelphia, and Boston, but such places scarcely registered out where most of us lived.

Such motes of history as are flecked here on the page, in actuality buttressed round with bookfuls of detail, were as present to their memories as memories of our own skinned knees and first loves are to us. No book can recapture but a shaving of a life's real panorama.

Chapter Fourteen

The Fleeing Dutchman

Family outing in Zeist, Netherlands, spring 1910. Neeltje (Nellie) and Anna, Tante (Aunt) Dora, Margaret with Harry, Oom (Uncle) Jaap (Nellie's brother) with daughter Thea.

FOUR THOUSAND MILES east of Good Hope and three hundred miles north of Paris, women in Holland wore bonnets, too. Darel was walking, talking, and emerging from the terrible twos when, on March 14, 1908, Hendrik and Neeltje Schuddeboom welcomed daughter Anna to the world in the ancient village of Zeist—first mentioned in an A.D. 838 document. Holland was picturesque, barely larger than the state of Maryland. Besides bonnets, her women wore billowy skirts, white aprons, and wooden shoes. Windmills lazily pumped water from lands below sea-level, while dikes held back the sea. "God created the world," the saying went, "but the Dutch created Holland." No little boy ever stuck his finger in a dike—the story didn't even originate in Holland—but the town of Spaarndam has a bronze statue of him anyway.

Anna's maternal grandfather was Jacobus Mandersloot, a railroad conductor, and her grandmother was Berendina Mandersloot, nee Tap. Her mother, Neeltje, grew up to pursue practically the only career open to women—homemaker—and accordingly married Hendrik Schuddeboom on December 20, 1906. A year and a quarter later, she duly delivered Anna to the world, and a year and a half after that, Margaret.

Hendrik had turned seventeen in 1900 and faced eight years of mandatory service in the Dutch militia. In 1904, he earned a bookkeeping certificate and went to work in a bank, but by 1912 or '13, was working as a road-paver. Pat, my older brother, said Hendrik (Gramps to us, Harry to most others) was in the reserves when World War I broke out, said to hell with war and whisked his family to America. But in September 1913, when he arrived, the war was still a year away and Harry's military obligation had long been discharged.

A partner in the paving concern had bid a job based on high-quality materials, then did the job with inferior materials. The job failed and blame was fobbed off on the junior partner, Harry Schuddeboom. He was ultimately exonerated but his prospects didn't recover.

The Schuddebooms in Medina, NY

A Mr. Malcolm, who owned an apple orchard in New York, had told Harry if he ever came to America, look him up. Harry likely didn't consider the move, at least partly because Neeltje—Nellie—wouldn't have considered it. But when things fell apart, the offer took on appeal. He made landfall in America in September 1913. Nellie, Anna, and Margaret came later, setting sail on Margaret's fourth birthday, October 17, and landing at Ellis Island. Their first American home was a house with a broad lawn in Medina, New York, where they lived from mid-January to the end of October 1914.

Anna rarely spoke of her childhood. The time was not happy. Her father was a stern disciplinarian. Locking her in closets was a favorite punishment.

She created an "inner garden" where no one could hurt her. It became a prison from which she never completely escaped. Margaret's take on their father allowed some grudging admiration. "My Dad," she said, "when he said something, he meant it." In 1992, Margaret recorded much of her and Anna's early history in an interview with my older sister, Helen.

Mr. Malcolm didn't have anything for Harry, but referred him to someone working on the Eire Canal, which flowed through Medina. The nature of the job is lost, but Harry told of concrete hauled in mule-drawn dump wagons. The contractor had trouble meeting his deadline and left equipment on the bottom of the canal as it refilled.

The contractor had a job in Baltimore and asked Harry to go with him. The family moved to Baltimore, the contractor disappeared, and, Margaret recalled, "Times got hard and wages were low. He worked on the Coca Cola Building for ten dollars a week." A clothing factory gave Nellie piecework she could do at home.

World War I had broken out in August, and DuPont opened a plant in Hopewell, near Richmond, Virginia, making guncotton, an ingredient of white gunpowder six times more explosive than black powder. DuPont employed 30,000 workers and produced over a million pounds of guncotton a day. Hopewell's population rocketed from a few hundred in 1912 to 40,000.

Harry "packed off for Hopewell," said Margaret, and there met "an experienced carpenter who was getting up in years" and offered to teach Harry the trade if Harry would do the heavy lifting. Harry agreed and went to work not making explosives but most likely working on the DuPont plant, or on Hopewell itself, or both.

Wife and kids stayed in Baltimore. A year later, December 10, 1915, Hopewell burned down—the whole town. Newspapers said the fire started in a restaurant. Margaret thought, "Somebody got in a brawl and upset a kerosene stove." Hopewell, she elaborated, was like the "old towns where they had bank robberies, and murders, and payroll holdups, and that sort of thing." Typically of the boomtown, there was a saloon on every block. Floating brothels plied the James River.

Harry got them an apartment in Richmond. Nellie bundled her daughters onto an overnight Chesapeake Bay steamer to Old Point Comfort. Harry was to have met them but had a bad cold, so Nellie decided she'd find Hopewell, and Frank's Sanitary Restaurant where Harry was staying, all by herself.

"Sanitary Restaurant" sounds strange today, but "Sanitary" was a selling point. The Sanitary Movement had originated in England in response to filthy living conditions in the Industrial Revolution. (A Sanitary grocery was still in business when Ma moved us to Alexandria after Pop's death.)

They took a train to Hopewell, which as yet had no station. The first thing they saw were two corpses on the railroad bank. "People killed," Margaret reckoned, "in a brawl or a shoot-out of some sort. You can imagine my mother, two years out of Holland, what that did to her."

Nellie thought American telephone poles looked "drunk," and that America must be very constipated because of all the laxative ads. Two corpses, however, weren't funny.

"And the mud," Margaret added. "Dad said he saw—no kidding—a mule drown in the mud. Well, it was shot because they couldn't get it out."

Nellie was flabbergasted. Harry evidently hadn't painted the picture in total accord with reality, and she hadn't realized what she'd be walking into.

A man took pity on her and her two crying children. "Every language under the sun was being spoken, because people of every nationality were there for the work," Margaret said. Her mother managed to communicate where she wanted to go. The man showed her a board across the sea of mud, and indicated the way to Frank's Sanitary Restaurant.

"We were so hungry," said Margaret, "that Anna ate a whole can of pork and beans and I ate a whole can of canned peas. We hadn't eaten for I don't know how long."

They stayed in Richmond until Hopewell was fit for women and children, then moved into a boarding house. They made the acquaintance of Charlie Smith, who lived there with his wife and two boys, and the children became playmates. Eventually the families rented a three-room house together—a sleeping room for each family, and a kitchen/living room. Sometimes all the grownups ate together, then the kids, and sometimes each family took its turn. That arrangement lasted until DuPont built its "Hopewell boxes," tenements of twelve-by-twelve rooms with "a door in front and a window in back," as Margaret described them. No sanitary facilities, a pump for water, and a common, outdoor latrine.

Acids used in the guncotton's manufacture befouled Hopewell's air and after about a year, they started troubling Harry. It was time to cast the family lot elsewhere. The Smiths had been to Roanoke. The Schuddebooms joined them, and again the families took a house together.

"I couldn't tell you what different kinds of work my father did," said Margaret. "What he could pick up he did. I started school during that time [1916]." Anna had started while they were still in Medina.

Harry was back in Hopewell, lying in a bunkhouse, when he heard somebody swearing in Dutch. It was a young sailor named Willem van Veert who had jumped ship in New York and drifted to Hopewell. When Harry returned to Roanoke, he brought Willem van Veert with him.

He became buddies with Anna and Margaret and took them on long walks. Once they picked wild, fall-blooming, purple asters. "We were wearing broad-brimmed Panama hats," Margaret said, "and we had long hair. When we left the house, I'm sure it was very nicely plaited and tied, but after a few hours, we looked like Little Orphan Annie. He took us to a photographer's and had a picture taken," purple asters and all.

Then he was gone. "The man had had pleurisy and got the flu," Margaret said. "He died at our house. There were so many dead people, and it was such a cold, bitter winter. The Red Cross had to bury him. We had no means. My father found his parents' address and sent his things back to Holland."

Willem van Veert, Anna, and Margaret

The Great Influenza sickened half a billion people, a third of Earth's population, killing ten percent of its victims. It caused 47 percent of all US deaths and lowered average life expectancy by ten years.

They moved to the west end of Roanoke and were there when the war ended. Kids were let out of school. Harry was working in Christiansburg, so Nellie took the girls downtown for the festivities. "It was something wild when that war was over," Margaret said. With the armistice, DuPont closed down and "everybody was out of work."

The family migrated to the coal fields of Mercer County, West Virginia, living in Bramwell, Simmons, Freeman, small towns central to the mining area in some of the region's ruggedest mountains. Harry worked building "bank cars," Margaret said.[**] He took Anna and Margaret into a mine a couple of times. "Dark," said Margaret, but her memory of the visits was vague.

With the war's end, demand for coal and steel slumped. The slump pulled other indicators down causing a recession, but by spring 1919, much of the country was amok in good times again as America filled European orders for goods whose production the war had decimated. Domestic demand, frustrated by wartime shortages, surged as well. That demand fueled inflation, and inflation sparked labor unrest, especially in mining and steel. By the end of 1919, stock prices had nosedived. By mid-1920, wholesale prices were in full retreat, and by fall, factory employment was down 30 percent. Four million workers, more than ever in US history, were jobless. There were bread lines in major cities. Such jobs as Harry could scrounge, plus the sewing Nellie took in, kept the family going.

Mercer County miners didn't strike, but in Logan County, sixty miles to the northwest, attempts to suppress unionization spawned the biggest civilian uprising since the Civil War, the West Virginia Coal Mine Wars, with some 5,000 miners facing 3,000 lawmen and strikebreakers at Blair Mountain. As many as 100 people were killed before President Harding deployed federal troops. Assured that they wouldn't be arrested, the miners ended the stand-off peacefully. The troops withdrew, and the miners were back at the mine owners' mercy.

The Coal Mine Wars had been a follow-up to 1919's "Red Summer" of racial unrest and rioting. African Americans had proven their valor on the battlefield during the war and returned home expecting their nation to uphold its end of the bargain. They were disappointed. White America quickly moved to reassert its privilege, but battle-tried black veterans weren't taking it lying down. The country descended into a summer of riots, lynchings, and property destruction.

A lynching took place every fourth or fifth day in 1919. In July, there were three days of deadly riots in Washington, D.C. and four more in Chicago. The *Washington Post*, the *New York Times*, and the *Wall Street Journal* all fueled

---

[**] I have not been able to discover what a "bank car" was.

the narrative that blacks caused the riots. The Justice Department fed the press "anonymous" tips that the Wobblies (International Workers of the World, IWW) and Bolsheviks had instigated them, though few blacks belonged to those "white" organizations. Black Americans ultimately found themselves still fighting the same old struggle against their country's baked-in Jim Crow culture.

Anna and Margaret knew discrimination firsthand. "We didn't run into it in cities," Margaret said, "but in small mountain communities where we lived for four or five years, because we were different...." She didn't finish the thought, but recalled a Jewish family named Abrahamson that ran a store who "weren't accepted. Not discriminated against the way black people were, because they went to the same schools and could go to the same bathrooms."

At age nine and ten, Anna and Margaret knew it was illegal for a black person to sit on a bus if a white person was standing, that when there were seats, blacks sat in the back. It was just how things were. Few nine- and ten-year-olds examine such details, but those details shaped the world they were growing up to inhabit.

Being a foreigner itself could be dicey. Somebody on a building site once dropped a cinder block on Harry's head from three stories up. Nobody wore hard hats then, but his felt fedora was said to be what saved him.

The Russian Revolution was no help. Americans feared that Bolshevism would do to us what it had done to Russia, and any outsider might be a Bolshevik. By what alchemy had a scruffy band of hooligans overthrown the 300-year Romanoff dynasty and established its own reign of terror? There were good reasons. Tsarist repression of the lower classes had generated resentment enough, but in the war, Russia suffered horrible reverses trying to repel the German invasion. Tsar Nicholas II took personal charge and pulled blame down on himself. It didn't help that he'd left his German wife minding the store. He financed the war by printing rubles on speed-dial, triggering ruinous inflation, food shortages, wage strikes, army mutinies, and street demonstrations. Bolshevik ringleader Vladimir Lenin crafted the chaos to his own ends. America invested Bolshevism with supernatural powers.

A Bolshevist rally in Washington, D.C., in February 1919, ignited the "First Red Scare," but what really fueled the Scare were anarchist bombs. It was just that most people couldn't tell an anarchist from a Bolshevist if they had to.

Anarchists believed government was not just unnecessary but downright harmful. With assassination as their working hypothesis, they had piled up an impressive kill list in 1890s Europe. Many, expelled for their deadly pastime, ended up in America and began assassinating people here. In 1901, one of them killed President McKinley.

Bombs started going off in earnest around 1914. The first, meant for John D. Rockefeller's estate, blew up the three anarchists making it. Another exploded in St. Patrick's Cathedral in New York. One was discovered and defused under the seat of a judge who had sentenced some anarchists. Another went off in a police station. The next year, a pipe bomb meant for an Italian pastor detonated while police were trying to disarm it, killing ten cops and a woman filing a robbery complaint.

The most spectacular explosion, however, took place in Washington, D.C., at 11:15 p.m. June 2, 1919, at the Dupont Circle home of President Wilson's Attorney General, A. Mitchell Palmer, the "fighting Quaker." The blast tore the porch off his house, shattered its windows, and blew up the bomber. Wilson's Assistant Secretary of the Navy, Franklin D. Roosevelt, lived across the street and dashed over to help. Palmer was unhurt but had reverted to his childhood speech patterns. "He was theeing me and thouing me all over the place," Roosevelt said. "Thank thee Franklin and all that."

Red Scare cause and Red Scare effect collided most notoriously on April 15, 1920. Two men were killed in a payroll robbery in Braintree, Massachusetts. Police suspected an anarchist "fundraiser" and arrested Nicola Sacco and Bartolomeo Vanzetti, both unapologetic anarchists. They were convicted and sentenced to death on July 14 the following year. The evidence was highly circumstantial and clumsily handled, and six years of unsuccessful appeals ensued. Theirs became an international cause célèbre, drawing succor from a galaxy of personalities including Felix Frankfurter, Jon Dos Passos, Dorothy Parker, Edna St. Vincent Millay, Albert Einstein, George Bernard Shaw, and H. G. Wells. When they were electrocuted in 1927, demonstrations erupted worldwide, as far off as Auckland and Tokyo.

Those were headlines as Anna and Margaret grew. On August 26, 1920, when Anna was twelve, Tennessee became the thirty-sixth and final state to ratify the nineteenth amendment, by which women won their 78-year struggle for the vote.

In Bramwell, West Virginia, Harry worked for the Booth-Bowen mines, but the family lived in a Buckeye company house because Booth-Bowen didn't have any vacancies. The Buckeye house didn't have indoor plumbing, but it was a bona fide, free-standing structure. They moved again when a Booth-Bowen house came available. That one had running water, four rooms, front and back doors, multiple windows, a porch, and an outdoor toilet. Bramwell had the most millionaires per capita of any town its size in America—fourteen in a population of 1700.

Nellie did sewing for many of the wealthy people, who in turn passed down their stylish cast-offs, which Nellie made over for Anna and Margaret. After they moved into the Booth-Bowen house, Nellie was hospitalized in Bluefield, ten or twelve miles away, for a hysterectomy. The mine owner's daughter-in-law drove her to the hospital. Nellie was there for three weeks. Mrs. Bowen took Anna and Margaret to visit her once, and also brought Nellie home.

Except for that one visit, Anna and Margaret didn't miss any school, and they did such housekeeping and cooking as got done because, Margaret said, "Dad couldn't boil water without burning it." The house sparkled for Nellie's return. Anna's one true culinary calling was pastry, and she made lemon pies and Margaret didn't know what all they *didn't* make. But when Nellie got home, she couldn't even look at it.

They attended the Methodist church in Bramwell, and one Sunday as service was letting out, a lady handed Anna and Margaret a chocolate cake, an act of kindness to the family in its time of difficulty. Sometime later, the Church was preparing for a convention and expected quite a crowd from the outside. Nellie had a good voice, and the minister wanted her to sing in the choir. He also wanted the family to put some people up. With only four rooms, and Nellie still recovering from her surgery, the Schuddebooms were forced to beg off. Nellie couldn't even get to church, let alone sing in the choir.

One Sunday, the minister said something about people who had gifts from the Lord and refused to use them for His glory. He may not have meant Harry and Nellie, but Harry figured he did. The next time they met on the street, they got in an argument and Harry punched the minister in the face.

The girls took piano lessons. Margaret stopped after a year and a half, but Anna continued four or five and played at some recitals with the music teacher. They were living in the hamlet of Shinbrier, a mile and a half west of Bramwell, when a brand-new, full-size, top-heavy, upright piano Nellie had scrimped and saved for showed up wobbling and fording a creek in a horse-drawn wagon. The only way out of there, Margaret said, was over a swinging foot bridge.

It was also in Shinbrier that Anna and Margaret decided to have chickens. Thornton's general store in Bramwell sold live chickens that customers brought in. Harry arranged with Mr. Thornton for eight old hens. Coming home from school, Anna and Margaret stopped and collected them. "Why he ever allowed us two kids to take them I'll never know," Margaret said. "We had a mile, mile and a half to walk along a little narrow path next to the railroad track, steep bank down to the creek, carrying two hens in each hand." They hadn't gone far when first one then the other wriggled loose. Anna and Margaret scrambled all over the creek bank and railroad track trying to catch them. Evidently, they did, because one spring day, they got an egg.

On May 13, 1922, Anna received an elementary-school diploma from West Virginia public schools. On May 26, she got another one from the school in Graham, Virginia. Why two diplomas has never been explained. Graham no longer appears on Virginia maps. It may have been swallowed by Bluefield.

Nellie and Anna outside, Harry and Shep inside Hudson touring car, Graham, Va., 1923

Tutankhamon's intact tomb in Egypt's Valley of the Kings was excavated during Anna's senior year. It was a worldwide sensation, triggering an Egyptian craze that took society by storm and influenced the Art Deco movement from fashion to architecture.

By fall, 1924, they were back in Roanoke. Somebody assumed that since Harry came from Holland with all the pretty tulips, he must know all about plants and flowers, and offered him a job tending gardens for a family in Salem, just outside of Roanoke.

It started with tomato plants. Harry didn't know a thing about setting out tomato plants, so he said he had to go "see a man about a dog [relieve himself]."

He found a secluded spot where he could watch how the others were doing it, and thus began his life's work—gardening and landscaping.

Margaret was having migraines and nosebleeds when high school started, still in Bramwell, and the doctor said she should stay out for two weeks. She crammed for her examinations and passed, but the migraines and nosebleeds returned, and she had to leave.

She didn't have much to occupy her that winter. The five-and-dime store sold baby chicks for five or ten cents apiece. She bought six and fixed up a box with a light bulb under an inverted flowerpot for heat. They had rented "a big old house," and she raised them in a spare room. They fed them mashed up boiled eggs, oatmeal and breadcrumbs, and those were Margaret's first chickens. As Harry went into gardening, Margaret went into chickens.

The family's locations and relocations are not fully cataloged. Anna told me she attended an average of two schools a year. Margaret's story of acquiring a dog adds a few stops. "We acquired a dog when we were living in Bramwell, kind of a shepherd, a black and brown and white stray, and he finally decided to be our dog. When we moved to Graham, and then Caswell, and then back to Graham and then back to Roanoke, we took Shep with us. As a matter of fact, we brought him with us to Baltimore."

They were still in Roanoke in March, but were back in the Baltimore area in time for Anna's senior year at Franklin High in Garrison, a few miles out Reisterstown Road.

The infamous "Monkey Trial" took place during the family's shift from Roanoke to Baltimore. Whatever the trial's effect on Anna when she was seventeen, she was a die-hard evolutionist by the time her children knew her.

For conservatives, few issues more glaringly highlighted the "evils of modernity" than the theory of evolution. In March 1925, Tennessee made it illegal to teach the subject in public schools. The American Civil Liberties Union (ACLU) advertised for a volunteer to test the law's constitutionality. Their one nibble came from Dayton, halfway between Knoxville and Chattanooga. A group of Dayton "Conspirators" saw a chance to raise their town's profile and asked John Scopes, the high school's science teacher, to volunteer.

Seeing a chance to take the field for the Bible, William Jennings Bryan—three-time presidential candidate, Woodrow Wilson's Secretary of State, foe of Darwinism—offered to join the prosecution. The ACLU wanted to keep a low-profile, but the Conspirators opened their arms to Bryan. When Clarence Darrow, "Lion of the Courtroom," learned Bryan was joining the prosecution, he couldn't resist joining the defense for free. The ACLU tried to discourage Darrow, but Scopes wanted him, and the stage was set—Darrow vs. Bryan, the clash of Titans.

The media made full use of this one sensation in a slow-news week. Anna's hometown paper, *The Baltimore Evening Sun,* assigned its cynic-in-residence, H. L. Mencken, to the story. Reporters filed 135,000 words a day, newsreel outlets chopped miles of film down to newsreel length. For radio, a Chicago paper created the first national hookup. Darrow made a mockery of Bryan's Bible-thumpery, but Scopes had violated existing law, and that decided the case. The *Sun* ponied up his $100 fine. The law was not repealed until 1967.

"Annie" Schuddeboom
senior picture

Her high school yearbook stated, "Anna joined us only this year, but we feel we have known her always....Anna's sense of humor is overwhelming, so much so in fact, that she was dubbed by authority at the start Giggleboom rather than Schuddeboom." Actually, they called her "Scoot." She sang with the glee club, played basketball and field ball, and became fast— ultimately lifelong—friends with fellow student Edythe Eckenrode, the class secretary, class pianist, editor-in-chief of the yearbook, whom the kids called "Eck."

While Eck entered Maryland University with designs on law school, Anna enrolled at Towson State Normal School (now Towson State University) just north of Baltimore, and on June 11, 1929, received a "1st grade teacher's certificate valid in the Maryland Public Elementary Schools, renewable without examination." On July 1, she

Best friends, Anna and Eck

signed a teacher's contract with the Baltimore County Board of Education.

Anna never learned to drive, but Margaret became a prodigious motorist. In the summer of 1928, she drove the two of them back to their first American home in Medina, New York. Their neighbors, the Rowleys, had invited them. Margaret's chickens had earned the price of the trip. She was eighteen, Maryland's age for a driver's license, and hadn't had hers very long. She and Anna were heading into Baltimore to buy some clothes for the trip. "And we had…*zoom!*" That's the way she put it. "*Zoom!*" She was driving Harry's car, and thought if you *had* the right of way, you *got* the right of way. They wound up in police court.

Anna and Margaret visiting Medina

Harry had told her, if she used his car and anything happened, she was responsible. Accordingly, the repair bill was Margaret's. They didn't buy any clothes, and the trip was almost canceled, until the owner of the car that hit them reimbursed her a week or two before their departure.

"My Dad, when he said something, he meant it," Margaret said. He would have had them lose the trip rather than go back on his word. "I thought he was awfully harsh, but I've grown old enough to appreciate it. It was a good lesson. I learned to be a careful driver when I was young."

From World War I to the stock market crash in 1929, America went through massive changes. The 1960s youth culture had nothing on the 1920s. The twenties brought the nation, kicking and screaming, messily and imperfectly, into the modern age—the airplane and the automobile, the radio and the movies, the phonograph, electric lights. The Great War had left deep disillusionment over the Victorian Era's smug assumptions about the mechanistic, closed-system nature of reality, suppositions that Albert Einstein and Sigmund Freud were tearing apart.

Youth was on the move. Flappers were the first liberated women. With the 1920 census, America became a majority urban society. Cities—movie theaters and automobiles—enabled sexual liaisons unheard of in small towns. Women had the vote. They smoked and drank in public. They shortened their skirts, rolled down their stockings, bobbed their hair—to widespread disapproval and sometimes physical retribution.

Zelda Sayre of Montgomery, Alabama, married F. Scott Fitzgerald, who made a career chronicling the youth phenomenon. Silent film star Lillian Gish said Scott and Zelda—young, gorgeous, flashy, daring—"didn't *make* the twenties; they *were* the twenties."

To many, flappers epitomized the decade's plunge into moral turpitude, which "caused," among other things, the murder of a 14-year-old boy by two rich, bored 19-year-olds, Nathan Leopold and Richard Loeb, the world's first "celebrity murderers." That senseless killing, just "for the thrill" of it, riveted the nation's attention as no gangland slayings (177 in the first half of 1924 in Chicago alone) could have. The killers were saved from the gallows by Clarence Darrow.

Prohibition, which had been in effect since January 1920, brought undreamt of opportunity. Illegal booze was bigger business than legal booze had ever been. In 1926, its profits matched the US government's entire annual budget. The press glamorized Al Capone, Lucky Luciano, Longy Zwillman, never failing to megaphone their dalliances with the likes of Jean Harlow and Mae West. Imported labels from the Caribbean and Canada, where booze was still legal, joined the rivers of domestic bootleg. Rum runners hired naval architects, and their boats regularly outran the Coast Guard. When New Orleans levees breached in the great Mississippi flood of 1927, bootleggers' boats were the first to the rescue.

Liquor shipments faced gauntlets of rival mobs hijacking each other's trucks. Unable to seek relief in the courts, they resorted to "concrete overshoes" and the Thompson submachine gun, affectionately called the "Chicago typewriter." Internecine warfare led some mobs to join cartels, establishing territories and fixing prices. A Seattle group held its peace conference using *Robert's Rules of Order*. But in many places, anarchy ran unchecked until Prohibition's repeal in 1933.

Among modernity's most clamorous foes was the Ku Klux Klan. The Klan had gone into eclipse after Reconstruction, but in 1915 a drifter named William Joseph Simmons, smitten by *Birth of a Nation*'s glamorization of the Klan, tried to revive it. But he was a dismal organizer, and his only public event was a 1919 veterans' parade where his "members" were twenty African Americans he paid to dress in sheets. By 1920, he only had a few hundred members.

That's when two public relations professionals saw financial promise in the organization and signed on as promoters. Their pitch aligned with majority American opinion: Protestant white supremacy, the Klan as the keeper of morals. They championed Prohibition and reviled the flappers. For enemies, they added Catholics, Jews, and immigrants to Negroes. They pushed boycotts of "wrong" businesses.

They backed and even ran political candidates. At their peak in the mid-1920s, they claimed four- to five-

KKK parade on Pennsylvania Avenue

million members. Under a gloss of respectability, their members no longer hid their faces. They organized high-profile parades, notoriously down Pennsylvania Avenue in Washington, D.C., in 1925, 1926, and 1928. By the last one, though, the organization had shrunk to little more than 30,000 members. Hypocrisy of the leaders—criminal activity, profiteering, drunkenness, and sexual adventurism—disenchanted its followers. The Klan sank back into quiescence until the civil rights movement of the '50s and '60s.

It would be irresponsible to neglect advertising's role in America's transformation. Consumerism mushroomed in the twenties, and advertising, flanked by credit purchasing, led the charge. Despite vast income inequality— the top tenth of one percent owned as much wealth as the bottom 42 percent— consumerism gave the illusion of a leveled playing field.

Modern advertising began with anti-German propaganda during World War I. Woodrow Wilson hired a muckraker named George Creel for the assignment. Creel hired Edward Bernays, a nephew of Sigmund Freud, to come up with the way of doing it. Bernays's insight was: how people *feel* about something is more important than what they *think*. Emotion is more primitive than reason. You don't just show the automobile, you show someone *enjoying* the automobile.

The most enduring image from Creel's office was the "UNCLE SAM WANTS *YOU*" poster, but it produced hundreds of others, from flag-draped beauties tempting, "Sow the Seeds of Victory," to the Hun as subhuman monster abducting Lady Liberty. The campaign was insanely effective. On German Americans, it was devastating. Creel titled his postwar memoir *How We Advertised America.*

Consumer products wasted no time catching the train. Listerine was a topical antiseptic whose fortunes were sagging until a member of its research team found the word "halitosis" in an old medical journal. Listerine had begun recommending its product for "bad breath," but "halitosis" put it on the map. Its advertisers quickly pitched it as the cure for that dreaded condition, which made you (gasp) unpopular! Sales went from 100,000 in 1921 to 4 million in 1927.

American Tobacco hired Bernays to redeem the image of women who smoked in public. He paid ten women to light up "Torches of Freedom" in New York's 1929 Easter Parade. Newspapers scrambled to finish the job for him, splashing that "bold protest against women's inequality" across their front pages—all while Bernays was urging his wife to quit.

The year before, he had published his groundbreaking *Propaganda*, which begins: "The conscious and intelligent manipulation of the organized habits and opinions of the masses is an important element in democratic society." Bernays's work strongly influenced Adolph Hitler's propaganda minister, Joseph Goebbels.

Racial violence lessened after Red Summer, as state and local governments began intervening. It didn't go away, but race relations began a slow, tectonic shift. Thanks to the Harlem Renaissance, black music, dance, and literature began infiltrating white awareness, taking the avant-garde by storm. The twenties were "Roaring," but they were also the "Jazz Age." President Warren Harding urged southerners to allow blacks the right to vote.

In 1992, Margaret told Helen, "A lot of people feel we haven't come very far. When I hear talk shows, and see documentaries on television, I see people saying, 'Oh, we haven't made any progress.' But, if you look back to the early part of this century, we've made lots of progress."

Anna dipped a toe in the multicultural pond during normal school. "Volunteers were called for to hostess tables for Hindu and African visitors. At that time there were few who could accept the idea of eating with colored people. I was one of the few who volunteered. They were students like ourselves, and thus interesting conversationalists. Since then, all such contacts have been with 'intellectuals' of dark skin. When I shook hands with that table full of Africans and Hindus, all of them men, I was doing something mechanically which my feelings couldn't accept, but the 'die was cast,' and I've never been sorry that I did it."

Chapter Fifteen

Almost Heaven

The farm near Good Hope, West Virginia, where Darel grew up

GRIMY AS THE COAL BUSINESS WAS, it was sited amid some of the nation's most sumptuous mountains. Not for no reason is West Virginia called the "Mountain State." The saying went, "If you flattened West Virginia out, it would be the size of Texas." Legion were the tales of mules with legs shorter on one side so they could plow the mountainsides, and of farmers falling out of their fields or needing ladders to climb into them.

While Anna and Margaret were emerging into adolescence among the coal fields' lofty peaks, Darel, in a landscape rubbed down to more undulating though still imposing hills, was emerging on a farm near Good Hope, West Virginia, pronounced "Goodope" by most, some 140 miles north of Bramwell.

He described "the green hills where I was born":

The smooth green hillsides where our cattle grazed, the hill on which the turkeys would come soaring down at evening, the hill with the 'little orchard' in the cove, the hill with the steep part where the 'little woods' grew. These were serene quiet hills with slopes and curves and groined supports, gentle and lovely as a woman's body.

Fecund but not rich, they supported grazing herds on bluegrass hillsides, produced the grass for pear-shaped haystacks on small fenced-in meadows, fields of corn and well-stocked gardens on bottomlands and benchlands, pigs and cows and all kinds of fowl, blocks of fruit orchards in coves and on hilltops, tangles of native berries, wild nuts and wild grapes, and native woods on the steep slopes; each variety of wood is known and put to long-established uses. There is enough small game for sport, an occasional change of diet, and a minor income from furs in the winter.

People work hard to make the land serve them, live honestly, are always ready to help a neighbor, are dollar-poor but never hungry, and, like the independent hills, wear no man's collar. They vote their ticket and worship their God as they want and declare that nobody can tell them which way to do either.…They believe in the state motto, "Mountaineers Are Always Free."

He was eight when Anna came to America in 1913, and decided that year to be a writer. He was the youngest of seven, and "not only the youngest but the most inferior as I looked up the ladder of size and capacity. It was incumbent on me to seek a field in which there was no competition. At the age of eight, I determined

Standing: Darel's sister Mamie, his father James, his mother Blanche, his sister Gladys. Seated: Darel, his brothers Frank and Harold. Probaly around 1911.

to be a great writer, like Zane Grey or James Oliver Curwood."

James Oliver Curwood's twenty-seven adventure novels, many set in the Yukon or around Hudson's Bay, left him the world's highest-paid per-word author when he died in 1927. His writings inspired 180 movies, most in the silent era. Zane Grey glamorized the Old West. The cowboy was America's chevalier. When Darel was ten, his oldest and favorite brother, Clyde, succumbed to the West's lure and went homesteading in Montana. The frontier was said to be closed, but the "West" motored on. Buffalo Bill's Wild West Show had only closed in 1913. Annie Oakley and Wyatt Earp yet lived.

Homesteading—"free" public land if you could stick it out for five years—was set up in 1862 to promote Western settlement. By 1909, most of the farmable land was claimed, so the government did the logical thing and doubled its offer from a quarter-section (160 acres) of good land to a half section of marginal land. Clyde joined the migration just after its peak (53,000 in 1914).

Homesteading is not ranching, and ranchers despised the sod-busting interlopers. Popular sentiment has generally sided with the

Clyde at his homesteader's shack

underdog farmers (*Shane*, *Little House on the Prairie*), but as things turned out, the ranchers were largely right. Absent commercial-scale irrigation, there wasn't water to sustain farming reliably.

More than rancher prejudice drove the honyockers[††] out of the Plains. Climate was their most implacable foe—drought, wind, flood, blizzard. We have almost no information about Clyde's turn at homesteading, but a snippet of family lore tells of a partner in the enterprise whose wife was a schoolteacher. One evening, walking home with their children, she was caught in a blizzard and they all froze to death. The story, if true, could certainly have contributed to the venture's demise. When the U.S. entered World War I in 1917, Clyde came home and joined the Navy.

[††] Hon-yocker: Cowboy slang for a failed homesteader. Almost as bad as calling a cowboy a sheepherder.

The Navy wasn't taking twelve-year-olds, so Darel joined the Lone Scouts of America. "My first and most important move," he wrote in his discontinuous diary, "was to join the L.S.A. July, 1917." A snapshot shows him in a partial uniform executing a most patriotic salute with a horse and a chicken in the background.

A most patriotic salute

The Lone Scouts served boys in regions too remote for the Boy Scouts, and encouraged them to contribute to the *Lone Scout* magazine. This Darel did with a vengeance. By New Year's, 1919, he had submitted 55 articles, of which five were published.

"There is something about paper and pencil that is fascinating," he diarized. "They are the tools of my trade, and I like to have an abundance of them. With the gloss of unspoiled paper under my hand, and a well-sharpened pencil in my fingers, there comes the thrill of desire to create. The pages must be filled with connected words and paragraphs which are ultimately to be molded into a story of great symmetry and beauty. It must be made to go out into the world and have its influence upon the minds of men who read, even as do the stories of masterful Kipling, the moralist Hawthorne, the impossible Stockton and the analytical Poe."

Elsewhere: "Writing is to me like doughnuts was [*sic*] to a man I once read about. Whenever he felt down-and-out, he always went to his doughnuts. 'Just a few,' he said—'only fifteen or twenty. They sort of keep me from getting lonely.' Sometimes when I feel badly and the blue color seems predominant, it is a great help to pen my stray thoughts in this little book."

He entitled "this little book" *Impressions*, which, he said, "it is to be hoped will someday be read in part by the public at large." In it, he listed story ideas and synopses—"The story of Lacke and Bill and how they fought each other, but *for* each other in the end"—character sketches, turns of phrase, potential descriptives: "The katy-did that sang its hoarse melody by the rain barrel near my open door during the summer months, and the methodical questioning of the hoot owl in the woods during the winter months, might make good local color in some story."

Somewhere in his boyhood environs was a pit that people swore had no bottom. One could drop in a stone and never hear it hit bottom. The story persisted until some enterprising soul climbed in and stood on the bottom, which was soundproofed with dead and decaying leaves, proving that there was no such thing as a bottomless pit.

The lesson was of a piece with two other epiphanies. His disillusionment when he found there was no Santa Claus, and his spontaneous conversion to agnosticism at age thirteen. He gave up on religion and took to the fields studying ants. His fascination with those nano-engineers never disappeared, even in adulthood.

Travel beckoned him. "There are two notable things about my home," he wrote in 1922, "the geese and the sound of the trains beyond the distant hills. There is something about a railroad train, a relic of childhood fancy, that manhood will never be able to efface from my being. They are a symbol of strength. Their lunging pistons and escaping steam, and the engineer perched in his cab I can never cease to regard with awe. But I think something deeper underlies it. I long to travel and the train takes me there, but no matter how long or how often I may travel I think that the charm that a train brings over my being will never grow old."

The entries betray a youthful innocence of that summer's railroad and mine strikes, of the bread lines forming across the country. European agriculture was rebounding, and the drop in demand for wheat and other foodstuffs hit American farmers hard. But the family farm could be as much a haven from as victim of fluctuating prices. Most food was raised and put up on the premises.

The march of technology gave him pause. "To think of the changes since my childhood," he remarked, "makes me feel venerable, although I am only sixteen." The journey from hot-air balloons to powered flight had taken over a century. From Kitty Hawk to aerial combat took eleven years. Tales of flying aces—Eddie Rickenbacker, the Red Baron—riveted public imagination. In 1918, the airplane started delivering mail. By 1921, radio was broadcasting news and concerts, even the World Series. The telephone and electric light were advancing into the countryside. The McConkeys apparently had a phone because, on May 15, 1922, his brother, Clyde, "came in evening. Helped moved [*sic*] phone in evening."

When the Victor Talking Machine Company's patents expired in 1919, gramophone recording exploded, bringing two- to four-minute songs into homes by the thousands. Darel began collecting albums, and "albums" they truly were—books whose "pages" were sleeves that held one record each.

He had been smitten by "Pomp and Circumstance," probably at a high school graduation. He later said, "I have always wanted to hear the 'Fire Bird,' ever since my earliest acquaintance with classical music. In the days when I was building my phonograph-record library I often looked longingly at the set by that title."

Almost single-handedly, D.W. Griffith transformed the way movies, "galloping tin-types," told stories, assembling scenes from montages of shots at different angles. Even Mack Sennett, of the zany Keystone Kops, studied Griffith. Sennett hired Charlie Chaplin, then wondered why—Chaplin was so *different*. But within a year, he was the world's first movie star.

In 1922, Darel recorded seeing *Hell's Hinges* with William S. Hart, the first movie cowboy in one of the first cowboy movies. It ran a little over an hour. John Gilbert had a bit part in it and went on to become a major silent-screen star and have a torrid affair with Swedish beauty Greta Garbo.

Darel learned to drive Clyde's Model T, though he also got around by buggy or on horseback. He occasionally braved the motorcycle, though whose we don't know, once reporting "2 of my spills."

Driving was a different beast in 1922. Ford had added an electric starter in 1919. Before that, you hand-cranked the engine, and even afterward cars came equipped with cranks. A backfire while cranking could break your arm. Before starters, cars didn't need batteries: once you'd cranked the engine to life, a magneto powered the spark plugs, the head- and taillights. The accelerator was a lever on the steering column. Another lever advanced and retarded spark.

Darel attended Unidis High School in West Milford, within walking distance of home. At the start of his second semester, 1922, the algebra teacher, Miss Ford, fell ill. Darel was in the middle of his sophomore year and filled in for her, making and grading tests and filing reports. She returned at the end of February and "everyone was glad to see her."

On April 4: "Finished 'Rubyait [*sic*] of Omar Khayyam.'" From the turn of the century through the twenties, the sensuous, live-for-the-day *Rubaiyat of Omar Khayyam* took American youth by storm, becoming an anthem for the licentious Flapper Era. "A loaf of bread, a jug of wine and thou...." Advertisers exploited "Omar" themes to great profit—Omar soap, cigarettes, and chocolates.

In February he tapped sugar maple trees. He tended a trap line, though the only thing he reported catching was a possum. He spent time splitting fence posts and some building fence. He hauled hay, manure, straw, and fodder, taking the last two to relatives, the Burnsides, for grinding. He plowed, he hoed potatoes and corn.

On April 29, "Repaired fence all day. Went to Milford to see Wild Rose Operetta. Pretty good. Rode Governor [their horse]."

On that same April day, 1922, in distant Washington, D.C., the United States Senate voted unanimously to investigate the biggest swindle in presidential history—Teapot Dome.

Even before Warren Harding's 1920 election, Interior Secretary designate Albert Fall and Attorney General designate Harry Daugherty had been scheming to defraud the government of its naval oil reserves at Teapot Dome, Wyoming. Teapot and its neighbor, Salt Creek, comprised the world's biggest known light crude oil field.

President Harding remained largely oblivious to Fall and Daugherty's connivance. His main concerns were the presidency's interference with his favorite hobbies: women, poker, and whiskey, which he indulged at a house belonging to *Washington Post* owner and publisher Ned McLean, a few blocks from the White House. Prohibition's enforcement arm, the Treasury Department, kept the house stocked with confiscated booze.

Laton McCartney, in his book, *The Teapot Dome Scandal*, wrote, "Once Warren Harding assumed office, this collection of swindlers, sharpies, con men, and extortionists descended on Washington like a pestilence." They came to be known as the "Ohio Gang."

Interior Secretary Fall cajoled the Navy Secretary into ceding control of the naval reserves to his department, then leased Teapot to Harry Sinclair of Mammoth Oil. Wyoming oilmen asked their senator why the contract hadn't been put out for bids. The senator asked Interior and got the runaround, so he introduced a resolution calling for full disclosure. By April 29, the resolution called not just for full disclosure but for full investigation. It passed unanimously.

Washington D.C. and Wyoming were far from Good Hope. Darel's diary for the next day merely says, "Hauled posts out of hollow and brot [*sic*] disk [a disk harrow] down from hill before noon. Took disk to Burnside's in afternoon." Two days later, he, "Drove to-day. Went to town to get glasses fixed....Got horse shod." That summer, he worked on the local gas pipeline digging "bell holes,"—enlarging spots in the trench to give workers room to connect pipe segments. He worked for neighboring farmers, moving from farm to farm.

He also "played music in afternoon," and, "Went to Good Hope to play with Homer and Aubrey." On July 2, he "did nothing except play music until evening." Playing music almost certainly meant playing records. He showed absolutely no innate musical talent in the time his children knew him. His oldest brother Clyde, however, apparently played banjo and fiddle.

On July 30, "Wade A. took me to Lost Creek to the train and I started for camp." The diary falls silent for a month. What camp is not specified.

That same day, Interior Secretary Fall sent Marines to close down an illicit operation on Teapot Dome that his fellow conspirator, Attorney General Daugherty, had let. The Daugherty illicit lease encroached on the illicit lease Fall had let to Harry Sinclair in return for Sinclair's paying off the Republican campaign debt. The Denver *Post* was there and got a juicy, two-column editorial condemning the action.

The day after Darel returned from camp, he "worked with Clyde in the mine," no further explanation. The McConkeys did work a small coal seam for their own use.

By then, the Hearst papers were reprinting the *Post*'s editorials, and in the White House President Harding was wondering what all the hoopla was about. Fall persuaded Hearst to stop running the editorials, but it took more than that—a million dollars from the Teapot conspirators—to shut the *Post* up.

The hoopla subsided. Back in school for his junior year, Darel played right tackle for Unidis. By graduation, he had already submitted copy to the Clarksburg *Exponent*.

Right tackle

In January 1923, Albert Fall resigned from Interior. In August, Harding died of a stroke and Vice President Calvin "Silent Cal" Coolidge, replaced him. Coolidge brought two rules to the presidency. 1) Do as little as possible. 2) Say as little as possible. "The things I don't say never get me in trouble….If you keep dead still," he said of White House visitors, "they will run down in three or four minutes. If you even cough or smile, they will start up all over again."

The Teapot Dome hearings began in October. Montana Senator Thomas Walsh, looking every inch the Wild West lawman, was the reluctant inquisitor. Though Fall's political opposite, he believed Fall to be honorable and doubted any corruption would turn up. After a week of inconclusive questioning—with Fall brandishing patriotism, Sinclair disavowing graft, and the Navy Secretary wrapping himself in amnesia—the hearing recessed for a month. Most Republicans thought it pretty much over. Instead, it was just the beginning of a process that continued by fits and starts for a decade.

The press perked back up in November when news of the million-dollar hush-money payment to the *Denver Post* came out. Plus, how had a nearly bankrupt Fall managed to buy a rival newspaper, pay ten years' back taxes on, and make repairs to his run-down New Mexico ranch? He said Ned McLean (host of President Harding's poker, booze, and sexual assignations) had loaned him the money. McLean, not being a Teapot lessee, looked clean, and committee members, friends, even the press, chided Walsh for not ending the inquiry right there.

But Walsh's inamorata, socialite Daisy Harriman, had something on McLean. At the time

Senator Walsh

Fall got his money, McLean was broke and couldn't have loaned anybody anything. Walsh deposed McLean under oath in Palm Beach, Florida and, yes, Fall's story had been a lie. So where had the money come from? Again reporters clamored for gallery seats.

Worried about his wife's health, Fall decided to fess up. He told Walsh that oilman Ed Doheny had loaned him the money.

Doheny was another recipient of a Fall lease, not in Wyoming but in California, though still a naval reserve. Doheny said he'd just been an incredibly rich man helping out an "old pard." The loan had nothing to do with the lease.

To United Press International, however, the scandal had leaped from "just another senate investigation" to "a throbbing drama."

The 1924 election was ten months away. Democrats were champing, Republicans terrified.

On January 28, Walsh gave the Senate six hours of evidence that the whole cabinet, including Vice President Coolidge, had been in on approving the leases. He and the other investigators now found themselves being tailed, their offices being ransacked, phones being tapped, mail being opened, family members threatened. The DC police sent a detective to guard the hearings. The Republicans smeared Walsh as a "public enemy." Coolidge appointed his own special prosecutor.

But on January 31, it was Republicans' turn to gloat when it emerged that William McAdoo, front-runner for the 1924 Democratic presidential nomination, had accepted a retainer from Ed Doheny. The retainer had had nothing to do with Teapot, but that didn't matter. The taint was on him.

The respite didn't last long. On March 24, senators voted, with only one dissent, to cite Sinclair with contempt of the Senate for refusing to answer questions "on advice of counsel." Sinclair sniffed that Coolidge's special prosecutor had supplanted the committee and the committee, therefore, lacked further authority to question him. "Gentlemen, I thank you," he smirked walking out.

Meanwhile, Burton Wheeler, Montana's junior senator, introduced a resolution to investigate Attorney General Daugherty for protecting rather than prosecuting Fall, Sinclair, and Doheny. That resolution also passed with one dissent, and transferred the intimidation tactics from Walsh to Wheeler.

Colleagues challenged him and the press challenged him, but Wheeler had a secret weapon—Roxy Stinson, ex-wife of the Gang's old bagman, Jess

Smith, who had either committed suicide or been murdered nine months earlier. Daugherty and his banker brother, Mal, had taken $11,000 from an account Jess had set up for Roxy. She told Daugherty if he didn't give it back, she would tell about the monthly deposits Jess had been taking to Mal's bank. Daugherty tried intimidating her, but Roxy wasn't cowed. Her testimony rallied the press again.

When Daugherty refused Wheeler's request for documents, Coolidge fired him. Walsh's inquiry fell off the radar but Coolidge's special prosecutors dug in with creditable if lower-profile diligence.

Darel graduated high school on June 4, 1924. He looks a dreamy-eyed youth in his senior picture. A week later, the Republicans, in "the dullest convention in American history," nominated Calvin Coolidge.

Two weeks after that, the Democrats mired themselves in history's *longest* convention—fifteen days, 103 ballots. Utterly unable to decide between anti-Prohibition ("wet") Catholic Al Smith, and "dry" but tainted William McAdoo, they finally settled on John W. Davis, the only West Virginian ever nominated.

A dreamy-eyed youth

Things looked up briefly for the Democrats when Coolidge's prosecutors indicted Fall, Sinclair, and Doheny for fraud, but it wasn't enough. After Teapot, the Democrats should have walked away with the election. Instead, their endless dithering surrendered it to Coolidge. Davis scraped but 29 percent of the vote. Humorist and social commentator Will Rogers said, "I am not a member of any organized political party. I'm a Democrat."

By heredity, Darel was Republican, but still an election shy of voting age.

He took a trip to New Hampshire in 1925, visiting the Old Man of the Mountain and climbing Mount Washington. "When I climbed Mt. Washington, I came, rather abruptly, on what is called Lake-in-the-Clouds. It is a clear little pool, surrounded by lichen-covered rocks, above the timberline, and occupies a hollow between Mt. Washington and Mt. Monroe, in the Presidential range.

"A stone shelter-house has been built beside it, and as I looked back from near the top of Mt. Washington it was like an opal in the bleak gray of the rocks; and the little stone house was like a doll's house beside it. Then a gray cloud swept down on me—a slow-motion picture of those which race past the crest of Everest—and I found it necessary to attend to the trail across the rocks."

The foxtrot, the Charleston, the black bottom scandalized polite society. The economy was red hot and the brakes were off. Wall Street was sky high and climbing. Newspapers splashed the exploits of Machine Gun Kelly, Baby Face Nelson, Bonnie and Clyde, Al Capone across front pages nationwide. The land was awash in bootleggers, speakeasies, and bathtub gin.

None of which doings slowed the march of science. In 1923, Edwin Hubble showed that "nebulae," bodies thought to be dust clouds within our own (and only) galaxy, were really other galaxies beyond ours, dilating our understanding of the universe by mind-boggling orders of magnitude.

Two years later, at Auburn, Massachusetts, Robert Goddard demonstrated a liquid-fuel rocket—more efficient and controllable than its solid-fuel progenitor.

Werner Heisenberg informed particle physicists that, no, you can't measure everything exactly—the better you know a particle's position, the less you know about its momentum, and vice versa. This was called the "uncertainty principle." Nobody understood it any better than they did Einstein's Relativity or Freud's Oedipus complex.

Sinclair went to trial in March, 1925; the judge proceeded to torpedo the prosecution's case, then take a Mediterranean cruise on Sinclair's yacht. The Circuit Court of Appeals reversed the decision but took fourteen months to do it.

Pressured by a muckraking journalist who had followed the case from the start, Walsh resumed his hearings. Eight years after they had begun, they finally produced results, only to have the Ohio Gang, which had committed rich-people's crimes, get rich-people's justice. Sinclair served seven months, Fall nine. Doheny's lawyer got him off. Daugherty lost his job.

Nineteen twenty-seven was a year of banner headlines. The first solo, nonstop flight across the Atlantic Ocean turned klieg lights on an intensely private man whom few had ever heard of. Charles Lindbergh was 25 when he landed on the grass at Le Bourget field outside Paris on May 21. Not even the first men in space, thirty-four years later, created a like sensation. Lindbergh hadn't known who if anyone would be there. Between 100,000 and 150,000 showed up. They pulled him from his cockpit and carried him aloft before dropping him and picking up somebody else who resembled him.

He was an instant and possibly the most reluctant hero in world history. The press ran a quarter million stories about him, streets and parks were named after him, parades and banquets were held in his honor, speeches were extracted from him.

Lindbergh was the quintessential "Lone Eagle," not disposed to play avatar to millions of fawning worshippers. At first, he tolerated the circus with patient good humor, but only alone and aloft in flying demonstrations did he truly feel at home. After five months of unrelieved adulation, he was bone tired and ready to quit, but realized to his dismay that he would never outrun his achievement.

In 1927, Babe Ruth set a season home-run record that stood for thirty-four years.

The talking movie, *The Jazz Singer*, premiered in October 1927. It was as beguiling when movies found their voice as it had been when photographs first moved at all. Mostly only *The Jazz Singer*'s songs really "talked." Speech was still done with dialogue cards.

Silent movies continued being made. A year and a half into the sound era, reclusive, quixotic billionaire Howard Hughes, filmmaker and aviation pioneer, having misread the tea leaves, was shooting the World War I epic *Hell's Angels*, one of the most expensive films ever made, as a silent when the truth caught up with him. Sound was taking the industry by storm. Hughes retooled and spent three-quarters again his original budget to bring the epic up to speed.

In 1927, the Mississippi River visited a flood of biblical proportions on the nation's midsection, inundating an area the size of Massachusetts, Connecticut,

New Hampshire, and Vermont, displacing 700,000 people and inflicting damage equal to a third of the national budget.

Rains had drenched the Mississippi watershed, which drains half the continental United States. President Coolidge sent his Commerce Secretary, Herbert Hoover, to organize relief. Hoover had earned a well-deserved reputation organizing food relief in Belgium during World War I, extracting agreements from belligerents on both sides of the conflict. Harding had made him Secretary of Commerce. Coolidge appointed him head of flood relief, then refused to have anything more to do with the effort.

As a consequence, Coolidge's reputation sagged and Hoover's soared, thanks in no small part to his exploitation of the press, something he had used ever since Belgium to promote his image. He now added radio to his bag of tricks. The publicity stimulated massive private donations, which was just as Hoover would have had it. Government charity, he held, would only stigmatize its recipients.

The Treasury Department had a record $635 million surplus, yet couldn't spare a dime for a disaster afflicting nearly one percent of the nation's population. Government could organize cooperation between private groups, Hoover felt, but it was for volunteer organizations like the Red Cross to do the real lifting. He had seen government overreach firsthand in Russia, and dreaded it.

Hoover's idea for reconstruction after the flood was pure capitalism. Credit. As engineers struggled to hold the levees, he drew plans for private "reconstruction corporations" to make loans at bargain rates. Businesses would buy stock in the corporations, creating capital for the loans. That was his only program, and it had a major flaw. Flood victims needed collateral to qualify for loans, and most people's collateral had washed into the Gulf of Mexico. Almost none of the capital was ever lent.

The inadequacy of response gave rise to a call rarely heard in America, for government to shoulder the burden. Republicans, Democrats, and newspapers begged Coolidge to call Congress into emergency session. Coolidge refused. Hoover, meanwhile, cajoled key personalities into dialing back their criticism, and declared his efforts a success. To the nation, he was a hero. As Hoover made one trip from the flood zone to Washington, Will Rogers quipped, "Bert's just resting between disasters."

"Bert" was priming for his chief goal in life—a run for the White House.

New York's famed Algonquin Round Table, peopled by some of journalism's most notorious wits—Dorothy Parker, George S. Kaufman, Robert Benchley, Robert Sherwood, Harold Ross, Heywood Broun, even Harpo Marx—was past its prime but still tickling the

The Algonquin Roundtable

national funny bone. The Roundtable's glittering repartee entertained the nation throughout the 1920s. All while America's "Lost Generation"—Ernest Hemingway, Gertrude Stein, Josephine Baker, F. Scott and Zelda Fitzgerald— wallowed in bohemian luxury in Paris, broadcasting their disillusionment following The Great War.

A few years are missing between Darel's 1924 high school graduation and his 1927 reappearance as a sophomore journalism student at West Virginia University, working on the editorial staff of the *Morgantown Post* with his own column, "Meanderings by Mac." He met Fannie Mae Craft there and the two were married July 2. "Together," she later wrote, "we helped open Ogelbay Farms in Wheeling, West Virginia, to public use."

Ogelbay Park, not "Farms," was a legacy of philanthropist Earl Ogelbay, who in 1901 had bought 25 acres from his mother's estate and spent the next quarter century developing them into an agricultural laboratory. He brought the first extension agent to the county and fostered 4-H clubs. On his death in 1926, he bequeathed Ogelbay to Wheeling "for the purposes of public recreation." The city had three years to accept. Wheeling dawdled for two, but the park went ahead developing its programs using volunteers and staff from West Virginia University's Extension Division.

Darel and Fannie Mae were among those workers. "It was Mac's story from the University Extension Division," Fannie Mae wrote, "that announced publicly the gift to the City of Wheeling in the *Morgantown Post*."

Pocono Peoples College held a winter session at Ogelbay; Darel taught journalism and did the school's publication. Pocono Peoples was a four-year-old experimental college based on methods from Denmark. Its main campus was a state away, near Stroudsburg in eastern Pennsylvania, but despite great promise, it lost out when the stock market crashed in 1929. Ogelbay Park survived and remains active to this day.

He continued doing the college's publication through the summer, but then he and Fanny Mae returned to Morgantown. Darel was back with the *Post* when the stock market crashed.

After "several months" there, he moved to the *Morgantown New Dominion*, where he stayed until June 1930. He was assigned to cover a lynch mob during that period. The mob had assembled to "liberate" a prisoner from jail. As the incident progressed, Darel became so caught up in the lynch-mob frenzy that he removed himself. That is all we've found out about that episode.

That summer, he spent three months in Topeka, Kansas, with his brother Frank. In the fall, he reenrolled in West Virginia University, working again with the Extension Division, writing a weekly "Farmhouse Fable" wherein "Ma and Pa Gandy" talked over improvements in agriculture. He also wrote a weekly editorial called "Guidelines on the Mountain State" regarding the same subject, and a weekly press release for the Allegheny section of the Society of American Foresters.

For one who later claimed never to have joined anything but the volunteer fire department, Darel was affiliated—perhaps honorarily?—with the Kiwanis Club, the Rotary Club, and the Lions Club. "They loved him!" said Fannie Mae. "He did the reporting for all their meetings—also reporting for the R.O.T.C." (There's a hint that he may have been in R.O.T.C.) "He was not only very greatly liked," said Fannie Mae, "but *trusted* and was a fine writer." Nat Frame, head of the University Extension Division, "thought so very much of him."

On Sept 8, 1931, they left for Elkins, West Virginia, to write publicity for the second annual West Virginia Forest Festival. "Then," said Fannie Mae, "on to Washington D.C." He stayed in D.C., she moved on to Ohio. Had she stayed, I might not be here to tell this tale.

Darel left no impression of the stock market crash. Nine days before it, Yale economist Irving Fisher declared, "Stocks have reached what looks like a permanently high plateau." That miscalculation crippled the reputation of an otherwise fine economist, but it echoed the "New Era's" received wisdom. For

Coolidge, capitalism had been religion—the factory its temple, work its worship.

Henry Ford crowed that mass production had tamed the business cycle, and the twenties' dizzying prosperity made the claim hard to gainsay. The assembly line had reduced the Model-T's production time from twelve and a half hours to one and a half, enabling Ford to halve its price. The economy validated Adam Smith's "invisible hand" which, left alone, would automatically fine-tune the market's every nuance.

Coolidge loathed government as much as he adored business. The biggest favor government could do business, he said, was to leave it alone. Classical economics claimed that government interference *caused* business downturns by preventing supply and demand from balancing each other out, and the twenties seemed to do nothing but prove the point. For seven years, from the post-World War I recession to the Crash, the formula worked beyond belief, and seemed it would last forever.

But classical economics was grounded in the pre-industrial world, and assumed an exchange process more like barter than finance, where money facilitated transactions but generally behaved itself. The rise of the factory had complicated things. Now workers fashioned goods én masse, not for sale directly to their neighbors but for sale by the factory to the distributor, by the distributor to the wholesaler, the wholesaler to the retailer, and the retailer to the customer.

It was money run amok, but conservatives clung to the old theories with a death grip. They were easy for voters to grasp and they favored business. But they couldn't account for money's exaggerated role in modern life, and the day of reckoning was nigh.

In truth, much was already amok when Adam Smith published *The Wealth of Nations*—the classicists' bible—in 1776. Long before the 1920s stock market craze, money itself had become a commodity, used to purchase purely financial instruments solely for reinvestment for no other reason than to make more money.

Herbert Hoover was hardly less of a capitalist than Calvin Coolidge, though he did decry Adam Smith's unrestrained capitalism and "the social and economic ills" resulting from "the aggregation of great wealth." Some Democrats, including Franklin Roosevelt, tried recruiting him to run for president in 1920, but he chose progressivism of Republican Teddy

Roosevelt's stripe instead. Harding made him Secretary of Commerce, where he couldn't help reorganizing the department in his own image, or pilfering functions from other departments, earning him the sobriquet, "Secretary of Commerce and undersecretary of everything else," until people wished he would just go away. Coolidge said of him, "That man has offered me unsolicited advice for six years, all of it bad."

Coolidge chose not to run in 1928, and Hoover—hero of Belgian relief and the Mississippi flood—practically sleepwalked to the White House. "We in America today," he exulted, "are nearer to the final triumph over poverty than ever before in the history of any land. Without the wise policies which the Republican Party has made effective during the past seven years, the great prosperity we now enjoy would not have been possible." The American people faced a choice, he counseled, between Republican "rugged individualism" and government control by the Democrats.

He pulverized his opponent—wet, Catholic Al Smith—better than four-to-three.

Doubtless Darel voted for Hoover, the first president he was eligible to vote for.

Hoover took office March 20, 1929. Seven months later, the bubble burst.

There had been warnings. Classical economics claimed that a lasting glut—unsold inventories—was impossible because supply created its own demand. If a glut occurred in eggs, it would be offset by production in coffee. Wages generated in coffee would then buy down the excess eggs. But in 1928 and 1929, unsold inventories trebled.

There were other signs: residential construction backslid, the increase in consumer spending slowed to a crawl, and, most ominously, wholesale commodity prices began falling. Farmers had never gotten on the gravy train to start with. The recovery of European agriculture after the War had set them on a downward slide that held through the decade. Yet, in September, sheer momentum carried stock prices to their all-time high.

Demand for stocks had been huge. The stock market frenzy was the biggest get-rich-quick scheme since the Gold Rush. Banks had sponsored competitions among employees to sell stocks. Customers bought on margin, ten percent down, balance due when the stocks rose. When the bubble burst, banks, that had bought at full price and sold for ten percent, called in their markers, but their investors couldn't pay and their stocks were suddenly worthless.

Wall Street laid its egg on October 29. Unemployment did not immediately surge to 24 percent. It took two years to reach 16 percent and another to attain 24. By November, 1932, 5,000 banks had failed, taking nine million accounts down with them. National income halved.

Darel continued with the extension service for two years. The September 1931 issue of *Greater Pittsburgh* ran his "Pittsburgh-Tableland Festival," for which he had done publicity. Following publicity for the Forest Festival in October, "the Depression closed out my job…and I went to Washington. There I freelanced for a time, with the accent on the first syllable."

Chapter Sixteen

Mr. D. Goes to Washington

PRESIDENT KENNEDY famously said, "Washington is a city of Southern efficiency and Northern charm." Darel's approach would most likely have been via US Route 50 from Clarksburg. Drawing near, he would have skirted Hoover Airport, on the site now occupied by the

Pentagon.[‡‡] Just north of Hoover was 14th Street Bridge across the Potomac. Partially obscured by the bridge's iron trusses, D.C.'s most striking feature was the gleaming, 555-foot-tall Washington Monument, the world's tallest obelisk, world's tallest masonry structure, world's tallest anything until the Eiffel Tower overtopped it in 1889. Some called it a fitting tribute to the man called the Father of His Country.

Far to the right, the Capitol dome rose above the city's low profile. Between the Monument and the Capitol, the Old Post Office's clock tower poked up. Zoning laws made it illegal to build above eleven stories, the height fire hoses could reach, giving the city an open, airy feel, like Paris, plenteously enriched with shade trees. The dominant residential style was the Victorian row house, most just two or three stories high. The Depression saw large numbers of those homes divided into apartments and rooming houses.

People think of D.C. as a town populated by bureaucrats, lawyers, lobbyists, congressmen and senators. The characterization is inaccurate. Cab and bus drivers, waiters and waitresses, carpenters, plumbers and electricians, busboys and hotel managers, green grocers and shop clerks, doctors and nurses, teachers, stenographers and typists—all the occupations that keep a metropolis running—far outnumber the lawyers and bureaucrats.

The average D.C. resident is not responsible for D.C.'s reputation. The ones causing all the trouble come in from outside. Still, the city's raison d'être is government. That's why it was created—written into the Constitution. Though residents' every waking minute is not consumed with public affairs, public affairs can't be escaped. Thanks to governmental presence, D.C. can be a festival of fairly-well considered intellectual discourse. It is one of the best-educated, most liberal jurisdictions in the nation.

Why did Darel choose Washington and not New York or Philadelphia, cities that *generated* art instead of just consuming it? Perhaps it was his congressman, Frank Bowman, whom he knew. Also, D.C. had more journalists per capita than any other city. Maybe that was part of the lure.

Darel introduced himself at D.C.'s seven daily papers. The earliest connection we have record of is with the *Washington Daily News*. On January 5, 1932, the paper's music critic, Ruth Howell, sent a giddy if somewhat

---

[‡‡] Before Hoover, "Washington Airport" was a single runway that crossed a street. Guards stopped traffic when planes took off or landed.

cryptic note to him at the family farm, Dixie, where he'd gone for the holidays. "Forgive me," it said,

> I was so goofy, when I wrote you yesterday. Forget it. The opera was lousy. The fiddles sounded like accordions, and Hansie nearly chewed his lip off with suffering.
>
> Pop Russell was tired, I was gay, the beans were good. Today I am very sleepy.
>
> You will get plenty of clippings—in a most scientific way—shortly.
>
> Write me, Ruth.

The *News* had a young advertising copywriter named Edythe Gordon, and before long Darel was bunking with her and her husband, a taxi driver named Sam, in a stable that had been converted into apartments in an alley off Biltmore Street, N.W. The structure's residents called their abode "The Alley" or "Starvation Alley." Rent was $32 a month. Darel contributed $12.

"The worst thing about the Depression," he said, "was feeling that one's young energy and talent were not wanted;" though "never but once did I feel like a revolutionary."

Resentment of wealth was stirring in the Depression. Intellectuals were looking soberly toward communism. "There has been more 'optimism' talked and less practiced," said Will Rogers, "than at any time during our history." Herbert Hoover, who had fed Belgium and brought relief to the Mississippi, seemed paralyzed in the face of depression. Two years in, his insistence that relief was bad for moral fiber, that government needed to get out of the way and let the economy recover by itself, his refrain that prosperity was just around the corner, were wearing thin. He said people were leaving their jobs because they could make more money selling apples.

Businessmen carped that unemployment was mere malingering. Henry Ford claimed unemployment insurance would just encourage a nation of unemployed. Harold Ickes shot back that Hoover, as President, had had no problem weakening "the moral fiber of banks and insurance companies" by handing them millions of dollars.

Barely six weeks after hitting town, in mid-November 1931, Darel reminisced, "With my last dollar and few cents, I was passing Harvey's

Restaurant on Connecticut Avenue and saw oysters advertised at 35¢ for the half dozen."

Harvey's, a few doors from the fashionable Mayflower Hotel, had been host to Washington's power elite since 1868. "Thirty-five cents," Darel said,

> seemed not too serious an inroad into my finances, so I went in and took a table. When the oysters and the chit were delivered, I was charged 50¢. I demurred but the man said they were 35¢ at the bar. So I thought I might as well do a job of it and have pie and coffee. The pie, appallingly, was 25¢, the coffee 10¢. So I blew the works, left a tip, and spent my last dime on a cigar on the way out.
>
> As I stepped onto the street, there was a wail of sirens, all traffic pulled to one side, and there came speeding a covey of escorting motorcycles and a long black limousine. In the limousine were Herbert Hoover and [Italy's foreign minister] Dino Grandi, in top hats.
>
> At that moment, I could have thrown a bomb.

Before marrying Sam Gordon, Edythe Gordon had been Edythe Eckenrode, "Eck," Anna Schuddeboom's best friend since high school. We can reasonably surmise that Anna, teaching first grade in Garrison, outside Baltimore, came to Washington to visit her friend and found Darel there. "I met your father in an alley," she used to say with a twinkle in her eye. He was smitten; she fancied the platonic relationship. He was twenty-six, she twenty-three.

Books, classical music, and solving the affairs of the universe drew them together. On their first date, Anna told me, Darel read her the entire *Crock of Gold*. I have trouble understanding how he did it. It's delightful, but over 200 pages long.

By January 7, 1932, they had listened alone to a radio concert, symphonic performances being among adolescent radio's most constant offerings. Separated by forty miles—D.C. to Baltimore—they critiqued broadcasts by mail. "The Overture to Tannhauser," Anna wrote, "was admirably executed, with the exception of the second violin section, which made a complete blunder of the first few lines carrying the melody of the Pilgrim's Chorus."

By summer, they were engaged in a lively and capacious correspondence, swapping newspaper clippings on the Riiser-Larsen Antarctic expedition,

Rutledge's unsuccessful Mt. Everest attempt, James Mattern's attempt to break the round-the-world flight record, and Auguste Piccard's stratospheric studies of cosmic rays.

There were descriptions of sunsets and other natural glories. "The post-sunrise sky," she wrote, "was like the smoothly shining surface of a pot filled with molten copper, and in its center was suspended the red golden sphere that presents us with such varying beauties."

He wrote to her, "I have just finished listening to Rimsky-Korsakoff's lovely Scheherazade Suite for the third time in the past four days. It was played as part of a Toscanini Fund concert from Hunter College in New York City. It was one of the many times recently when I have longed for you. To have had you here to listen in the silent companionship you know so well would have been to make the afternoon period one of perfection. You are, little blond Dutch girl, the finest girl companion I have ever met."

"I was most delighted to find your letter with its account of Sunday's concert," she answered. "That is the joy of having someone who gets similar pleasure from music willing to write."

His freelance career showed life in April when the Washington *Star* ran his piece, "Three Generals Washington Fired," without byline.

Nineteen thirty-two was the year of the notorious "Bonus March." Darel recalled, "I was in Washington when the bonus marchers were run out."

The "Bonus Expeditionary Force" was a contingent of Great War veterans who arrived in Washington to petition Congress for immediate release of bonuses that had been promised for payment in 1945. In May 1932, a group in Portland, Oregon, desperate to feed their families, began asking why not get the bonuses now, when they really needed them? Led by an unemployed ex-sergeant, Walter Waters, they set out for Washington, riding the rails, living on handouts. Along the way, other veterans joined them, and they reached Washington a thousand strong, with more still arriving.

They camped on Anacostia Flats. D.C.'s Superintendent of Police, General Glassford (he'd been America's youngest brigadier-general in France), went into action arranging food and tents, organizing ball games, helping maintain discipline, holding the police at bay. He supplied a thousand dollars worth of food with his own money.

A bill for payment passed the House of Representatives on June 15.

Veterans, by now twenty-thousand strong, awaiting the Senate vote on the Capitol grounds, grew restive through the hot day and into the evening. President Hoover wanted to emplace machine guns, but General Glassford dissuaded him. Finally, their leader, ex-Sgt. Waters, mounted the steps. "Comrades, I have bad news."

The Senate had voted the bill down. "Comrades, let us show them that…we are patriotic Americans. I call on you to sing 'America.'" After the song, the veterans formed up in regiments and marched back to Anacostia, emptying the Capitol grounds in thirty minutes. Some left town, but fifteen thousand, many with wives and children, stayed, hoping Congress would change its mind.

Hoover had refused to meet them. Secretary of War Hurley complained that they were too law-abiding; an incident was needed making it possible to declare martial law. On July 28, District police moved to eject veterans from some abandoned buildings on Pennsylvania Avenue. Waters counseled a peaceful exit. Two hours later, a second incident left two people dead of police gunfire. An order to "Stop that shooting" from Glassford quelled the violence.

The city quieted, but the District Commissioners asked for federal troops. Four cavalry troops, six tanks, and an infantry column, led by General Douglas MacArthur and his aide de camp, Major Dwight D. Eisenhower, cleared the downtown with teargas and bayonets. As evening fell, they moved on Anacostia Flats. Allowing an hour for inhabitants to evacuate, they moved in, gassing pockets of resisters and torching their shelters. The conflagration silhouetted the Capitol dome. Eleven-week-old Bernard Meyers, who had been born in the camp, died in a hospital.

"General Glassford was quite a fellow," Darel recounted. "I didn't see the bonus violence, but I remember riding an old-fashioned open-air streetcar that night along Pennsylvania Avenue toward the Capitol. The violence lingered in the air—an electric tension like that I had once felt in a lynch mob in West Virginia. The streets seemed deserted, yet palpable mutiny hung in the air. The lighted dome of the Capitol seemed like a vacant glaring skull, without mind or intelligence or will."

While the Bonus Expeditionary Force sweltered on Anacostia Flats, Darel's engineer bother, Wendell, lost his job working on the Pennsylvania Turnpike. Hearing of a "contract let for construction of an earthen breastwork for a town reservoir," he wrote Darel, "I am going to try for a job even though I can get nothing better than laborer." His family moved to a house with space for chickens and a vegetable garden.

In mid-July, Anna was vacationing in Connecticut. Darel hoped to join her. "Events have conspired to keep me from Connecticut, but I have high hopes of leaving Washington next week.

"A story I had hoped to sell to *National Geographic* came home day before yesterday with four others from various magazines. I had hoped to realize about $100 from it. I then took it down to *American Forests*, hoping to sell it for $25." It was wrong for *American Forests* too. He had spent weeks working it up, and "it was the hardest blow I have taken since getting into this field. But by rewriting, *American Forests* may buy it. I want to submit another story I am writing for them on assignment, after which I hope and believe I can get to the vacation land which you now occupy."

The writing life is not easy. An article starts with an idea. Publications have needs all their own, and woe betide the author who ignores them. The freelancer must study the publication and tailor his idea accordingly, then craft a query letter to pitch the idea, then wait for the rejection slip. "You can paper your walls with rejection slips before your first acceptance," goes the dreary refrain. Darel saved 65 rejection slips from 1932 alone, about one for every five days of work, though often the same piece gets rejected more than once.

Look what work that represents:

It begins with research—the library, interviews with or letters to experts, requests to institutions for materials—gobs more than you'll ever use. Then you sit down to write. Per another refrain, "There is no such thing as good writing, there's only good rewriting." Some writers have the gift of getting close right off, others struggle. But unless your name alone can sell an article, no first draft will pass editorial muster. And no article is ever "finished." At a point, you declare it done and stop working on it.

After you write the article, you prepare the manuscript. The page needs to be free of typos and has to be struck with a fresh ribbon and clean typewriter keys. Nobody cleans typewriter keys now, but in the day that tedious chore was paramount. The remedy for mistakes that can't be fixed with a typing eraser is to type the whole page over. Darel was an accurate typist and took pride in the skill. You keep a carbon copy. The original and the carbon or carbons (up to three or four) are the only copies. If you want more, you type them over from scratch.

Finally, you write a cover letter, enclose it with the manuscript, haul all to the post office for weighing and stamping, and mail it. All for 1,500–3,000 words that might net you $25.00.

The writer is ever on the prowl for stories. Few leads pan out. Ernie Pyle, managing editor at the *News*, told Darel of an airmail pilot who had dropped flares to warn a railroad engineer of a burning trestle ahead. Darel wrote to the pilot, who agreed to meet when he came to Washington, but there's no sign of further work on the story. Pyle later gained fame with his World War II "GI-Joe" dispatches, until he was killed in the Pacific just short of the war's end.

There was no mistaking Darel's love of language.

The language we speak is intriguing. I have pondered how interesting it would be to study its roots and branches, its history of words and phrases. How glibly we use quotations the origin of which we have forgotten or never knew, how choice bits of literature have been woven into folk language; how many forgotten heroic and interesting happenings have become part of our vocal and written equipment, its meaning unknown alike to speaker and writer; time is joined in everyday language; words built and made current on the tongues of Sanskrit herders are brought together with the most currently coined phrases; pidgin-English and Creole; Indian and stately Latin, Saxon gutturals and stylish French phrases, polished Gallic sonant mingled with the choppy Anglo-Saxon, and so infinitely, time and history and nations and people lost into the questionable oblivion of death talk in the more-than-phonographic tongue of today.

But I shall not pore over dusty tomes seeking the far dusty trail of root meanings; temperamentally and by personal preference I am fitted to be the popularizer, the humanizer of knowledge made arid on the tongues of those who seek and in the measured mechanics of seeking find their salvation. I am the romanticist, the flyer of kites, the walker on the high places of dusty research. Not that I find the dust uninteresting, but I would pluck the most iridescent bits, magnify them under a bright and vivifying lens, and call all to look how lovely is this grain of dirt.

Though she never cited cases other than her father's locking her in closets, Anna let us know that her childhood had not been happy, and she had set about creating an "inner garden" where no one could hurt her. That enclosure frustrated Darel. She was still on vacation in Connecticut when he wrote, "I am incurably the romanticist and the lover." He longed to display his affection. She was a dear companion, he said, but their relationship would be the sweetest if only she had the will to love. He longed for her, but it came as a shock suddenly to think that his advances might be met with shrinking by her. He had no wish to hurt her, but the things they already enjoyed together…must their relationship stop there?

Her defense of platonism came back cryptically. Reading the Plato in question, her mind had strayed to a quarry hole half-filled with water opposite her window, and a large frog that amused itself by plunging in with a splash then climbing out again. Wasn't its attitude toward life typically platonic? Its driving interest was acquiring food and seeking a proper balance between wet and dry states. Its sensual pleasures, though liberally indulged, didn't dominate. Was she referring to her own childhood when she generalized that many people suffer almost unbearably from another's thoughtless act?

Some of those people, she said, went on to fuller happiness anyway, but many became misanthropes. She thought the difference was due "largely to the fact that some have straws at which to grasp and others have none. The frog always seemed to have a straw."

It struck Darel as a curious abstraction. "I am puzzled by your Aesopic presentation of a Platonic philosophy as exemplified by the viewpoint of a Connecticut frog." He, in fact, didn't believe there was any such thing as a true platonic relationship. To him, sensual pleasures were necessary to a rounded relationship. Maybe to her they were not. Maybe she could get everything from the froggy attitude she described. But even in the frog, he said, there was the urge to reproduce, notwithstanding its other hungers and equilibriums between wetness and dryness. If she preferred the platonic attitude, he would respect it, but such an arrangement would be incomplete for him.

She replied that her "froggy attitude was not clearly set forth." She had been very sleepy and had not meant to speak in parables, but she couldn't remember ever having been obsessed with the idea that a relationship could ever approach completion. Yet the straw was no abstraction. She had meant that a platonic attitude could help some rise to great greater happiness despite injury, rather than add to humanity's embitterment. That, she thought, was the most valuable thing in the platonic philosophy. "To me, the world is good," she said, "and I wish that all could know it."

Darel asked her not feel that he gained nothing from their friendship. No doubt a platonic relationship was good for him; he'd had few. He possessed, in fact, something of a "Don Juan" reputation. Perhaps he overly esteemed the importance of sex. Perhaps, with years, certain changes would become normal, whereas a vigorous sex life was now normal, and hence (as with the frog?) neither right nor wrong. Her feelings about sex and about him were normal for her, and thus right and worthy of respect. It didn't matter if her feelings inconvenienced him, for he valued her friendship and companionship above physical intimacies.

He nevertheless failed to comprehend how Nature had created such a lovely and attractive person "without the usual arrangement of desires," but if he could bring her happiness in any way, he would be "vastly pleased."

The plan was for him to attend a retreat at Colebrook, Connecticut, stopping to see her on the way. On inspection, however, Colebrook was diagonally across the state from Groton, where Anna was staying, so he wouldn't be able to see her even if he got to Connecticut before she left. And anyway, he was "going to make a determined effort to handle publicity for the National Symphony Orchestra."

Just because you are working "for yourself," you are "your own boss," unbeholden to anyone else, you don't have the luxury of playing hooky. Leads are precious. They are food, clothing, and shelter. Especially trying to break into freelancing, especially during a Depression, you neglect them at your peril. The National Symphony's manager was on vacation. Darel was going to wait till he got back. If he got the job, he would work in D.C. for the rest of the summer. "If I get a flat negative, I shall probably depart at once for Connecticut.

"I have turned in two stories to *American Forests*, with a fair assurance of their being accepted, and have an assignment from *American Motorist* which must be in by July 28. So I should not be entirely without financial blessings by the time you return. I have been tasting the savor of poverty practically ever since I saw you. It doesn't bother me too much. I know it well and can call it by nicknames."

The Symphony rendered its verdict a week later. "My summer's fate, which the gods have so carefully kept from me, unfolded with a bang yesterday. I found, quite suddenly, that the National Symphony job was already taken. A man with a salary of $60 per week gets $1000 extra for this work. 'Them as has, gits—'

"So today I am rushing about like an ant disturbed by a puff of smoke, gathering books, clothing, and all loose ends together so I can leave for Connecticut at 2:45 Saturday morning."

His spot was an abandoned lumber camp named Three Trees near Colebrook, his cabin a dilapidated logger's shack. "My first letter from Three Trees goes to you," he wrote Anna on August 1. She was back home with her parents in Garrison, outside Baltimore.

How you would love the life I am leading up here! You get up when you feel like it; go down to the brook; take an invigorating scrub before breakfast; drink a cup of coffee in the sun; do such things as may please you until the mail comes; then occupy yourself in whatever way you choose until it is time for a swim, a sunbath, or a nap in the afternoon; dinner is not till 7 where I have been staying; candles are lighted and dinner eaten very leisurely, with the final cup of coffee on the stoop just at twilight; then there is the evening to read aloud in the light of an oil lamp as long as you feel like it.

The town of Colebrook had an interest in Three Trees, and perhaps was trading rent for sweat equity, but we can't be sure.

I am half a mile from any house, almost as far from the road, and here is such peace and quiet as you would find in but few places. The camp itself—my portion of it—is two rooms in a lumber camp that has not been used for 17 years. It is old and rickety and dingy. Curtains are one of my first considerations. There is a pile of wood on the porch to move when I feel like it. Bushes and grass to cut.

I must excavate a bathtub in the brook. I must explore to the spring. There I shall probably be detained by huckleberries and raspberries. Then, of course, I must get to writing again. Thus far I have been so utterly lazy— and loving it—that there has not been room for anything else.

Returning one day from errands, "I found my landlord and another man had been here, and had amused themselves by hooking a bottle of my beer from the brook-refrigerator," which he had stocked in merry disregard of Prohibition. "I was glad they had helped themselves, for I had been uncertain about their attitude toward me, and I happen to know that men do not invade another man's beer supply when he is not home unless they have a friendly regard for him."

But even paradise is temporary. On Sunday, August 28, he wrote, "Things have worked out so I will probably return to Washington the last of the week. It looks like I will get to stay here only long enough to see the total eclipse of the sun on Wednesday." In actuality, totality brushed Cape Cod but missed Colebrook by a few minutes of longitude. There is no further mention of what writing he may have done while there.

Freelancing can take a toll on relationships. Explaining the creative drive frustrates both the creator and the creator's friends. Friends understand the demands of "regular" employment; self-employment's demands not so much. Sam and Edythe were going to visit Anna in Garrison the last weekend in September, and Darel, resettled at The Alley, elected to use the solitude for work instead of going along.

"I shall not be over with Sam & Edythe this weekend," he told Anna. "I am devoting myself entirely to work, and feel that this is too good an opportunity to miss. I am sorry. The press of economics is not the only reason—there is an inner compulsion that I may someday explain to you. To Sam & Edythe, & to others who may wonder why, I say only that I am aweary of poverty and am starting out to make money."

His poverty was relieved by occasional parcels from home—canned garden produce and blankets. "We sent out the covers today," wrote his sister Gladys, "and we hope you will not have to be cold any longer."

A few months later, he reread some letters he had written to his mother: "Intended to convey exuberant optimism, they now seemed to me to carry a note of desperation. I wondered if the folks got that impression, too." His sisters, Gladys and Mamie (who was severely retarded), and his mother, Blanche, remained at Dixie, the farm, cooking and cleaning for the owners. They wished Darel would come back home, or at least write more often.

He, Sam, and Edythe planned a trip to Dixie in early October, and urged Anna to join them. "You would love my mountains in autumn." He thought of staying at Dixie to finish two projects, but before they could leave, a September 28 telegram changed everything.

Chapter Seventeen

On the Road

"I had myself Kodaked."

NINETEEN THIRTY-TWO was election year, and Darel's congressman, Frank L. Bowman, telegrammed an offer he couldn't refuse—driving and doing publicity for his campaign. "Anna," he wrote, "I am going to play traitor to you for the dear old Republican party. We will be on the highroad till election."

In mid-June, the Republican Convention had overwhelmingly renamed Herbert Hoover its presidential nominee. As June turned to July, the Democrats chose New York Governor Franklin Delano Roosevelt. Roosevelt didn't hurt his cause by taking the unprecedented step of accepting the nomination in person, or the equally unprecedented step of arriving by air. He had been the predicted nominee, but few foresaw the rout that lay ahead.

Darel was to meet his congressman in Petersburg, West Virginia, on October 2nd. (In 1932, one month of campaigning was enough.) Sam drove him to the bus station, but "information that Greyhound had a bus at 3 o'clock proved entirely without foundation."

Sam suggested that Adolph might drive him. Adolph Whitener was an Alley resident and possibly the building's manager, as he had the authority to turn the electricity off and on, and once mentioned possible carpentry work for Darel. He was a difficult personality, but it was no small act of generosity to drive 150 miles to Petersburg and return the same distance.

If they talked of the reason behind the trip, whether they sensed the political watershed that loomed, no record survives. Adolph's interests were select. Anna noted that he knew something of calculus.

"We started at 5:15," Darel wrote, "and drove into a brilliant, blazing sunset. I felt out Adolph to see if he had any appreciation of that display, but found him unresponsive. We sped on, mile after mile, in windy silence."

Finally Darel asked, "How long do you think it will be before it will be possible to get a rocket ship and follow a sunset around the world?" Adolph perked up. "He thought that with present materials, it would not be possible to reach a speed of more than 600 m. p. h., whereas to keep in view of a sunset for 24 hours would require a cruising speed (at this latitude) of about 800 M.p.h." Adolph calculated that the two of them, traveling west at 50 miles per hour, were getting more sunset than those sitting in Washington. "It figured, in his mental arithmetic, a gain of the 500th portion of a day, or about three minutes. But there was too much beauty in the sunset to pursue those calculations further.

"Finally, there were the mountains, lying low and lavender beneath the sunset sky, and I thrilled at the sight of them, as the born mountain-man ever must." They made Petersburg at 9:30.

"There was only a breathing-spell and we were away to Morgantown. There were long hours of conversation, in the course of which I absorbed much political information and studied rather calculatedly this man with whom I am to travel for the weeks to come. We reached Morgantown at 3 a.m."

Bowman's man-on-the-make persona seduced Darel. "It is wonderful," he wrote, "traveling with a politician. There is great psychological insight, and I have been by no means idle. Everybody is out to get what he can. *So am I* [emphasis added]. I study the man, inflate his ego, and feel for means of doing the work in such a way that he will be convinced that I can be valuable to him."

He was struck by the "genuine Communistic sentiments" people were expressing, while the politicians he heard mixed "an outworn patriotism" with the capitalist's loathed terms, "Red," "Bolshevist," "Communist," "Socialist." Yet the average American, Darel believed, was "a Communist at heart." He just refused "to give his sentiments their proper name." Darel doesn't tell us exactly what people said to show those sentiments, but it's not hard to think some of it could have come straight from *The Communist Manifesto* with little modification:

"The capitalist," said Karl Marx in 1848, "has resolved personal worth into exchange value." Capitalism had "stripped of its halo every occupation hitherto honored and looked up to with reverent awe. It has converted the physician, the lawyer, the priest, the poet, the man of science, into its paid wage laborers." Capitalism had "torn away from the family its sentimental veil, and has reduced the family relation to a mere money relation."

It would have been easy for the hungry, cold, and dispossessed to relate to such sentiments. One in four was out of work. Roosevelt supporter Donald Richberg told a Senate committee: "Although the conspicuous money-makers who presume to advise you have proved their ability to make themselves wealthy, it is far more important for this committee to realize that they have also proved their ability to make millions of people very poor."

Darel made his own thinking clear: "Unless there is relief from this depression [*sic*, uncapitalized], if people suffer economic stress enough that they feel it is not temporary, that sentiment will flare to a revolution. Not a disciplined revolution such as Russia's, where Communists were disciplined through secret meetings for years, but it will burst forth so unexpectedly as to frighten the participants themselves. Unless the Republicans are returned to office, and permitted to carry out their program of reconstruction, a Democratic administration might precipitate the outbreak."

Herbert Hoover led the Republican charge: the top priority was protecting American business from foreign competition. Protect business and the economy would recover on its own. The Smoot-Hawley tariff, passed in 1930, taxed imports, making them more expensive than the same goods produced at home. Hoover signed it with five gold pens.

"I have been exposed to the high tariff side of the question so much that I can claim no knowledge of what it is all about," Darel said. "I know the arguments on one side pretty thoroughly, but am in ignorance of the other."

The flaw in the high-tariff side is that other countries invariably respond with tariffs of their own, which hurt American exports. The debate can get complicated, and doubtless Darel was subjected to its complications, but history concludes that Smoot-Hawley exacerbated the Depression, though by how much is not settled. It slashed foreign trade fifty percent, but foreign trade was a fairly small part of the economy to begin with.

The nation's highways were being paved at an accelerating pace, yet, driving the congressman, Darel could still talk of "miles of rough, rocky road, until one wonders where God got all the rocks to pave them."

"From excellent hard road (3 miles of it) we turned up Deep Hollow."

"I drove back to Elkins—30 miles of mud each way."

Those grueling miles were driven in 1930s cars without power steering, power brakes, automatic transmissions, or even turn signals. "It snowed, and the windshield wiper refused to function."

Yet those Appalachian byways had their compensations.

The Indian Hammock

"In the early moonlight, we topped the Allegheny Front. There, as we wound down the mountain, lay the Indian Hammock under moonlight.

"It is a long perfectly symmetrical notch in the backbone of a mountain, one of the most pleasing sights to be found in my country of the hills. It was the first time I have seen it under the moon. Cursed with the necessity of driving through this mystical country this time of year, with the need to reach a certain point at a certain time, I lost much of the beauty I might have enjoyed, given time and leisure, and such companionship as yours."

He sent Anna a hand-tinted post card.

There were car troubles. "It rained *sans cesse*. Our car got some vital parts water soaked & refused to operate. We borrowed the postmaster's Chevrolet, which is nice to drive, & I almost enjoyed the mud and rain as we threaded miles of rough country roads."

"Near Kingwood the left front tire exploded with a most unbecoming bang. But it was within 100 yards of a garage, so dark found us rolling down magical sunset aisles of painted mountain & woodland to Morgantown."

"Well shod with two new tires in front, we started again this morning."

Ten miles from Fairmont, on a mountain road with not a filling station anywhere, the car coughed, sputtered, and refused to operate. We thought that, in the rain, it had gotten wet, as had happened near Charles Town. I walked a mile back to a place called the Mountain View Inn. Across the hills the lights of Fairmont glowed under the clouds.

The innkeeper was the only person who ever cussed me out in a manner that I actually liked.

I asked about a mechanic. He said none nearer than Fairmont or Grafton. He was a huge fat man. He had a fierce brindled dog.

Could I call Fairmont? No, the switchboard closed at 9 o'clock and nobody was supposed to call unless in case of severest necessity. I allowed this was a considerable necessity.

He took the attitude that I was trying to put something over on him. I began to get riled. Why the hell should I try to put anything over on him? He said, "People try to pull all kinds of stuff. You can never tell a crook." And I, "Do I look like a crook?"

And he, "You can't never tell: crooks dress up and look nice too."

He asked me for my operator's license. As a matter of plain fact I have been driving for ten years without one. I said it was in the car. "Listen, I'm driving for Congressman Bowman. He's sitting down there in the car now waiting for me. You're in a public business, and it seems to me you should show a little courtesy when people stop in."

He asked that I show some identification. I hadn't a scratch on my person, but started to look, getting madder and madder. I put my papers back, saying, "Hell, I don't have to identify myself to you!"

"All right!" says my eloquent friend. "There's the road, and you can get out and use it. And your congressman—if there really is one—can sit in his car and rot for all I give a damn!"

Meantime, I began to get amused. Unless this man helped me, God knew which way I would turn. People don't stop on the road past midnight without good reason. I couldn't stand on my own or anybody else's dignity. Amusement was the only thing I could resort to. The man's independence was amazing. I even found it admirable.

We continued to talk for a while. He said, 'You say you are traveling with a congressman. You feel that I should know you. Well, I don't. And you don't seem to have any idea of the stuff people try to pull on a man in my business in the middle of the night.' So we began to understand each other.

Finally, he said if I put up 20 cents, he'd call Fairmont. I furnished the 20 cents. He did the talking himself, so it would only cost a dime, and refused to keep the rest of it, though I insisted. So I shook hands with him as I left, and promised to come back. I will, too.

The wind blew a fierce gale as I trudged back down the road and found the congressman sound asleep and snoring. After a time, a wrecker arrived and towed us to Fairmont.

We routed out a mechanic. Bowman suggested we see if there was any gasoline. We vetoed the suggestion, for we had bought gasoline before we started. But I sneaked around for a look. The cap was gone. The tank was dry! Someone had stolen most of our gas at Clemtown, and hadn't even the grace to replace the cap! To learn that cost $12.

Darel's congressman "drank wet and voted dry," as the saying went during Prohibition. Darel, too, observed the law in the breach. One night he got "delightfully drunk," and wanted to tell Anna about it, "before I recover from that laudable condition. The North & South Branches of the Potomac River," he wrote,

join the Potomac at Cumberland, Md. In the angle at this intersection is Ridgeley, W. Va., just across the river from Cumberland. It was there that our first day's campaigning in this county ended.

After the speech, we followed State Senator Abe Helmick at hotfoot across the bridge into Cumberland, to the home of one Mr. Williamson, second in command at the Western Maryland Railway, a very fat man smoking a cigar, seated next a large radio. There I learned how little geographical boundaries matter in politics. For Williamson of Maryland was called on to smooth out certain political functions in West Virginia. And what I first judged to be a wealthy gourmand changed suddenly to a keen, analytical businessman.

Drinks were ordered & consumed. Drinks were served again. Then fudge, made by a good fudge-making daughter, too modest to appear in pajamas. Then more drinks, while a Mr. Fess, of Republican persuasion, tore a Mr. Roosevelt, of Democratic persuasion, into the tiniest of shreds & scattered them over any dissociated floor you may associate with these gentlemen.

Then—suddenly—symphonic music on the radio!

"Keep that," says I, getting on toward demolition of cocktail No. 3. "That's good!"

Mr. Williamson casts an appreciative glance at me. "You like classical music?"

"I love it!"

"Thank god!" he bubbles. "At last someone who likes good music. Woodie doesn't like it." (Woodie being his henchman, on whose shoulders fall responsibility for sifting out this political intrigue across the river.)

So, I settle me down to listen. I bubble over about the transmission of the tone of every instrument.

Williamson gets started. "I'm a nut," he says, "about radio. If there's anything better than this, I'll buy it. Most people can't be nuts like I am, because they can't afford it."

I pause to wonder how much this setup costs. Twenty-eight condensers (whatever they may be) on this single radio, he tells me. I nod intelligently and give up mathematics, because my attentions are being divided between some divine music and the recital of the most opulent radio nut I have ever seen.

"I get two octaves higher & two octaves lower than the average machine," he informs me.…Oh! Lovely pure music!…

"See this! Loud or soft, it never fades or gets louder."

Brahms, give but a moment for your 2nd Hungarian dance!

"Now here's the absolute latest in radio tubes. Let me show you."

And so, endlessly. The congressman & Senator Helmick drift out for some private confab. Woodie & Davis mutter about the Ridgeley political tangle.

"When this is over," Williamson adds, "I'll play to you on the concertina."

"Let's go," cuts in the congressman.

"He's got to hear the rest of this symphony," protests Williamson.

"No! Let's hear *you* play," urges the congressman, hoping to expedite matters.

Woodie cuts off the radio. The little wife brings out the baby accordion. The fat man rises wheezes out a false note, then plays "Abide with Me," swaying rapturously with elephantine grace.

"He never plays except when he's drunk," says the wife.

He was prevailed upon to play in imitation of bagpipes, to everybody's amusement. Then—mingled church bells of a Sunday morning. Then—

"Let's go! Let's go!"

Goodbyes.

Standing invitations to return.

Anna, don't judge me too harshly—I never wrote you an unsober letter before.

Anna replied, "A letter from Eck was almost as entertaining as the intoxicated epistle you sent me 10 days ago."

October 20 was a day off. The congressman had a conference in Washington with President Hoover. The day before, while Bowman speechified, Darel worked in the hotel on a statement for release following the conference. He shot a note to Anna, "Tonight, I imagine, I shall sleep once more in Starvation Alley."

After their interlude, she wrote Darel, who was already back in Morgantown, "Last night was the happiest evening I have experienced in a long time. I had been wishing for a share of your companionship, but I had not even remotely thought that you might appear. I wish you could have stayed longer. You looked tired and it was lovely of you to take hours from needed rest to give me such a happy surprise."

She was happy but continued on guard. Where Darel could write, "Anna, I'm lonesome as hell tonight. Not since Hector ceased to be a very small puppy can I recall being more lonesome," and close his letters with, "Kindest goodnight thoughts to you," hers concluded matter-of-factly, "My best regards to you," and "Good night and best regards."

As the campaign drew to a close, he reflected, "I have driven, I believe, several thousands of miles with the Congressman in the past month. At no time have I been able to enter into an intimate conversation with him. Always I have found it necessary to inflate his ego, and to talk interminably of politics. The adjustment has all been on my part. I have not resented that too greatly, for it was part of my job.

"But it gave rise to this question: What is the barrier between the one generation and the other?" The congressman believed it was diversity of experience. But, Darel asked, "are not all human experiences basically similar? Do we not all meet with successes, defeats, love, labor, laughter, and, ultimately, death? Are our experiences really sufficiently diverse to explain the difference?"

Darel thought terminology might be part of it. Scientific advances arranged facts into different patterns. New names and new knowledge put the rising generation's view through a different prism. Psychoanalysis was highly topical with Darel's contemporaries (Anna was taking a psychology course at Johns Hopkins), and so the younger generation treated "ego," "complexes," "libido," "sex," almost as the new slang. The older generation might learn the essentials, but they never get the hang of terminology. The two spoke different languages, and so drifted apart, unable to reconnect.

"The Congressman heard me through, in silence," Darel said, "as we followed our headlights into the dark. When I was done, he said, glumly, 'I think you're all wrong.' It was dismissed thus. I made no attempt to express myself further."

The congressman was twice Darel's age and had election on his mind. The post-Great War generational gulf was driven largely by technology—radio, automobiles, movies, telephones, electric lights, airplanes, relativity and psychoanalysis. The gap wasn't equaled again until the sixties, and maybe not even then.

November 8 was Election Day. "I had feared it would be a strained, irritable day. But the campaign is over, and the voters are deciding. The

Congressman is in a fine, kindly humor, and the family seems generally happy. Unofficial reports make the election look good in Morgantown."

By morning, however, "We have all the returns we want and then some." My man was snewed [*sic*] under with every other Republican in West Virginia.

Depression lassoed a Democratic rout. The Republicans lost 197 seats in the House of Representatives, nine in the Senate. Franklin Roosevelt and his running mate, John Nance Garner, who cordially despised each other, won the White House by nearly eighteen percent. Will Rogers reported, "Two democratic contenders made up. Yes sir, they made up and decided to bury the hatchet. They decided to bury it in the Republican president."

"It was an unpredictable debacle," Darel said, though with historical perspective, it's hard to believe it could have been otherwise.

"The telephone is the most exquisite instrument of torture ever devised," he told Anna. "From 8 o'clock Tuesday evening until 3:30 the following morning I never left my post. Telephoning and tabulating, tabulating and telephoning, hoping against hope that something might stem the tide of Democratic votes."

But the congressman had "fought out his battle and now is more happy than he has been in eight years in Congress. He is glad to be away from the demands, from taking a slap first on one cheek and then on the other."

Work for the congressman, as a congressman, was over, but a strand remained. For six years, Bowman had dreamed of telling the humorous side of public life and had collected some 150 stories. A newspaper syndicate had turned them down, but now he revisited the dream. "This country needs humor," he said. "It has never needed it as it needs it now."

"He is right about that," Darel agreed. "We will write them in collaboration—both of our names will be used. I will do the writing, he will furnish the material. It may resolve into a sizable undertaking."

"I'm glad that you've come to such a satisfactory arrangement with the congressman," Anna told him. "You'll spend some interesting hours at that work, I imagine."

"I will probably go home [to Dixie] for a day to a week. I have not been there since Dad's death in March." (This letter contains his only references to that event.) "But where I shall want to be is in the Alley—with you, and Sam, and Edythe."

Chapter Eighteen

From Dixie with Love

Home at Dixie—Darel's mother.

NOVEMBER 12, DIXIE: "Anna, I have just finished a country bath. I feel, frankly, more virtuous than cleansed.

"If you don't know what a country bath is, it represents entering into precarious contact with an adequate bar of soap, a full-sized washcloth, & a basin of water not sufficient in size to immerse one foot (that is, one of mine; feet didn't cost anything when I got mine, so I took a big pair). When your ablution is completed you feel that if the cleansing was commensurate with the amount of soapsuds, you ought by rights to be cleaner than ever before.

"I came home night before last. It was bitterly cold at Dixie, and a powdery gray snow sifted down all yesterday. Today continues cold, & I toast my toes before Dixie fires, consume much rural food, & sleep into the large hours. I could not prevent an occasional twinge of thought about you—and the Gordons—a dream that will include you, if you wish it. But I must refrain from dreaming it aloud until it becomes more than the evanescent shadow it now represents."

He wouldn't tell his family about Anna until their relationship was better cemented.

She reminded him, "The country bath and all of the attending country joys constituted a substantial part of my early experiences" in the coal fields.

Anticipating returning to D.C., he asked, "When are you coming to the Alley again? Honestly, I'm so hungry to see you! Don't be surprised if I make love to you, for I am more love-hungry now than at any recent period in my experience. Being celibate is bad medicine.

"How hundred fold good to think of being with you once more! Then I shall begin building myself back into the niche our companionship evolved in The Alley. How little I realized before that this West Virginia interlude, while in some respects stimulating, has been for the most part rather unhappy. I can admit it to myself now, that I am so happy at the prospect of seeing you— sweet person—very soon."

He was back the day after Thanksgiving and loosed a fusillade of love letters Cyrano de Bergerac would have envied.

Last night I dreamed about you. There was the sweet satisfaction of having you near, of touching the soft gold of your hair, the balm and forgetfulness of troubles your sweet presence always brings.

Anna, sweetheart, my little Dutch girl, I love you with a love that throbs its message to the blue heart of Sirius himself. It seems to me the binary suns in the body of the Great Bear, and the Great Nebula in Orion, must know how I love you: the opalescent gem in the Hunter's belt, and the jewel in the hilt of his sword send back the clear glow of the great light there is in my soul for you. It cannot be written, any more than Betelgeuse can be placed on the page of a book. Somewhen, after I have taught you the meaning of love, you will recognize the cosmic wordlessness that lives in the thoughts and emotions of one person for another. The astral symphony of the ancients will then become comprehensible to you, and in your heart you will question its music no more.

Knowing you has added fragrance to living. Comradeship such as yours, in thought, in beauty, I have never known. To yearn for you is to know poignantly of urgent need, yet it is pain I should not care to miss. To be with you is to know such human harmony as I should not have believed possible. Your ready interest in things, your receptiveness to the myriad voices of beauty, are qualities which have endeared you to me past all descriptive language.

I love the enigmatic blue of your eyes, I love the sunlight of the Netherlands that shines always upon your hair, I love the sweet slenderness of your graceful body, I love the colors and textures of the clothes you wear, and, surpassing all these things, I love you.

She came to him, and something happened—just what is left ambiguous, presumably for delicacy's sake. On Monday, after she'd gone home, Darel wrote: "This morning at breakfast, in your blue tam and dress, in spite of my unshaven face, unbrushed teeth, and punctuated before-breakfast feeling, I thought you a dream and a vision of loveliness. There was a glow about you that made you seem so fresh and vital. How I wanted to take you in my arms, and kiss your face until none of it could feel neglected, and then to love you until our world might go out to join the radiant beauty of sunrise.

"It was more than pleasant to see the sunrise with you. Something sweet and dear and precious went away when your blue-toqued figure melted into the perspective of distance this morning. I saw so much before the hill hid you from view."

It was Friday before she wrote back, thus cryptically: "You can't know how I regret the severe results of that three-day visit. It's good to suspect you of feeling more animated and happy. I hope the suspicion is justified." Perhaps those words hid meanings that only two lovers could know.

By Sunday, any hint of regret had vanished. "Was not Friday after Thanksgiving a perfect day?" she asked. "I could spend many days like that, and be infinitely happy even lacking some necessities of life. At least that's my opinion while I live under the present circumstances."

"Present circumstances" had their own meaning. At twenty-four, she was still living at home, and had now secretly violated her parents' morals.

That was where the subterfuge began: "I'll have to be in possession of a very good reason to leave here in peace next weekend," she told Darel. "Can you invent an art exhibit or something?"

"It won't be necessary to invent an art exhibit," he wrote back. "On Friday evening there is a free concert, enthusedly announced by Edythe, at which the finest amateur piano-playing in the city is done by a certain Mrs. Something-or-other Emerson."

He suggested Anna tell her parents it was a two-night event for which Edythe had been gifted four tickets, justifying Anna's need to stay over Saturday. Saturday, of course, was the lie, but there was always the Alley's kaleidoscope of personalities: Eck, the gifted pianist, whose opinions some found "brutally frank;" and Sam, the taxi-driving junkman's son, rough on the outside, who enjoyed scientific discussions. There was Adolph Whiteman, who had driven Darel to Petersburg. Despite Adolph's holding Darel, as Darel put it, "in high contempt," they managed a provisional cordiality. Adolph's wife, Evelyn, and Betty who suffered bouts of amnesia but also played piano, eagerly subjected themselves to Alley psychoanalysis.

Whether Dr. Sprowls, a psychologist with a column, "Everyday Psychology," contributed to those sessions we don't know. The name, Moats, came up, without specifics to identify him. When bridge games erupted, Darel took the opportunity to write unmolested. He often visited nearby Charlie Wood, another writer he had met at Three Trees in Connecticut, who remarked, "If you wait long enough, somebody will write your book for you, and save you the trouble."

Beyond the Alley lay Washington's galleries, museums, and parks, plenty to fill the hours of two young lovers.

"The loveliness of having you here lives in my heart like music," Darel wrote. "You seemed to me more beautiful than ever. I look forward with joy to the pleasances, and satisfactions, and happiness that wait for us, folded under the wings of sleeping tomorrows, as, one by one, these birds of unknown color, and shape, and luster, are wakened by the dawns of tomorrows, and fly away toward the sunsets of an unrealized range of yesterdays."

Back home in Garrison she wrote, "I arrived here in the same state of lethargy which possessed me when I left you. The Alley is a much better place for such a condition than this."

He told her, "Sam came home Sunday afternoon [after leaving Anna at the train] and said, 'The last thing Anna said was, 'Tell Darel to be sure to come over for Christmas.' To which I said, with fullest fervency, 'God bless Anna!'"

"Yesterday was so perfectly delightful," she elaborated. "It is so gratifying to enjoy a companionship such as yours, which appreciates my general silence and yet is so ready to discuss and explore those delectable realms of ideas suggested by almost every human contact and books. I miss you tonight."

On Dec 6, a humor story was finally ready for submission, and he faced typing "6,000 words, very correctly," but, "ere I grow tired of this miniature Juggernaut (typewriter) I propose to devote some time to You."

He thereupon drew back Cupid's bow and let fly his sleekermost arrow. It should be read in full:

I often think how often I write you from midnight on. That is the hour of our companionship. That is when we can be together, just you and I, and the rest of the world fades into the lamplighted darkness of a city, stretches unhindered over leagues of quiet country, and eventually wraps itself around your abode, and looks in the window to see you, reading late. Sometimes, I believe the crepuscular substance of it carries something from my lighted window to your lighted window, and brings something back to me. And our messenger through the cavern of darkness, I think, gathers a ray from Betelgeuse, and a spear from Sirius, and a feathered shaft from far Vega, and a trident of silver from the path of the new moon; I think it wanders in the far pastures of the heavens and plucks a red ray here, a green ray there, like a child picking flowers, and hurries to reach through the transparent pane to place a bouquet of brittle beauty on our tables, that each may see the loveliness the other sends through the nocturnal vacuum of uninhabited darkness.

At least I hope the messenger does not lose himself in the astral meadows where Orion hunts, having so faithfully brought me the rayed pattern of loveliness that comes from you when night grows still. My inmost thoughts whisperingly urge that the rider of velvet night seek far and far into the blue beyond until he comes to the rare, poised comet-flower, and pluck it and bear it gently to you, that he find the nebula-rose with the most exquisite whorls, and handle it carefully, that it not dissolve until the sunrise blossom for you in a new day; that he gather, with exceptional care, rays from the most vari-hued stars in the upper and nether fields of distance, and bind them meticulously with a band from the inmost ring of Saturn, and place them where you may look at them after you have gone to sleep. I hope the messenger has not dallied at his task. For there can be no chastisement of the messenger. The fault lies ever with he who sends....

Reluctantly, I light a fresh cigarette—a stick of incense burned in the temple of night to my love for you—and come back from the world of fantasy. Of split infinitives I have been oft-accused, and justly; I have been tried in literary tribunal for metaphor-mixing, and found shamelessly guilty; but both of these are among the harmless sins of the rhetorical Eighteenth Amendment. But let it earnestly be hoped that I never become a Bactrian, with two humps, straining through a needle's eye toward fading beauty when the genie of fantasy has departed. Before committing this venal sin, I bow willingly before the nine-lashed whip of gingham phraseology.

But, though my own lamp of inspiration gutters on its wick, I can turn to the close-writ lines of your dear letter, and kindle anew in my mind the fires of beauty, and analysis, and abstraction.

"Last night when I came home I found your letter of Monday evening," she wrote. "It is beautiful and full of poetry and philosophy. Your writing has been a fathomless source of joy to me."
Yet she remained enigmatic.

Anna, I am going to ask of you something which you may or may not feel like doing. But I am going to ask you to write it, because I know you would not be likely to express yourself so fully in conversation.

I look upon you, and see the lissome gracefulness of your body, see the warm gold of your hair, see the unfathomable blue of your eyes. I look upon you with warm wonder, and adoration, and a sincere depth of love. But on your Lisa-like face I read so little, and in the blue background of your eyes I do not find an answer.

Will you tell me, frankly—coldly, if need be—just what you think of me, and what you think of our companionship as it has spelled itself out to the present time? Are you disappointed? Expectant? What?

I hope my curiosity is pardonable. You have, after all, been quite noncommittal. You may, I realize, be in a state of indecision, or suspended judgment. You may feel that you have nothing to say, orally or in writing, in answer to the things I have asked. I leave that all up to you.

She ventured, "Darel, I've never experienced quite so satisfactory a companionship as this with you. You may have noticed that I have a great deal of difficulty transcribing my feelings into words, and therein lies I think the cause for my silence in regard to our relationship. I really would prefer to tell you my opinion of you orally rather than in writing. Regardless of what I think of your powers of analysis, I'd be quite prone to say exactly what I felt, hence there would be no need for analysis; but I never manage to say or write just exactly what I feel or think. If this is rationalization, I'd like for you to tell me, for it is an attitude of mine that has often puzzled me."

And she added: "That lovely lyrical letter of week before last touched something in me and obtained a response that I even at this time cannot voice, but that is often my response to experiences with you. I'll try to be more expressive on the subject when I see you, I hope next Saturday."

Despite the imbalance of romantic sentiment, they equally shared the passion for intellectual discourse. Sam and Eck figured prominently in the connivance. They discoursed on the psychological theories of Adler and Freud, drew on Will Durant's *Pleasures of Philosophy*, waxed as ever ecstatic—and critical—over classical music programs. They pondered monogamy versus polygamy, and geographical influences on language. At a point, Darel was moved to write whimsically:

I have been impressed recently by the dilettante manner of some of our discussions. It seems that some of my dissertations have been very sophomoric, bound to comparatively few facts; that they did not appreciate the complexity of social & psychological questions. We are all circumscribed by duties that make it impossible for us to explore these orchards of thought & pluck the accumulated wisdom in as large baskets as we carry, full of questions longing to be displaced with factual matter.

It has never been my intention to be positive in my epistolary dissertations—they are based on a few primary facts which are woefully inadequate. If they are of passing interest in your quest for the fruits of knowledge, sprinkle them thinly over the bottom of your basket, & cover them with the more substantial & less runty berries of learning when you pluck them. But be assured that the green fruits I offer are passed on with a welcome, complimented with the apology, "they're the best I have, this early in the season."

Chapter Nineteen

Post Office

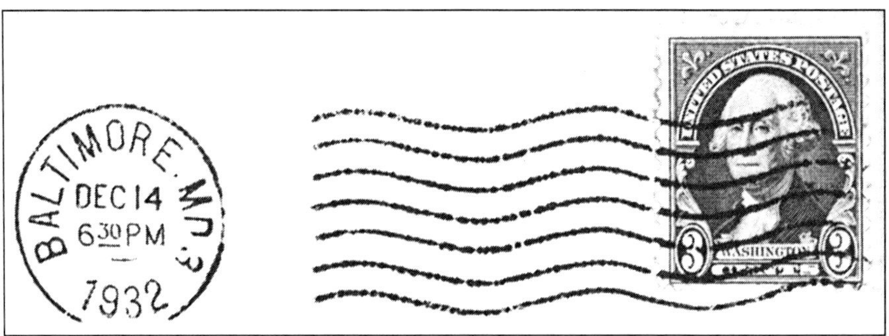

BY MID-DECEMBER, his money from the campaign was all but gone and hopes of generating more were trending futile. He continued submitting manuscripts and ideas, largely to *American Forests*, his mainstay. Companion pieces, "Tree Immigrants" and "Tree Emigrants," were set for January and February publication. He wrote the odd book review for the *News*, worked on Bowman's stories, going round to see Louisiana's demagogue, Senator Huey Long—the megalomaniacal "Kingfish"—and being turned summarily away. The congressman's secretary had promised him Christmas-rush work at the post-office, to start December 20 and last two or three weeks. There would be no pay until the job was done, but he found much to like in the work.

It has been utterly delightful. I distributed the greater part of 20 bags of mail over a marvelous range of homes, and carried back to the central office a sheaf of insured receipts of a size sufficient to wad a cannon.

I would tell you of calling on a Russian princess, but the princess, unfortunately, had moved her place of residence, and I had not the pleasure of meeting her. Of the finest Massachusetts Avenue chateaux, where liveried butlers of colorful nationalities appeared at the door to sign for packages. Of one cadaverous English butler, than whom no caricature of the most typical English butler ever put on stage or screen, could have been better drawn. Of a marvelously pleasant apartment house on New Hampshire Avenue, where I went from door to door, delivering packets; and where everyone was gracious, and kind, and grateful, from the dear old Dutch lady I first met to the gorgeous Tekla Van Norman, as exotic and feminine as her name. Of being chased by a humorous little Scotch terrier in Wesley Heights. Of being sworn at in broken English by a French valet, whose delicate senses had been disorganized because I did not content myself with ringing the doorbell once, discreetly, and waiting for his wuship to come, long moments later, to the door.

Of being smiled upon with heavy-lidded invitation by a siren-like army colonel's young wife. Of a two-minute conversation with a broguish old Irish woman, who wished me "Merry Christmas" with all the spirit of Erin we found in "Playboy of the Western World." Of servants, predominantly Negro, but including also those transplantations of Russian, French, Austrian, Japanese, and Filipino. Of one dear old Negro charwoman who thanked me graciously and simply for the packages as if she had been a princess and I had presented her the gift of my own volition....And an amazing range of kaleidoscopic impressions of people, and personalities, and human abodes.

I am really looking forward to working on Christmas Eve; from all accounts that is the interesting time, when Christmas spirit is at its height, and gifts run all the way from a nip of liquor to whole quarts to take home, and from dimes to dollars. I want that experience, much though I shall miss your sweet companionship, and the pleasant atmosphere of your home.

His post office check arrived January 5—$32.86. "I felt financially relieved, but was brought back to earth when it came to me that I owed Sam $22 and Edythe $11.20. A little figuring will convince you just what my minus balance is."

Chapter Twenty

"Free" Lancing

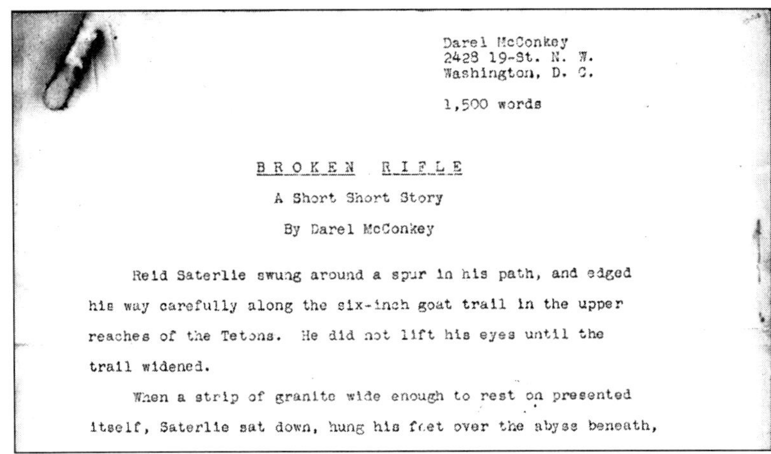

DAREL RETURNED to his typewriter, and Anna struck out on her own. She had moved to another school, Highlands Elementary in Baltimore, but her trolly took an hour and a half each way, and her parents were moving to Silver Spring, Maryland, outside D.C. Anna's room with her new landlords, the Blancks, was in Lansdowne, next door to Baltimore and not far from Johns Hopkins University, where she was taking night classes.

Mr. Blanck was a British consul stationed in Baltimore. Darel, Sam, Edythe, and Adolph's wife, Evelyn, helped Anna move. Darel "enjoyed the Blancks tremendously." He thought Mrs. Blanck a "lovely person" and Mr. Blanck "a brilliant eccentric."

Mr. Blanck, in turn, "put each of you into a pigeon hole," Anna said. "Evelyn occupies the most favored position with you a close second, and Edythe and Sam in the background. He says Sam is completely submerged in Eck and more or less asks her for permission for everything. Eck, he says, talks a great deal and is better informed than Sam. Evelyn he considers quite intellectual and you are headed for fame."

At twenty-five, Anna reveled in her freedom. "There is no one to say me nay if I read or work at math until the small hours. The atmosphere is conducive to all the things we enjoy. I wish you were here. Every evening, Mrs. Blanck gives me a drink of Spanish Port which I imbibe with great pleasure." As representatives of the British crown, the Blancks had diplomatic immunity from Prohibition's depredations.

Just as Anna was spreading her wings, Darel was bogging down in discouragement. The day his post office check arrived, he told her, "I am very much in need of ego-bolstering. One gets such a rotten feeling sometimes, feeling he has useful talents for which there is no market which pays a reasonable return.

"Forgive the tone. I hate to impose it on you yet dislike to miss writing you. Though floundering in the Stygian abyss, I can yet look upward, see the sunlight on your golden hair, catch a gleam of your lovely windblown figure, reach upward with longing, still utter 'I love you' with sincerity, though feeling unutterably alone and without hope.

"But it is temporary. I know my moods. Tomorrow I shall fling a banner of happiness to sunlit winds and repeat, 'I love you!' with the ardor of an avianite newly come back to answer the challenge of the spring."

Two days later, "Anna, darling, I told you I would fling a banner of happiness to the sunlit winds! I think that I have rarely been more pleased to compose for you than this night."

He had completed the first draft of a Bowman story and shown it to him. "He and Mrs. Bowman were very kindly, friendly, and agreeable. He is going to write his own version, then we will combine them. I like that, for I can dress up his written ideas better than I can drag them out of him. I excused myself for five days to get out the *American Forests* yarn."

A fissure appeared in The Alley. "Sam feels that Edythe is being gently let out at the *News*," Darel wrote. "He is considering driving a new cab, ten hours a day, no days off. He is also considering a proposal made by the Whiteners that they exchange apartments with us. Adolph's mother is coming to live with them, and they haven't room for her. Sam is very much in the dumps. I feel intensely sorry for him. Edythe is inclined to poke fun at him, which doesn't help matters."

A salaried means of survival bent Darel's attention. Darcy Wilson—with whom he had collaborated on a pageant in Somerset, Pennsylvania, during extension service days—wrote offering him four months of training in social work in New York at $60 a month with a raise once the job began. The money was attractive, but Darel had reservations. Would not such a move be a retreat from his hard-fought investment in writing? Should he take the offer just while the economy recovered? What might that do to his life's trajectory?

"I want to be a writer," he told Anna, "Not a social worker."

D.C.'s half million people were crowd enough for him; New York's seven million too many. But his greatest objection to "going metropolitan," as he put it, was the distance from Anna. Anna's reaction was the same. "I hope you won't go so far away," but her hope was, "due purely to my desire to be undeprived of your companionship."

Still, he might consider, if he could finish the current Bowman story, if he could wait to hear back on a book proposal. Or wait to learn whether publicity for the National Symphony Orchestra was on or off.

He was still angling for that post despite the previous summer's unsuccess. His symphonic dissertations to Anna read like dress rehearsals for the part.

He had contacts that should have helped. The *News*'s music critic, Ruth Howell, had once referenced "Pop" Russell in a note, and Pop's wife was at least as significant as Pop. Plus there was Charlie Wood....

But let Darel tell it: "The first time I heard the Glink number I was with 'Pop' Russell, that fine old man I have often mentioned. The concert was by the Philharmonic, with Bruno Walter conducting." Critic John O'Rourke, the National Symphony's publicity man, had likened Walter to "Charlie Wood drying a head of lettuce."

"When I first met Charlie, in Connecticut, I said, 'Oh, yes, you're the fellow who dries lettuce!'

"Well, it recalled the Russells—dear Mrs. Russell, who was so kind to me. When I was near starvation, she would invite me to her place and urge upon me all manner of food. And Mrs. Russell's insistence to Kindler [the National Symphony's music director] and others, that I was the man to handle publicity." Certain "recent events," (unspecified) had occurred which Darel thought removed the obstacle to his applying for the job. It paid $1,000 for the season, "and could I use $1,000!" He wrote Mrs. Russell, asking to see her. "I believe this time there is a good chance."

He waited nearly three weeks. At the beginning of February, the Symphony's marketing manager, Mr. Cappel, told him that on Feb 9 the symphony was offering a five-number program. Darel was to write five stories, subject to Mr. Cappel's approval, each featuring a number, to send to Washington's five top papers. Darel would be paid when they appeared. Cappel promised further work and, significantly, had not yet chosen the season's publicity person.

"Here at last is the opportunity I have sought! It is only a precarious toehold, but I have so much faith in the idea and my ability to carry it out, that I see work of this kind right through the remainder of the season. I think I can make myself sufficiently valuable to stand a good chance of stepping into the publicity position for another season."

When Darel arrived in Mr. Cappel's office, who should be there but Pop Russell? He and Darel shook hands, impressing Mr. Cappel. Like everyone else, Mr. Cappel greatly admired Russell. "Where did you meet him?" Mr. Cappel asked. Presumably Darel told Mr. Cappel, but alas did not tell us.

Mr. Cappel gave generously, discussing ideas, and letting Darel show how to slant a story. They touched on the "Pathétique." Darel confessed he hadn't heard it live but had listened to a broadcast, whereupon Mr. Cappel declared that there was something about a live performance that couldn't be got via radio, something about the soloist, about the conductor's entry, his charging the symphony, and the symphony's giving something to the crowd. "It is a living miracle. I have seen it in the faces of people coming out of the hall, [but] I don't know how to present the fact."

To which Darel chimed, "I know how. Let us first become curious as to this 'living miracle.' What causes it? Who could tell us? A psychologist! I would invite an eminent psychologist to the concert and interview him afterward. He would say the thing you want said. I know Dr. Sprowls, who has written several books on psychology and writes 'Everyday Psychology' for the *Star* and other papers." Darel didn't reveal his personal opinion of Sprowls, but Sprowls had a big name and would jump at the chance to enlarge it further.

"See him about it," said Mr. Cappel, then mentioned a scientist at the Bureau of Standards who photographed sounds and scoffed at the idea that a Stradivarius would have smoother tones than newer instruments. "I thought of engaging him in an argument with our music director, Dr. Kindler, but Kindler is so busy I don't want to take his time."

"There's no need to take his time," Darel suggested. "Just get him to make a statement and have your scientist disagree; then have the respective sounds photographed, settle the argument, and, incidentally, get some publicity out of it."

Darel mentioned a blind man he had seen at a concert.

"Do you think there's a story in that?" Cappel asked.

Darel did. Cappel showed him a letter from the National Library for the Blind acknowledging receipt of six tickets to be distributed to six blind people. "Take that letter along," he told Darel. "Make a story out of it."

Darel bubbled to Anna, "It is a new world I'm looking at tonight. I'm happy about it, and happy that there is such a person as you in it." Among the gems he unearthed in researching the articles was a duel Handel had fought over playing harpsichord for an opera.

Writing is one thing. Getting published is completely different, and there lay the rub. Darel wrote the pieces, but Cappel wasn't paying unless they were published, and it was up to Darel to get them published.

The *Evening Star* building, 11th and Penn, N.W.

At the *Times-Herald*, Sunday editor William Moore was not in due to illness, but Mabelle Jennings, who wrote the "lowbrow" theatrical column, was there and took a story. Darel blessed her for that.

The "very young and inexperienced Sunday editor" at the *Washington Post* liked the material but didn't know if there was a place for it. He would show it to the managing editor and let Darel know on the morrow. "On the morrow," the Sunday editor had not yet been seen, and we don't know whether he ever was.

Darel visited the marble-facaded *Evening Star* building on Pennsylvania Avenue, across from the Old Post Office, both of which have escaped the wrecking ball some ninety years on. The paper's music editor was out but

Darel resolved to track her down. The next day, when a call failed to find her, he decided to put off seeing her until he had something else ready.

The *News*'s music critic, Ruth Howell, told him his type of writing belonged in the symphony's program notes, not in the newspapers. She wished Darel could do the notes. "Tell Mr. Cappel that the present ones are lousy." She also had reservations about the "living miracle," live- vs. radio-performance piece with Sprowls.

But Darel was nothing if not optimistic. He told Anna, "I am not discouraged by what happened today. [The *Times-Herald*'s] Mabelle Jennings took his Bach-Handel story with no questions. I want to study these other personalities and see what they require." The *Star* used one piece.

Mrs. Russell finally got back to him. John O'Rourke, who had likened Bruno Walter to Charlie Wood drying lettuce, was not going to be used again. Mr. Cappel was training a young man whose experience consisted of four years at The George Washington University's student paper, *The Hatchet*, to write things the way he wanted them. Darel was optimistic to the end, but the post did not pan out. Mrs. Russell told him, "If you can keep your head above water in these times, you are more than good."

Chapter Twenty-One

Trouble in Paradise

WINTER HAD THE ALLEY in its grip. "Feeling rather absurdly brave," Darel wrote Anna, "as I shiver beside a tepid radiator. Very little has happened in this Polar Region of Washington today.

"I look forward most eagerly, darling, to seeing you this weekend, though I may not be quite up to par after braving the rigors of this Antarctic Alley for the past week."

Dr. Sprowls proposed that Darel rewrite some of his "Everyday Psychology" columns for him to sell as pamphlets on newsstands. "I could write several people's books on that basis. All of which is very pleasing to the ego, but doesn't pay the bills."

Despite cash flow's unreliability, Darel managed to squeeze out the "mazuma" for seats to the Pulitzer-prize winning play, *The Green Pastures*. Though written by a white playwright, it presented eighteen biblical scenes ostensibly through Negro eyes. The Lord, sometimes walking among people and sometimes watching them from afar, was both a guide to and an observer of humanity.

There were no white roles. Even God was black. "I have for about two years," Darel told Anna, "had an intense yen to see this play, and I know you would enjoy it too." After seeing it, they raved over the Hall Johnson Choir's accompanying spiritual numbers.

Three years later, Warner Brothers released a film version, a rare all-black Hollywood production, and it mirrored the day's race relations. What strikes modern sensitivities is the stereotyping of black dialect and society. Had that aspect struck my parents, I'm sure they would have said something, but they didn't. The movie showed white conceits of Negroes.

Yet blacks largely applauded the film. They were starved, waiting year on year, decade on decade, century on century, to see themselves reflected, recognized, validated in the mainstream. Finally, there they were, not in small roles subordinate to whites, but as the story's main characters. They settled for the stereotyping to get the movie out. The cast comported itself with dignity, and the film was a box-office success.

Still, progress was excruciatingly slow. The next major all-black film, Metro-Goldwyn-Mayer's *Cabin in the Sky*, waited six more years, until 1943. But *Green Pastures* had not been first. In 1929 MGM had released *Hallelujah*. In fourteen years, three mainstream movies, but a body of black, *non-*Hollywood cinema, including westerns, stretched back to the silent era.

The Alley fissure widened. Edythe was going on about homosexuality. Sam refused to believe she had lesbian traits, and Darel thought what she called lesbianism could be explained otherwise. Edythe objected, "Darel, in the letters you write to Anna, you use the same endearing terms that I used in writing to her several years ago."

She had said the same thing to Anna at the Blancks. Anna hadn't answered, and Edythe evidently took silence for agreement.

The situation clarified over the next two months. Anna had been Edythe's cherished friend since high school. As Anna and Darel's relationship blossomed, Edythe felt sidelined. There's a hint that when Darel first appeared, Edythe thought his attentions were on her, not Anna, and as the truth emerged, she lost that connection, too. Edythe generally blamed Anna, but Darel wasn't totally immune from her blandishments.

Dr. Sprowls "strolled in this evening with his customary scowling aloofness," Darel wrote to Anna, "and inquired as to the whereabouts of the Alley inhabitants." He recited the various "whereaboutses."

"Has Anna Schuddeboom gone back?" Sprowls asked.

"Yes."

"She is a beautiful girl."

"I know it."

"Cold as hell, though, isn't she?"

"Ummmm. More or less," Darel said. Then, "Doctor, how would you explain that?"

"I don't try to explain it. Why the hell should I?"

"It is in the realm of psychology," Darel said. "I thought you might know something about it."

His knowledge being challenged, Sprowls came out with his answer: "Homosexuality. Most accepted theory."

Did he think that the right solution in this case? He did, but wasn't interested.

"But I am," Darel said.

"Then take what I tell you or go on in your ignorance."

Would a girl like the one in question have an active relationship with some other woman?

Nary a doubt of it.

Would she admit it?

"Rather die first. Rather commit suicide."

"So you have been tried in your absence," he told Anna, "on a charge of lesbianism, and convicted in the Sprowlian court of last appeal."

"I pity the man. How could anyone in his line be so colossally ignorant of human nature?"

Anna and Darel began avoiding Edythe when together. Edythe responded well to the selective exposure, giving Anna and Darel hope that the rift might heal. Sam continued friends with both.

Initially, there was a sense of mischief in getting past Edythe. "Anna, darling, your getaway this morning was perfect!" Darel wrote. "The conspiracy worked so superlatively that no one could have guessed it. Your first two steps on the stairs bothered me a little, but after that I could not hear another sound. The amused content of our strategy's success has been with me all day."

Sam was a willing confederate, and seemed to get as much of a kick out of the subterfuge as Darel did. He told how Anna had reached the train just in the nick of time. Later, Sam and Edythe dined with Anna's parents, and Sam almost choked when Harry asked him about taking Anna to the train, but Edythe didn't seem to hear.

"My belief that she is feeling better continues," Darel wrote. "I think you should write her early this week. She has, after all, many endearing qualities, and I don't want to lose her friendship any more than you do. The tiff seems to be wearing off, but I still think it would be unwise for us to see her together."

Anna responded, "I'm happy that Eck's attitude is improving." She invited Edythe and Evelyn to spend a night with her at the Blancks in Baltimore, but wished "we could all enjoy 'The Alley' together again."

Sam had a talk with Edythe, and Darel thought he saw improvement. Sam felt he could bring her around in a week or two.

They kept hopeful, but Edythe could not bring herself to compromise. She continued treating Anna coolly, like a casual acquaintance—retaliation, Darel thought, for the hurt she felt Anna had done her, and protection from being hurt again.

Nor was Darel immune to her blandishments. He came home to find Sam and Edythe finishing some pecan rolls that Betty had left. Darel lied that he'd already had some then gone to see Bowman.

Edythe, suspecting the lie, laughed. "Oh! That's too good!"

"I played the innocent," Darel said, "looked blank, but things were happening to my emotions." Later, Edythe explained herself. She had told Sam, "Let's hurry up and eat the rolls before Darel comes." And as he entered, there she was she was chewing her roll all around so he couldn't ask for any of it.

Sam confirmed the explanation. Edythe joked about how badly she treated Darel, who took that as the nearest thing to an apology she could manage. Sam agreed.

"Sweetheart," Darel wrote Anna, "try not to be disheartened about the Alley situation. I shall watch it for signs of improvement, and for any opportunity to help."

Anna's hope soldiered on. On February 8, she wrote, "I had a communication from Eck today. She is delightfully frank as usual and I like her the better for it. She is a dear person and I feel optimistic about the return to our old Alley relationship." Edythe was an intelligent conversationalist and an accomplished pianist. Often, she entertained the Alley with Beethoven, Tchaikovsky, and others. "I appreciate," Anna told Darel, "the care with which you have gleaned information to help me with my part of this problem. She says I'm welcome at the house."

Anna visited the Alley over the weekend while Darel busied himself elsewhere. "I hope," he said, "that your first weekend since the armistice in Edythe's company has been pleasant and promising of a return to the Alley days gone by."

But by February 27, hope dimmed again. "The Alley situation continues pleasant insofar as I am concerned," Darel wrote, "but there is apparently very little change insofar as *we* are concerned. Sam says Edythe could be very happy granting a favor, but would bridle if asked for it. She must feel magnanimous, and so far she has not felt like granting us the use of part of her house. She is apparently enjoying the power to withhold, recouping some of the injury she feels was done her.

"I am trying to be as considerate as possible but feel little hope of getting back to the old basis. Edythe is so thoroughly complexed on the subject that she will not change. This weekend was proof of it. You and I took advantage of last weekend's pleasantness by using the apartment this weekend while Edythe went to the theater. She knew how the interval would be utilized."

It threatened her control of the situation. Edythe told Anna not to come for the opera broadcast the following weekend because she wasn't working—i.e., would be at home—and Anna would not be welcome.

Anna's father ratified the others' suppositions. "Whatever your relationship with Anna may be," Harry told Darel, "it is that which hurts Eck. She believed Anna's sole interest was in her, and after you became intimate with Anna, that was broken down. I might say that the same thing is true of you—Eck believed that your principal interest was in her."

Another part to that conversation opened concerns that grew in significance as Anna and Darel's relationship entered its next phase. Harry told Darel he had not "bothered his head" about their relationship—though he had tried to keep Anna's mother from worrying. He hadn't said anything because "young people go their own way (I went mine)."

"I was a little stupefied," Darel said, "but admired him for his attitude. Here was an unexpected demonstration of parental broad-mindedness. He revealed a knowledge of the underlying psychology which I thought quite keen.

"This conversation did reveal that your mother is worried about our relationship, which I hadn't apprehended, but it gave me favorable insight into your father's attitude. I doubted the likelihood of parents—or even one parent—being so broadminded. Mayhap you will find things in it I didn't see."

Anna did find things. It was nice that her parents assumed a broadminded pose, but her father was just as worried as her mother. All they had in America were their children and a few friends, and they didn't want to lose the respect of either. Those few friends were more like those they'd known in Holland than your typical, smug church-goers. Her parents would sanction her and Darel's relationship so long as it didn't "transcend barriers which they consider necessary to real happiness."

Sexual barriers? What else? And, "Could they be convinced that my happiness will not be impaired, and also rationalize the situation to friends and relatives abroad, they would endorse our situation whole-heartedly." As long as Anna was happy, and friends and relatives weren't scandalized, it was OK.

Anna and Darel were still inventing stories to hide the more intimate aspects of their relationship from her parents. For one weekend visit, "Make it a piano concert, something that wouldn't be in the papers. Here's a good one: Mr. Cappel gave me tickets to a special concert, admission by invitation only. You don't know who the pianist is, somebody local, but good."

At the end of January, Adolph lost his job, and with it his braggadocio that "anybody can get a job." He floundered "in the depths of a blue funk," was "completely whipped." Evelyn refused to take his suggestion that she look for work. All he'd do if she did, she said, would be to "sit around and act licked."

She hung on for nearly a month, but on February 22, Darel wrote to Anna, "The final act, apparently, in the Evelyn-Adolph tragedy played this afternoon."

It started when Dr. Sprowls dropped in on Sam and Darel. They adjourned to Adolph's and sat down to a game of rumme [*sic*] with another Alley denizen named Davis. At a point, Darel was 70 cents ahead, having started from nothing, but staked it all on one hand, which the doctor won.

Sprowls felt so good he said he could play any man's game, so Darel introduced him to blackjack at 5 cents a hand. When he'd won 40 cents, Sprowls said he 'didn't like that game.' Sam came in, and they played draw poker. Then Adolph came in bearing "a thunderous scowl. 'I want to see you,' he told Evelyn and they went into the hall."

When they came back, Evelyn said, "Adolph is mad. He doesn't want you-all to play while he isn't here. He says it causes talk."

Darel and Sprowls retreated to a sea-food counter on Columbia Road and downed 20 raw oysters and clams. The doctor bought an extra dozen for Sam and Evelyn, but Evelyn didn't want any, so Sam and Darel ate more, and put the rest in the icebox for Edythe.

Darel was in the bedroom talking to Sam. Evelyn came in to borrow a bag. She was going for "a little visit." She didn't disclose her destination, but they figured she was going to spend some time with Betty. It looked like Evelyn's matrimonial bridges had been burned.

Davis and Adolph drank and played the radio loudly all evening. When Davis tried to leave, Adolph wouldn't let him, and suddenly Darel felt sorry for him. "Few people," he said, "could be more lost than Adolph. But," he added, "that marriage has always been hopeless. I hope there will be no further attempts to patch it up."

Davis tried again to leave. Darel could hear them in the hall. "I don't feel sorry for you," Davis said. "You'll have to crawl in there and sleep alone tonight." The radio "was going like a locomotive" and Adolph boasted, "I'm goin' to keep the whole neighborhood awake," A bottle bumped down the hall and collided against Darel's door.

Chapter Twenty-Two

Down and Out

Roosevelt's inauguration

MARCH 4, 1933, was Inauguration Day, where Franklin Delano Roosevelt famously asserted his "firm belief that the only thing we have to fear is fear itself." That event strikes us as a parting of clouds, but for those living through it, the day began and ended like hundreds before it.

In Germany, Adolph Hitler had been Chancellor for two months.

Darel had been hoping for inaugural work of some kind through National Geographic, but it didn't materialize. Sam's junk-man father was planning to sell sandwiches because the license was only a dollar, where it was $25 for balloons and souvenirs. National income was less than half its pre-crash level. A quarter of the work force was scrounging for jobs. State relief and private charities were running out of money. Darel was eating 16¢ meals at the Penny Restaurant. "Migawd, but I am hungry!" he once exclaimed. "Excuse it, please, while I go up to Mr. McZilch's tramps' kitchen for something to eat."

Anna had met an elderly woman who "was a most piteous victim of the depression. She lives in a large capacious house with the remnants of excellent furniture. She lives however in its basement and has been selling her furniture to eke out an existence. People at one time befriended by her will have nothing to do with her, and her loneliness was forcibly expressed when she wept with pleasure at a simple invitation to a P.T.A. meeting."

For Darel, freelancing was OK as far as it went. Few people ever pressed it harder than he did. He conceived a book, *Magellan to Mattern*, about the history of global circumnavigation, timed for release at the end of James Mattern's attempt to break the round-the-world flight record. Around that same time, he discovered Lewis and Clark, who were not then well known, and started developing plans to retrace their route and write a book about that, even drafting a Guggenheim grant application because "no satisfactory book on their journey has ever been written."

He put great effort into a short fiction, "Eros and Psyche." Scribner's Magazine rejected it. He advertised as someone who could read to invalids, the elderly, and children. Freelancing was OK as far as it went, but it wasn't going far enough.

He told Earle Kauffman, assistant editor at *American Forests*, he wanted a job. Kauffman had heard rumor of a public relations position opening at the Forest Service. "A job could hardly be more fitted to me," Darel wrote to Anna. "It pays $3000."

Kauffman would check it out. "I tried calling him this evening, but his phone is unlisted, so it must wait for tomorrow. Meantime, I ponder what splendid disposition I could make of $3000. I *want* that job, and propose to have it if there is such a thing."

But in the Depression, dozens vied for every opening. We hear no more of Forest Service employment.

Into the mix of potential jobs fell a "camp for peregrinating youth," nineteen miles outside D.C., being organized by General Glassford, hero of the Bonus Expeditionary march. After Darel's work at Ogelbay Park and Pocono People's College, who better than he to bring experience to such a venture? He would, in fact, take anything, even secretarial work.

Charlie Wood's identity remains stubbornly elusive, but it was he whom Darel asked to make the contact with Glassford. Darel was shy approaching Charlie on the subject. Their association had not been based on personal economics. "It was hard for me to talk of earning an occasional couple of dollars typing in Glassford's office, and working in the camp at subsistence plus 10 cents a day. It is hard to tell what will happen, but there seems a pretty good chance of picking up a stray dollar doing stenographic work, and entering camp life on a dime-a-day basis."

But nothing lay down that way either. His mother, confusing Glassford's project with Roosevelt's Civilian Conservation Corps, said "I am glad you did not get in on the Forest camp work. I hear it is very demoralizing for the boys." She had told him to "be sure to vote for the drys," i.e., the Republicans. She took a different tone later, however. "Mrs. Roosevelt is so nice to help people out. Go to her if you cannot manage. She may find you a buyer for your book or help you in some way."

From the bottom of the financial pit, any few shekels brought exaggerated relief. When Anna's father asked Darel to write an ad for him, you'd have thought the heavens had opened. Another time, news that *American Forests* had accepted a story sent him into such a paroxysm of laughter that Sam worried for his sanity.

There's no record of Darel's ever having joined a bread line, but he ate often at the Penny Restaurant and left a rare personal glimpse of that establishment:

Sam and I drove to the Penny Restaurant in the 1900 block of Pennsylvania Avenue and got breakfast. The place is operated by Guy Glassford, son of the General, and is financed by Bernarr McFadden.[§§] We had a bowl of cracked wheat each, with brown sugar and cream, a square of whole-wheat apple pie, and coffee. It cost exactly 16 cents for the two

---

[§§] A celebrated health and fitness advocate.

of us and was a most satisfying meal. The coffee costs 1¢ a cup, with a penny extra for cream and a like consideration for sugar.

This evening he dropped me off at the restaurant again. I had two hamburgers, a bowl of baked beans, cracked wheat with cream and brown sugar, two slices of whole-wheat raisin bread, butter, and coffee, for 13 cents. It was a complete, wholesome, and satisfying meal. I want to take you there the coming weekend. How about Saturday dinner? Even with paying my fare on the trolley to come back home, I had a very fine meal for exactly 20½ cents.

It is cafeteria style. About 50 people were being served when I was there, five or six of them women. You eat from your tray while standing at a tall table. The average person was of the white-collar variety, slightly threadbare, of much higher type than you would expect. I suspect that some of the better-dressed people were those affected by the bank moratorium.

Two middle-aged men of the lean but slightly shopworn white-collar variety were at my table. I caught the phrase "he's just a figurehead to justify the evasion." It was far from Bowery language, and I listened. They talked earnestly, communistically. I failed to catch the thread of their discussion or I might have joined them. But I was interested in the other people in the place.

Some few were working men, in rough clothing, but clean. Two or three were cab-drivers. One was a Boy Scout. Perhaps a dozen were very well dressed. The women were mostly of the government-worker clerical type, though two were of the type of Sam's mother. There was one man with his little girl. At least two of those patronizing the place were patently students.

It is amazing to me that such things could be. I could satisfactorily eat 3-cent breakfasts the rest of my life, provided grapefruit and oranges might be substituted in their season. They are feeding from 2,000 to 2,200 people a day.

His reference to the bank moratorium suggests he ate there during Roosevelt's "bank holiday," March 6 to 9, to stanch the hemorrhage of banking assets. It was the new administration's first act.

Banks hold only enough depositors' money to cover daily transactions plus a buffer. The rest they invest in interest-yielding loans, mortgages, securities.

Those instruments are carried as assets though the money itself is out with the borrowers, not physically in the banks. When the stock market crashed, depositors raced to retrieve their deposits and banks couldn't cover them. Thus, the bank failures and contraction in the money supply. On March 9, an emergency joint session of Congress authorized the Federal Reserve to supply banks with the currency needed to meet demand. The stock market rebounded fifteen percent, the largest one-day gain in history. By the end of March, two-thirds of the money withdrawn had been redeposited.

Two weeks after Evelyn's breakup with Adolph, Darel walked down Massachusetts Avenue, "grand with its rows of trees" as Anna once put it, past Thomas Circle, to 11th Street to see her for the first time since she left the Alley. She looked "quite chic," Darel said, "in a tailored brown suit and pert little hat" with an air of self-assurance he hadn't seen before. She pitied Adolph. Not enough to go back to him, but she had agreed to see him the coming Saturday. Darel advised her not to.

She advised Darel, in return, to leave the Alley. He'd told her the events of two weekends past, and that he had given up attempts to resurrect the old companionship. He hadn't moved, mainly for financial reasons, but she reminded him there *were* rooms as reasonable as the one he had. If he could get within walking distance of the Copper Cafeteria, he could live quite reasonably. She urged him to make the shift when *American Forests* paid him.

"I have been struggling with the problem of moving," he told Anna, and have just about concluded to do it. I no longer belong here. I am the mote in the eye, the fly in the ointment, the hair in the soup. Evelyn said, 'The Alley gets to you,' giving it almost a sinister, animal, personality. 'I liked it too,' she told me. 'But it gets you.'

"It looks like a rebuilding and rearrangement of living. The next thing you know I will be doing carpentry for Adolph or pecking a typewriter for Glassford. At other times I may be researching stories for *American Forests*. Between the three, I may be able to pick up stray bits of change which will allow me to live."

On March 15, he took a room in the old Capitol Hotel, 1015 13th St. "This hotel had its splendor in days long past. Its architecture is passé and its halls and rooms are dingy as a black silk suit, frayed at the cuffs and lapels. My room is small but clean, third floor, fronting on 13th, facing west. It is probably the best I could do for the money, and by dint of some things to hang on the walls I believe I can make it livable."

A communal bathroom was down the hall. "I like the deliberate, kindly, pachydermal manager, and hope to wheedle a few extra comforts from him in time." The hotel was diagonally across K Street from Franklin Square Park, seven blocks from the Copper Cafeteria, four from the public library, and within walking distance of most downtown places.

"Were you ever alone with God in a blowsy hotel room?" he asked Anna.

"That is where I am. God and I were about to sit down, smoke a cigarette, and talk it over, but it suddenly occurred to me that I should much rather talk with you. So I opened the window and God obligingly flew out.

"Surrounded by the most miscellaneous collection of baggages, I dedicate this room to an uncertain future. Before Saturday, it is incumbent upon me to earn $3 for next week's rent. With the utmost brazenness, I paid $1.50 for the remainder of this week, with the assurance that we could start from scratch and make it regular."

On April 1, Sam and Edythe left the Alley for a Georgetown apartment—P St. just off Wisconsin Avenue. Georgetown was not the upscale neighborhood it is today. I've heard people say it was a slum, but have found no documentary support for that description. Many residents were poor, but people of means lived there in great houses. As late as the 1960s, students could find affordable housing there. Industry lined Water Street—a lumber yard—still doing business when I bought my first house in 1971—a flour mill, a cement works, a foundry, a meat rendering plant you could still smell all the way to Foggy Bottom when I started college in 1962.

Baltimore and Ohio locomotives distributed smoke and freight along the river front. B&O sold its defunct C&O Canal to the Park Service in 1938. Up the hill on M Street were two hardware stores and a Woolworth's. P Street, where Sam and Edythe moved, is still farther up.

Chapter Twenty-Three

Silent Partner

ANNA AND DAREL continued sorting issues, Anna much the silent partner, to Darel's ongoing puzzlement. "I have wondered how it happens that I spend hours and pages telling you about my personal predicaments and successes, whereas you never breathe a word about the things you encounter at school, etc."

"Am I stimulating to you? You so seldom say anything that it is hard for me to tell." And yet she was able to write "beautiful letters that have great depth of thought and understanding, and great beauty in them. Do I talk so much that I don't give you a chance to express the things you are thinking? If I do, please say so, and I'll take steps to curb my verbosity."

"No," she said, "you never talk too much for me. I always enjoy your conversation." She then bored to the crux of the matter. "I've been trying for quite a while to overcome the habit of making mental rejoinders without expressing them verbally. I think I know how it started, and though I can find no trace at present of the reasons I once had for keeping my opinions to myself, the habit persists." As children, she and Margaret were looked down on as foreigners. Adopting a cool, indifferent, enigmatic persona had gotten Anna a place among her schoolmates, but she'd been trying to overcome her silent rejoinders ever since.

Darel took a stab at psychoanalysis. He thought a negative childhood father fixation had induced her to adopt a pattern of not having or showing great affection to anyone. "I make that statement with a certain hesitancy and mental reservation," he said. "I don't know enough about psychology and must maintain an open mind until the matter is proved to my entire satisfaction."

We never learned the extent of her father's abuse. There's no evidence it went beyond stern discipline, but she was unequivocal about having had an unhappy homelife growing up. To cite a Native American writer whose name escapes me, "When you've been abused, it makes you afraid to love someone; you feel like you're damaged."

After a weekend visit, Darel remarked, "Threshing out the gloomy side of our personal situation had its favorable aftermath. We chewed the gall, made wry faces, protested having our noses held while castor oil was administered. But we swallowed it, and its cathartic effect became operative. We were ready then to leave the psychological sick-bed and become enjoyably alive again.

"You were more communicative, as if the articulation of our desire to voice conflicting opinions had released something of your personality too long submerged. I liked your assertiveness. Please keep it up. I pray that I may not inhibit you; don't let me. Stand up for your own verbalization, and know that you have my inner applause."

Anna "appreciated you even more than usual this weekend, if that is possible. There is one thing that could have made it more perfect and that is more time with you."

Another visit built on that one. "This has been a very happy weekend, Darel. It has given beauty and contentment, and has passed leaving the feeling that many problems have been solved and that 'God's in his heav'n; all's right with the world.'"

She wrote, however, "May the day soon arrive when there will be no chance of your thinking that I am paying a price in our relationship. As near perfection as your companionship has been, there is incompleteness when I am aware of a need in you that I seem incapable of satisfying, and I want with all of my being to learn how to fill that need."

Darel shot back, "Sweetheart, I have never meant to imply that I thought you felt you were 'paying' for our relationship." He had only posed "paying" as one explanation, to himself, for her unresponsiveness.

I am more than assured by what you have said. Please, darling Valkyrie maiden, trust me and have faith in me, and in time I shall introduce you to a realm of experience which will make life more deep, and full, and meaningful to you.

Never before have you made the expressions of endearment that came from you Friday, and never have you with such sweet confidence cushioned your head on my shoulder, and nestled there with such apparent security. It is difficult to say how these things made me feel, but it was sweetness beyond expression.

I think it was these things which made parting from you so poignant tonight. Your going seemed a departure it had not in times before. It was with a feeling of absolute aloneness that I saw you go. And it has taken me hours to recapture the stability, the sereneness, and patience that can shorten the days ahead.

There was such an upwelling that I wanted to pour out to you. A thousand endearments struggling for expression, a mesh and a lacery of emotions that paralyzed my vocal organs, and the only things I could find to say were merest banalities. And when your dear face, framed by the window, moved beyond my vision, there was a vacuum, an abyss, a void that cried for you, and made all other things of no import.

But now I can think of you, slender and graceful and straight, crowned with Holland's gold, moving across your days and meeting with happiness the beauty life brings you, and it heartens me to look on my own coming days with more sereneness, and friendliness. Yours is a strengthening soul, and the thought of you lends beauty and strength.

She wrote back to him, "I wish I had some way of telling you of the complete satisfaction I've derived from your companionship.

"I grow more fond of you and miss you."

She continued having trouble giving in to intimacy, but Darel told her the intellectual intensity between them more than made up for the deficit. He was consoled, too, by something Evelyn said. "Anna is a person no one will ever possess."

"Possession," Darel said, "is the wreckage of many man-and-woman relationships."

At the end of March, she told Darel, "Having told three different people that I don't want to teach next year, I returned to school today in a more settled mental attitude."

In the midst of the Depression, she would forsake the security of job and income and move to D.C. to risk poverty with a married man whom she loved, to live (in words from the screwball comedy, *Blessed Event*) "without benefit of clergy," more common in those days than we tend to imagine.

Margaret told Helen, "You have no idea how much that hurt the family." Anna had been tutoring private students of evenings, and her landlady, Mrs. Blanck, suggested she advertise to help immigrants preparing for naturalization. "If I enjoy it and am successful, that may provide a means of livelihood next winter."

At Easter, Darel took Anna home to meet the family. "There will be mountains, and lovely valleys, and trees in bud and blossom, and flowers beside the road, and the inviting sweep of panorama and sky," he told her, "and, presently we shall be at Dixie, and you shall glimpse the home which 'borned me' and reared me and guided me into that indeterminate something I represent today. You will find joy in the round green hills of my nativity, and beauty of line and color in the land of which I am organically a part."

When it came to the actual visit, there's not a word on how the family took to Darel's girlfriend. Anna interested Darel's sister, Gladys, in learning the "pianna." Three weeks later, his mother wrote Darel that she hadn't seen enough of him while he was there.

Chapter Twenty-Four

Roosevelt's Moral Equivalent of War

Civilian Conservation Corps Camp

SPRING WAS COMING. Anna's school year was still in session, and she'd not yet made her fateful move. Darel found landscaping work for Anna's father.

Darel took *Magellan to Mattern* to Jesse Hildebrand, assistant editor at *National Geographic*. That an editor would talk to a writer is totally at odds with current practice. Today they rarely even bother with rejection slips. But Hildebrand not only sat down with Darel, he gave him some top-tier advice.

Darel wanted to popularize the history of global circumnavigation, but Hildebrand told him that wasn't what the public was looking for. Besides Willem Van Loon, a popular author of youth literature, had already done what Darel contemplated with *Van Loon's Geography: The Story of the World*. The difference between Darel and Van Loon was that Van Loon's name alone would sell his work, whereas Darel's might only get him a library reference.

"He marveled that I, ten years in the newspaper game, should so run to librarian's methods," he wrote to Anna.

"Instead of an idea," Hildebrand told him, "you want to group your efforts around a person or a place." There was demand for explorers' biographies. Lewis & Clark should do well.

"The book that is waiting to be written," said Hildebrand, "is the rapid development of commercial aviation." The industry might even subsidize a book showing how accessible air travel was.

Routes already established were almost as impressive as railroad routes. Airlines wanted people to think of flying as normal as travel by rail or bus. Airport architecture was as distinctive as the architecture of railroad stations. What was involved in buying tickets? Could you eat and sleep on a plane? The airlines would back such a book. The new drama of the air merely waited the writing.

There's no indication that Darel followed the lead. It would take time to adjust his point of view, he said. He hadn't wanted to believe that the "frothy, casual, evanescent newspaper type of thing" was all people really wanted. Somewhere there must be a readership eager to "get up to their necks" in ideas. Hildebrand, "one of the best minds in the editorial business" had schooled him otherwise. Darel told Anna, "If a change in my way of thinking will result in sales, it will be one of the best things that has ever happened to me."

Bowman was getting into the coal business and couldn't seem to focus on his stories unless reminded. That lack of interest affected Darel's motivation to work on them. At a point, Bowman mentioned an out-of-work newspaperman who had started his own syndicate. Thinking Bowman meant to have the fellow syndicate the stories, Darel met him at the swank Willard Hotel, waited while he talked to various "sensuous, sloppy, selfish, assured business men" in the lobby. "It had been so long since I had seen this type that I suddenly found how far removed from them I had come to be."

The guy gave Darel an aggressive spiel, but Darel saw only a man who had 'no conception of what it is to slave for bread; who didn't know what insecurity was; didn't know what the depression could do to one; what it felt like to have your last dollar in your pocket with no certain dollars ahead; what it meant to face starvation.'

"I wanted to escape his cocksureness, to bury myself in library and books. I realized what this depression has done to me; how blow after blow, deprivation after deprivation, it has led me to seek security on any terms, no matter how humble; how it has unfitted me for economic warfare. I was conscious of unpressed trousers, too-large collar, unshined shoes, no hat. I fled the influence that made me conscious of these things."

Bowman had not, in fact, thought of hooking up with the fellow but of going in with Darel on their own syndicate. But, "He has really been pushing his coal business, and says he has made more money than if he had been in Congress."

Darel stopped by the Forest Service where he'd left a job application. "A girl said, 'Yes, Mr. McConkey, we are holding the place for you until you are available on June 15. Didn't you get our telegram?' It sounded like Greek to me. 'What's this about June 15?' I asked. She looked up the wire. It was to a T. W. McConkey at Ithaca, N.Y. My own application, apparently, has been shelved."

He kept his typewriter keys clean, but seems to have saved fresh ribbons for manuscript submissions, using old ones for personal letters. He pounded the keys so hard they left indentations—as visible on the back of the page as on the front—but little ink, and they were almost impossible to read.

Then, "Out of the blue came a vital connection that would join two things and make a first-class story," he wrote Anna. "I have told you of William James's essay, 'The Moral Equivalent of War.' Something suddenly clicked! '*Roosevelt*'s Moral Equivalent of War!'"

In 1906, American philosopher William James had proposed satisfying our warlike impulses by conscription into service in "the immemorial human warfare against nature" instead of in warfare between nations. He would use military discipline, barracks life, physical conditioning in those programs. "New energies and hardihoods" must carry forward "the manliness to which the military mind so faithfully clings."

The hardihoods would be applied to the physically demanding work of manufacturing, construction, farming, fire-fighting, and the like. Upon discharge, recruits "would have...done their...part, they could tread the earth more proudly, the women would value them more highly, they would be better fathers and teachers of the following generation."

Earle Kauffman at *American Forests* had told Darel of the demand for stories on the Civilian Conservation Corps (CCC), the first and most successful of Roosevelt's New Deal programs. Darel would apply James's ideas to the Civilian Conservation Corps, and up the appeal by adding military flash and parade, things by which the Army built esprit de corps. The Army held competitions between squads. The best-drilled won ribbons, were the first dismissed at parade. Perhaps the CCC could pit camp against camp for most trees planted, lengths of trail built. "Russia," he pointed out, "has used competition to build enthusiasm and effort."

"The more I thought, the more I realized how critical my article would be of the conservation corps." Criticism might make the article sell better, "but another possibility opened out. Why not work out a full-fledged plan, present it to Fechner [head of the CCC], and get myself in a position to do it?"

He took the idea to Charlie Wood. Charlie thought it a good story, but Fechner surely had suggestions aplenty on how to run his business, and Darel's would just be filed with the rest. Fechner, upon investigation, was opposed to military methods anyway. Charlie recommended shopping the idea to a syndicate or possibly the *New York Times* Magazine. Darel settled on the latter. To augment its credibility, Charlie suggested trying to get the story out under General Glassford's byline.

Coincidence brought Darel personal contact with the CCC. Ever since January, he and Anna had schemed to rent a summer cabin in Virginia's Shenandoah Valley. Darel told Charlie, Charlie liked the idea and thought he might join them. "How'd you like to drive over there and shop around?"

So they went, though it was 70 miles each way, and stumbled on Camp Roosevelt, the first of the CCC camps, just getting established. They saw bronzed young fellows, smiling and happy. "It's great out here" and "we like it fine," they told him. Now Darel could say from observation that Roosevelt's moral equivalent was bringing fitness, health, and cheer to young men of the nation.

He wrote Anna, "It was 2:30 this morning when I got to bed, but I couldn't sleep. My thoughts were in the Shenandoah Valley—and how to overcome the need for money, to spar for time until the 'Moral Equivalent' story be written, sent out, and paid for. How to write it to best effect. How to pass on to the next, and the next. And I thought of sending my story to Fechner *after it is printed*, as an example of my work, and how I could help propagandize his Conservation Corps."

For hours my mind ran on, would not stop. Then, out of the darkness came the first sleepy twitter of a robin. The twitter swelled to a chorus as the birds sang their matins to the rising sun. I saw the street lights switch off at 4:30, the sky grow lighter. I went to the other side of the house to watch the sunrise.

The latticed clouds were darkly blue, the protractor-shaped moon was yet gold. But a sunrise is sunset reversed, and the steel blue of the clouds must alter. I saw the moon fade to silver, then tarnish to white. Through the light loosened lattice of the sky I saw a lavender-rose glow in the east, a faint glow behind the blue of the clouds. Then the rose became mauve, the mauve purple, and the low clouds became gray, misty, luminous. High above the roofs and trees there floated wisps of flame. And they floated there for long minutes as the purple deepened to scarlet, and spread its glow upward to color the interior of the inverted eggshell into which I looked. The light spread, metamorphosed gradually from crimson to gold, then, as I stood and watched, faded to a pale yellow in the east. I ceased looking then, but, back in my room, could see that the western sky was tinted, purple clouds with golden rims, royal colors for the regal flotilla of the heavens. Then it was that I could sleep.

The next day, "I went to the Forest Service to find out all I could about the Civilian Conservation Corps and came home loaded with mimeographed matter. Now I am ready to marshal my material, outline the story, and wade in. If I can keep up my present confident frame of mind—and I think it would be hard to destroy—this story, and the next and the next, are going to be clipped off in pretty short order, and then we are going to the Shenandoah Valley!"

On May 18 Congress passed the Tennessee Valley Authority act, another measure of Roosevelt's first 100 days. The plan included dams for flood control and hydroelectric power along the Tennessee River, plus the introduction of fertilizers and other agricultural improvements. Congressman John Rankin called it "the most profitable investment…since the Louisiana Purchase." It planted the seed for Darel's next article. "After 'Moral

Equivalent' I want immediately to write a story which would probably carry the headline, 'IS THE OHIO VALLEY NEXT?'" A 1906 "Wickersham Report" had mapped out development of the watershed above Pittsburgh. Would the administration adapt a TVA-like plan to the Monongahela and Allegheny River Valleys—which joined at Pittsburgh to become the Ohio River Valley?

Darel initially thought of pitching the story to a single Pittsburgh paper, but expanded his scope to include as many papers as possible, first just for the Ohio Valley, later with two more versions for the Monongahela and Allegheny valleys.

"Perhaps the Administration is coming closer to my background and interest," he declared, "but the fact is that I now have three corking story ideas based on things made timely by Government events. These Roosevelt stories should all sell."

On May 22, he mailed 'Moral Equivalent' to the New York *Times*, and turned his attention to flood control. At the Library of Congress, the Flood Commission report was off the shelf. Only members of Congress could check books out, and the Library couldn't reveal who had it. Darel tracked it down to Representative Riley J. Wilson of Louisiana, chairman of the House Committee on Flood Control. They lent it to him.

While poking around the House and Senate, he picked up a tip that the Army Corps of Engineers was making a survey of all US rivers. So, the next day he dropped in at the Engineer Corps in one of the "temporary" buildings on the Mall.

"Temporary" buildings on the Mall
Washinton Monument top, left of center

Those "Temps" were one of D.C.'s longest-running jokes. They were built during World War I to serve the nation's wartime needs and designed, some said, to fall down after a few years. They were the brainchild of Woodrow Wilson's Assistant Secretary of the Navy, Franklin Delano Roosevelt. In 1941, Roosevelt expressed regret. "I didn't think I would ever be let into the gates of Heaven, because I had been responsible for desecrating the parks of Washington." The buildings hung on year after year, through World War II, Korea, and into Vietnam. When built, apparently, the art of planned obsolescence hadn't been refined to today's keen edge. President Nixon finally demolished them in 1970. Today, Constitution Gardens and the Vietnam Memorial occupy the site.

Darel interviewed Capt. Casey of the Engineers, who had drafted a report on the Allegheny and Monongahela basins. His report had not been made public, and recommendations from a 1911 study, if implemented, would have cost $40 million more than they were worth in flood control. Darel persisted nonetheless.

On May 25, "'Moral Equivalent' came trotting dutifully back from the *Times*. I did it up and immediately shot it out to the New York *Herald Tribune*. The darn thing costs 24¢ every time it goes out." On May 30, the *Herald Tribune* returned it, and he sent it to the *Philadelphia Ledger*.

On June 13, "The globe-galloping [*Magellan to Mattern*] tale came cantering back home from the *Times*." On the 15th, the *Chicago Tribune* Syndicate returned "Moral Equivalent."

In mid-June, the *Clarksburg* (West Virginia) *Exponent-Telegram* published the Monongahela Valley version of "Is the Ohio Valley Next?"

Chapter Twenty-Five

"Without Benefit of Clergy"

THE LETTERS STOPPED as if shut off by a spigot. Anna wasn't returning to work in the fall, and the two planned summer in the Shenandoah Valley, though given the results of Darel's article submissions, it's likely that they didn't go. Darel was still married to Fanny Mae and so, between bigamy and adultery, he and Anna chose the latter. This may be when Anna hid Darel in a closet on her father's unannounced arrival, and maybe Harry's trying to run Darel down with his car. Anna worried whether "thorough deception" was kinder than the truth. "I'm not at all sure which would be conducive to the greater happiness of Mother and Dad."

Anna found work tutoring and told me she didn't mind bringing in money while Darel got $25 for an occasional article. Just how much she brought in is not recorded, but it apparently freed Darel to finish a novel, *The Earth-Speaking*, by the end of 1933. It is set on a fictional island in the South Atlantic inhabited by a pre-industrial, dark-skinned race whose men can't grow hair on their faces. Darel seems to have searched then-obscure lexicons for place and person names. The hero is named Svastika, which in Sanskrit means "good luck."

Apparently in 1933—the year Hitler came to power—Nazism and its swastika ensign weren't yet seen as the menace they later became. The island's volcano erupted when Svastika was born, an omen that he was destined for great things. The island boasts of a legendary giant named Maha-rishi, the Wise-one. In Sanskrit, a maha-rishi is, literally, a "great wise one." The swastika itself is an ancient religious symbol of India and other far-flung places. There's a fisherman named Desara. Desara is a Hindu festival.

The islanders grow a unique plant called saumana that supplies a coarse fiber suitable for sandal soles, a fine fiber more sumptuous than silk, an edible tuber, a tea, a perfume, and a serum good for everything from scrapes to snake bites. The other miracle is the bronze mine. Only on that island can you mine bronze. Elsewhere, copper and zinc must be mined separately and alloyed to get bronze. But the mine is secondary to the story. It is saumana that attracts the hairy-faced white men.

"Book the First," sets an idyllic scene with a reference to the white men's toehold—a mill churning out saumana textiles that the islanders formerly created on hand-looms.

In "Book the Second," the white men send Svastika to New York for education, hoping to turn him to their own ends. In "Book the Third," with Svastika back home, the ploy fails, though not before the hairy-face tries to drown Svastika.

At the end, imperialism and the island's Edenic idyll compromise with each other, reflecting a Depression-era refrain: the small guy prevailing against the greedy and powerful, as in the movies *Meet John Doe* and *Mr. Smith Goes to Washington*.

In October, 1933, Germany under Adolph Hitler withdrew from the League of Nations.

Soon after the New Year, Darel bundled off to New York for a week to show publishers and agents the manuscript. He recorded his first impressions of Gotham. "Got here yesterday afternoon. *Bien fatigue* after the long journey. The sight of great works of steel and mortar on entering N.Y. was almost too much. The road crosses a great high viaduct, miles long, then goes for more miles under concrete braces and buttressings, then dips into the bright yellow gloom of the Holland Tunnel. It was so wearying—as if myself had been made to build it alone."

He stayed with Charlie Wood's sister, Doris Ware, who told him to tell Anna she was taking good care of him. Gardiner Wood, a brother, recommended he see journalist/novelist/editor Lucian Cary, who referred Darel to his own agent, Carl Brandt.

Another agent, Annie Laurie Williams, saw a movie in the book, though she thought "Book the First" led one to expect a different kind of story than the one that emerged. Darel subsequently revised "Book the First".

There were other contacts up and down Manhattan—and a stop to admire the Chrysler building's "gargoyles"—actually oversized hood ornaments—but *The Earth-Speaking* ultimately wound up like most first novels, stuffed unpublished in a file-cabinet drawer.

Chapter Twenty-Six

The Federal Emergency Relief Administration

Library of Congress: Main Reading Room

JULY 10, 1934:

"Dear Mr. McConkey:

"Due to slackness of work at this season it will be impossible for me to make further use of your services at this time.

"I regret very much that this is necessary, but I have had to lay off several men, and unless conditions improve must dispense with the services of others. It may be possible for me to provide you with work later.

"Very truly yours, H. Schuddeboom"

Darel may have penned the letter himself. Sometime in 1934, he cast an eye on the second of Roosevelt's New Deal programs, the Federal Emergency Relief Administration (FERA). The letter suggests Harry was helping Darel document his lack of employment.

Roosevelt's approach to the Depression was that any action, right or wrong, was better than no action. If one thing didn't work, try another. His "make-work" programs reaped thunderous criticism from business, which accused him of driving up wages and wrecking the nation's moral fiber. But Roosevelt saw little choice between relief and revolution, and within a year, communism was having trouble competing with the New Deal. Journalist Martha Gelhorn, Ernest Hemingway's future third wife, attributed those gains to idolatry of Roosevelt. Will Rogers chimed, "If he burned down the capitol we would cheer and say, 'Well, at least we got a fire started anyhow.'"

Business, while blaring relief's ruinous effects on morale, offered no alternative; and New Deal wages were, in fact, deliberately kept below prevailing rates.

FERA had been set up to give grants to states to create unskilled jobs for the unemployed. A year later, unemployed teachers were teaching adult-education or relocating to country schools in danger of shutting down, and Darel found work as a Library of Congress researcher and cataloger. "I rapidly became a New Dealer," he said in 1959, "and have remained one."

Americans pride themselves on self-reliance, and many saw federal jobs as hardly better than the dole, something you'd have to be both morally and financially bankrupt before considering. I can imagine that Darel aligned with those who saw government-sponsored scholarship as refreshingly enlightened. He was assigned to Earl Hyde, a Library supervisor, to assist collecting and collating data on colonial statute law.

Darel stood in awe of Hyde, whom he called "the last universal genius." Pat once said Hyde could catalog books in 200 languages. Darel, Anna, and Earl Hyde became lifelong friends. Anna became a Library habitué, researching Lewis and Clark, toward whom *National Geographic* editor Jesse Hildebrand had pointed Darel.

The Library of Congress's main reading room is a cathedral. Octagonal in plan, two hundred twenty-six polished wooden desks array in concentric circles around the librarian's station. Two banks of tall, arcaded galleries encircle the room, one at floor level, one above that. Around a third, unarcaded level, tall statues of ancient literary, scientific, religious and other figures keep silent vigil. The eye drifts yet upward to arched windows filtering natural light into the space below. Floating above all is the sheltering dome, topping out 160 feet above the floor. After two years of privation, Darel was getting a paycheck in that hallowed temple.

Today the public is banned from that room, to forestall vandalism, which is sadly too predictable.

FERA's pay, by law, was above relief but below prevailing wage, so people wouldn't be tempted to leave regular jobs. Direct relief would actually have cost less, but the Depression was as much a crisis of morale as of dollars.

Harry Hopkins, Roosevelt's right-hand man, believed paying able-bodied men to keep idle couldn't help but corrode morale. Either approach would infuse needed money into the economy, but jobs helped allay the dole's stigma. The pay scale was designed to ward off cries of foul from business and conservative politicians, who cried foul anyway.

FERA made a New Dealer of Darel, but another Roosevelt program, the National Recovery Administration (NRA) made a Republican of Anna's father. Harry was intellectually liberal, but he was also a small businessman, and took a dim view of government's meddling in his affairs.

NRA was created to engage business in the fight against Depression through fair-practice "codes" designed to prevent cutthroat competition and encourage shorter hours, better wages, and holding prices down so rising outlays wouldn't neutralize gains in income. In return, government would exempt businesses from antitrust regulation.

To forestall court challenges, NRA's director tirelessly negotiated voluntary structures industry by industry. A massive campaign publicized the "Blue Eagle"—a banner with a thunderbird graphic—which

complying industries could display to help consumers choose their products, and that's where Harry parted company.

Of paramount importance was bringing the "big ten" industries—from steel and textiles to coal and automobiles—into compliance. All the automakers agreed but one: Henry Ford. Ford had pioneered better wages and shorter hours in his Model-T plant so his workers could afford the cars they made. Independent, eccentric, irascible, he refused to participate.

The administration insisted that NRA was weakened without 100 percent compliance, but at last proceeded sans Ford. Family lore puts it that Roosevelt's "making" Henry Ford fly the Blue Eagle (it was available as a flag) made Harry a Republican, but Ford never actually flew the Blue Eagle.

In 1935, the Supreme Court declared NRA unconstitutional. It violated "delegation of powers" prohibitions. The executive branch, the Court pointed out, had no authority over interstate commerce. That belonged to Congress. Six weeks later, many of NRA's codes reappeared in the National Labor Relations Act—elimination of child labor, minimum wages and maximum hours, labor's right to bargain collectively and strike. All survived court challenges. But during NRA's brief life, industrial output rose twenty-two percent.

FERA didn't stop Darel's writing. In October, *American Forests* accepted his "The Health of John Peavey," about the CCC's effects on a scrawny city boy; but in November they rejected "Sassafras Voyage." On December 23, the *Washington Post* published his article on the destinations of the Magi after visiting baby Jesus, as told in Persia to Marco Polo around 1260 A.D.

He went home to West Virginia in early November. Anna stayed back, not to advertise their living arrangement. "Had I begun to write an hour ago," he told Anna, "I should have said, 'Anna, darling, home is where you are.' For I felt, in the depth of melancholy, that Dixie was no longer my home."

Right now I still think home is where you are, but I do not feel as thoroughly disowned by Dixie.

Since my coming here, I have looked with horror upon what transpires in the thoughts of country folk. It is story after story of misfortune, struggle, pathetic incident, death, marriage, birth, economic lack, more miserable poverty than ever before I have seen in my home, and again, of last moments, and funerals, and how corpses look.

I was mute before it. I listened, and smoked, and tried to read the signature of the flames, and sought to untangle it all. I seemed disowned and miserably alone.

And then I bethought that they talked as much because I talked so little. And I told them the Moncacht-apé story. And theirs was a live and living interest and they were lifted out of themselves and have just retired happy at the hour of eleven.

Moncacht-apé had shown up in the Lewis and Clark research. Sometime in the first third of the 1700s, a French planter in Louisiana had recorded the story of a Yazoo Indian named Moncacht-apé who claimed to have journeyed to the Pacific in the late 1600s, over a century before Lewis and Clark. *American Forests* published Darel's account of the odyssey (though not until November 1936).

I'd be derelict if I didn't say that the story held a glaring defect. No less an historian than Bernard DeVoto pointed out that Moncacht-apé claimed to have gone up the Missouri, then down the Columbia, with nary a rock, never mind a Rocky Mountain, to stub his toe on, calling the account into serious question. It was disheartening to learn my father's fallibility, but we must learn to demythologize our parents. He was merely twenty-nine years old, and had personally only visited as far west as Wichita, five hundred miles short of the Rockies.

House painting fetched Darel's oldest brother, Clyde, 50 cents an hour. After the first of the year, he got a three-month job with Federal Housing, surveying properties in Clarksburg, West Virginia, but after one month was back looking for work. He'd had a job on the police force but lost it, his mother opined, "on account of being on the wrong side. I guess the Dem's are dyed so deep in the wool that a recommendation from them does no good." She was averse to "the Dems," obviously, but not to FDR's Social Security, or Darel's contacting Eleanor Roosevelt for assistance. By the end of April, it looked like the police job might return, but in mid-May, Clyde went "back to the tower"— a fire-tower lookout?

To stay on the farm, Gladys and Blanche cleaned and cooked for the farm's owners, Judge and Mrs. E.G. Smith.

Working for the post office again, Darel stayed in D.C. for Christmas, to his mother's chagrin. "We would have loved to have had you here but it seems we are destined to spend that season alone anymore." The only one to pop by was Clyde, after spending the day with his wife's family. "Well honey I am glad for you as you have so patiently and hopefully went on trying your best and almost giving up in despair. The depression has been a handicap. Hope you may please them [FERA?] so well they cannot do without you."

Gladys traded her "pianna" for a radio. "It was worth all of that little piano," she said, "to hear the lovely Christmas carols and all at Christmas time. My ideas are the same as yours when it comes to jazz. I do not like it! Music to me must be kinda unusual like Hwan [Hawaiian—popular at the time], good string music and some symphony music would be good. We have had some mighty good gospel music from Pittsburg [sic]. We have heard some good acts from Hollywood by Mary Pickford."

Hollywood was one industry that boomed in the Depression. Pickford was "America's Sweetheart," married to Douglas Fairbanks, but glances swung often to screen siren Mae West—whose innuendos ("When I'm good, I'm very good, but when I'm bad, I'm better.") ran afoul of Hollywood's censors. In 1935, West was the highest paid woman in America. The year before, Hollywood's top draw had been homespun humorist, columnist, and vaudeville veteran turned screen actor, Will Rogers. On August 15, 1935, Rogers and aviation pioneer Wiley Post were killed in a plane crash near Barrow, Alaska.

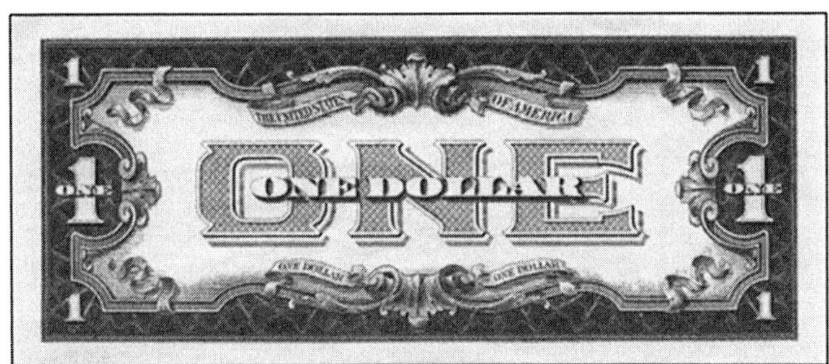

In 1935, the pyramid with its all-seeing eye was added to the back of the dollar bill. Pre-1935 bill shown here.

In violation of the Versailles Treaty, Adolph Hitler announced a six-fold expansion of Germany's "defense" forces. Britain, France, Italy, and the League of Nations—from which Hitler had withdrawn—condemned the action but did nothing to stop it.

Sometime in mid-1935, Sam and Edythe parted ways. Sam took up with a lady named Dorothy. A Dorothy Gresch was floating around during that period, but whether it was she who married Sam or another Dorothy is not answered. The two remained united until death did them part forty years later.

Nineteen thirty-five was the year that Darel contributed four sections to that American Forests book, *American Conservation*, which I later found in Burke Elementary's library.

And it was then that Anna and Darel set up housekeeping on an island in the Potomac River near Cabin John, Maryland, just above D.C., perhaps, for Darel, a spiritual return to the Three Trees retreat in Connecticut, three years earlier. The site came equipped with a cabin. Candles supplied illumination. The island accommodated them and one other occupant, a Mr. Walter. Access was via the landlord's rowboat. Downstream lay Snake Island. In 1959, Snake Island was incorporated into Little Falls Dam, which must have inundated Anna and Darel's island, as no island fitting its description appears on present-day maps.

The Dust Bowl

In 1935, dust from the Midwest darkened skies over Washington, D.C. For the fourth year in a row, drought was desiccating parts of Texas, Oklahoma, New Mexico, Colorado, Nebraska, and Kansas. Before April 19, 1935, Congress had taken little note of the Dust Bowl, victim of one of history's most harebrained agricultural theories—"rain follows the plow"—trumpeted not by agriculturists but by land speculators. Buoyed early on by atypical rainfall, cultivators had plowed up miles of the prairie grasses that had held the soil in place for thousands of years. In 1931, the rains tapered back.

Without the grass, topsoil began blowing away, often in spectacular dust storms that blackened skies for miles. Each inch of topsoil was a thousand years of nature's work, yet few remarked the devastation until Black Sunday, April 14, 1935. On that single day, nature scoured twice as much topsoil out of the Dust Bowl as had been excavated in seven years building the Panama Canal. It was the following Friday the 19th, before the airborne mass reached

D.C., spurring Congress at last to action. Within a day, legislators created the Soil Conservation Service, which reassigned 150 CCC camps to it from the Forest Service and ultimately sent 20,000 people to work on soil conservation. Anna and Darel cannot but have witnessed the phenomenon, but managed not to say so.

Nineteen thirty-five's "Labor Day Hurricane" was the only category 5 storm to make landfall on the United States until Camille in 1969. It struck the Florida Keys September 2. Small in diameter, its damage was relatively confined, but the storm surge swept an eleven-car evacuation train off its tracks and demolished the village of Islamorada. The death toll was 408, including 256 war veterans in the CCC building the Overseas Highway. The railroad had been the main transportation link for the island chain. Nearly bankrupt anyway, it was so badly damaged that it sold out to the state of Florida. Much of the roadbed was used in the Overseas Highway.

Chapter Twenty-Seven

The Writers' Project

TWO YEARS INTO Roosevelt's first term, unemployment was down five points. The Dow had recovered 200 percent of its all-time low. In April, 1935, Roosevelt signed the $4.8 billion Emergency Relief Authorization Act. Out of it grew the Works Progress Administration, WPA, which ended FERA and took up where FERA left off.

Economic theory called—and to an extent still does—for more public works during economic contraction, and less during expansion. The Great Depression was the worst contraction in US history. Few living Americans had seen anything like it before. The Panic of 1893 had gone as deep, but only lasted four years. When Roosevelt created WPA, the Great Depression was six years old with no end in sight. After the freewheeling twenties, it had staggered

America. WPA hired millions of mostly unskilled men to build roads, libraries, airports, dams, bridges, and other projects. At its height, it was America's biggest employer, employing 8.5 million people.

Artists, the administration concluded, were just as hungry as factory workers, and for their sake WPA carved out Federal Project Number One—"Federal One"—which employed artists in four categories: writers, painters and sculptors, musicians, and actors. Naysayers screamed that art was not real work, and FDR himself was lukewarm to spending money on it, but First Lady Eleanor was all-in and kept her husband pointed in the right direction. Paying artists for their work was still better than the dole. Darel wasted no time applying for the Federal Writers' Project.

Roosevelt had put his right-hand man, Harry Hopkins, at the head of the whole, sprawling, WPA agglomeration. Hopkins was a colorful figure much in the public eye throughout Roosevelt's administration. He put Henry Alsberg, a rumpled former foreign correspondent, playwright, and director of the Provincetown Theatre, in charge of the Writers' Project. The Project got housed of all places in the now-vacant Florentine-style mansion of Ned and Evalyn Walsh McLean. Its grand ballroom, oozing nineteen-twenties opulence—crystal chandeliers, mahogany paneling, silk wallpaper—became littered with desks and filing cabinets. Life-size statues became coat racks. The staccato rap of typewriter keys proclaimed the building's reduced circumstance.

The Project's most celebrated product was a series of guidebooks, one for each state plus Washington, D.C., Puerto Rico, and Alaska. Spun off from a successful guide to Connecticut produced under FERA, the set has been considered by many, even now, to be among the best ever produced. Its scholarship, emerging under national rather than state auspices, often debunked local myths that had shown states in more favorable light than they deserved. The approach invited cries of foul, but the editors largely stuck to their guns.

Trading on America's love of the automobile, each book featured a section on driving tours. There were 22.6 million automobiles in America in 1936, one for every 5.6 people. (Will Rogers had quipped, "We are the first nation in the history of the world to go to the poorhouse in an automobile.")

Among the Project's accomplishments, researchers under the direction of Alan Lomax, and later Benjamin Botkin, collected oral histories from over 2,300 ex-slaves. It was the only project of its kind ever undertaken.

On September 17, Darel joined forces with some 6,700 writers, editors, critics, researchers, and historians. With them, he'd had to take the "pauper's oath"—show he had no money, property, job, or prospects, yet still show his writing chops. Alsberg put him on the road not as a writer but as a field supervisor, sorting issues in offices around the Southeast. Doubtless he would rather have been a writer—the Project helped the careers of Saul Bellow, John Cheever, Ralph Ellison, Zora Neale Hurston, Kenneth Rexroth, Studs Terkel, Richard Wright, and many others—but in the Depression, a job was a job. Maybe Darel's extension work, or his work for Congressman Bowman, had suggested other uses for his talents, and on the road he went.

"How long my sojourn in West Virginia will take I cannot guess. I think I will need to come back to Charleston [the state capital] to see the state WPA administrator, but I have avoided him so far because I need to spy out the land first. I do hope to wind up the W. Va. business before I get away; the Virginia situation is more complex—I need advice and policy, then go back to do something final & definite."

In Charlottesville, he encountered the politics which were virtually built into the Project. Competition among local factions for the contracts could be intense. "There is a pretty interesting situation here," he wrote Anna. "I haven't been permitted to see the other side. There *must* be another side, but I probably won't get to see it unless tomorrow morning. There seems to be one pretty strong clique, and they are trying to get the Writers Project. It will probably end with their getting it unless something much to the contrary turns up, for it looks like they are the strong party. This has been a very interesting trip. There has been opportunity for the exercise of one's native wit—if any—and to probe into and guess at men's motives."

When he traveled by rail, the Project sprang for Pullman sleeping-cars. "The cuisine on the C&O is more than passably good," he told Anna, "for which be thanks, since I must travel on it considerably." He gave expansive descriptions of the passing countryside. Departing Charlottesville on a crisp autumn morning, he saw, "the sun rising in fiery fury, a white frost on the landscape, and miasmas rising from the river known to Jefferson & Lewis."

He spent October's mid-section in D.C., but on the 21st was bound for Louisville and Nashville, where he boarded the Louisville and Nashville's crack, all-Pullman "Pan American" for New Orleans to meet established author Lyle Saxon, director of the Louisiana project.

What he found worth transmitting to Anna had nothing to do with politics or writing and everything to do with a party from which he got back to his hotel at 4:30 a.m. As with campaigning with Bowman, this was another side of the Writers' Project, with one caveat—booze was legal again. Prohibition had been repealed in December, 1933. This party began with dinner at the home of archaeologist Franz Blom.

Mexican artist Rique was there, along with "Gonzales and his wife." Saxon and "Shad" arrived well primed, having "spent the latter afternoon soaking up three Planters punches." Darel's letter to Anna was, by his own admission, "drunken insane," penned on his arrival back at the hotel. At the Bloms', they dined on turtle and rice. "Delicious. These people are lousy with money & live in a magnificent place.

"Well, after[ward?] we went with Ricci [Rique] and the Gonzalez's for coffee, then for Benedictine then for taquila [*sic*], Mexico's native drink, taken with lemon & salt. 'Tis somewhat as I think vodka must be. And I had three. Most aphrodisiac. But I return to the Monteleone [his hotel] thoroughly virginal & true to you, & that's a thing for both of us to be thankful for.

"And Lyle meantime is a grand person & at this hour, filled as I am with taquila & a final scotch & soda—this last soothing as compared with taquila— I love him as man—not homo—loves man, and I have felt so only toward one previous human being who is now dead. But that may be due to the Planter's punch—a beautiful drink—or to Blom's whiskey & soda, or to taquila, or to the final whiskey & soda.

"Though I gave my crooked pipe and tobacco to Ricci—and promised a gift to Gonzales & to his wife, & traded my venerable belt to Ricci for a red sash which I now wear. He is a beautiful (illegible word), this Ricci, and I should not write when so perforated with drink—but so 'tis."

In Darel's movements around the land, there were trains but also airplanes. "I flew to Jackson, Miss., today & back in time for final dinner with Lyle." Commercial air travel was barely a decade old in 1935, and he confessed to a "childlike delight" in flying.

It was wonderful! I left there at 5 p.m. Soon the sun, a clean-cut ball of flame, went down somewhere beyond the Mississippi. Its last rays played on the trees, giving them spring or autumn tints which they had not in daylight. And some were hoared with Spanish moss.

It was my first sunset from the air. When the sun was gone, subdued tints lay along the flat skyline. Then an oval wisp of cloud flamed to gold. Others picked it up till the Mighty Painter had laid a scroll upon the sky. It deepened to crimson, scarce changing shape, then to rusty red, then to mauve, and stayed long, reluctant to depart. Then it was dark, and a solitary star came out.

The plane flew low & smooth, its right wing just above the sunset horizon. There were fires burning in the woods. The smoke from them rose column straight, then streamed off horizontally in the direction we were going. Then I knew why we flew so smoothly. The pilot's airspeed indicator stood at 110, the compass almost due S. Sometimes the smoke spread over fields like new-sown & unsettled bonemeal [a widely used soil conditioner]. Then I saw five fires burning. They were bright in early twilight and their smoke was a pattern of loveliness.

Then I was tired and dozed. There was a bump. The ship rocked. We had hit directly conflicting currents of air. We climbed. Gradually we smoothed out. Beacons flashed. Crawling cars and Christmas-tree towns winked up from below.

Then we were crossing Lake Ponchartrain. It must be near 50 miles across, taking from 6:15 to 6:40 to cross [actually 40 at its widest]. Then, long after, a jeweled & fairy city burst upon us. Fabulous New Orleans! There it shone and glittered, such sudden and swift-gone beauty as to leave one breathless & awed, with no words.

We came over Shushan airport, circled back over Ponchartrain, banked low till it seemed a wing must cut the vague gray water,

Ford Tri-Motor

the gemmed city slanted, then slowly righted, & we hopped over the levee & were down.

Then taxi. Then learned I'd missed a giant shooting star over Pontchartrain that lit up the whole lake. I'd thought it the flash of a beacon.

That Darel could read the airspeed and compass suggests that the ship was a Ford Tri-Motor, with the plane's cockpit open to the cabin. Its cruising speed was around 110 mph, and family lore had it that Pop actually had flown in one of those dinosaurs. It was one of the world's first all-metal planes. As the Model-T had been the "Tin-Lizzy," so the Tri-Motor was the "Tin-Goose." It carried eight to thirteen passengers plus the pilot, co-pilot, and a flight attendant. The cabin was uninsulated and the engine noise was deafening. The plane revolutionized air travel when it went into service in 1926, but by 1935, the Boeing 247 and Douglas DC-2 were leaving it in the dust.

Early November found Darel back home, whence he was dispatched forty miles up the pike to Baltimore. "Most of the afternoon I spent with Dr. Wheeler in the Pratt Library," he wrote Anna. "I have done what others seemed afraid to do—ask him to take the project as state director. He is worried about the character of relief personnel. I gave him some reassurance based on my morning spent interviewing.

"So I may be able to get the state as well as city going in short order." Ultimately Wheeler's name does not appear in the finished guide.

"It's darned lonesome without you, and the first thing anybody knows I won't be able to pay my room rent. So I am going to append an order to Mrs. Hawkins so you can get my check. Borrow or steal enough money to come to Baltimore, and arrive at the Southern Hotel around 5 p.m. Then we'll dine out. You may stay the night if you like, and we'll return to Washington the next day."

On December 19, he was in Atlanta checking the status of the Georgia project. "This is pleasant-unpleasant," he told Anna. "Key [the state director] is rather a good egg. I haven't had a chance to get away from him yet"

The next day, on a train to Charlotte, North Carolina, he wrote, "Atlanta has been a tough situation, but I have an idea I'm leaving it in a lot better shape than it was. Key did pull a pretty bad one, but I am going to recommend his continuance unless something untoward develops.

"This is the coldest Pullman I've ever been in. Gone to bed to keep warm. I haven't been to bed earlier than 4 a.m. for the past two nights and I'm just about dead."

Back in Atlanta after New Year's, things looked different. Key was not working out as thought. "Key came to my room at about 2:30. He is a winning devil, well groomed, and had quite a lot to show. I set out to be hard boiled with him but failed miserably. I was, however, very direct. He left at 4:30.

"I called Mrs. Dillard. We had coffee and then dinner. She told me about developments subsequent to my last visit. Key has been drinking; he precipitately fired a local supervisor at Albany; promised a Historical Survey job to a person who cannot possibly take it; has messed things up with Miss Ruth Blair, State Archivist, whom we want to take it; and insulted WPA people. I have a lot of fixing to do.

"Tomorrow, after getting the story from Miss Shepperson, WPA administrator, I propose to swing the ax. I'll give Key a chance to resign. If he doesn't, I'll wire [Writers' Project director] Alsberg and get him fired, then start reorganizing. I haven't yet told Mrs. Dillard that she would be the new state director. She is distraught. Key carried a gun and threatened suicide, even told her she was the reason he drank. She has mostly gotten over these things but they've worked on her. She thinks it rotten to tell all this about the man who got her the job. No hysterics, just feeling rotten."

The next day, Darel and Miss Shepperson "deplored the necessity of firing Key, for all agree he is a very winning and capable person when sober. Everybody has tried to help him, but he has piled mess on mess. It was necessary to be sure we had a case that could resist appeal to any possible source, political or other. Miss Shepperson gave him 3¾ days of vacation due him and promised to make a place for him on another project if he stays sober. I then interviewed Miss Fitzsimmons, Mr. MacDougall, and Mr. Boggs.

"By that time I had a complete case and went in to Key. I asked him why Miss Blair has cooled toward the Historical Survey—and he evaded. That was all right. I called for complete correspondence on the case of Miss Jarrell, at Albany, whom he fired without apparent justification. (I'll have to go there on Thursday and try to clear that up. Miss Shepperson will rely on my judgment.) Then I said, 'Mr. Key, I'm sorry, but based on the Jarrell matter and some other things, I find it necessary to ask for your resignation. I think it would be better if you wire Mr. Alsberg and submit it of your own volition.'

"He took it on the chin, like a gentleman. I admired him. He asked me to write, in proper form, his telegram of resignation. I did and left him.

"When I came back an hour later to Miss Shepperson's office the wire had gone out. Mrs. Dillard was waiting to see Miss Shepperson, as per arrangement. She was asked to take the directorship, and in a few minutes I wired Alsberg asking him to authorize her appointment. We had a fine chat for an hour. Then had coffee with Mrs. Dillard and she went home."

After making reports in preparation for Albany—which had two district supervisors on payroll thanks to one of Key's inebriate actions—he had dinner with the Dillards.

"It was a very pleasant soirée. The steak, due to lateness, was like sole leather, but, also due to lateness, tasted like filet mignon. I told Fielding Dillard I was eloping with his wife. 'At what time?' said he. 'Nine o'clock,' said I. 'There's a train at twelve-something tonight,' he suggested. But there wasn't such a train so we leave tomorrow morning.

"That means returning here Friday. Then I think I'll get off to Birmingham Friday night. This Georgia thing is taking a good while, but I'm taking care of myself, & the work is valuable. I think I'll be feeling pretty fit once I hit New Orleans."

By the end of the month, Mrs. Dillard worried that Alsberg would let Key back on the project. Darel called her from Birmingham and "told her to stick by her guns." He would write Alsberg and work it out, unnecessarily as things turned out. Key showed up at the D.C. office drunk and penniless, having run up large hotel and long-distance phone bills, and twice asked Alsberg to pay them.

At the second request, Aslberg slipped out leaving his assistant director, George Cronyn, to deal with Key. Cronyn gave Key money for a shave, a cup of coffee, and phone change to call his sister, who lived in the D.C. area, and hoped he wouldn't spend it on booze.

Darel routed back through Charleston, West Virginia, with a layover in Charlottesville. Anna caught a train and met him. "Twas lovely, darling, that little interlude in Charlottesville. The lovely supple roundness of you, the sweet giving-resisting of your body was like fresh-drawn nectar. And to be with you, & see you, & hear about things you are doing, for those short few hours was worth such price as may be incurred.

"I love you, Dutch Girl."

Darel arrived in Charleston, West Virginia, January 19. The project was going nowhere. After consulting with Project Director L. W. Burns, and later with Clyde Billups, State Professional and Service Director, and with Bob Bradford, regional supervisor of Professional and Service Projects, "It didn't take long to tell what was wrong. Burns is as slow as a snail, feels lost in the job." He "is painfully moral, doesn't let his secretary smoke, has wavered & hesitated on getting Herbert here because of Herbert's reputation! I told him we didn't care a damn how much a man drinks so long as it doesn't affect his work."

Darel was indebted to Jimmy Herbert for the first three steps he ever took toward writing. He fails to tell us what the steps were, but the first stabs we know of were as a Lone Scout in 1917.

Darel made Burns nervous. While he used Billups's secretary to prepare his report to Alsberg, Burns haunted the office next door. When Herbert finally showed up on the 23rd, Burns was "really steamed up; he put on an exhibition in my room here a few minutes ago that tickled me no end. My visit has helped him. He even says 'darned' now."

Darel had meant to leave on the 22nd, but Alsberg was dissatisfied leaving slow old Burns and tipsy Herbert in charge. He wanted Darel to find someone else. He and Billups went to see Ross Johnston, who was in charge of an historic and scenic road-marker project.

"Ross is eminently capable, thoroughly interested, & we worked out a nice little scheme: Ross (I've known him for years—he's put out state guide books for ten years) is to quietly supervise the whole thing, so that in case Burns is slow & Herbert on a binge the project can still go on. Everybody was enthused, even Alsberg. I merely suggested to Burns & Herbert that they call on Ross with his materials & knowledge; and they were happy to do so. They have known him longer than I have."

Alsberg then sent Darel to Louisville. "So the trip drags on, another state is added. Haven't any idea how long I'll be in Kentucky. I'm not allowed to move now without Alsberg's approval."

Anna and Darel had been scheming to meet in New Orleans when next Darel went there. Anna wrote how marvelous it was "to think upon New

Orleans, and I still allow myself a thrill of anticipation." On January 27 she was writing while "steaming and pressing a black velvet dinner gown, which has been contributed to my New Orleans wardrobe. It's amazing how everyone wants to lend me clothes. Helen, Joran, Evelyn have all been most generous."

Helen had remarked, "I think it's grand the way you [and Darel] spend all your money on books, but why don't you use libraries and spend on clothes instead?"

Darel responded from his hotel in Louisville. "I had thought of Little Rock next, but now I'm in Louisville, & find it more economical to go on to Birmingham. I'll probably go there next, & thence to New Orleans. That will make New Orleans sooner, & seeing you sooner, but we'll probably miss Mardi Gras.

"Of course all this is subject to Alsberg," he continued. "He seems to be holding a tight rein on us."

The phone rang as he wrote. Two special delivery letters were being brought to his room.

"—Yes, very much depending on Alsberg," he resumed. "The first special delivery says that Alsberg is flying to New Orleans, 'so you will please postpone going there until further notice from us.'

"Now I ask you—ain't that hell? Honestly I'm all busted up. Our Mecca, our Dream city, blasted from under us. And not a damned thing to do about it. I thought you might meet 'Rique & all the rest. Oh goddamn! Alsberg has so tightened up that I can't even leave a place without his permission—or go to one either. Such freedom as this job once had is lost, & I'm almost ready to say 'to hell with it.'

"I must call up Col. Beckner & do some work on editorial matters this afternoon. I'm so disgusted about this New Orleans business that I've got to go & get interested in something else."

A wire from chief field supervisor Reed Harris confirmed that Alsberg had departed. "That means no New Orleans for us."

"Do you want to wait for another time, or do you want to take a small shot at what is probably nearest to New Orleans—Mobile?"

"I'll be at Birmingham two or three days. Need also to go to Montgomery. Then I'll find Mobile needs a two-day visit if you want to do that. It's a poor substitute for New Orleans. The people aren't there. Wire me at the Redmont,

Birmingham. I can conspire with Miss Miles & work out a scheme for getting on to Mobile & wire you back when to be there.

Canal Street, New Orleans

"If you want to do it. I want to arrange it if you think the trip would be worthwhile. Personally I feel pretty damned sick about it. There wouldn't be people for you to stay with as in N.O., but you could get back to Atlanta & see the Dillards."

Three days later the prospect brightened. Alsberg had a bumpy flight to New Orleans and only planned to stay one day. "So maybe we'll get to go yet."

Anna was overjoyed. "May the gods grant us New Orleans. I long, darling, to be with you again, and how more perfectly could we meet than in the fabled city?"

But the gods disappointed. When Anna arrived on February 7, Darel was stuck in Jackson, Mississippi. "Dearest darling," she wrote him from New Orleans, "I'm so, sorry that you're missing this, but I couldn't regret coming though it is alone."

The Writers' Project took her under its wing. New Orleans was her first meeting with the South's fabled hospitality, and it mesmerized her. "Aunt Cammie showed me beautiful Indian weaving and her own weaving done entirely with plantation materials. She's trying to make an industry of it here on the plantation."

Then there was state director Lyle Saxon, beloved author of books on Louisiana. First Darel and then Anna were smitten by him. I picture him, hypothetically, the courtly southern gentleman. His velvet-drawled "nigger" lands outrageously on modern ears. The drawl I guess at, but the word is in print. Both races used it widely then, and we scratch our heads in wonder at 1930s race relations. After meeting Saxon, Anna toyed with the word herself— temporarily thank goodness.

There are hints that Anna and Darel arranged a visit after all while she was in New Orleans. She wrote him near the end of March, "It seems that last night's tears were due to the time of the moon, and so this morning I arose with the knowledge that the chance I thought we took *in New Orleans* [emphasis added] was no chance at all." That and one other passing reference is all we get, yet the day-to-day exchanges seem to leave no space for such a visit.

New Orleans was over quickly. "There are no thanks for such a lovely experience as this trip has been," she wrote. Homeward bound, she described the swamps passing her train window, the oaks with Spanish moss, palmettos sparkling in the morning sun, cypress trees with their gangling root systems reflected in still water, knees poking up at intervals. An arm of the Gulf was ornamented with whitecaps and distant sails, and later "long needle pine country," all new to Anna.

In Atlanta, Project people greeted and feted her for a day, then she was back in Washington.

Darel had left the Charleston office under the nominal direction of slow Mr. Burns and drunk Mr. Herbert, with Ross Johnston pulling strings backstage. In mid-March, Darel was back to deal with the firing of Burns. *Attempted* firing, as things turned out. The man had a following, "and folks are fearful to kick him out. He would make a terrific noise." Clyde Billups took over from Johnston, improving things, Darel said, but ultimately it would "never work amiably with Burns in it—he is an impossible old coot. Billups is very quiet, but he has an iron hand under his suede gloves. Herbert also emerges as a leader, and I believe that between them they will make a go of it."

Chapter Twenty-Eight

Deluge

I T HAD BEEN one of the coldest winters in US history. Darel's folks back home at Dixie had their first white Christmas in years. His mother wrote in early January, 1936, "I wish you could have saw the beautiful Chris. trees we had all around. The pines was white and green, and the holly trees was covered with snow and the red berries peeping thru. I had a hard time to keep feed out for the birds. The snow would come and cover it up." On the 21st, Gladys wrote, "We had the biggest snow come last night and yesterday we have had for years. There must be fifteen inches in depth. I just thought yesterday when we were having such a blizzard how nice it was to be able to turn on the radio and have church services and entertainment from the outside."

February temperatures had often dipped below zero, but toward the end of the month things began warming up, and the snow began melting. Streams swelled, though not yet enough to raise alarms. As early as February 8, Darel reported that he had seen "a good deal of flooded land on the upper waters of the Pearl River," but that was the deep South. Darel was in Mississippi, and things were warmer there.

On March 2, Germany remilitarized the Rhineland, a buffer between Germany and France, which the Versailles Treaty had demilitarized. Hitler said he did it because the toothless 1935 Franco-Soviet Mutual Aid Treaty made him nervous.

As winter ebbed, Anna glowed with accounts of spring-like weather. "The day has been beautiful," she wrote on March 5. "The little silver fir in the park at 13th & K was like a melody for strings by Bach, rare and lovely, and straining delicately to the gray blue sky. I saw a cardinal singing lustily on the top of a gnarled old oak. Oh it was good, the sun and birds and trees and the flower vendors in the street. And tonight a large golden moon sends a soft glow through high mist."

But snow melt had things rumbling up the Potomac. A Mr. Talmadge, whom Anna encountered on a trolley, told her and she told Darel, that "the high water and ice haven't hurt our place [on the island] at all." March temperatures were higher than normal; weather was unsettled. By mid-month, D.C., Baltimore, and surrounding areas had gotten an entire month's worth of rain. On her birthday, March 14, Anna went out to look at the Island. "The water has risen very high. It flows entirely through the depression between our half and Mr. Walter's half. It was fascinating to watch."

March 17, St. Patrick's Day, was arguably Darel's favorite; he would don his "antique" green tie and raise a toast to his adopted kinsmen. On that day, a powerful storm up from the Gulf of Mexico dropped five inches and more of rain in the Blue Ridge Mountains.

By stages, the rising Potomac wreaked its fury—$3 million damage in Cumberland, Maryland ($50 million today), cresting 17 feet above flood stage at Hancock, washing out a bridge at Shepherdstown and two at Harper's Ferry, damaging the bridge at Brunswick, destroying the one at Point of Rocks. On that same day Anna, lacking perhaps a radio for late-breaking reports, wrote to Darel, "'Tis a stormy March 17 and St. Patrick's Day, so merry returns to you. May it bode you much happiness. It's been a balmy spring day with trees budding to burst and grass green and greener and lovely clouds chasing each other across the sky. 'Tis beautiful dear person and I wish for you much of the same beauty."

The flood reached D.C on the 19th. It was the city's worst ever. Only one other, during World War II, has surpassed it, and the height at Great Falls has never been topped. Darel wrote to Anna from Nashville, "I read about the floods in the Potomac. You are safe of course and comparatively undisturbed, but I wonder what's happening on the Island. Our shack ought to stand up, I suppose. I do hope nothing bad happens. You told in your letter about high water, but neither of us thought things would get this bad. I can't imagine Memorial Bridge closed, or any of the things I've been reading about."

That same day, Anna wrote, "How are you Darel? Have you had any flood troubles? Oh how I hope not and that you won't. Washington is prepared for the crest of the Potomac at 1 p.m. today. A dike is built to the river beginning at the Washington Monument. I want to go down and see it." The Civilian Conservation Corps had built the dike. Water had invaded the Mall, threatening Federal Triangle, which lies below sea level.

"I hope our Island dwelling will be safe," she said. "I'm going out now and mail this airmail special, though airmail probably won't do any good for the airport is flooded." The airport, where the Pentagon now sits, was under six to eight feet of water. "Radio report just announced that all summer cottages along the canal [the C&O Canal, which paralleled the Potomac] are covered and some of them are floating down the river. I'm anxious to go out this evening. I believe it will be possible through upper Georgetown to Reservoir Road."

Eight friends piled into a car. "There was no Island," she told Darel. It was completely submerged. "No anything, just water all the way up to Tucker Brewster's old home. A few thin trees were left; most of our lovely big ones were carried away. The lockhouse is still there but that row of houses to the left as you come down the hill is gone. The old watchmaker said that the first one in that row went when a tree was impounded against it, and the others just went before it like so many toothpicks. Mrs. Clokey's house, our house, Mr. Walter's house, those others along the canal and feeder are all gone. We saw trees sway, sag, and snap off, then swirl away as we stood there."

For the others of her party, it was exhilarating, but Anna felt sick. "It was grand in a way," she said, "but they hadn't seen our moonlight fairyland. We came back to town through two hours of traffic. I think all of Washington was out on Reservoir Road to view the flood."

Darel wrote her back, "Sorry I was to hear of the fate of our shack, and wondering and thinking ever since what we must do, and thinking it probably best to get us a tent and go there this summer should that prove suitable to Skinker. I have me doots he will want to build again. Darling, don't you worry about floods down here. The Ohio can pour all its floods into the Mississippi without flooding the Lower Mississippi unless a lot also comes in from the western tributaries. I have been looking for signs of such a condition but haven't seen any in the papers. I feel pretty sure I won't run into any trouble. I suppose the house on Snake Island went too, did it? Maybe we might tent there, huh?"

A couple of nights later, Charles Brooks, working on the Duchess County, New York, guide, and Alsberg's assistant director, George Cronyn and his wife, pitched in to throw a dinner party for Charles's friends at Anna and Darel's apartment, though Darel was still on the road. Charles was a well-connected Harvard graduate—"lousy with money," Anna said. He had a car.

Anna invited an impoverished poet from D.C.'s Federal Arts project, Julian Lee Rayford, whose painted plaster busts of Uncle Remus, Davy Crockett, Mark Twain, Casey Jones, and John Henry found a home in the John Easton School in Georgetown. He didn't even have taxi fare, and didn't make much of an impression until he started reading his verse. He grew on them then, and the party evolved into a spirited session of readings and responses.

Anna was proud of the way it worked out, lacking only Darel's presence to make it complete. "The more I see of Marian and Bill Dove the more I wish that they could know you," she told him. During the evening, she had tried convincing Charles that coercion wasn't the best way of trying to change a person's opinion, but he refused to budge. "I found out later that he was pretty well lit," she said, "which I think explains much."

It was a good crowd, but at 3 or 3:30, as the last consignment—Charles, Julian Lee, the Doves—was leaving, Murray Godwin took off his coat and said, "How about some coffee?" Jerre Mangione, author of *The Dream and the Deal* about the Writers' Project, described Godwin as a "personable...orange-haired disciple of James Joyce who...when aroused to action, could demonstrate the anarchic streak that was the hallmark of any writer worth his salt."

Anna assented to the coffee, but Charles needed to leave, and the others depended on him for transport. Anna started brewing coffee but told Murray that if the others didn't wait for him, he'd have to get a cab. To which he offered, "You don't have to make coffee, you know." Since it was nearly made, Anna said, he might as well have it unless he wanted to try catching Charles. No, he was tired of riding around with other people.

A knock came at the door. Charles, Julian Lee, and Bill Dove had decided Murray's intentions toward Anna may not have been honorable, and Charles undertook the coercive route to change Murray's opinion, demanding that he come immediately. Murray sat down and said, "Try and take me." Anna asked them all to have a cup of coffee and then go, but that wouldn't do.

Before she knew it they had Murray in the hall. She heard, "Take off your glasses," and a fight erupted. She tried to get them to come back and have some coffee, or let Murray come back while they waited, but the thing had acquired momentum. So she closed and chained the door. Murray was finally left on the stoop outside with a bloody nose, hailing a cab. He sent the elevator boy back up for his hat.

"My feeling is that I never want to see Murray Goodwin [*sic*]*** again," she wrote to Darel, "unless he is completely sober. It was ugly, and it had been such a brilliantly conversational party. It just made me sick. How I wished for you. I just sat for a long time feeling stunned. Believe me, I'm not having any more Murrays up here unless you're here too…I'm through socializing for a while." (She wasn't.)

That was Saturday. On Monday Charles went to the Library of Congress where Anna was researching Lewis and Clark. He took full responsibility for the fracas and apologized. Then he called Julian Lee and took him, Murray, and another party guest, D'Arcy McNickle, assigned by the Writers' Project to the Bureau of Indian Affairs, to lunch at La Paree, and all were friends again.

D'Arcy and his wife, Joran, were among Charles's friends. They had a daughter, Antoinette, 'Toinette or, even more diminutively, "Tony," who was apparently one of the children Anna tutored. There must have been regularity to the tutoring, for she refers more than once to "my job." She very much enjoyed the "McNicks," but D'Arcy and Joran felt they no longer had much in common and were staying together mainly for their daughter.

*** Different sources spell the name with or without the double "o."

Chapter Twenty-Nine

Matrimony

A T THE END OF MARCH, Darel was home for a seven-week respite. He and Anna bought a commodious army surplus tent, set it up on the Island, and happily reestablished housekeeping. Pictures show plenty of trees still standing. Anna called it, "An Elysium for beauty and soft coolness in the evening, home of such mortals as we are." They ordered a ten-foot sailing dinghy kit, but it didn't arrive until mid-August, by which time Darel was in Atlanta confronting "a messy situation" which involved "that redoubtable character, Annie Laurie Hill (from all accounts her name would best be spelled without dotting the I in the last name)."

Cohabiting "without benefit of clergy," Anna and Darel had caged their status. She return-addressed her letters "Mrs. Darel McConkey" from their winter quarters, an apartment at 19th and M, N.W. On January 13th, his divorce from Fanny Mae had come through, the decree stipulating that he not remarry for 60 days. Earl Hyde reckoned the stipulation was there to be violated, to earn more work for the lawyers. Anna and Darel managed not to oblige them. On May 9, Darel's thirty-first birthday, he and Anna visited a justice of the peace and quietly tied the matrimonial knot.

Ten days later he was back on the road. Anna wrote thanking him for freeing her from her family. He told her, "You need not thank me for 'freeing you from the family.' What was done was done wholly & free-heartedly. I am glad if it makes you happy." So low-key was the event that it took Darel's mother until June 1 to welcome Anna "into our humble family. Hope you may never have cause to regret it." Anna wore a thin, unadorned, white-gold wedding ring.

One of Anna's closest friends, Mary Barrett, head of the Writers' Project's essays division, thought Anna had nerve to cast her lot with a married Irishman with a Don Juan reputation. "I answered," she told Darel, "that your attraction is stronger than the thrusts of those who had tried to warn me agin you— Edythe, Betty, Kitty etc. It is not my nerve that made me want to live with you, but just you as you are, because you have so much that I find endearing and attractive and that warnings of any kind mean nothing at all. I've known more happiness in my life with you than I thought it possible to have and that is literally true."

Darel replied, "I don't know how Mary got her information. The only thing I can think of is a conversation we had at coffee about types of women, her favorite being the 'big blond type of woman.' I took exception to the idea that physical types make much difference in personality and cited a few 'types' I had known, including the 'ex.' I must not have made it clear that I hadn't 'known' them 'biblically,' for I hadn't. I think Mary surmised more than was necessary."

Anna opened up frankly. "Will it help you to see my loneliness for you when you remember that there was not even an affectionate family in my background, and that you have taught me so much of what I have missed, that when I see you after a trip, I'm so full of the love that is trying to make up for those lost years that I just can't even begin to get enough of feeling you [word illegible] your hand on mine or on my arm, or just getting close and feeling at rest with you who really love me. I'm sorry that these other people whom I really like get the brunt of my longing for you. I long to be just with you, even if you sleep, I can be with you what always seemed to me before was only true of unreal folks.

"I can learn to be, I think, a really affectionate human being. But darling even now when I kiss you often it seems that this can't really be me. You see, warmth & demonstrative affection of any kind just weren't in a Dutchman's world, but I believe all people should experience their delights, and all of this does make me understand that your philosophy about showing warmth to folks is different from my feeling about it, but it helps oh so often to understand and I love you for being capable of something so infinitely desirable.

"I want life to have love and affection. I've learned to love you and you've been the greatest of teachers. So dearest won't you let me love you much, even too much, and so perhaps learn not to be embarrassed about my own warmth for the world? At present I have no desire to do more than love you, but I'll try to learn (and I really think I've made some progress) about the world the way you feel, because it seems so happy. Goodnight Darel sweetheart.—Anna"

Chapter Thirty

Absence Makes the Heart Grow Fonder

Norris Dam, Tennessee Valley Authority

IT COULD BE EASY to think that all of Darel's assignments were vexed, but meetings in Knoxville near the end of March had been rewarding. "We worked out a complete cooperation between TVA and the Writers' Project in the seven states that fall within the Tennessee Valley. TVA has a Recreational Development Survey modeled on the outline for the Guide and covering practically the same ground. I framed a letter to the state directors in Tennessee, Kentucky, Virginia, North Carolina, South Carolina, Alabama, and Georgia to send TVA all pertinent material that they have. The TVA survey is to end on April 10, and after that we can begin to ask them things. I think it is a swell swap, and both sides seem well pleased.

"Elder & I got back to Nashville this morning, 7 a.m., and had an editorial Sunday school in the Hermitage Hotel. The best heads of the staff were there, and it turned out to be a vastly congenial and apparently a very helpful conference. I was personally surprised at how well it turned out, since I felt I had mostly said everything in the previous one."

On the train from Knoxville to Nashville, he "worked over manuscripts till 1:30 a.m." and from Nashville wrote, "This is a very intelligent editorial board, eager to learn just what is wanted. I'm feeling particularly good about Tennessee—and one reason for it is that I worked out the TVA cooperation— a thing K.K. scratched at when she was here. Result: nothing." K.K. was Katherine Kellock, national head of the books' tours sections, a respected researcher but prone to errors in grammar, Darel said.

"There are a few flies in the ointment. The Knoxville project, an important one because of TVA, is very weak, with a pestiferous woman at the head of it. I understand Memphis is also weak. Elder & I go there tonite & will spend tomorrow. Then I'll go on over to Little Rock."

In late June, Darel was wrestling with West Virginia again. "Waiting for Glenn Callaghan to come over for Scotch, soda, and conversation on the problem of Mr. Burns," he wrote. Callaghan was state director of West Virginia's National Youth Administration. The "problem of Mr. Burns" was replacing him.

West Virginia's WPA administrator, Frank McCullough, was a Burns advocate, but Alsberg wanted a better man. Glen Callaghan suggested Page Pitt, head of journalism at Marshall College in Huntington. Pitt was a friend of McCullough and was willing to take the post. McCullough had, in fact, already tried recruiting him, but McCullough was now on vacation. Darel would take the matter up with Deputy Administrator E. C. Smith and let Pitt know the outcome.

On August 1, on a jaunt to Nashville, Darel could report nothing more consequential than waking in his hotel room with chigger bites:

It is with a pardonable lack of pride, and an unpardonable lack of modesty that I must tell you I have something more than fifty chigger-bites. If you remember how the symbol of the cross originated you must agree that they are either religious chiggers or that they are punishing me for seditious utterances among churchgoing people, for I have a bite on each of those three parts from which Fraser says crosses were first made.

I wakened to the sad state of facts this morning and besought a waitress in the coffie shoppie to get me some salt. She didn't, so I pocketed a full salt cellar, emptied it in the tub, and soaked myself for about an hour. Whether or not it helped I don't know. So far I have refrained, with a courage worthy of the Spartans, from scratching. Tonite, in my sleep I shall probably mangle myself horribly.

While Darel itched, Negro athlete Jesse Owens won the first of four gold medals at the summer Olympics in Berlin, where Adolph Hitler had expected nothing less than total Aryan triumph. On four consecutive days, Owens set three world records and tied another. To avoid shaking hands with the blackamoor who had humiliated his Aryans, Hitler declined to shake hands publicly with anyone at all.

Darel was home for a couple of days, then flew to Charleston, again. Anna saw him off at the airport. "May you have the memory of a good trip! The blue and the clouds were lovely as your plane rose and circled westward."

Aboard the plane, he watched her recede as he gained altitude. "I saw you in white down there at the airport, watching us go. And a feeling swept over me—with what childlike longing she watches this thunderbird soaring away, and so wishes to be in it! And how she would see the little airport, and the white blobs beside it, the Monument, and the Capitol, and spread-out Washington, and the Potomac."

In Charleston, Page Pitt had replaced Clyde Billups, who had replaced Ross Johnston, as chief puppeteer. "I think I have seldom been more amused and pleased than this morning at the conference which Pitt called," Darel wrote. "He *said* Mr. Herbert was the boss, but Pitt told him what to do. He outlined a regimen for himself whereby he will keep a definite schedule in the field (thus indicating that Burns will be expected to do the same). This is the humor and cajoling he used in taking authority and making everybody like it. I leave West Virginia looking better than it did and am happy about it. Page Pitt is just what the project needs."

Pitt also nudged an effort of Darel's to have a section on "Hill Country Humor" included in the West Virginia guide. Pitt told Darel that the president of Morris Harvey College, a Dr. Riggleman, would be on his plane to Cincinnati, and conversely told Riggleman that Darel was on it.

"We got together and told hill-country stories all the way. The day was misty, visibility was poor, the trip bumpy, and we were both glad to have conversation. Dr. Riggleman has a fund of stories. One of them I intend to write to Henry:

"A North Carolinian, visiting in West Virginia, stood agape before a rugged and beautiful scene. He was annoyed by an old man, a native, who came up selling apples. 'I'm enjoying this beautiful view of the mountains.' 'Yes,' said the old man, 'it's purty, but mighty rough. Now I've got a boy down in North Carolina and he writes me they have some fine scenery down there.'

"He told about a man's coon dog: It was winter, just at the time for cutting ice to store away in the ice-house. The man noticed a coon's track in the ice but thought nothing of it. He cut the ice and put it away. The next summer, when that piece of ice was brought out, with the coon track still in it, old Ring happened to be there and don't you know he picked up the trail and had that coon treed in less than thirty minutes."

A few such stories appeared in the West Virginia guide, but not a dedicated section. In 1937, however, the Writers' Project issued an anthology by Project members entitled *American Stuff*. It included Darel's "Hill-Country Wonders," but erroneously attributed it to C.S. Barnett. It also included a piece by Murray Godwin.

"At Cincinnati I parted from Dr. Riggleman and got into a big two-wing Condor (rather old-fashioned) and thence to Louisville. I left Cincinnati at 3:15 and arrived in Louisville at 3:11! believe it or not! The time changes somewhere along the way."

Curtiss T-32 Condor

Louisville was the heart of Bluegrass Country. "Clarke took me out to see the horse farms. The pièce de resistance was Man O' War." You'd have thought he'd visited a Wonder of the World, and maybe he had.

After seeing him, all else pales to insignificance. Man O' War is probably the greatest horse alive, 19 years old now but more magnificent than one could dream a horse could be. In his racing days he won 20 out of 21 races and untold sums in purses. He is insured for half a million and is used now only as a stud horse. A single service costs $25,000. It seems futile to try to describe his magnificent proportions, the burnished golden bay coat, the regal bearing. Man O' War is a big horse, but even considering his age he is supple, graceful, and—well—magnificent. You just run out of words, but it would be worth a million, if you had it, just to go out and look at him every day.

We drove through thousands of acres of bluegrass horse farms—the Whitneys, the Bradleys, the Riddles, the Fishers (of Body by Fisher), the Wideners, etc. They are fenced with miles of white painted fences. The fields and woodlots are as clean as if swept, and some of the fine old mansion's date back to 1830 and 1840. [Sam Riddle owned Man O' War, whose son, War Admiral, lost a ballyhooed match race to underdog Seabiscuit on November 1, 1938.]

But, coming back to town through Louisville's squalid outskirts, I could not but wonder at the disregard of values that exists in those thousands of artificially-kept acres, those inflated values on horses, and the gentility of mansions and broad acres set against the day-by-day values of the people who live in that poverty-stricken fringe. They constitute a commentary not lightly to be looked on.

Darel was eager that Anna share the flying experience. "I've just been thinking it's too selfish for me to go galumphing around all over the country in planes and you never up in ary one." In mid-August, he suddenly decided Anna needed a vacation and "ordered" her to fly to Elkins, where his brother, Clyde, would meet her at the airport, and she would visit his mother and Gladys at Dixie. "Buy yourself a few pretties to wear to Dixie. The rest I leave to you—but remember—this is orders." He somehow managed to figure that the trip would cost less than staying home.

Anna was delighted. "Sweetest Darling you're the most precious person in the world! And then you come along and give me a vacation and to fly. It's a beautiful idea and you're lovely to think of it, though very bad."

Three days later, however, "The Dixie farm was sold last Sat." Blanche's word drops with virtually no warning. "Of course we do not know just what we are to do," she said, "or when we will have to get out of here as there is no definite arrangements made yet." So much for Anna's flying vacation.

It sounds like a foreclosure or a tax auction. "The deed will be made today to *whoever gets the place* [emphasis added]."

"We hate so bad to think of going from here, but He who cares for the sparrows will take care of us. Gladys is down at Smith's every day helping. They are packing and getting ready to move out."

There was one slim chance. "We are going to try to rent here if we can. We will find a way somewhere or some way. Will let you know soon as we can."

By September 8, things had settled down, at least temporarily. "Guess matters have come to a definite end at last," Blanche wrote to Anna. "The deed has been signed and Strawther wins, and we took your advice and rented here." Darel had offered to pay the rent. "I am so glad we do not have to move this fall anyway. We get the house, lawn, and chicken lots and free gas for $12 a month. That seems high. If we had taken the garden it would have been $15. We decided we might have some of the yard in garden. That would be as much as we would be able to tend. The Smiths goes away the last of this wk. or the first of next."

Darel was sorry Anna's vacation didn't work out. "I *want* you to make a flying trip," he said, "and I mean for you to. Mayhap Elkins in October. That would be gorgeous." Intentions to the contrary, Anna never flew a day in her life.

While Anna was missing out on flying, Darel was missing out on the Island's natural beauty. "There is soft rain falling," she wrote of an evening, "and the candle flame sways gently in the breeze. The black shadow, more real almost than my pen itself, moves silently in the yellow glow. The Katy-did symphony is at its height and the tree frogs are a chorus in the distance." And of a morning: "I hope you slept as beautifully as I did. There is sunshine on the wet leaves and the mist is white and bright over the river. The tufted tit mouse peeps in, and I have no crumbs.

"I must bring something out for him & Pat and the cat bird and all of our other folk. And oh yes—I'm afraid that Cyrano has gone to other climes. I haven't seen him for weeks. Not since you've been gone. The Phlox is still blooming strong and there is a lovely little orange flower that I haven't seen before, and the beautiful water plant with its leaves that we like so well has flowers of which I send you one."

She could catch a trolley all the way to Cabin John. Frequently others gathered with her, and someone would have a car. They would grill steaks over an open fire, drink scotch, swim naked in the river, expostulate learnedly over current events, history, literature, the theories of Adler, the art of Whistler.

Sometimes she preceded the guests. "I added stones to the fireplace so it would accommodate two grills, and then gathered wood. At about dark, I built the fire and loved its crisp smokiness in the cool air. In the tent I lighted candles and prepared food. I was so happy to have all of that time to be doing things alone. Then I heard sounds across the feeder. My guests were arriving."

She rowed over to get them. "In a moment they were all busy mixing drinks, holding and turning the grills, and before very long we were eating steaks, and the pungent odor of coffee made glad anticipations for the after dinner smoke. Millions of stars shown brilliantly. There was no moon. The fire by then was a bed of coals and the candle light glowed lovely in the dark. And there was time, as I saw the whole, for an ache to rise at your absence."

He wrote back, "I miss you darling, and wish for you particularly in Island hours," and added, another time, "Ye gods, here you're doing all these interesting things at the Island, the McKnicks, the Sterling Browns, etc., and me not there!" Sterling Brown, a Howard University English professor, was the Project's national editor of Negro affairs.

She recounted a conversation about the Irish situation, which at that time consisted of a tariff war with England. A Professional and Service man from Michigan, Mr. Stannard, British and an unapologetic imperialist, explained that Ireland was England's "back door" and needed to be conquered. Anna's friend, Mary Barrett, asked why conquer? Why not partner? The question was naïve. British rule of Ireland could have taught the Jim Crow South a thing or two.

Stannard said the Irish would never partner. He admitted that English landlords exploited the Irish, but the Irish wanted "too much independence." Few Americans knew Ireland's tortured history with England, but Murray Godwin—of the bloody nose back in March—was an exception. The English first invaded Ireland in 1171 to solve labor problems, and that was when the exploitation started. Not until England became an imperial power, however, did her "back door" need protection, and she flexed imperial muscle to get it.

Ireland perversely declined to cooperate. "And so on & on," said Anna. "I was highly entertained."

Another time, she and Mary Barrett discussed nature vs. nurture. Mary favored nature 52 to 48, while Anna was the opposite. The difference put Mary in the eugenics camp—sterilizing human "delinquents" to improve the race, or breeding for "positive traits" as we do with animals. Anna didn't think we knew enough to predict outcomes. They talked for hours, ending on the accommodating note that they had different outlooks and that eugenics was an open question. The subject was debated seriously in the '20s and '30s, until Nazi perversions of the theory during World War II resulted in the extermination of 6 million Jews.

She shared office gossip. "Yesterday at noon I met Don Corley and spent an afternoon with scotch and soda at the Toltec. He is certainly a character isn't he? Most of the afternoon was spent in Don's defense of Henry Alsberg against Mary. She dislikes him [Alsberg] more than ever. Don did attack Carita Corse [head of the Florida Project] as a competent historian in somewhat the same way as Monroe did. What is your opinion?"

On another day: "I've just come from the office where a vociferous battle between Henry & George [Cronyn] was in process. George, by being calm and holding on to his reason, was gradually allowing Henry to wear himself out and it seemed to be going more smoothly. When I left, Henry was still shouting petulant remarks at George & George would go on calmly with whatever problem it all started from."

Darel responded, "Don't worry too much about the tiff between George and Henry. They are of rather frequent occurrence. My main reaction to them is that it's a damnable shame two people as fine and intelligent as they are can't work together."

But the next day, "The Henry & George quarrel seemed to clear the air. No one has mentioned it, but many people heard it. Due to that or some other cause, the atmosphere in the office is healthier, more open and happy than I have ever seen it. This morning George, Henry, Mrs. Gilbert and someone else were having a conference that simply exuded good spirit. The District Guide seems to be moving along beautifully now and all in all things in this office have a bright aspect."

She later added, "Everyone notices that the office has a better atmosphere. The door between Henry & George's offices are nearly always open now and they are in and out of each other's cubicles. I hope it lasts. The whole place has a healthier, happier look than it has had for a long time."

In a larger vein, she commented to Darel on an Ernest Hemingway piece in "American Points of View." Italian dictator Benito Mussolini, said Hemingway, did not want war in Europe because the first dictator to provoke war and lose would lose the Continent for dictators for a long time. "This was written during the early part of the Abyssinian trouble," Anna said, when Mussolini, trying to resurrect the Roman Empire, had invaded Abyssinia (Ethiopia), sandwiched between the Italian colonies of Somalia and Eritrea.

America cheered Abyssinian Emperor Haile Selassie's defiance of Mussolini until he was forced into exile. "War is made by…demagogues and dictators," said Hemingway, "who play on the patriotism of their people to mislead them into a belief in the great fallacy of war when all their vaunted reforms have failed to satisfy the people they misrule."

A year later, Hemingway was reporting on the gruesome Spanish Civil War, which had begun as a coup attempt on the elected, left-leaning "Republican" government, and stretched over the next three years. Fascist dictator Francisco Franco emerged victorious and ruled with an iron hand until his death in 1975.

Hitler and Mussolini had come to his aid, testing advanced war machines like the Stuka dive bomber, in rehearsal for blitzkrieg by which the Nazis conquered most of Europe beginning in 1939. Officially, America stayed out, though many private citizens volunteered for the Republican side, to whom only the Soviet Union and Mexico tendered official support.

When that war came, sixteen-year-old history student Carlos Bosch left the University of Barcelona for France, thence for England and Oxford, until World War II displaced him to Panama and ultimately Mexico City, where he became an expert on pre-Columbian Mexico and US-Mexican relations. As a Guggenheim fellow in 1947, he met Dale Morgan, and through Morgan met Anna and Darel, introducing tortillas to their family in 1951, and becoming a fixture in their Mexican sojourn.

"Honey," Darel wrote, "I always love your accounts of conversations, tho I often don't comment on them at great length. Yours with Mary on problem cases and their cure [eugenics] interested me profoundly."

Mary Barrett sometimes bunked with Anna at the Island, and Anna sometimes slept at Mary's apartment in town. They were constantly borrowing money from each other. The whole office did it. We even see Anna paying $8.71 for the Cronyns' electricity. George and Frances Cronyn were frequent partyers at the Island, and they and Anna often ate out in D.C. or at the Cronyns' home. Anna visited the office so regularly, and was on such familiar terms with the people, that it sometimes sounds like she worked there, though she didn't.

The plane that flew Darel to Atlanta on August 21 was a Lockheed Electra. "It is built like a big Douglas," he told Anna, "but it is smaller—only ten passengers." (The "big" Douglas, the DC-2, carried fourteen.) "A beautiful, trim little ship," he said. Airplane cabins were neither heated nor pressurized, so top cruising altitude was little more than 12,000 feet. Amelia Erhart, the "female Charles Lindbergh," disappeared in an Elektra trying to break the round-the-world record the following year.

He was in Atlanta for a week. The inebriate Mr. Key was gone, and the project must have been moving satisfactorily, for he reported little more than reading reams of copy. He was on to Savannah, then finally logged about a week of Island time back home, assembling the boat kit while there, then soaring off again, this time to Jacksonville, Florida, beholding the limitless Atlantic from the air.

Boatwright, Anna's parents in background

The ocean, when seen first from the air, is an awful sight, in the true sense of the word. It is as if the world broke there at the white shoreline and beyond was an abyss of blue mist. For the ocean is a vast nothingness of water. You find yourself doubting its corporeality. You watch its blue-mist surface anxiously to reassure yourself that in truth it is water, real water, like you swim in. And presently you are out over it, and there is nothing under your side of the ship except a blue void that people say is water.

So you look, and seem to see a rippling swell, and you are glad then, for it really is water, and you feel like clapping your hands when a whitecap breaks, yet you watch hopefully, for it may be a white bird. And when presently it is a white bird, you are not sure it is a white bird for you are so high it is probably a boat or a buoy. And you look away out there, and find almost undecipherable lines on that unbelievable deep and you think, 'This is really the ocean, the kind the early explorers sailed on, and I am seeing it from a crow's nest higher than they ever had on the tallest-masted ships.'

And you seek far out, and fill in land where there is no land, for your eyes simply will not admit there can be anything that is nothing. But land there is not, nor horizon even, for this mist and the cloud-mist are sewn together so artfully you cannot even find the seam. And there is a gnawing fear inside you as you look out over to the other side of the ship and out the other windows. But there, thank God! is an animated pastel relief map of brown wide winding rivers coming down through algae-green swamps and there really is something that is something after all.

He spent a day in Jacksonville "answering vexatious questions popped at me by Dr. Corse and Carey Thomas," and in talking over the vexed Historical Survey problem. The Historical Records Survey, about which more later, had been separated from the Writers' Project and set up as an independent entity. "Mrs. Corse is, or says she is, glad to get rid of the Survey." Carita Corse was the Florida Writers' Project director.

"Mrs. Hahorner, the present [Survey] head…is rather young (about 27 I believe) and rather too ready to talk, which I told her seemed true, and Mrs. Southworth head of Women's and Professional Projects, is a bluff, hearty, cards-on-the-table woman, fortyish and fat, whom it was a relief to meet, for I felt I could say flatly what I had to say. The others seem devious and too careful to say no more than they should. Mrs. Southworth is calling a conference tomorrow morning to get us all together, and then we'll see what happens."

He doesn't bore us with the conference details but does amuse us with his visit to St. Augustine, America's oldest city, of his prowling the Spanish fort, of swimming tentatively for his first time in Atlantic surf, and enjoying the best seafood of his life. He crossed for a day to Tampa and Fort Myers on the Gulf coast, flying in "an old noisy Stinson (8 passengers) which you suspect may fall into bits at the next bump." He was able to borrow the airways map from the pilot to keep track of where he was.

Then something new—Topeka Kansas. "I've just finished dictating my report," he told Anna, "and I'm to be called for at four for my second and last swim in Florida salt water before leaving tomorrow for Kansas—of all ungodly places to go."

Anna asked Alsberg when he was going to send Darel to a more glamorous spot than Kansas. Alsberg answered that none of us could do what we wanted, and Darel did, after all, have Florida. "There was an engaging twinkle in his eye when I suggested that Santa Fe would be nice."

Chapter Thirty-One

Kansas

The "big Douglas" DC-2

DAREL'S FLIGHT as far as St. Louis was a red-eye of numerous short hops. "The less said about that night flight, napping on planes, napping in airport waiting rooms between hops, etc., the better. I was tired when I left Florida and absolutely frayed when I got here." Still,

Our big Douglas started its long smooth glide into St. Louis at about 6 this morning. There was a streak of pastel sunrise above the line of clouds, and down below was an enchanted prairie. There was a softness about it, to deceive the eyes, a quality of blown white sand, which made me wonder if this could be the dust-storm country. Then I realized that the whole land was covered with a low thin fog, above which single trees and clumps rose in a misty green. It was a land of sheer enchantment which the eye could scarce accept by reason of its almost immaterial beauty.

From there on I did not sleep, for this was the entry to Lewis and Clark country and I wanted to see it from the air. Besides, it had a loveliness that drove sleep away.

The last time I crossed Missouri [visiting his brother, Frank, in 1929] it was in a bus, and took a full day. This time it took one hour and thirty-six minutes. All the way across from St. Louis to Kansas City, the winding broad ribbon of the Missouri River could be seen from our altitude, which I estimate at 9,000 feet (because westbound planes fly at odd thousands).

My eyes followed its great bends hungrily, tracing out the channel we will one day putt-putt along, trying to visualize how hilly the shores might be, and imagining immobile water birds watching us go by, then stirring to unhurried graceful flight. [They still dreamed of tracing Lewis and Clark.] Even from aloft, where great graceful bends go for miles out of the way and become all but lost to sight, or covered under a lake of fog, this river has a quietness that engendered such visions.

I was happy in watching it, and seeing the tall yellow bluffs at one point, and broad sand beaches, and channels that wander from it, and sandbars, and islands, and once a side-wheel boat pushing a barge. But I wished ever so much I might go back across it before the land was pieced into farms, when herds of buffalo would be scattered living patches of black below, and a colorful straggling caravan would be an Indian village on the move.

Once I saw an eastbound train cometing across the landscape at unbelievable speed (about 250 miles per hour, apparent; that is, our speed of perhaps 190 plus his 60, since we have no feel of speed at all) with a long silver plume reaching straight out behind.

And almost too soon we were losing height and before long came smoothly down into the black dirty mist that covers Kansas City, banked for a close look at the river, and sat down on the black runway of the K. C. airport. What followed was a train trip [to Topeka] on a lousy day-coach, without breakfast.

"I had just thirty-two dollars. The old seersucker is so worn that I cannot with self-respect use it again, so I am going to send it back for such slovenly summer wear as it will endure next year. I do not seem out of place, just yet, wearing white trousers, but their days are numbered (it was 90 here today). Will you send me the blue linen trousers? I have to buy a fall suit, like it or not. That will mean about $15.

"I will probably be here all week, and I know I won't have enough money. Can you rustle up $20 or $25 for me and send it right away? I'm sorry as all get out putting this burden on you. I feel perfectly rotten about it.

"When do you plan to move back to town? It's only ten days to October now, and it must be getting pretty cool on the Island."

Weather, it turned out, was not the only issue. "It is not politic for me to stay on the Island alone," she wrote, "so to obviate any unpleasantness, I'll confine my nights to the city unless someone goes with me. It seems that from a most unexpected source I can expect difficulty—our neighbor [Mr. Walter] on the upper end. If I simply don't stay alone any more, all will be well and no embarrassment will ensue. That seems to me to be the right time to put an end to something that may mean poor relations with a neighbor."

Later, however, "Don't be bothered about Mr. Walter. The situation didn't get far. I just wanted to avoid having to make an unpleasant break with a neighbor."

Kansas epitomized Writers' Project politics at their worst, and Darel minced no words expressing his opinion. Two days after his arrival, he told Anna, "I am feeling very much in the dumps about Kansas. So much that I went to a movie to escape myself. What will have to be done I don't know, but something will. I'm beginning to recover my Irish and I'm about ready to wade into this. I'm getting plenty of sleep now—at least these Kansans leave me alone.

"But God! Their copy is unutterably lousy.

"Were it not that they leave me alone it would be as bad as Little Rock. As boring, I mean."

The next day, "Another day with dull people, another day with rotten copy, another evening at the movies, and another evening poring over hopeless stuff."

Slowly he began getting a handle on things. "The Kansas situation is one of the most intricate and interesting I have encountered. It involves literally days to even disentangle the facts. Now I think I have a fairly good picture, which is a cross-section of politics if ever there was one. I'm waiting to see what my next move is, but I think I'll delay the march of the politicians for a month in any case.

"It is more fun than I expected, and fun of a totally different sort than anything I foresaw."

The day before Darel arrived in Topeka, two people resigned from the Kansas Project for political reasons. Nineteen thirty-six was election year, and Kansas governor Alf Landon was the Republican nominee. Landon had been one of just two Republican governors in the nation to win re-election in 1934. An anti-Landon book, *Meet Mr. Landon*, had appeared over the byline of state Writers' Project Assistant Director, John Wells. Wells resigned, presumably so as not to be seen trying to curry favor with the Roosevelt forces.

The other resignee was project supervisor E. W. Parkes, who had actually written the book but couldn't take credit for it owing to blots on his character, including a stretch in prison and "certain radical activities."

Wells had convinced Darel's predecessors, one of whom was Larry Morris, that he was a capable administrator. Morris was assistant to Ellen Woodward, the head of the entire Federal Project Number One, or "Federal One," the whole WPA arts division, including theater, music, and visual arts along with writers.

When Darel arrived, the Kansas office was in disarray, ostensibly thanks to Wells's absence. There had been no blowback from the book—which wasn't selling well—so Darel explored the possibility of bringing Wells back. Kansas's Democratic committeeman saw no problem politically and suggested that Darel and Wells talk it over with the State WPA Chairman, Evan Griffith. Mrs. Harrison Parkman, state Director of Women's and Professional Projects, also favored bringing Wells back. She offered to make the case to Griffith, but Darel insisted on making it himself.

Afterward, he took the proposal to state Writers' Project Director, A. Q. Miller. Miller had already lamented to Darel about losing a good man; Darel now asked him if he'd like to get the man back. Surprisingly, Miller opposed the idea. Wells and Parkes had failed to get Democratic Committee backing for their book, so they had solicited money from Project staff. It hadn't sold well, and they'd gotten staff members to sell it for them. Darel suspected Miller may also have been jealous of the influence Wells still held with the staff, though Miller himself had assented to Wells's ongoing casual affiliation.

Miller told Darel to ask the "Cabinet" about reinstating Wells. Clarence Cook, the managing editor, didn't think Wells would get the work done. The office consultant, Jennie Owen, was reluctant to weigh in—her loyalties seemed to be with Miller, but Wells had gotten her the job. Ralph Hukill, the office manager, was also ambivalent. "Through time," Darel said, "the other side of the picture began to come out."

Darel took Wells to see State WPA Chairman Griffith, who had supported bringing Wells back, and there revealed Miller's opposition. "Wells was flabbergasted," Darel said. He watched the man struggle between being philosophical and heaping abuse on Miller. Griffith suggested that Wells wait a month and see what happened.

The deeper Darel dug, the less promising Wells looked. He was a former chairman of the Kansas State Democratic Committee who'd "had to be placed," and the "placement" had been as the Writers' Project assistant director. He had come to the job thinking it really was the boondoggle its enemies said it was—to keep people happy regardless of output. As a result, that was just what it became: a "dumpheap" for misfits, as Darel put it—one of the worst in the country.

"Reading copy has convinced me that the entire Kansas Guide has yet to be written," he said, "with the exception of two or three pieces by Hukill, Cook, and Project Supervisor Harry Ross." When Wells left, the office consultant, Jennie Owen, had been put in charge of a group "which she handled as a kindergarten teacher would have," complete with morning and afternoon recesses. She had "no capacity for handling people," though she appeared to be a capable writer. Rehabilitation of the project through competent work "had in no sense of the word been attempted."

Project Director Miller took it on himself to convince the National Democratic Committeeman for Kansas, Lynn Broderick, that reinstating Wells was not a good idea, and reported the move to Darel the next day. By now Darel was fully convinced and said as much to Women's and Professional Projects Director, Mrs. Parkman. She concurred and relayed the information to State WPA Administrator Griffith. Miller announced in conference that Griffith had telephoned him his vote of confidence in the decision.

In fact, the Democratic powers in Kansas were afraid to antagonize Miller before the election, November 3. Miller was a Republican and made it clear that if Wells came back, he would resign the project and blow the whistle on

Wells. This, even though he had been happy enough to travel while Wells handled administrative troubles right up to the time of his departure.

There remained "bitter disagreements on quota, assignments, payrolls, and practically everything involved in administration of the project." Mrs. Parkman arrogated to herself control over *all* the Federal projects, theater, music, and visual arts as well as the writing. A personality clash existed between her and Mr. Miller which Darel doubted could be resolved. She had told Wells she was going to fire Miller after the election. State WPA Administrator Griffith was tired of her and determined either to reduce her supervision to a minimum or be rid of her entirely after the election. In any case, Darel could see no possibility of doing much before Election Day. He told Mrs. Parkman he would try to return to Kansas at about that time.

Darel thought the office manager, Ralph Hukill, was the best prospect to replace Wells. Hukill, though not a writer by profession, had written most of the Kansas copy that got approved in Washington. He was serious about doing a good job and believed it would be possible to inspire the staff to turn out good copy. Darel left him in charge of personnel. If by November 3, he had gotten good copy from them, his appointment as Wells's replacement could be justified. He'd only been on the project six weeks, and a promotion now might encounter opposition. "If, however, on the basis of performance, we can promote him in early November, we have a perfect comeback for politicians."

Jennie Owen would be made tour editor with responsibility for the form and finish of all tours. She was an experienced writer and expected to be happier and more productive in that capacity.

"Mr. Miller," Darel said, "is honest and well-meaning but he has no conception of the job before him."

He asked Alsberg to let him return to Washington to discuss Kansas, but Alsberg wired back, "STAY KANSAS MAKE COMPLETE STUDY AND SEND REPORT ALSO USE PHONE IF NECESSARY STOP TRIP WASHINGTON WOULD BE USELESS."

"So now I'll be off somewhere else" until after the election. "Where, only Alsberg knows." When he learned it was Arkansas, Darel said, "That was the most unkindest cut of all. Alsberg knows my sentiments on the subject, yet he sends me there. I thought that was a closed book."

Anna wrote back, "I hope that Little Rock is not too bad. Your work is valuable. I know it is considered so by Henry. He as much as told me so the other day when he said, half laughing, 'So what if he doesn't like Little Rock? He's the one who can do it.'"

Chapter Thirty-Two

Arkansas, Georgia, West Virginia

Bernie Babcock, Arkansas Writers' Project Director
Bernie Babcock Photograph Collection UALR PH 0060

H E HAD BEEN BORED in Arkansas in February, and hadn't had a good opinion of the state director, Mrs. Bernie Babcock. "She is a sturdy picturesque, oaklike old lady, young in spirit, with colorful rural use of words. It didn't take long to find that she was a dry & a few other idiosyncrasies, tho on some points she is very advanced—a liberal of the Jane Addams school." His second encounter, after Kansas, didn't initially improve his outlook.

Deadlines seemed to be "how things were going." Babcock was rushing to complete "stuff" related to tours, cities, points of interest, and maps by October 1, "but the darned old fool has Fulks and Charles J. Finger, her only capable writers, slaving away on Introductory Essays," which were not under deadline at all.

He had seen copy, he said, "bad enough to justify issuing a memorandum that 'all copy intended for Washington must pass over the desk of Clay Fulks, Editor-in-Chief, before being sent to Washington.' I've passed the point where that old lady can talk my ear off. I've made up my mind she won't load Washington with a lot of tripe just to say she met the deadline."

The next day: "Say, didn't I raise a storm today! I told you last night I was going to. I wrote a terse memorandum to the effect that all copy intended for Washington must go over Clay Fulks' desk and bear his initial.

"Then I went to see Dot Kennon, director of [Arkansas] Women's & Professional Projects, to let the memo sink in. While I was there, Mrs. Babcock called. Mrs. Kennon said to tell her she was in conference. She waited, but when we decided to let her in, she was not to be found. Then Floyd Sharp, the administrator, wanted to see us. Bernie had taken her troubles to him, and he had countermanded my order."

Darel had underestimated his Bernie Babcock. She was nobody's fool. In a life that stretched from 1868, the year after Darel's father was born, to 1962, the year after Darel died, she published forty books, among them the historical novel, *The Soul of Ann Rutledge*, based partly on interviews with people who had known Abraham Lincoln personally.

When it appeared in 1919, it went through fourteen printings and was translated into several foreign languages. In 1903, she had been the first Arkansas woman listed in *Authors and Writers Who's Who*. She had founded the Museum of Natural History in Little Rock. She had been a Prohibition activist, and those were just a fraction of her accomplishments.

"It developed," Darel continued, "that Frank Wells [Darel's predecessor] had agreed, when he hired Clay Fulks, that Mrs. Babcock would edit all his copy. I'd never heard of this, and have reason to believe that Henry [Alsberg] hadn't either. Naturally, Mrs. Babcock, who did know it, and Floyd Sharp, who also knew it, were up in the air over my memo." Fulks's copy was to be reviewed because of his radical history, his connection with Commonwealth

College, a cooperative farming and educational community based on socialism.

"Well, I realized I had stuck my neck out," he admitted, "but I grinned with a certain joy in the fight, and the foreknowledge that something would come of it to improve the situation.

"Fulks came up to my room and I outlined to him what had happened. He was amenable to the situation, and I admire his attitude. He met honesty with honesty, and I feel there will be no trouble on his part whatever."

"I need to pay a tribute to Bernie. She was exceedingly nice to me this morning and I believe can stand the gaff better than I thought. I deliberately left the way to Washington open. She could have appealed to Henry [Alsberg] or, more devastatingly, to Senator Joe. T. Robinson."

Robinson was Senate Majority Leader. Had she chosen to take Darel's memo up with Robinson, there's no telling what might have happened. Darel himself hadn't "whispered" to Washington; he wanted to work it out first on his own. "Apparently Bernie has kept her peace. It would have surprised me to find a mean streak in her. Right now I don't believe it's there.

"This copy," on the other hand, "drove me so nutty last night that I went to see a movie, *My Man Godfrey*. By all means see this show. It is one of the most charming and amusing—nay even uproarious—sophisticated comedies I have ever seen." It starred William Powell, a great of American stage and film, most famous for his role in *The Thin Man* film series. Yet still, Darel felt like "a very uninteresting resident of Little Rock. The town just does things to a fellow. Wish I had time to get drunk—and you to get drunk with."

On October 4, he wrote from Charleston, West Virginia, "Presumably I'll be back in Washington a week from now. We had probably better move to town. If you can find an apartment and make a down payment of say $10 to hold it, we could finish the first advance payment on the 15th."

And, in a week, back in Washington he was. He had been on the road for a year, and the Project rewarded him with two weeks off. Anna had found winter quarters, an apartment at 15th and M Streets, but it was November 19 before she was all moved in.

Darel left for a Writers' Project conference in Raleigh, North Carolina, and gave a talk at an ancillary meeting in Ashville. He reckoned everyone was pleased with its brevity, "for it was the last before lunch."

After a "dinner of banquet proportions," the WPA Symphony played "'Flight of the Bumblebee,' with zest and precision," and a Negro chorus opened with "Swing Low Sweet Chariot." The all-male ensemble was led by a woman, Nell Hunter. Only when its third number was a too-polished rendering of "Lo Hear the Gentle Lark," did Darel "disapprove"…until Nell Hunter began to sing. "I forgot everything but the richness, roundness, and power of her voice," he said.

"Now you shall never hear the end of my praises for Nell Hunter. If she were not a Negro, she would be in the Metropolitan—I am convinced of it. She sang in the chorus of the staged Green Pastures, but has done little else, so far as I can learn, commensurate with the superlative gravity of her voice." In 1939, President Roosevelt brought her to the White House to entertain the king and queen of England.

November 3, Election Day, Darel was in West Virginia. Franklin Roosevelt had defeated Alf Landon in the most lopsided popular-vote victory since James Monroe ran unopposed in 1820. Landon carried just two states, not including his own, Kansas. Roosevelt reckoned he had a mandate to continue the New Deal.

Darel had left Slow Burns and Drunk Herbert in "control" of the West Virginia project, with Ross Johnston pulling strings backstage. In March, Clyde Billups had replaced Johnston. By August, Page Pitt had replaced Billups. Herbert was turning in creditable copy, but Burns continued an anchor chain. It was time to get serious.

Darel and Billups went to WPA's West Virginia administrator, Frank McCullough, who promised to huddle with Senator Matthew Neely, to see if something else could be found for Burns. Then Darel and Billups lunched with Ross Johnston, who expressed willingness to take Burns's job, as long as the move didn't hurt Burns, though he probably wouldn't be able to come in until mid-December in order to finish his current project.

Darel then traveled to Huntington to get Page Pitt's angle. They drank and talked shop until the wee hours, but Pitt, lacking information from the field, couldn't add much. Darel was back in Charleston the next day, Thursday. On Sunday he wrote, "Things drag on here at a disgustingly slow pace. McCullough was supposed to have news on Saturday, but he came back from Washington without seeing Senator Neely. I was as mad as a wet hen, for I had called a conference Sunday afternoon to include Ross Johnston, Page Pitt, Clyde Billups, Jimmy Herbert, and myself, but there was no conference today."

Darel was also disappointed to learn that Herbert had not been doing satisfactory work. He hoped that once Burns was out of the way, things would improve.

In the midst of all, Alsberg asked the minimum number of people needed to run the program. Burns, Herbert, Billups, Pitt, and Darel met and framed an answer which Burns would send back after a study, striking off those who were inefficient or no longer needed. At a point, Pitt declared that "by damn" he was ready to quit if he couldn't get more cooperation. He understood that the program might be shut down, or at least "suspended" for a few weeks, an idea that McCullough, as state WPA administrator, supported. It was not a matter Darel had meant to raise, but he was glad Pitt did. "It may implant in Burns's mind the importance of either doing something or resigning."

Finally on Tuesday he could report that Senator Neely felt W. W. Trent, the State Commissioner of Education, should find something for Burns. Billups tried to call him but he was out of town and wouldn't be back until the next day. If Trent failed, Darel said, he would ask Burns to resign. If Burns refused, Darel could recommend closing the project temporarily.

On Wednesday, Darel said, "I think I begin to understand what it means to be a State Director. I find myself cast in approximately that role, and the days are wearisome with delays, yet when I look on them without impatience, I realize that things move a little." He went over three manuscripts with Herbert and found them in need of editing. He talked to Ross Johnston about rewriting the US 40 tour. He sat with Billups until he called Trent again.

Trent wouldn't be back until Thursday now. "Let no one tell you that Mexico is the real *mañana* land!" There had, however, been a letter about Burns—from Neely, Darel suspected—and a note on Trent's desk from his assistant saying, "See me about Mr. Burns." Maybe something was afoot after all, but to add to all the other headaches, Billups's supervision over federal projects had ended the day before.

Chapter Thirty-Three

DAREL HAD ASKED to go to Kansas after the election. He soon wished he hadn't.

"It all came about with a bang," he told Anna, "for Henry wired me to call him at 10 this morning. I did, with misgivings, for I expected him to be in a dirty humor, but he was very kind. The Kansas situation was bothering him, so I agreed to let W.Va. stew for a while and run out to Kansas. And here I am in Chicago, én route.

"Yesterday I got all worked up over the futility of trying to get things done in West Virginia, and decided that today I must tell of some progress even if it meant going direct to Burns and asking him to resign."

Alsberg had wired before Darel could act.

In Topeka, he found that Ralph Hukill's promotion to the assistant directorship had not gone through. It had been approved all along the line, by

State Administrator Griffith, by Alsberg, and by Mrs. Woodward, the head of Federal One, effective November 1.

It was now November 22, but Mrs. Harrison Parkman was holding it on her desk. Her recalcitrance offers a clue to the bees' nest Darel was heading into. She was the head of the Kansas State Women's and Professional Projects and may have thought her position gave her a state-level authority analogous to Mrs. Woodward's.

Many, taking a "states' rights" posture, resented federal oversight, even though The Writers' Project was clearly a federal program with standards the states had to meet to qualify for funding. Whatever Parkman thought, Darel was "pretty sore." He went to Deputy Administrator Allaman who "promised that the promotion would go through that day."

Darel was overly reassured. He told Washington that Hukill's promotion would go through. He also told them that quality of work would be the basis for keeping people on the payroll, and he announced stricter rules for attendance at the office and on visiting within the office, by authority of the state administrator.

The next morning, Hukill's appointment was still on Mrs. Parkman's desk. Darel wired Henry: the appointment—approved by him, Administrator Griffith, and Mrs. Woodward—was being held up in the state division of Women's and Professional Projects. He asked if Larry Morris couldn't do something about it.

Larry Morris was Mrs. Woodward's assistant at Federal One. He spent much time in the field and had been one to report favorably on John Wells. Morris, Darel thought, would fix Mrs. Parkman.

"But great is the resourcefulness of the opposition," he discovered. He had been asked to go see Miss Ann Laughlin, state director of the National Youth Administration (NYA, a WPA project to find jobs for sixteen- to twenty-five-year-olds).

Ann Laughlin told him that unless Hukill was dropped from the project, she would take her workers and leave. She had seen a letter by Hukill to Miss Jennie Owen which contained, as Darel put it, "nasty implications." He was sure Hukill had written the letter to "cheer Miss Jennie up," he said, but "she is 51 years old and it is silly to suppose that Hukill was making a play for somebody that old." Nevertheless, several women from NYA had complained to Miss Laughlin about Hukill's off-color cracks, and she had made up her mind that if Hukill didn't go, NYA would. "This would create a scandal," Darel said, "that would be ruinous to the project."

He could see no way out but to ask Hukill to withdraw as deputy and find someone else to run the project for "poor old ineffective Director Miller."

He asked Deputy Administrator Allaman to chew it over and went to lunch. On Monday he would question every person about Hukill's conduct, taking the women first. If that didn't bring out the truth, he didn't know what would. Then he would present the results in open conference to Administrator Griffith, Allaman, Mrs. Parkman, Miss Laughlin, Miller, and Hukill.

After lunch, Allaman called for him. "Too quickly," he had found someone fill Hukill's position, a Dr. MacGregor of the NYA. Darel said he wanted to investigate the charges first. Allaman and Miss Laughlin agreed to wait.

Saturday afternoon, Hukill and a Mr. Torrey, whom Darel had met on his previous trip, came to Darel's room to "use up some Scotch." Torrey was "a clear-minded, fair-minded chap" who worked closely with Mrs. Parkman. As the Scotch loosened him up, things began to clarify. MacGregor was a high-priced NYA man whom Miss Laughlin wanted placed advantageously.

That cleared up her angle, while the Wells and Parkes *Meet Mr. Landon* business was being used to discredit Hukill. "Torrey said an affidavit existed to the effect that Hukill boasted he had made three gray-haired women pregnant, all of them past 50!" Darel was the subject of innuendo himself. "Apparently I like Hukill because he gets me drunk and furnishes me with women!"

As the picture emerged, Darel got his Irish up. He would see this through, sanely and openly, and then "see what we shall see."

When he returned to his room that evening, an anonymous note was in his box: "McConkey: Hukill being investigated by Federal authorities and in all probability will be arrested within a few weeks."

That night he noticed a queer metal gadget about three inches square attached to the side of a locked door into the next room. Wires ran into the gadget, down the side of the door and through a hole in the wall to the next room. Powdered plaster on the floor under it made him think the hole had been drilled recently. He had never seen a Dictaphone and didn't know whether it was one, but he unfastened one wire and bent it up, then went to breakfast, to see if anybody refastened it while he was gone. He was out most of the afternoon. When he came back the wire was still bent up. He was determined to find out what it was.

Anna's information from Washington was that Mrs. Woodward, not Alsberg, had ordered Darel back to Kansas. "You need not wonder," he wrote her, "that when I got your letter saying Mrs. Woodward's office had sent me, it brought some questions to mind: Am I being put on the spot? Did [Mrs. Woodward's assistant] Larry Morris decide I should come, or did someone else? If somebody else did, why? Did Mrs. Parkman ask for me? If so, why?

"Do these people think I am a callow youth, easy to handle? (They do, I gather, for which I am glad, for it gives me an advantage.) I dined alone, for I don't want my social contacts misinterpreted."

On November 24, he wired Anna frantically: "PLEASE DEAR COULD YOU WIRE ME TWENTY DOLLARS WEDNESDAY. I'M GETTING TOO LOW ON FUNDS TO GET AWAY FROM HERE AND HOW I WANT TO GET AWAY. THREATENED WITH ARREST TODAY. HAVING LOTS OF FUN. LOOK FOR SEMI SHOWDOWN TUESDAY. REMEMBER ME IN YOUR PRAYERS. MEANTIME I LOVE YOU"

He elaborated in a letter.

"Intrigue piles upon intrigue, prison bars loom for Hukill, jail bars for both of us!

"Today I went about the business of investigating Hukill's morals. I questioned the entire staff, and a stenographer took it all down. It took most of the day. The office buzzed. One man refused to answer my questions because he is an applicant for the position. Another refused to answer because he is not sworn, and went out laughing and shouting and causing a commotion.

"Midst all this Torrey called saying I must see him at once. I found him with Parkes, author of *Meet Mr. Landon*. We drew aside for a little talk. He told me the postal authorities are ready to arrest Hukill for the letter he sent Jennie Owens [it is illegal to send obscene material through the mail], but Mrs. Parkman was stalling them off 'till afternoon. The day passed and Hukill was not arrested.

"Parkes nailed me after Torrey left. 'There are a few things I think ought to be straightened out,' sez he. 'Neither John Wells nor I want back on the Writers' Project. I don't understand what all the shooting's about. Never have....'"

"'Pardon me, Mr. Parkes,' sez I, 'but I beg to disagree with you. You know damned well what it's all about. You and John Wells have played a damned dirty game in this thing. And that's all I've got to say to you.'"

Wells, former chairman of the Kansas Democratic Party, "placed" in the Writers' Project, treated it as make-work with no standards. "Pencil-leaners," after the "shovel-leaners" of the construction projects. "SEND SHOVELS," the joke went.

"OUT OF SHOVELS," came the reply. "TELL MEN TO LEAN ON EACH OTHER." Wells larded the office with people regardless of ability. He and Parkes had solicited staff donations for *Meet Mr. Landon,* and had them selling the book for them.

"As I walked away," Darel said, "he protested weakly, "But that isn't true."

"When I came back from a pretended necessary trip to my room he was still sitting there, planning mean dirty guttersome things to do."

Mr. Miller invited Darel to lunch where, with Mrs. Parkman's representative, Henry Sticher, they discussed the program's needs. Then back to the interviews.

After they were over, Darel and Hukill went to Washburn College to see Hukill's old friend and counselor, Dr. Collier. While they were there, Hukill's wife called. Warrants had been sworn out for the arrests of himself, for his secretary, Violet Peterson, who had taken notes during the interviews, and for Darel.

They spent long worried moments while Dr. Collier's puzzling serenity made them feel like a couple of raw adolescents.

Darel called Miller and asked to come to his room. There Miller changed Darel's opinion from "poor old ineffective Miller" to, "he is wonderful, that old boy! His serenity under adverse report restores one's confidence. I could have hugged him. Knowing about warrants, he set out to prove that there couldn't be one. He called the county attorney, thru whom warrants must issue, and settled it once for all. The story had been started by the man who refused to answer questions and stormed out."

A woman in the office told it to Hukill's secretary—Violet Peterson—who called Hukill's wife, who called Hukill, "and so the news was toted from Ghent to Aix."[†††] Hukill and Darel were jumpy enough to accept the story at face

---

[†††] from Robert Browning, a book of whose verse Darel had with him

value, "but not old A. Q. He's been doing business in a state putrid with politics too long to be fooled."

By now, Thanksgiving was two days away, and Darel told Anna, "I look with much disfavor on Thanksgiving in Kansas! It ain't right, but I fear me 'twill be. If it does, I just won't do it: I'll go to Kansas City, Mo, and get thankfully plastered—for being out of Kansas one day!

"By the way, the electrical gadget is still unhooked as I left it. Hukill suggests I steal it, for a souvenir. I think I'll just do that, by gar!"

The next day he wired: "BUSY GETTING PLASTERED WITH TORREY. FIGHT WAXES WARM WITH NEW SUPPORT FROM WASHINGTON AND CHICAGO. DICTAPHONE IS ONLY A BUZZER AND ALL IS MERRY ON THE KAW RIVER."

Anna gave him the office's take. "Everyone seems to know that there is excitement in Kansas, and they're constantly asking me what I know about it. This morning Mr. Alsberg talked to me. Honey, he has confidence in you, I can tell. Just you keep on with your head above water & I'll bet that if there's anything of this organization left after January 1 [congressional opponents mounted endless challenges to Federal One's continued existence], there'll be a place in it for you. I'm to talk to Larry Morris for a few minutes later today, & if he knows anything, I'll let you know. Henry says he expects to hear from you Monday, so I suppose you'll be in Kansas at least that long. Then, another stop in W.Va. will put you well into Dec. before coming home. Keep well & happy."

On Tuesday, Darel gave Director Miller, Deputy Administrator Allaman, and Mrs. Parkman the results of his investigation. Twenty-eight of the 35 women in the office had no objection to Hukill's behavior. Only two said anything derogatory, while the others thought it a matter of opinion. He then reviewed the history of the project.

From April to late September, all copy sent to Washington had been returned as unacceptable except a piece written by Hukill. Since September, when Hukill was put in charge, a number of pieces had been returned with favorable comment, for slight revision only. If quality of work was the basis for judging a project, Hukill's output should be taken into consideration.

His listeners fell silent. Mrs. Parkman changed the subject.

Darel had ridden to the conference with Miller and asked him who he had in mind as Hukill's successor. Miller hadn't wanted to say until he heard from the others. In the conference, he said only that he didn't feel Hukill could be of value after all that had happened, then turned to Mrs. Parkman for her opinion. She didn't hesitate. *Miller's own recommendation* to her—Henry Sticher—was good.

"These people are more cunning than I," he told Anna, "and this I do not regret except that it puts me in a hole." When Miller took him to lunch with Sticher, Darel just thought they agreed on what needed to be done. But when Mrs. Parkman approved "Miller's recommendation," after Miller had refused to tell Darel he even had one, Darel suddenly realized that a game was afoot beyond his ken.

He doesn't tell us the specific objection to Stitcher, beyond that he was an old friend of Miller and was Mrs. Parkman's representative at Darel's meeting with Miller. Stitcher was a 25-year newspaperman and a Presbyterian elder who spoke at Rotary clubs.

"They arranged for Hukill to stay to the end of the month, and for Sticher to join in planning how to clear out the undesirables.

"Frankly I was so dumbfounded I hadn't the presence of mind to object, except to tell them that of course I would have to get in touch with Washington. 'Twas a bit of a love-feast with everybody in it except me. Now if they desire to show me up as incompetent, as one who plays both sides of the game, they can."

Frankly I have never been more lonely in my life than I was this afternoon.

These politicians are doing everything they can to discredit and embarrass me, not only here but in the home office. I wasn't as smart as they, and the realization is a severe wound to the ego.

The worst of it was that I let myself be drawn into that lunch with Miller and Sticher, where we discussed the malcontents, and who should be fired and who shouldn't. Oh I was vulnerable! A mere novice, a child, in their hands.

I hot-footed back to the hotel and called Alsberg. It was quite clear to him how they'd boxed me in. I told him they were trying to put Sticher over on me, and that all the young blood was being squeezed out. DeWitt Gilpin, a young and accomplished writer, will probably leave after Hukill does; he will be strangled by the atmosphere.

Henry said, 'They can't put in somebody you don't think can do the job.' He advised me to call Mrs. Florence Kerr, Regional Director of Women's and Professional Projects in Chicago, which I did. Both she and her assistant, Russell F. Bender, were on the wire and sounded swell. Bender told me to wait till Monday and he would be here.

Well, with Washington and Chicago backing, I thought I had scored. I called Miller and asked him to dinner. I told him that Alsberg would not approve Sticher, an old friend of his, and he at once put the blame on me. Meantime Torrey came over to discuss the situation, and it was then that we discovered that the "Dictaphone" was a buzzer.

Torrey came back with some gin at about 8:30 and while he was here Mrs. Parkman called. I told her that Alsberg would not approve Sticher and also let drop that Bender would be in town Monday. She was pretty well flummoxed. Both Torrey and I had fun while I talked to her.

The next morning, Darel learned that Jennie Owen had turned Hukill's letter over to the postal inspector. Hukill told him it had made the papers. Darel went to see the inspector, who assured him there would not be a prosecution.

Miller had gone from "poor old ineffective Miller" to, "he is wonderful, that old boy!" to adversary. He did an end run around Darel, writing to Alsberg himself—at Mrs. Parkman's request—telling how it had been "agreed" that Sticher should be approved, adding his own commendation. Darel called Alsberg and urged him to contact WPA State Administrator Evan Griffith, who was then in Washington, to see if they could work it out between them.

"Now I'm scared," he told Anna. As he wrote, his handwriting got shaky. It had been a mistake to trust Allaman. He'd told Allaman he thought Mrs. Parkman was the "meanest God damn woman I ever met." Allaman noted that his stenographer sometimes took down what people said. Miller, additionally, had wondered to Darel what Mrs. Woodward would think of the states'-rights issue—whether local people shouldn't be allowed to make their own choices. (This was a favorite argument against Washington's insistence that the Guides not descend into provincial boosterism. Massachusetts complained— unsuccessfully—that more space had been given to Sacco and Vanzetti than to the Boston Tea Party.)

Miller had charged that Darel's meddling was taking time away from the Guide. The charge had gotten back to Darel. Miller also suggested that "it might be better that Mr. McConkey not know about our disagreement on Sticher." Darel doesn't say who was in disagreement or who Miller said it to, or how he heard about it, but the threat of those and other innuendos ("the meanest God damned woman") getting back to Mrs. Woodward panicked him into thinking the Kansas machine might be nudging him toward "changing his mind" about Sticher—"a species of blackmail if you please."

"Well, I *had* to see *somebody*, so I popped in on Torrey and threw the thing in his lap. He was swell, of course, and assured me that I was making them jittery too. He believes they think I have a pretty long head,[‡‡‡] and are as scared of me as I am of them. It looks like they are trying to put me in a bad light before Bender comes.

"So we worked out a plan: Tomorrow morning I'll tell Mrs. Parkman that Alsberg said he would close the project before he would appoint Sticher, so now what would she suggest? That will give her a chance to do something on her own and have everything sweet and lovely when Bender comes Monday. Torrey did not feel they could attack me in any significant way, and I bethought me that if I let myself be blackmailed on Sticher, they would have me more firmly than if I went out and did a straightforward job of scrapping. I guess Miller is scared about his job, and Mrs. Parkman is scared about a blowup that would cause an investigation."

Anna reassured Darel that Alsberg had confidence in him. He wrote back, "Darling, your assurance of Henry's confidence is heartening. You know how I need it. I have not been so discouraged in the life of the project as I have been out here."

He visited Mrs. Parkman in the morning and felt he had won her somewhat to his point of view. Miller, however, still stood on state's rights, and insisted that Sticher be put in, and that Mrs. Parkman and the State administrator stand by him. Miller said he would go to Washington at his own expense to take it up with Alsberg personally. He told Mrs. Parkman he would discuss the matter with Darel and Bender on Monday. That was Saturday.

Mrs. Parkman told Darel she would call him Sunday to see if he'd changed his mind. He thought that he wouldn't. When Bender arrived on Monday, they'd see what they would see. He spent the weekend reading copy.

[‡‡‡] "Long-headed": having unusual foresight—*Webster*.

"I feel sort of low on the thing, for Miller is a canny old devil. I used to trust him, but I don't now. He has something up his sleeve, and I can't figure out what it is. Mrs. Parkman's call may reveal something. I think Miller means to threaten me with my statement about her. They are afraid of Bender and want to settle this before he comes."

The next day he wrote, "Another deadly Sunday in Topeka. Please god it may be the last—ever.

Hotel Kansan

"Mrs. Parkman called me, but said nothing about the local situation. Talked about quota, etc., but seemed to be giving me a chance to open the subject. They have something up their sleeve. I won't know what it is till tomorrow. They will probably hold what I said about Mrs. P. over me. Well, let them. I'll admit it—and so what?

"I always have the feeling I am being watched. I used to see Parkes patrolling the block where the Kansan [his hotel] is, at least once or twice a day. I don't believe I've seen him since Thursday, when that newspaper story about Hukill came out.

"Honey, I'll be so happy when I start out of this town! If I can get Bender to suggest it, by any subtle means, I'll ask permission to run up to Chicago."

On December 1, he was able to say, "My departure from this hell hole may be a matter of hours.

"Russell Bender came in this morning [Tuesday, not Monday]. We had a long talk and out of it came Bender's recommendation that I suggest to Henry that Gaer or Reed Harris come out here to study this situation, & that then we could have the backing of the regional office in whatever step we take." Joseph Gaer and Reed Harris were the big guns of the Project's field supervisors. Gaer had visited at the Island. Anna had borrowed money from him. Everybody borrowed money from everybody.

"I would be so happy with such a solution," Darel said, "that I would do it willingly—just to get away from here. I have done an honest if tactless job and am willing to stand by it. So that is what I am going to do, and maybe I'll get sent back to W. Va., where perhaps I belong more than here."

Bender's coming sparked the machine to a last-ditch maneuver. A buxom lady name Peggy Beard, one of the malcontents weeded from the project, tabbed Darel on the street and asked if she could come up to his room. He said he didn't have time, that she couldn't come up in any case, and what did she want? To ask some questions. He told her to call after five the next day. She could ask her questions then or not at all. Hukill called him a moment later and said she'd been at the office asking where he lived. The ploy was utterly transparent. Peggy Beard never called back.

Bender thought Darel may have leaned too heavily toward Hukill. Darel still thought Hukill was doing a good job, but regretted that his support had been damaging.

He and Bender dined together, and afterward went with the Hukills to interview a Mrs. Gartside, a possible successor to Hukill. Then they picked up DeWitt Gilpin, one of the "boys" on the project, at the railway station and went to Hukill's for drinks. "Gilpin is a Communist," Darel said, "and a very keen young man. He is one of the few good writers on the project." Darel did not think Gilpin would stay after Hukill left.

"Well, maybe the shooting will be over, as far as I am concerned, by tomorrow."

Anna reassured him. "Honey, I'm sorry you're having such an unhappy time, but I know it will come out all right. Alsberg is sending you backing in the form of Reed Harris. I was in the office a while ago & Alsberg said you're doing good work in ferreting things out, but he thinks sending Reed down in answer to your reports will show Kansas that the WPA means business. I know that anything the politicians might do to represent you as playing a double game will not be credited by Alsberg or Larry Morris, & they after all will have more to do with what Mrs. Woodward thinks of you than does anyone in Kansas."

On December 3, at last, "Here sit I in Kansas City, waiting for Reed. He should be here a little after 9, or nigh to midnight.

"I've been here since 1:30 this afternoon. Left Topeka at 12:30 on the Streamliner, the

first streamlined train I have ever rode on. It is painted yellow. I had a very good lunch—shrimp salad, coffee, pie, and more coffee—all for 50¢. This was my introduction to the new reasonably-priced meal idea on trains. The flat Kaw Valley slid rapidly past, with an occasional view of the winding, broad, sand-barred Kaw River, and my coffee was hardly finished before we came to Kansas City.

"I had to borrow a couple of dollars from Bender and $10 from Ralph Hukill to get out of Topeka. So here I am with less than $2 in my pocket, feeling like getting pie-eyed alone, but without the necessary resources."

He was no longer worried that the Washington office would feel he hadn't done well. He was glad it was Harris coming—Harris would be more charitable than Gaer. He was deeply disappointed to learn from Bender that the state office knew of every visit he'd had with Torrey. He'd thought Torrey a "swell person," but this news let him down.

"I heard a Beethoven quartet," he said. "The Stradivarius string quartet in the Library of Congress. The music did me a lot of good, but not so much as seeing Reed Harris! He just left after a two-hour harangue from me and it did me a heap of good. Reed will support me in this thing, and I believe that eventually some good will work out of it. At least I've saved somebody a lot of time learning the ins & outs of the mess.

"Reed says I'm to go back to W. Va. to clear that up—it's still hanging fire. He wasn't feeling well & went off to bed after I'd barely told him my Kansas story. We will probably spend half a day tomorrow going back over it, & then, if possible, I'll take a plane to W. Va."

We hear almost nothing of Topeka again. Anna could only relate this snippet of scuttlebutt: "It seems that Reed Harris just followed the path of least resistance and let it go at that."

Chapter Thirty-Four

West Virginia

WHEN DAREL ARRIVED back in West Virginia, Burns had resigned, but the politics of getting a new director vexed the project. Frank McCullough, WPA's state administrator, gave Ross Johnston the once over, then decided Jimmy Herbert should get Burns's place. Johnston had been a "pretty militant" Republican, though he was now a New Deal supporter. "We all who know the project," Darel said, "know that

Herbert can't fill the bill," but McCullough left town before Darel could argue the point. Billups suggested that Darel try persuading Senator Neely. McCullough would listen to Neely.

Darel called Alsberg and asked him to go see Neely. Alsberg called back saying Neely wasn't in Washington but in Fairmont, his West Virginia home. Darel wired for an appointment, then waited all day and half the night with no reply. He finally reached the Senator by phone the next morning, only to learn he was going to Washington the next day. He did, however, agree to meet Alsberg. Darel wired Alsberg, then sat back to wait…again. "If Alsberg can sell Neely on Johnston, we ought to be able to settle down to work."

The politics disgusted Darel profoundly. "There are barriers like this everywhere," he groused. "Just when it seems time—and *is* time—to settle down to a real job, the political issue crops up. Why must people so lack foresight that they fail to see the political value of a good book? I am made deeply unhappy by problems such as this—especially when this one follows on the heels of Kansas, from which [a week after his departure] I have not heard." On December 12, a Saturday, he wrote,

> Wait, wait, wait!
> Have I done anything on this trip but wait?
> Alsberg was supposed to have seen Senator Neely in Washington this afternoon. I have waited to learn of the outcome, if any, but nary a word. Did Henry see Neely or didn't he? If he did, was he able to persuade him in favor of Johnston? No answer to these questions. Nor is there any answer to this—did Neely contact McCullough, and what did he say? What should I say to McCullough in case I see him tomorrow? When will this damnable waiting end and there be a chance to begin doing a job? Honestly, I would rather be given a job of writing the State book myself than have all this waiting. Then at least I could get my teeth into something.

He waited until twenty past noon Sunday, then called Alsberg in exasperation. Alsberg had failed to see Neely, meaning Darel would have to. He got an appointment in Fairmont at eleven Monday morning. "Whether I'll be able to sell him I don't know, but I surely am going to put on a sales talk. I'm relieved to have something to put my teeth in. If I don't carry it off, I shan't blame Alsberg if he feels I have not done so well. But I shall do my best, and let the record rest on any merit it may have."

Neely did not impress him. Darel started with the importance of a good guide to West Virginia, but the Senator cut him short and insisted he cut straight to personnel. He asked Darel to interview a Dr. Davis. If Davis wouldn't do, appoint Johnston. But when Darel affirmed that Davis wouldn't do, Neely retorted that Johnston was "opposed by some of my friends, and that's enough for me."

"That's how much dependence you can put in a politician's word from one ten minutes to the next," Darel said. "The whole thing was political, and I couldn't get it out."

Darel called Henry, who stuck to his guns. "He isn't scared of the wolf of politics in W.Va. He told me to carry on the fight. Johnston or close the project." Or, Darel could stay and run the project himself. "I told him I hoped that wouldn't happen." Darel returned to Charleston to take the battle to McCullough.

He saw him on Tuesday, and used a Billups tactic, complimenting him on his sartorial finish, saying he looked like a page out of *Esquire* magazine. The meeting was pleasant but accomplished nothing. Darel wanted Ross Johnston. McCullough told him Johnston was not approved of politically.

When Darel said both he and Alsberg considered Johnston the best man, McCullough asked him why they were forever coming up with Republicans, called his publicity man to try finding a Democrat, and suggested Darel call him at 4:30. Darel tried three times but got no better reply than that McCullough would be unprepared to talk before ten the next morning. "So that's another day shot to pieces." At least McCullough was "more tractable with the approach I used today."

One Leroy Mosby recommended Bob Plummer, a former newspaperman and great organizer currently working at a WPA sub-district office in Wheeling. Darel and Mosby went to see McCullough. Darel pointed out that where Johnston already knew the operation and could take over smoothly, bringing in a new person would lose time and might jeopardize a planned Forest Guide.

McCullough got mad. "All right!" he snapped. "If you want Johnston appoint him, but it won't be on my recommendation! And you will have to take the heat when it's turned on! Bob Plummer is my recommendation [presumably a good Democrat]."

"What do you mean, 'the heat'?" asked Darel.

"You'll find out!" snapped McCullough. "Go on and appoint Johnston, but not on my recommendation."

Darel said he'd call Alsberg about it, admittedly feeling a little exultant, "for now a real organization could be put together." Even if "the heat" meant Neely lambasting them in the Senate, even if it meant someone going after Darel's personal scalp, even with all that, he felt they could count it a victory.

Alsberg, however, was leery of "the heat," and told Darel to give Plummer a look while he discussed the matter with Mrs. Woodward's office. Plummer arrived on Thursday. He was capable but couldn't take the job because he didn't want to leave his aging father in Wheeling. Darel told McCullough, and McCullough asked to see him in the afternoon, "Then we'll make another move." Darel concluded that that meant scraping up another Democrat, with more delay and more interviewing. He lunched with Glenn Callaghan, (state director of West Virginia's National Youth Administration) who suggested Larry Hamby, one of his NYA county supervisors. Hamby sounded better than anyone Darel had heard about yet, so he tucked the Hamby card up his sleeve, to pull out if McCullough was adamant on Johnston.

He reiterated to McCullough how impressed he'd been by Plummer and waited for a reply. "I suppose," McCullough conceded, "you might as well use Johnston. Make him acting director if you like, to give him some power. I have no one else to offer."

"So there 'twas," said Darel, "tossed in my lap." It remained what to do about Page Pitt, who had been steering the program from behind the scenes. Had Pitt moved to the associate director's slot, he'd have qualified for $2,000 a year. With that out of the picture, he could still be made a consultant, which commanded $1,200. Darel felt sure Pitt would agree and told McCullough he'd effect the change by the first of the year.

"The galley proofs of the District Guide are in," Anna wrote, "and everyone is busy reading proof." The race was on to make the D.C. Guide the first in the nation, as Alsberg deemed proper, but it was no simple jog to the finish line. Way out west, a self-willed personality named Vardis Fisher—who called Alsberg the "director of indigent writers"—was turning out Idaho's guide almost single-handedly and was as determined as Alsberg to be the first.

As crunch time approached, Alsberg began insisting on more and more changes to Fisher's copy, slowing him down. A phone call between the two got so profane that Fisher's staff feared he'd be fired. Around the end of October, Alsberg sent George Cronyn to Boise to straighten things out. An apocryphal story has Fisher getting Cronyn drunk and putting him on a train back home. Jerre Mangione repeated the story but saying only that a "trusted assistant" had met Fisher.

Anna's take on the episode was, "George apparently had little if any difficulty with Vardis Fisher. It was simply a personality trouble that needed the human element to smooth it out." We'll probably never know for sure. Years later, Darel wrote that the D.C. Guide came out first, but in fact it was Fisher by a nose. Both books appeared in January, 1937. The D.C. Guide was printed on slick paper and weighed 4½ pounds. Alsberg said he feared learning in the papers that Harry Hopkins would be found in the Potomac with a copy of the book tied around his neck.

For the first time in a year and two-thirds of married life, Anna and Darel celebrated a holiday together, sharing Christmas with Darel's family at Dixie. They had an entire month, the longest stretch since getting married, to test their nuptial wings. Both took great joy in the time.

Back in November, on his second trip to Topeka, Darel had picked up a copy of Carl Carmer's 1934 best-selling *Stars Fell on Alabama*, now remaindered to the dollar table. The author was a New York state native, but his book was a cultural collage based on six years teaching at the University of Alabama. It covered folklore, religion, superstition, and race relations including lynching and the Ku Klux Klan.

"I have been pondering a possible book," Darel told Anna. "*West By God Virginia*, based on the same idea," and he worked on it for the rest of his life. *West by God Virginia* was never far from our awareness growing up.

Sometime around the end of the year, Anna and Darel discovered an account of a seventeenth century French Jesuit's attempt to reach China by land. The Jesuit was Pére Avril, which Darel translated literally as Father April. The account was in French. Darel copied it and over the next few months, with his high school and college French, translated it into English. The translation, which he named *Father* April, stood shelved in a three-inch binder from early in my life to the end of Darel's. On the cover, our old cowboy playmate, Joe Colgan, rendered a Jesuit father. People praised the book. Darel never managed to get it into print but, like *West by God Virginia*, it loomed over our childhood.

Expectations were high as they dove into the project. Darel took the translating on the road and said of it, "Let not anyone ever say that translation is not creative work! I got into the swing of that wonderful flowery letter of dedication, and was carried away by the flow of it. Definitions in a dictionary must not be considered pat and final. The spirit of a thing must decide word choices: a dictionary can only be suggestions."

Anna spent joyful days at the Library of Congress researching background material with enthusiastic support from Earl Hyde. "When I turn to Mr. Hyde with a very tiny question, and he takes me hither and yon over the Library until so many new avenues are opened, that I must needs sit down and think of where I was and fit in the new possibilities. He says to tell you that Père Avril could not have a better or more appreciative narrator of his travels than he has in you." She told Darel, "It seems almost impossible to get too tired to work."

The story fit an interest of Darel's about how travel routes originated. Often migratory animals blazed "game trails" over paths of least resistance that were later used by aboriginal peoples, growing betimes into major byways and trade routes. That interest may in part have led them to trace Moncacht Apé and Lewis and Clark. After Father April, however, Lewis and Clark lost position.

Meanwhile, the Writers' Project was considering a *Project Prodigies* book of short works by Project members, and Darel pulled out a story, "Heavy Haulin'," which he'd written in 1932, and submitted it. Unlike *American Stuff*, which included his "Hill-Country Wonders" under the wrong name, *Project Prodigies* never flew.

Darel was back in West Virginia at the end of January, 1937, and learned that he'd been investigated "from top to bottom; my personnel record dug up;

with it the fact that I'd worked for [Republican] Bowman; my political motives questioned, etc., etc. It is evident that someone was out for me."

A Mrs. Miller, whom we only encounter in the context of this episode, "did a wonderful job of soothing them down, persuaded them that I was just interested in doing a real job." Frank McCullough, WPA's state administrator, who had opposed Ross Johnston for state director, now argued for Darel "to come back and set things aright, find somebody not Johnston, and put buzz in the program."

So, Darel began interviewing candidates and presenting them to McCullough. His first meeting was "friendly on the surface, but I felt I was walking on hummingbirds' eggs. If I can overcome my anger at the effort these smiling hypocrites made to get me fired, (who the hell are they to investigate a Washington field person?), and get to carrying every pin-prick to everybody to be sure they feel all right about it, I think things will move off all right. The challenge is for me to overcome. I hope I can. I'm going to get pied with Glenn Callaghan this eve and see if that helps."

Not only had they investigated his background, they were tracking his movements. The Writers' Project secretary confided to him that Mc-Cullough's secretary had asked her when he'd gotten back from Washington, where he was staying, when he had left for Clarksburg, where he stayed while there, and when he got back to Charleston. Kansas all over again.

"I have no disposition to run out on this," he told Anna, "but it is evident that Senator Neely & McCullough want to have revenge on me [for prevailing with Johnston?]. If Mrs. Miller will come down and work the thing thru with me, I'll stay. (She told me she would if I needed her.) Otherwise I shall not stay unless I have an understanding with McCullough that I am to go ahead on the basis that I am trying to do a good job for the State, for WPA, and for the sake of a good job. If not, I shall ask someone else to come in." He expressed the intention of asking Alsberg to send Mrs. Miller back to go over the situation.

He did call Alsberg, though we don't know what they said. The point became moot a day later when Page Pitt arrived from Huntington with his candidate for state director, John L. Stender. "Stender took everybody by storm, including me. He is a fine clean chap, 32. It looks like he is it. I hope so, for the combination of a high class person and one thoroughly agreeable to everyone would be hard to duplicate."

McCullough's offensive shriveled. Alsberg and McCullough both approved Stender who, by mid-February, was undergoing orientation at Darel's elbow.

Chapter Thirty-Five

Fidelity

A TENANT IN THEIR BUILDING was hassling Anna. "I'm afraid to keep the door open for ventilation," she wrote Darel. "A man has whistled and called and done all sorts of things to attract my attention. He comes out when I go to the elevator. I told him I'd report him if he didn't stop, and he had the effrontery to say his word is as good as mine. I had the door open just now and he whistled. It is probably just over-jitteryness, but I put our door on the hook."

Darel wrote back, "I'm sorry about the masher who moved in." He said she should tell management she'd move out if it didn't to stop. "Failing that, have Mr. Hyde come up and sit inside the door. Leave the door open, show yourself moving about, and wait till it starts. Then leave the rest to Mr. Hyde. Tell him I'll pay his fine if there is any, which I feel confident there won't be."

In another day it was over. "Don't worry about the masher. The room is empty again."

But of course, it is never over. "I do get a sort of sick feeling sometimes at the way I get followed around at night. I've had Mary Jansen, & others too, tell like stories." She was philosophical about it. "There must be many people that lack a feeling of social responsibility"—but the philosophy got a little imprecise—"for even though this is evidence of only one irresponsible facet, it is probably indicative of a personality built on the same plan. But that is the world we live in, so it behooves us for our own peace of being not to be too rebellious."

She was philosophical, too, about two slips of paper she found containing women's contact information. "One has Millie—34-329," she told Darel. "The other I can't find any more—but it was something like Eliz. Bolivant with an address on 17th St. N.W. I hope it can be replaced if you want it."

After some pages about her Father April researches, she decided elaboration was in order. She was obviously in earnest, but America's mixed-up sexual attitudes—trying to say something without saying it—may have affected her penmanship (never the best to start with) and lain at the root of her trouble keeping pronouns in line with their antecedents, or making sure they even had antecedents.

Darling, I've felt so good and full of joy that I don't see any possibility of ever feeling otherwise, but I know these things don't last forever, and I want to say now that I don't ever intend even in my most emotional moments to be a [word illegible] to you. I dislike such an idea [being a?] [word illegible] [to you?] with the greatest intensity.

But you know as well as I that things do happen. Sometimes the simple juxtaposition of a few chance remarks or acts will bring ideas into my head that aren't too pleasant. I don't say this to make you feel self-conscious, but simply in explanation. I hope that you're feeling as exuberant as I am so that this won't make you feel shadowy, but if it does, just come back with as much Irish steam as you feel. There is nothing in this that detracts from my belief in your basic integrity.

I'm just stating what happens while I'm in the best state to be honest about it, and mean quite frankly and truly that I don't want you to feel in any way encumbered or obligated to me or by me. Or, if it suits you, just forget that I wrote any of this, because if my emotions sometimes don't agree with this policy they'll have to learn. It just boils down to the fact that I like my feeling of freedom and I want you to hear it too, on account I love you and nobody else and it doesn't seem right for me to feel so good all by myself.

Darel moved to re-cork his Don Juan reputation.

Darling, I want you to raise doubts if you feel like it. What with a masher on the same floor and these persistent attempts at pickups, it is easy to understand how you must think upon my past and have occasional doubts. Especially when something like Millie and 'Eliz. Bullivant' turns up. I told you of the party when some of Page's friends came to my room.

One of them was a girl named Millie, whose brother Charlie I particularly liked. He had no phone so I took her number. Later, as I also told you, Dean & I went there for an evening, with the understanding Charlie would be there. He wasn't. That's the whole history of it, & you may rest assured I will have no need for her telephone number.

Elizabeth Bullivant was in school with me at D&E [Davis and Elkins] back in '24-'25. When I was in Elkins last trip here, I was hobnobbing with the hotel man, also a D&E man. Somehow one asks about everybody in a little school like that. He said "Elizabeth Bullivant's in Washington." Not to seem disinterested, I took her address, never expecting to do any more than that.

Anna, sweetheart, please try to believe this, for it is truer than anything of its kind I've ever said to you: with you as my partner I no longer desire the pursuit of women. I think you should also know that I have never done so in those obnoxious ways that have been used on you, & which must have reminded you of the instability of men.

In your sweet person, and in your lovely slender body I have found sexual fulfillment far more satisfying than ever before. There must have been times when you doubted this, but it is nonetheless true. I suppose it is because of my conquest of you from an entirely frigid state to one of full sexual realization.

To me the psychic gratification of giving joy is greater than the purely physical one of receiving it. And I am but speaking the candid truth when I say you are more beautiful to love than anyone I might ever expect to find. I also speak the truth when I say that even in difficult times when I need emotional release I find antidote for that need in the joy of remaining true to you.

In working with you and staying home long enough to become effective in your behalf, I was so happy in that month with you that I could so cheerfully have foregone ever setting foot inside a train again. We were more livable for each other than ever, I think.

So darlingest of all persons, I understand how you can doubt, and I cannot say I blame you. But at the same time, you can see how I try to live down a past that haunts you, and perhaps anon you may understand how I suddenly hit the ceiling when I am doubted.

Anna wrote back:

Sweet-heart, it is most dear of you to be so willing to explain things and I love you for that willingness. I was truly not perturbed about the pieces of paper with names for they dropped out the first day I went to the Library and it had not been uppermost enough for me to remember to send them to you until I lost one and now I've lost the other, but its all-right if you don't need them.

I was really feeling intoxicated with the world in general that evening and I suppose that my sub-conscious desire to manifest my confidence in you and feeling that nothing wrong could happen, was even more apparent than I thought on reading it the next morning. Dearest person it is such happiness to have you so sweet and willing to understand things. That is what makes you such a satisfactory person to live with.

Darel, dearest I want you to know that I do believe all the things you say of yourself and more than that, I've never associated you in any way with the obnoxious things that have happened to me. You probably remember that I told you that most of my contacts with men had been the obnoxious kind and you immediately became the person outside of that class. It is true that I was attempting to demonstrate my feeling of freedom from emotional entanglements, though you were probably correct in seeing at least a subconscious hangover from other states.

Darel answered more than she had verbalized.

Darling person, your lack of experience in the realm of sex is precious to me. I suppose every man has that 'will-to-be-first' and prizes virginity in the woman of his choice more than he is willing to admit in this period of more than average sexual freedom. It is to admit a selfishness to admit that our sexual love is fine and dear and lovely beyond anything to me because, I suspect, I can feel in it a firstness and oneness and onliness not to be found anywhere else in my experience.

So long as I can feel that your whole life-in-sex appertains to me, I can feel real pleasure in keeping myself only for you. That is putting it pretty baldly, but I suspect it is mostly true. But in my feelings I seem to find more to account for it, which escapes analytical language, and mayhap eludes any language soever.

There is that about your clean lovely slenderness and your sweet luscious breasts which gives me a totality of answer to bodily seeking. Honey darling sweetheart preciousest person—*you suit me*! You fit my needs, not alone in what I receive but in what I give. And I joy in the giving, and calm reposeful spirit is the answer when my giving is good.

And honey if betimes I seem matter of fact about sex, it is not because I lose interest, but because usually other things have sapped my energy. I want to make it lovely and changing and iridescent, totally awakening and completely satisfying to that awakened. So, I do say and think and feel now that when I am back, we may experiment and vary the play to our mutual endearment and joy, and I mean not ever so long as I am a capable man to let it become stale or flat or dull to you.

To which Anna replied, "You are a dear, darling person, and I love you. It was sweet of you to explain so many puzzles to me and I want to tell you that I experienced more satisfaction and beauty out of our relationship during the last month at home than ever before, and I most earnestly will try not to be bothered by things that don't seem quite so."

Chapter Thirty-Six

Sweet Home Arkansas

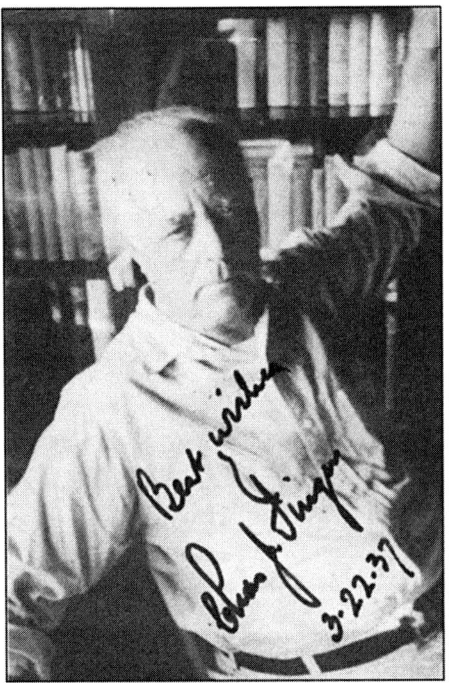

Charles Finger

THE STATE GUIDES weren't the only Writers' Project productions. They put out dozens of smaller books—individual city guides, guides to recreational areas, *Birds of the World, Outlaws and Desperados*. Darel thought a West Virginia State Forest guide would be ideal. He proposed it first to the people in charge of the Forest Festival, but they weren't interested in taking it on. He took the idea to Project staffers, and most liked it, even McCullough. At the very least, it would employ a few more out-of-work West Virginia writers.

A Mrs. Garlitz of the Project was working to arrange a conference with Representative Jennings Randolph, who had replaced Bowman in 1932. He had headed the journalism and public speaking department at Davis and Elkins when Darel was there. Darel angled to take charge of the project himself and planned to bring Anna for some life together. His mother looked into getting his residence changed—presumably to qualify him for West Virginia's Project—but she didn't find anything helpful. Delay on delay getting a director installed, however, frustrated the effort. The project fizzled amid the press of other business.

George Cronyn and Katherine Kellock were thinking of sending Darel to Arizona because, Anna told him, "their copy is lousy and you are the only person who knows how to dig in and pull out the trouble." Instead, they sent him to Arkansas. By March 2, 1937, he was in Little Rock. He had once asked to be sent to Kansas, and Kansas had soured. He had recoiled at going to Arkansas, but, contrary to expectation, in his five days there he found a home.

When he arrived, the state project's chief editor, Charles Finger, was at loggerheads with state director, Bernie Babcock, over the Guide's shape. Anna had wondered, "Why don't they send Lyle?" Lyle Saxon, director of the Louisiana state project, who had so enchanted Darel and Anna. Well, they *had* sent Lyle, and the visit, in Darel's word, had been a "fiasco."

Neither Charles Finger nor Dot Kennan, Arkansas's state director of Women's and Professional Projects, who conducted Darel around on this visit, had cared for Lyle Saxon. He had told them that Project Administrator Floyd Sharp had never seen Darel's October 2 memo that all copy destined for Washington had to cross Clay Fulks's desk. This was untrue, as Darel had discussed the matter with Sharp personally. "But that's all rather unpleasant detail," he told Anna. "It reflects on Lyle, and I shan't go into it now, but will tell you of it when I see you."

There he leaves us dangling as regards that incident. There may exist papers—a field report, perhaps—explaining what wheel got oiled by that falsehood, but documentation has proven elusive. Nor was Fulks any longer with the Project. They'd fired him for drunkenness. He'd been suspect to begin with for past radical associations, though he'd been a competent editor and writer.

Dot drove Darel the nearly two hundred miles from Little Rock to Fayetteville to see Charles Finger. "Dot was as funny as she could be," Darel wrote Anna. "She may be in Washington about mid-April and I want you to meet her. There's only one Dot Kennan." Darel brought along a bottle of White Horse, which the two "used out of on the way."

Charles Finger was a colorful Arkansas favorite son, born not in Arkansas but in England in 1867. He was a prolific author of largely young-adult adventure books, based largely on his life in South America herding sheep, panning for gold, working among gauchos on the Pampas, guiding an ornithological expedition in Tierra del Fuego. In 1896, he came to America, became a citizen, married the daughter of a sheep rancher, found work as a boilermaker's helper in a New Mexico railroad shop, moving to the position of auditor in the general manager's office.

He began having success as a writer in the late nineteen-teens, and moved to a homestead, called Gayeta, near Fayetteville in 1920. His writing style was breezy and compelling, reminiscent of Arthur Conan Doyle and Rudyard Kipling. If his letters tell us anything, words flowed from him in a torrent. His endless fund of knowledge and experience richly larded his endlessly entertaining monologues. He and Darel took to each other immediately.

"At Gayeta Lodge, springtime is coming," Darel wrote. "There are lambs in the pasture, and I heard chickadee and tufted titmouse out in the trees, as I sat by the fireplace with Mr. Finger and talked over guide topics.

"He was smoking the straight Bertram pipe when I came, but put it away at once for his new one, which pleased him as much as a boy would be pleased over a present.

"When we settled down, I found out what the trouble was. Mr. Finger had all the instructions he needed, but he simply hadn't assimilated them. I felt myself in a most ridiculous position, a raw youngster telling a seasoned veteran of 23 published books that he must study his lessons. But I did it, in a much more roundabout way of course, and he took it most gracefully. He agreed that a certain uniformity in State Guides is desirable, that possibly he might assimilate instructions and so be rid of them as a hampering force, and free to write."

That was it? That was why the Project had sent Darel to Arkansas? And it fixed the problem? Like the Lyle Saxon prevarication, this seems pretty thin. There was just this bit more, and it came in a March 9 letter to Finger, by which time Darel was in Providence, Rhode Island. Darel had noticed cattle being allowed to roam freely on the highways, and felt that the Arkansas tours should warn visitors of this practice. But for the moment, instead of elaborating the business side of his trip, Darel settled luxuriantly into recounting his personal visit with Finger.

"We covered the ground as far as I dared without insulting a truly great mind's intelligence. And then we talked of everything under the sun. Both Mr. Finger and Helen [his daughter] were interested in Père Avril, the translation, and your research. An interest in these old things is an opening to their hearts, meaning especially Mr. Finger's of course. That was one of the most delightsome afternoons I have ever spent!"

Finger's 1925 *Tales from a Silver Land* had won a Newbery Medal for juvenile fiction. "He showed me his Newbery Medal, which he prizes highly. He showed me Mitchell Kennerly's 'perfect book'—an illustrated folio volume of one of HG Well's stories. And he brought out from his safe a book in beautiful dark green leather, the only one of its kind in the world! It is an illuminated hand printed text on parchment, with illuminated letters and colorful pictures, dated 1531. It is in French, and relates to church usage. I have never seen as beautiful a book.

"And he showed me a copy of RB Cuninghame Graham's book, 'A Vanished Arcadia being some account of Jesuits in Paraguay 1607 to 1767,' London, Heineman, 1901. In keeping with your thoughts on the Jesuits, it might be worth looking into.

"Honey sweetheart, I shan't try to tell you all about the Fingers now, but I want them to come to Washington so you can meet them! They are among the finest people I've ever met up with. And I'll tell you more verbally when I'm home again. Already they like you and want to meet you. And I shall be most proud of you then!"

Chapter Thirty-Seven

New England and Then Some

Maine lobsterman

DAREL ARRIVED back in D.C. March 7, 1937. The next day, he stepped off the train in Providence, Rhode Island. "I got orders to remain here till further instructions," he told Anna. "It looks very much like R.I. would need somebody to help them with tours." He bounced around New England for the next two and a half weeks—Providence, Boston, Manchester, Portland, focusing on copy. Anna told him, "Mrs. Kellock says that Maine copy is very bad and full of error." He wrote her back, "Tell George (Cronyn) I'm working like hell, and that gradually I'm getting the 'loveliness,' the 'beautifulness,' the 'fineness' and the 'charmingness' and all such indefinite adjectiveness weeded out of N.H. copy. This will be a really good book." From Manchester he wrote, "Just to make Alsberg feel bad, I wired him that I'd handled 160,000 words of copy, reducing it by 10%."

In New England, field supervising dropped out of the picture and the job became full-time editing. Editing had always been interlaced with the supervising, and by Darel's own word he seemed to consider that his more important function. He frequently mentioned reading reams and mounds of copy on trains and in hotel rooms, but for story-value editing can't compete with politics.

Nevertheless, the job's scale took even him into new territory. "I just didn't realize what slow work there was in going over copy with a fine-toothed blue pencil," he wrote from Manchester. "Having worked intensively this evening, I still have two more cities to do. I'll save them for tomorrow, since it's so late.

"There are yet tours to do, and the size of the portfolio makes it look like a sizable task. The best I can hope for is to get to Portland Tuesday evening, which provokes me, for it makes the home-for-Easter idea look more and more unattainable. I have an even harder job to do there—checking for facts on copy I know nothing whatever about."

He acquired a 35mm camera and began taking pictures: fishermen in Providence, the architecture of Harvard, Russian and Greek Catholic churches in Manchester....The film-advance was knob-wind; the camera had a range finder, much trickier than the reflex viewfinder. The range finder didn't show focus. It consisted of two spots of light which, when brought to superimposition, told you the subject was focused. The camera lacked a light meter.

Film came packaged with a sheet suggesting exposures for different light conditions, and Darel seems to have had his best success in that department. But too many shots were out of focus. Too many were blurred because he jerked the shutter release. As much as he tried, as much pride as he took in the job well done, despite exposing miles of film, despite not quitting to the end of his days, despite a number of worthy compositions, he never became a consistently good photographer.

Anna was sorry New England was dragging on and looked back "with happiness on our little interlude in this hectic existence"—their one day between Little Rock and Providence. "Your being bandied about so much of late makes me realize what fortune is mine to have my days free for research such as I'm doing."

And what wonders she unearthed, enriching their appreciation for Father April's time. It was the age of Louis XIV, the age of poison in the court, poison for "divorce, abortion, legal prosecution, the fulfillment of every wish that someone was out of the way. It is from such a land that the good fathers went out to carry the true faith to the Orient," she said.

"No wonder," Darel replied, "that Père Avril put Louis's name in capital letters and called him the greatest king on earth."

Anna learned that Giovanni Cassini had devised a way of determining longitude using the moons of Jupiter. North-south latitude was reckoned by how far above the horizon certain stars appeared. East-west longitude demanded comparing positions in terms of Earth's rotation. Lacking instant communication over distance, the sun can't help because it occupies different places in the sky depending on your position along the east-west line.

But eclipses, being extra-terrestrial, aren't affected by Earth's rotation. Their timing is the same everywhere they are visible. Galileo had actually suggested using them, but Cassini was the first to do it (and, so doing, shrank Louis's France). Clocks are easier but need to gain or lose no more than ten seconds a day. Back then, they couldn't do that.

Part of Father April's mission was calculating the distance from Paris to Beijing. His account discussed the eclipse method, but he never got to use it.

The Jesuits were set on spreading the Word worldwide. The Chinese had proven receptive. It seemed, at least in part, that their interest was in European science, not religion, but they were willing to take the religion in order to get the science. The Jesuits were willing to impart the science as long as the Chinese took the religion. The sea journey was hazardous in the extreme. Far more missionaries were lost at sea than arrived in China, so there was much interest in finding a land route. Father April was one who tried.

March 24 in D.C. was "so beautiful and springy." The weather reawakened thoughts of the Island. "Last evening, as the last of sunset color was in the sky, I saw a Cabin John trolley and it seemed we should be getting on it and going out. Perhaps during April and May, should you be home long enough, we might go out on Saturdays and Sundays and begin setting up."

In Manchester, Darel woke "to a two-inch 'maple-sugar' snow. That is what we New Englanders call a spring snow along about sugar-making time." The snow must have made the Island seem all the more desirable.

"The Island!" he wrote. "What a thought! I seem so far away from it. We could get the boat under cover and get the painting done, and perhaps be ready to use it when we are ready to move."

He still hoped to make it home for Easter, March 28, but on the 26th, Alsberg wired him: "IMPORTANT YOU GO MAINE GIVE EDITORIAL HELP THERE. WIRE ME."

Darel wired back, "PLAN COMPLETION OF ASSIGNMENT AND GO TO MAINE TOMORROW."

"It made me a little sore," he told Anna, "because I've been working three shifts a day here, morning, afternoon, and night, and wanted no end to get away. But I still want to do a real job. I don't think Henry realizes what a careful job I'm doing, or what is involved in a survey of a 200,000-word book."

"Please God I can come for Easter—but I doubt it. Washington is too sure of Maine's inaccuracy to bring me back so soon. I am personally certain of Westall's desire to do a real job"—Dorris Westall was Maine's state director— "but I hardly think Kellock is. If ever I have seen one, that is a feud between an unattractive woman (KK) and an attractive one, Miss Westall. Maybe I'm wrong, but it carries to such points as naming Bangor capital of Maine when Augusta is. That makes our office look foolish and I'm in the embarrassing position of trying to smooth it over. So where am I? The feeling is pretty bad. I'm inclined to leave it alone…after suggesting that sources be sent on everything."

Alsberg wired Maine to send all completed copy to Washington. Darel wired Alsberg that since the copy was going to Washington anyway, he couldn't see any reason to stay in Maine.

Alsberg wired him home. Darel wired Anna, "RETURNING WASHINGTON SEVEN FORTY FIVE EASTER MORNING. GOD BLESS US. CAN YOU GET EASTER SCOTCH."

Westall's credentials were thin—she'd worked for her hometown paper at $12 a week and been fired for smoking—but she ran a tight ship in Maine and, despite problems with the copy, was among the Projects best administrators. The year, 1937, had been the deadline for all the guidebooks. Only five made it, Maine among them. Alsberg had set the deadline because Congress's blessing was never assured from one year to the next.

In April, Darel was settled back at the McLean mansion, working under E. M. "Doc" Barrows organizing the Project's Cities Division, to handle individual cities within each guidebook. He continued signing his official correspondence "Field Supervisor." Barrows was the author of the successful *Great Commodore*, about Commodore Perry, who "opened" Japan to commerce with the United States.

On April 28, the Potomac flooded again, and on May 6, Darel's mother wrote, "Am sorry your island home prospect has been washed away." But the prospect had not washed away. By the end of May, Anna and Darel's mail drop had changed from their apartment on M Street to the Project's headquarters in the mansion.

At the beginning of June, Charles and Helen Finger visited Washington. Finger later recalled singing "Amsterdam Maid" on the Island, raising a twinkle in George Cronyn's eye. Before arriving, Finger had promised, if an open fire were available, to prepare steaks Patagonian style for Alsberg, Cronyn, and Barrows. Whether he did or didn't is not recorded. He swore he'd regale Alan Lomax—famous for his collection of indigenous folk music under Federal One—with his half dozen published songs, and the cowboy song and the sea shanty he'd "invented." He was greatly taken by the Project people. Being an accomplished pianist, he gave a recital at the Library of Congress. He expressed to Darel, "By the Seven sacred Cats of Egypt, I swear that the gods work out destinies in strange ways! Who'd have thought that all of this could have come out of our first meeting?" Finger was impressed with *Father April*, was certain there would be no trouble finding a publisher, and promised to do what he could to further that end. He also read Moncacht Apé and found nothing wrong with it.

On May 6, the Zeppelin Hindenburg burst into flames while docking at Lakehurst, New Jersey, after crossing from Berlin. Of 97 passengers and crew, 35 perished. Spectacular newsreel footage and emotional eyewitness reporting by Herbert Morrison of WSL Radio, Chicago, electrified the nation, punctuating the end of rigid-airship travel.

The world's longest and tallest suspension bridge, The Golden Gate, opened on May 28. The Lyon Street approach to the bridge was built entirely by WPA workers.

On July 2, Amelia Earhart went missing near Howland Island in the Pacific, while attempting the first round-the-world flight at equatorial latitudes—making it the longest

The Hindenburg disaster

circumnavigation ever. In 1928, a year after Lindbergh, she had been the first

Amelia Earhart

woman to fly—as a passenger— nonstop across the Atlantic. In 1932, she became the first woman to solo that body. She was wildly popular, the "female Charles Lindbergh," to whom she bore a passing resemblance.

On December 21, Walt Disney premiered *Snow White and the Seven Dwarfs*, the world's first animated feature-length film.

In July, Anna and Darel took a vacation. Darel had been much taken with New England. His thought was to stay somewhere within striking distance of Harvard, so they could pursue the Father April studies. A project member told Darel he had an idea for a swanky place. Anna was alarmed at a "'swanky' summer vacation idea. Does it lack the element of simplicity? On account Swanky seems so overstuffed. I'm sort of scared of it. Maybe I misunderstand, though."

A Dr. White suggested Rockport or Marblehead—both had beaches and were accessible to Harvard. Duly, July 12 found them at Rockport. On the 21st, Darel's mother wrote them, "Well my dears, am glad you are having a good time if you are working some. Think you ought to take more time to rest and get away from the pen." Margaret had contemplated joining them, with overtures toward driving them home, but instead they voyaged down the coast from Maine to Norfolk, thrilling to the sight of porpoises gamboling alongside their vessel.

August 12 found Darel in Louisville. Anna wrote of some confusion she was finding in a 1674 book, *Cosmography*, by Peter Heylin, which they had acquired. It contained four magnificent period maps and fit right in with *Father April*. A person had offered some antique books for sale, including *Cosmography*. They bought it. Anna later described the person as a possible "fly-by-nighter." Reports circulated of a theft of books from the Library of Congress. Anna and Darel wondered if *Cosmography* had been one of them, but didn't ask. (The book was not, they learned through Earl Hyde, highly valuable. Too many copies were floating around.)

In September, they folded their tent and set up winter quarters in an apartment on Mintwood Place in D.C.'s Adams Morgan neighborhood, a short walk in one direction from the Alley, and in the other from George and Frances Cronyn. A variety of income levels peopled the area, but it was racially segregated and far from the vibrant, bohemian hearth it later became, where Anna lived her final days.

They again closed out the year celebrating Christmas at Dixie.

By February, 1938, their base of operations had shifted again, to an apartment above Dupont Circle.

Nineteen thirty-seven had been the first year of Roosevelt's second term. Unemployment was down from 25 to 14 percent. Production, profits, and wages had recovered much of their pre-Depression levels. Roosevelt profited from the economy's brightened aspect.

Contrary to accusations from the New Deal's enemies, Roosevelt was, philosophically, a fiscal conservative. He believed in balanced budgets. But in desperate times, he'd been willing to try desperate measures. Now, with the Depression seemingly on the run, with unemployment sinking and production rising, between 1936 and 1937 he cut federal spending 17 percent.

The Federal Reserve and the Treasury Department took their own steps against a fancied threat of inflation. Economists still debate the causes, but by June 1938, unemployment was back up to 20 percent and production was down by 32. Some blamed the budget, some thought it the normal business cycle manifesting in the midst of depression. Others, naturally, blamed the New

Deal. In 1938, Roosevelt abandoned the balanced budget and the economy improved, though not to '37 levels.

Employment and production did not fully recover until World War II exacted government spending at levels the New Deal never dreamed of. Anna and Darel left no impression of the economic picture during what some called that "Roosevelt Depression." Presumably the Writer's Project shielded them. (Those working in government relief programs were, officially, still classified as unemployed.)

In March 1938, Adolph Hitler annexed Austria into Nazi Germany. Britain formally protested, but neither she nor France did anything.

World War I had broken up the Austro-Hungarian Empire. Both Germany and Austria favored reunifying with each other, but Britain and France, fearful of a strengthened Germany, insisted that the Versailles Treaty forbid reunification. Reunification sentiment persisted until Hitler came to power in 1933. Then the Austrian government severed economic ties with Germany. Hitler, Austrian by birth, continued pressing for reunification.

Now, in violation of the treaty, he began rearming and to that end eyed Austria's iron, coal, and skilled workers. On March 12, 1938, the German military—the Wehrmacht—invaded Austria, unopposed and largely welcomed by the people as liberators. Within days, 70,000 members of opposition groups had been sent to prison or concentration camps. Four hundred thousand more were stripped of voting rights.

America heard those rumblings faintly beyond the horizon, but largely considered itself removed from them. That same month, Anna and Darel traveled to Florida. It was a working vacation. Copy for the Florida Guide was approaching final form and needed Washington's input. Darel photographed Seminoles in Florida and Catawbas in South Carolina, and submitted samples of his work, captioned after the fashion of the professionals. In seedy, bohemian Key West, they visited Sloppy Joe's, the saloon where Ernest "Papa" Hemingway hung out with his "mob" of literati—John Dos Passos and others—and where he did much work.

Maybe Darel eyed striking up an acquaintance. Hemingway, struggling with back pain, worked standing at the bar. He entered in a flurry and slapped his material down, announcing his arrival. Anna and Darel thought the behavior unnecessary and left with a view of Papa somewhat diminished from the one they'd arrived with.

The Florida Project introduced them to Roland Phillips—Phil—who later became our "Man Who Came to Dinner" at Burke before we went to Mexico. He was one of the people on whom Darel bestowed a pipe from Bertram's, makers of D.C.'s finest briar smoking implements, cardinal accessories to the male ensemble. "But honestly," Phil wrote them, "I didn't expect you-all to make me a present even though my natal day happens to be next week. Thanks a million. If you desire an alligator or perhaps a photo or two of a Florida chamber of commerce, just make your wants known."

Zora Neale Hurston

In April, Zora Neale Hurston joined the Florida Project. Anna and Darel were much taken with this magnanimous, stylish woman. She had joined reluctantly. Where Darel, still looking for his big break, had seen it as an opportunity, to Hurston, with three books published and a fourth on the way, it was the dole, not something to be proud of. She was, in fact, a Republican and opposed to the New Deal.

But her books, short stories, and articles weren't sustaining her, this woman with an Associate's Degree from Howard University, mentored by Franz Boas—the "Father of American Anthropology"—at Barnard College and later as a graduate student at Columbia, who did ethnographic studies, including documentary film work in the Caribbean.

Details of the friendship between my parents and Zora Neale Hurston are maddeningly sparse: four letters—hardly more than notes, two concerning an eight-dollar loan to get her car registered—three signed and two unsigned first editions. "Anna and Darel McConkey," she wrote on the *Mules and Men* flyleaf, "the 'Her' and 'Him' God had in mind for a pattern."

Anna told of visiting the ladies' room with Zora. "Anna," Zora said, "give me your coat."

"Zora," said Anna, "you don't have to hold my coat."

To which Zora replied, "If somebody comes in here and sees us, you'll find out why I have to hold your coat."

That story, four letters, and three inscriptions, are the sum and total that we have.

On July 1, 1938, Reed Harris abruptly resigned from the Project. Alsberg was shocked; Harris had been his most trusted associate. But Harris sensed trouble from leftwing elements in the New York Project. New York had been a hotbed of mainly union activity almost from the beginning. Though their disruptions had mostly abated, he felt that keeping the agitators on the New York payroll would end up jeopardizing the whole Writers' Project. Alsberg, for his part, didn't think meddling in local administration was his job. Even if he had, the law forbade him from firing people for political affiliations. Harris was getting out before the trouble started.

He may have been more prescient than he knew. A month after his departure, the House Rules Committee formed a subcommittee to investigate un-American propaganda. It was chaired by Texan Martin Dies. Though a Democrat, Dies was an implacable New Deal foe. Ted Morgan, in his book *Reds*, calls him "a big, blond, beefy fellow with a face the color of boiled ham." Like Joseph McCarthy after him, Dies was a demagogue with little regard for the truth or fair play.

At the end of July, he demanded an investigation of the Theater and Writers' Projects based on "startling evidence" that the projects were "a hotbed of communism" and a "link in the vast and unparalleled New Deal propaganda machine." It was the beginning of an attempt to "discredit the entire New Deal," through what Dies considered its weakest points. Few in the press—and not even Roosevelt—took the threat very seriously.

Darel bought his first car in 1938. His brother, Clyde, was working as a mechanic in Clarksburg and had found a four-year-old candidate. "It seems the best thing that I have found," he wrote. "It is a '34 Plymouth similar to mine only that it is a little later model of the DeLuxe type, longer wheel base and rides better than mine, upholstery in good condition, and mechanically in good shape with few exceptions which I will have them correct. The color is gunmetal gray. Tires in fair

1934 Plymouth

condition, about as good as can be expected in a used car. Price $285.00. I chiseled them down from $295.00." The dealership delivered the car to Washington in August. Anna and Darel drove it to Dixie in October. By the time they turned homeward, it was burning a quart of oil every fifty miles. It needed new engine bearings, two new pistons, a ring job, and a water pump. Total cost, $63. It also needed a new clutch, a brake job, and a new tail light which, Darel estimated, would bring the total to around $75. He suggested to the dealership that they abate the last $65-plus in car payments. There's no record of whether they did or didn't. My parents stuck with that car for the next ten years.

Caricature of Charles Finger by his illustrator daughter, Helen

Darel told Charles Finger of his intent to become a self-sustaining writer, and Finger, the elder, the mentor, applauded that intention in a rambling disquisition mainly about his own qualifications to judge people. That said, seemingly oblivious to Darel's history that had begun with 55 submissions to the *Lone Scout* magazine some twenty years gone, to his newspaper work in the 20s, to the hungry freelancing years before FERA, Finger grandly concluded, "I emphatically say that when you start (when you *start*?), when you settle down, when you feel assured that you can succeed working for yourself, you will win.

"It will take a little time to get under way, to set your course, to decide definitely on the haven to which you steer, but once under way with your mind in accord, you cannot fail." Somehow Finger's personality enabled him to get away with such grand pronouncements. He was a force of nature. He was one whom Darel gifted with a Bertram's pipe.

Finger brought his compendious knowledge of publications and editorial boards to bear on the disposition of Darel's "dainty and quaintly humour, thought-packed" *McAesop's Fables*. "Let me suggest you try *Ken*, addressing Gingrich the owner."

Ken was a short-lived, politically controversial magazine begun in 1938 and disappearing in 1939. "Also try the *Nation*," Finger counseled, "addressing Frieda Kirchway. Doubtless you've tried Harper's and been rejected—not because of any inferiority of work, because there's none—but because of all excellent magazines they favor an old and proved style."

Finger pointed to Heywood Broun's publication, *Broun's Nutmeg*, and it is probable that Darel submitted it the fables; Anna later told me that Broun had said he'd try to do something with them. Broun was a noted journalist whose syndicated column, "It Seems to Me," had run in the Washington Daily *News* (Sam Gordon's paper) among others, and as "It Seems to Heywood Broun," in *The Nation*. Along with wits Dorothy Parker and Robert Benchley, he'd been part of the Algonquin Round Table, which thought his disheveled appearance made him look like "an unmade bed." In 1930 he had run unsuccessfully for Congress as a Socialist, on the slogan, "I'd rather be right than Roosevelt." In December 1939, he died of pneumonia at age 51.

Now Hitler accused Czechoslovakia of atrocities against its German-speaking minority in the Sudetenland and insisted on the "need" to take the region over. In Britain, appeasers fretted that war with Germany would be military suicide. On September 29, Prime Minister Neville Chamberlin met in Munich with Hitler, Mussolini, and French Prime Minister Daladier.

The four signed the "Munich Agreement," which gave Hitler the Sudetenland in return for agreeing not to "need" anything else. Chamberlain returned to London calling the agreement "peace for our time." Winston Churchill said the British Empire had suffered its worst military defeat without a shot being fired.

On October 30, Orson Wells broadcast his radio play, "War of the Worlds," from the Mercury Theater of the Air. Thousands panicked, thinking the play was a news account of an actual invasion from Mars. Wells swore that result was utterly unintended. Only about 2 percent of the network's audience had actually listened to it, but newspapers, struggling against upstart radio, ginned up the panic in hopes of giving its challenger a black eye. Anna and Darel were at Dixie. Neither of them even mentioned it.

Eight days later, a Jewish teen assassinated a German diplomat in Paris. Two nights after that, Nazi storm troopers "spontaneously" rampaged through Jewish neighborhoods all over Germany while authorities stood by. The "demonstrators" damaged or destroyed nearly 1,000 synagogues and ransacked 7,500 Jewish businesses. Thirty thousand Jewish men were sent to concentration camps. News reports sent shockwaves across the globe.

The following spring, March 15, 1939, Hitler's forces occupied Czechoslovakia in open violation of the agreement signed in Munich the previous September.

Britain and other nations cautiously began rearming. At the end of March, Chamberlain announced that Britain and France "would lend the Polish Government all support in their power" should Hitler invade.

On April 9, Easter Sunday, celebrated Negro contralto Marian Anderson, denied booking at Constitution Hall in D.C. because of her race, sang for 75,000 live fans at the Lincoln Memorial. The performance was broadcast nationwide. Constitution Hall was owned by the Daughters of the American Revolution. First Lady Eleanor Roosevelt resigned her membership in protest. On May 9, Darel's birthday, he and Anna heard Anderson at the Rialto Theater as part of the Howard University Concert Series.

Anna, by this time, was growing large with her and Darel's first child. It was time to start thinking of bigger digs. A July 24 postcard from Dixie addressed to 1603 19th St., where they had lived for a year and a half, was redirected to 222 North Pitt St., across the Potomac in Alexandria. Even now, that block of Pitt retains is original cobbles, giving such a teeth-shattering ride, even on pneumatic tires, that one wonders how anybody could ever have thought cobbles were a good idea.

On August 23, Germany and the Soviet Union signed a nonaggression pact. It promised Stalin half of Poland if an invasion succeeded. All Stalin had to do was not interfere. Britain stuck with her promise of "all support" in case of German aggression. At any point—when Hitler remilitarized the Rhineland, when he annexed Austria, when he grabbed the Sudetenland, invaded Czechoslovakia—Britain and France, with Russian support, could have stopped him but did nothing.

It was no secret that Hitler had designs on Poland. Geographically, neutralizing Poland would secure his eastern flank, freeing him to concentrate on Western Europe. Accordingly, on September 1, 1939, the Wehrmacht, employing blitzkrieg—"lightning war" with planes, tanks, and infantry, first tested in the Spanish Civil War—quickly overwhelmed Poland's poorly equipped military.

Britain initially threatened Hitler with a declaration of war if he didn't withdraw. Hitler didn't, and Britain dithered before making good its threat on September 3. France declared the same day. The Second World War was off and running.

Chapter Thirty-Eight

Patrick Darel McConkey

Anna and Pat

THE NEWS FROM EUROPE was starting to raise jitters in America, but Anna and Darel were otherwise preoccupied. On September 1, the day Hitler marched into Poland, Patrick Darel McConkey emerged into the delivery room's cold, harsh light.

Birth of the first child is a bewildering mixture of awe and terror. Anna left no record of the event's effects on her, but Darel wrote a ten-thousand-word essay, "Footnotes for First Parents."

"You may have read widely, and on divers subjects," it began, and named history, opera, astronomy, and Sanskrit among those subjects, "but all this will profit nothing when the time comes for bringing home the first baby from the hospital."

Right up to delivery, he'd managed to nourish the fancy that the marriage was still between him and Anna. New life hadn't been kicking the insides of *his* ribs.

When the time arrived, Darel quickly got perspective on the nature of his position. Anxious to be of use, he lobbied for a private room. It cost twice as much as a ward, but nothing was too good for his wife. Anna figured what the heck, care in the ward would be the same and cheaper to boot. The doctor sided with Anna, and as the process advanced, Darel came to agree.

"Private-room mothers," he said, "seem a bit wistful. They read magazines, play low-tuned music on a little radio, or watch the narrow bit of hall through their door."

But ward mothers, once they awoke from anesthesia, found the ward's camaraderie buoying. Maternity's pageant flowed ceaselessly around them, there was always something to engage the interest. They were impatient to sit up, to swing their legs over the sides of their beds. They enjoyed comparing notes and borrowing cigarettes from each other.

But, said Darel, "Hospitals have scant use for fathers. In fact, they do not seem to believe in them. The architecture and furnishings…are sufficiently indicative of the low esteem in which fathers are held." The ward was accessed by a long, curvilinear corridor "so built that any but a doting husband, new father, or white rat trained to mazes would be efficaciously lost. A little table, with one chair, was provided for the nurse in charge; new fathers should be quite comfortable standing. He should not wear a hat (all but universal for men), or should finger it nervously, for there is not where to hang one. Nurses rustling by were disposed to regard him as something that ought to be combed out of their hair.

"The doctor obviously understood the scope of the *ameublements*[§§§] and attentions lavished on the *papa novo*. 'I suggest,' he said, 'that you kiss the little lady good night, go home where you can be comfortable, and I'll call you half an hour to forty-five minutes before something happens.' It was past midnight when he departed D.C.'s Garfield Hospital—now Washington Hospital Center—and drove home to Alexandria. It was dawn before he could sleep. The call came three hours later.

"Half an hour to forty-five minutes" stretched agonizingly to an hour and a half. Had something gone wrong? Something must have gone wrong!

The doctor appeared. "You have a nice big nine-pound boy, practically perfect."

"What do you mean, *practically* perfect?"

"Well, he hasn't much hair."

"Yes, yes, doctor, but how is she?"

"Fine, she's fine! She won't be out of the anesthetic for a while, won't remember much that happens today, but came through in fine condition."

He'd seen plenty of relatives' babies, and always thought they looked "parboiled, or like something out of a rotten log." His own had the color of ground liver, but good lungs, and was all right, and the mother was all right, and "the singing feeling begins."

Pat, his color improved, came home at 12 days. "There are ominous overtones to Bringing Home the Baby," the essay continued. "The doctor writes in his instructions: 'Sleep baby on stomach.' 'But doctor,' says New Father, 'isn't there danger of a baby smothering if you let it sleep on its stomach?' 'Yes,' replies the doctor, 'and there is danger, if the baby sleeps on its back, of mucus draining down its throat and choking it. Whenever you have a baby, you have danger.' *Whenever you have a baby, you have danger.* That sentence is a bar sinister[****] across the parents' thoughts as they drive carefully home."

Amazingly, the little thing seemed to know how not to smother itself. However, having been caught in a wave of diarrhoea that had swept every infant hospital in the city save one, Patrick arrived home less than full-strength. There ensued a problem feeding him, until a neighbor showed how to enlarge the holes in the bottles' nipples by piercing them with a hot needle. By then,

---

[§§§] furnishings

[****] a rare instance of his misusing a term

however, he was losing ground fast. Anna and Darel bundled him off to an infant hospital at midnight.

By morning, it was clear that only a series of transfusions would save him. Darel's blood type didn't match. Anna offered hers, but the doctors said a boy baby needed male blood. Darel tried calling a couple of friends but got no response. He called the office, from which he had inconveniently been separated the day before Patrick arrived. He was told to stand by for five minutes.

Beyond the horizon of the empty hospital hall, then, a human miracle happens. New Mother and New Father, bleakly enduring, know nothing in the five eternities that go by. The phone rings. 'Eight men are on the way to the hospital! We commandeered every phone in the place. They are coming to help you.' New Father and New Mother sit weakly down, too dry-eyed to cry, too numb with the unbearable futility to apprehend the sunshine that suddenly broke on the world.

It was not, indeed, until afterward that they realized how streams of strong blood were converging toward the hospital, how reckless men were breaking laws in the traffic to bring help to their baby, to the pinched little face, to the blue little lips, to the weak little form that could no longer cry. And this miracle of human warmth was no less a miracle than that of new blood. Within twelve hours they return to a rosy, round-cheeked infant, peacefully asleep in his little bassinet, but capable of raising a lusty howl when time comes to eat.

Patrick needed three weeks of transfusions before going home. And, said Darel, "hospitalization…is no trip through the ten-cent store." The first month of Patrick's life cost $500. Rent went begging. The car needed gas. Darel haunted personnel offices looking for work without result. Things got so ridiculous that at one point he and Anna were convulsed with laughter.

"Then, with as silly and capricious logic," he said, "Dame Fortune calls off her dogs, and everything turns for the better." A friend wrote them a $100 check. They discovered the Community Chest's Health Administration, which helped negotiate medical bills. The landlady eased off pressure on the rent. The mechanic tuned up the car for free. And sometime in the first half of October— around the same time Patrick was discharged from his second hospitalization—

the Project called Darel back, "at the same insufficient old salary, which now seems like a king's ransom." His salary for each of the previous two years had been $2,900.

Darel tried selling that good-humored essay, but nobody bought it.

On January 27, 1940, just as Anna, Darel, and Pat were leaving for Salt Lake City on Writers' Project business, Darel's oldest brother, Clyde, died of pneumonia, three weeks shy of his 49th birthday. Penicillin, which had been in development since 1928, could have saved him, but wasn't available for another two years.

Chapter Thirty-Nine

Utah

Darel, Pat, and Anna at Salt Lake

NINETEEN-FORTY was election year, and Roosevelt sought an unprecedented third term. On February 7, Gracie Allen announced from the "Burns and Allen" radio show her candidacy for president on the "Surprise Party" ticket. The stunt won her thousands of write-in votes.

Around the first of the year, WPA head Harry Hopkins became Commerce Secretary. A no-nonsense, retired army engineer, Colonel Francis Harrington, replaced him. Harrington had little use for Federal One or for Henry Alsberg. He was the picture of military discipline while Alsberg was a rumpled old bear with a ramshackle style, whose genius had been his vision of what it was possible to extract from a rag-tag band of irregular writers and editors. In four years, his Project had produced some three hundred books and pamphlets, all to critical acclaim and good sales, with more to come. But forces were converging on him. Not only had he made what many thought a too-conciliatory appearance before the Dies Committee, both Harrington and the Project's congressional enemies were champing to gut Federal One entirely. Additionally, Alsberg had replaced Reed Harris with a former field supervisor who seemed to draw to himself all the trust and support that Alsberg had once reserved for the staff, and the staff resented it.

Harrington wanted Alsberg's resignation; Alsberg said he had no intention of leaving until the last of the guides were in press. Harrington gave him until August 1, then replaced him with John D. Newsom, another ex-military man who had headed the Michigan Project. Newsom had four books of his own to his credit and proved an able administrator.

WPA was up for renewal July 1. Congress had no stomach for putting thousands of teachers and construction workers out of work in an election year, but it renamed the Writers' Project the Writers' "Program" and turned it from a federal into a state program, making the states responsible for at least 25 percent of the funding and making each program responsible for finding sponsors. Washington retained final approval on copy.

The reorganization, in August, cut the D.C. staff in half. That was when Darel had been let go. A new rule stipulated that no employees be retained more than eighteen months and prevented them from being rehired for at least thirty days after dismissal. Those rules most likely explain Darel's August furlough and October rehire.

On February 2, 1940, some three months after resuming his duties, he, Anna, and five-month-old Patrick arrived by train in Salt Lake City to help get the Utah guide back on the rails.

The Utah guide had gotten off to a promising start in 1936. In the first month, under the direction of *Ogden Standard Examiner* staff writer, Maurice Howe, the office outlined half a dozen sections and by May had sent the national office a page make-up dummy and a full outline with space for essays and the placement of illustrations. In July they sent drafts of several sections. But Utah suffered disproportionately from the Writers' Project's built-in maladies.

Generally, state offices were staffed with people of widely varying abilities and writing styles. Turnover was high, and the result was great unevenness in output. To ensure uniformity, review and approval were centralized in Washington, but the flood of material created bottlenecks. Manuscripts got so bogged down in review that a piece approved with minor edits, once corrected and resubmitted could find itself deemed totally unacceptable. Small wonder that the following poem, a takeoff on Joyce Kilmer's "Trees," circulated among the projects:

I think that I have never tried
A job as painful as the Guide.
A Guide which changes every day
Because our betters feel that way.
A guide whose deadlines come so fast
Yet no one lives to see the last.
A guide to which we give our best
To hear: "This stinks like all the rest!"
There's no way out but suicide,
For only God can end the Guide.

Through mid-1937, Utah fired off drafts for review and approval, but they only made the bottleneck worse. Utah was further disadvantaged by being a small western state, lower in priority than the more populous coastal states. As Utah spewed forth fresh copy, its submissions filtered into peripheral file drawers as D.C. grappled with more pressing concerns.

At the end of June 1938, Washington shanghaied Maurice Howe for its own ends, though he continued directing Utah via correspondence for another year, until he was deployed elsewhere. Even then, he continued as an unpaid Utah consultant. Charles Madsen, who had been with the guide almost from the start, became project director.

Under him, production slowed to a crawl. His failure stemmed from an inability to delegate. He worked—indefatigably—trying to do everything himself, tending at the same time to view staff initiative as a personal threat. Relations between staff members—each responsible only to Madsen— deteriorated. One observer marveled how so much energy could result in so little output. In the fall of 1938, with many of the other guides going into production, someone in Washington—apparently unaware of the material already submitted—asked Vardis Fisher, who had beaten Alsberg to the finish with Idaho's guide, to crank out a Utah manuscript.

The following spring, Fisher reported that the material on hand was too fragmented for use. In mid-August, he said an acceptable book should be possible by the first of the year, then left. Madsen's staff still couldn't disengage from politics, so Madsen asked Dale Morgan, historian of the Historical Records Survey, to leave HRS and come to work for him. Morgan, already struggling with a nearly impossible workload, declined. In December, Washington, fed up with the imbroglio, told Utah they were sending a consulting editor—Darel McConkey. Ahead of Darel's arrival, Madsen was able to get Morgan to critique the guide's historic essay. Morgan reported that the essay, though "ably written," was riddled with errors. He appended thirteen pages of them.

That was the situation Darel found in Salt Lake City on February 2. He had with him Maurice Howe's behest to involve Dale Morgan, who "knows more about Utah history than any living person. Sounds like a big order, but the boy has the real stuff." Dale was 25 years old.

Like Fisher, Darel found Utah's writings utterly inadequate and Madsen's office helpless to fix them. Focus on Dale Morgan intensified, and a new scheme hatched. Rather than plucking Morgan away from Historical Records, how about sharing him? Darel convinced the state's WPA director of Morgan's value to the guide and proposed that Morgan split his time between that and Historical Records.

The HRS head pled Morgan's value to Records, but in the end, all agreed to let Morgan spend mornings editing essays for the Writers' Project and afternoons at HRS. The arrangement, in fact, gave Morgan two part-time jobs—effectively full-time. At HRS, Project rules had limited him to 90 hours a month. He readily agreed.

Meningitis had stolen Morgan's hearing at age fourteen, launching a years-long exercise adapting to forced isolation. Deprived of his inner ear, he'd tortuously had to relearn walking using visual cues. He had loved school and been a top student, but his illness and recovery made him sit out an entire year. His intelligence remained, however, and served him well.

A scholarship in 1933, the year Roosevelt took office, enabled him to further his studies despite the Depression. In college, unable to hear lectures, he got by cribbing notes off his seatmates. He developed the facility of reading books—comprehensively—at a few seconds per page. His ability to recall details seemed limitless, and he cultivated the ability to commit them to paper with a speed few others could equal. Deafness had one positive effect: it enabled him to concentrate in a way denied his hearing peers.

In his sophomore year, work on the college paper allowed him a toehold back to the hearing world. Off campus, the *Salt Lake Tribune* printed his story, "The Atheist," that won the *Tribune*'s free-lance award for short fiction.

Over his college career, the student literary magazine published eight of his pieces. But after graduation, frustrated by Utah's Depression-era unemployment (around 30 percent, among the nation's worst), he drifted for a year, trying to find work in advertising, writing a weekly book review for the *Sunday Tribune*.

In July 1938, Maurice Howe offered Morgan's friend, Jarvis Thurston, an editorial position with Utah's Historical Records Survey. Thurston, otherwise gainfully employed, declined, but recommended Dale.

Dale's interest in history, Utah's particularly, burgeoned at the Records Survey. The survey was not an idle undertaking. America's public records were a shambles. From state to state, county to county, town to town, there was no consistent way of cataloging them if they were cataloged at all. Often, they were just shoved into random spaces, basements and attics. Researching them could be a nightmare.

The National Archives in Washington, D.C., opened in 1935, made the first attempt to centralize *national* records, a need owned since the Continental Congress in 1774. WPA's Historical Records Surveys extended the undertaking to the states. Different categories of records were to be accompanied by essays, and it was in editing those that Dale's interest bloomed. He was quick to spot historical errors and was soon engrossed in corrective rewrites surpassing anything his coworkers did. In particular, he found that nearly all of Utah history had been written by, of, and for the Mormon Church.

Pioneer diaries often revealed quite different stories. Dale made it his mission to bring Utah's history into line with the raw data. Thus, Maurice Howe's estimate, by 1940 when Darel arrived, that Dale at age 25 knew "more about Utah history than any living person."

Darel and Dale hit it off immediately. Howe told Darel, "He certainly likes you. He says he found you a kindred spirit right from the first day." The feeling was mutual. Around the first of March, while Darel and the Utah staff sorted, typed, edited, and rewrote, Dale tackled the guide's historical essay, and by the end of April had an 89-page manuscript.

By mid-May, things had smoothed out sufficiently that Alsberg's replacement, John Newsom, asked Howe to sound Darel on assuming directorship of the Utah project. Darel declined, but recommended Dale in his place. Not even Howe had contemplated such a move, but Dale's abilities had attracted notice on both the state and national levels. He had an independent streak arresting in one so young, however, and would only accept the directorship on condition:

"If I do take over the project," he told Darel, "I should like to take it over lock, stock, and barrel. I would like full responsibility for making it run as I think it should be run. I would like to be directly responsible for quantity and quality of production; and therefore, I should like to have full control of the processes of production."

On June 18, while talks were ongoing, Dale left for two weeks to reconnoiter Nevada's Humboldt River, which he had a contract to write about from the publishers of the *Rivers of America* series. On June 21, Darel wrote him care of general delivery in Wells, Nevada, "You're IT!" and Dale Morgan was director of the Utah Writers' Project.

As for the old director, Charles Madsen, Washington had never confirmed his appointment to begin with; he'd never advanced beyond acting director. It was a simple matter, in recognition of the exemplary work he'd actually done, to find him a non-supervisory place in the state administration. Madsen was unhappy, Darel said, but "he took it very bravely."

Darel had yet "to meet a man as objective about himself" as Madsen. Madsen asked Darel "what was wrong with him," and Darel said that his "Sherlockian bent" to see everything to the finish personally was "poorly fitted to a job that was in a hurry." He'd needed to delegate and had been unable to do it.

Dale returned to Salt Lake City on July 8 and took command on the 12th, showing a flair for both supervision and organization, and a maturity beyond his years in interpersonal relationships, all with people needing communicate with him via handwritten notes.

He wrote to Darel, "Friday morning I had a sense of being two persons, a guy who was sitting behind a desk talking to people like God, and another who was standing incredulously by, asking what the hell this fellow was doing here.

But after a general declaration of policy to the staff, I got into the spirit of the thing and now am state supervisor, big as life and twice as real."

Anna and Darel missed a personal farewell, having entrained for home on June 28. Charles Finger had met them in Salt Lake City, presenting Darel with a *Roget's Thesaurus*. Darel is hardly likely to have mentioned that he regarded the thesaurus as a cheat. Six months later, at age 71, Charles Finger died of influenza and a heart attack.

Once back home, Darel sent Dale a detailed, single-spaced, six-page letter on the personnel situation he would find in the Utah office. Darel then dove into pruning the guide's 325,000-word manuscript down to publishable size. In three weeks, he excised some 30,000 words of an anticipated 50,000. For the next four months, a lengthy and lively exchange of letters—mixed business and personal—passed between the two men until the guide was done.

In West Virginia and Kansas, Darel had dealt with politics and personnel. With Utah, it was the messy process of whipping material into publishable shape. Maurice Howe had wrested Utah's submissions—technically "under review" for an entire year—from the national office and sent them home; but this piece needed that and that piece needed this. Eliminate this source in that essay, but add another source in a different one. This tour was good but that one had problems. This piece was too long, that one…well, rarely if ever was a piece too short.

All was being cobbled together by fluctuating personnel of uneven abilities and styles. Everything had to pass muster with the Mormon Church. The introductory essay, "The Contemporary Scene," which Dale ended up calling "The Contemptuous Scene," flew back and forth between D.C. and Utah more than any other piece. Darel had revised it once while still in Utah and again after his return, but Writers' Project director Newsom felt the essay should

Dale Morgan signing the Utah Guide for Governor Maw

bear the finish of a real Utahn, so back to Salt Lake City it went. Dale completed the final version when the rest of the book was already at the publisher. Darel's work on the guide, meanwhile, was interrupted while he did a second-edition edit of another Writers' Project book, *Our Government and How It Functions*. It's a wonder the guide series got finished at all, let alone emerged as a celebrated production.

For all that, Darel wrote of it, "God knows it has been picked and scratched a great deal, but though some of the feathers are sticking out at odd angles, it's the same bird as the one that was so frequently 'gone' in the dear, long-gone days in Utah." When the galley proofs arrived from the typesetter in December, he said, "we need not shrivel in shame, despite the pinpricks this office has given me about the book. 'Contemporary Scene' and 'History' look noble in print."

Chapter Forty

War

German invasion of Holland, May 1940

ANNA AND DAREL had had a secondary mission in Utah. Anna's maternal uncle in Holland, Thom Mandersloot, dealt in building materials, importing from Germany many that were unavailable in Holland. When Hitler invaded Poland, German supplies dried up. Oom (Uncle) Thom wrote his sister, Nellie Schuddeboom, to see if she could find suppliers in America. Nellie put the question to Anna and Darel as they were leaving for Utah. On a layover in Chicago, they happened to dine with an employee of the American Paint Company, who put them on the trail of a Utah supplier of gilsonite—one of the materials on Oom Thom's list.

They tracked down a firm in Mynton, Utah, but Project business prevented their forwarding its name until early May. On the tenth of that month, the Wehrmacht rolled into Holland and communication with America ceased. Not only did Oom Thom not get his gilsonite, the American branch of the family had no idea what was happening to the Dutch branch, and didn't until the war ended five years later.

Maurice Howe had similar worries. His wife was British. On May 18, he wrote Darel, "Everyone is heartsick over the war situation. Looks like we may all be in uniform or bombed before the year is out. Lucie has had no further word from England."

In April, Hitler had invaded Denmark and Norway. When he invaded Holland in May, he also overran Belgium and Luxembourg to get at France, which he subdued in six weeks. France's fall left the British, French and Belgian rearguard stranded on the English Channel at Dunkirk, threatened by vastly superior German might. The Germans paused their advance for three days, possibly to consolidate their position.

Germany, being land-based, may have thought its prey had nowhere left to go, but to the sea-faring British, the Channel was their escape route. It wasn't a clean getaway. The Luftwaffe strafed the beach, and artillery sank 243 of 861 vessels, but between May 27 and June 4, 338,000 British, French, Belgian, and a few Dutch troops escaped across the Channel.

Hitler now turned his sights on Britain. On July 10, readying for a cross-channel invasion, he ordered blockades of British shipping and the bombing of her ports, coastal airfields, radar installations, and aircraft manufacturing. He failed to reckon on three things: the Royal Air Force, the British people, and Prime Minister Winston Churchill, who famously told his cabinet that he had "nothing to offer but blood, toil, tears, and sweat."

Britain fought back, and not just defensively. She sent bombing raids over the Rhur manufacturing region, over Berlin, and other targets. When some bombs fell wide into a Berlin residential area, Hitler ordered the Luftwaffe to retaliate on British cities. On September 7, four hundred bombers and six hundred fighters attacked London. The Blitz was underway. American newscaster Edward R. Murrow, the "father of broadcast journalism," began his reports live from London rooftops.

Hitler had conquered Europe in nine months, and Americans were wondering: if Britain fell, could we stop Hitler if he came for us? Following

World War I, the "war to end war," our military had sunk to eighteenth in the world. Congress, suddenly sensing danger, granted Roosevelt's full request for rearmament.

While Congress was all for rearming America, it was less enthusiastic about aiding Hitler's victims. To skirt congressional recalcitrance, Roosevelt drew from existing stockpiles—a quarter million rifles with 130 million rounds of ammunition, 800,000 machine guns, 900 artillery pieces, 140 bombers. Some White House aides thought Roosevelt, standing for his third term, was committing political suicide. The War Department fretted for its independence. Joseph Kennedy, US ambassador in London, voiced grave pessimism for Britain's prospects.

Roosevelt further risked reelection by coming out in favor of America's first-ever peacetime draft when the public was ten-to-one against it. But we couldn't wait, he said, for a crisis to happen before starting to prepare. We would need an army at the ready, and it would take a year to get there. Amid great acrimony, the draft became law on September 16.

The first lottery number was drawn on October 29. Roosevelt called it a defensive "muster," evoking Lexington and Concord more than London and Dunkirk. Roosevelt promised mothers that "Your boys are not going to be sent into any foreign wars." But, "We cannot remain indifferent to the philosophy of force now rampant in the world."

Isolationism's champion, Charles Lindbergh, warned that America's meddling in other people's conflicts was just asking for war. Roosevelt retorted that Hitler's propaganda minister, Joseph Goebbels, could not have said it better himself.

The Royal British Air Force fought the Nazis to a standstill. Hitler turned his eyes eastward, broke his pact with Stalin, and invaded Russia. Roosevelt declared that arms sales to Britain, as well as China and the Soviet Union, made America "the great arsenal of democracy." Isolationism was losing ground. When Roosevelt signed the draft law, the sentiment had slipped to 50-50. By November, it was a minority position.

Churchill buoyed his nation, "We shall fight on the beaches, we shall fight on the landing grounds, we shall fight in the fields and in the streets, we shall fight in the hills; we shall never surrender."

As required by America's 1930s-era Neutrality Acts, Britain had been paying cash for equipment, but she was running out of money. Churchill begged for help and Roosevelt desperately wanted to give it, but needed a way to skirt both the Neutrality Acts and congressional opposition. His solution was Lend-Lease, in which, he said, we would lend, not sell, the arms Britain needed, and Britain would pay us back in kind after the war.

He likened the idea to lending a neighbor, whose house was on fire, a garden hose which he would return once the fire was out. The idea was specious at best. Who would need, or want, all that war junk back once peace returned? But, as Roosevelt also said, "There can be no reasoning with incendiary bombs."

His arguments had their effect. Despite shrieks of protest from die-hard opponents, Lend-Lease passed Congress with comfortable margins, and Roosevelt signed it on March 11, 1941. The measure also aided Russia, battling the German invasion, and China, battling invasion by Axis partner Japan. Four days after signing Lend-Lease, Roosevelt told an audience, "Let not dictators of Europe or Asia doubt our unanimity now."

Lend-Lease not only supplied Jeeps, tanks, and warships, it built destroyer and seaplane bases in Ireland and Scotland, helped build Ford's Willow Run bomber plant, Chrysler's Detroit tank arsenal, and Kaiser's California shipyard. Industry, nevertheless, needed time to tool up. Lend-Lease opened the pipeline, but it took months to fill it. As important as anything else, the program supplied Britain with hundreds of tons of food.

Those were reports from the war front. Anna and Darel, home from Utah in July 1940, resumed housekeeping in same old Alexandria, different address. Darel told Dale that the house, their largest yet, was "built on a scale almost too spacious for us to endure. Pat, instead of growing, gets smaller and smaller as we put him into larger places."

He described the "livestock" in the back garden: ants, a moth, and "a middle-size praying mantis (look the critter up if you don't know him) who turned his head and looked at me with curious bovine alertness."

Dale wrote back that he had never seen a praying mantis, but had "read about them and seen photos, and I think if I should see one, that I would flee to the cellar and lock the doors."

Darel responded, "The praying mantis is a fellow with a certain charm. He is built like an attenuated katydid, and has the unusual faculty of turning his head. This gives him a seeming alertness and intelligence not common to insects. Two feet are held out in front in an attitude of prayer, but what that critter is praying for is that some fellow-insect get within reach. If the mantis were thirty feet long, I shouldn't like him quite so well, and would join you in the dash for the bomb-proof cellar."

Alexandria, he informed Dale, was "just across the dusty Potomac from Washington. A radio station," he elaborated, "used to say it was just across the sparkling, broad, sunlit Potomac. Now they are building an airport on a pumped-in plain, and the Potomac is literally dusty." Washington National Airport was a-building, employing many WPA workers. It opened in June 1941, and by 1942 was the nation's third busiest.

Washington National Airport

"Got the car back from mechanic and inspection today, and it hums a goodly tune. It cost $55, but is probably worth it. A good machine is a joy, not forever, but for the moment, till it has to go back. One day, as soon as may be, I shall tackle the Alleghenies in it, and feel sure of getting over."

He did. In August, the Project gave him a vacation, and to West Virginia he went—no longer to Dixie but to West Milford, where he'd gone to high school. Gladys had bought a house there with a legacy from her aunt Laura. Darel's mother had moved there with her. Anna's mother came along to visit, and Anna and Darel left Pat in the care of grandmothers and aunts and went sniffing out country real estate, the first recorded act toward Darel's lifelong dream of returning to the soil.

>None of us can step out of his own experience (he wrote to Dale). I had a childhood on the farm, and it gave me certain things for which I would not exchange millions of dollars. There is a training in simplicity that cannot be matched by unfulfilled wants engendered by, for instance, a child going through a ten-cent store. I was raised a pioneer, and some of that spirit is damn well needed to cope with life and its problems.
>
>I feel, in some very deep way, that this is the best answer for me, for Anna, for Pat, for Pat's brothers and sisters, should they run to that

plurality. "The earth does have grace and beauty," as you say, of which qualities our time has not an oversupply.

I question whether the return to the earth will ever be final. I know that it will not. We will miss the people we know in metropolitan centers, but if we can draw from the earth some grace and beauty, we shall have more with which to work out success in the metropolises without having to live in them.

Perhaps it is my destiny, if any human can claim such a grandiose purpose, to speak for West by God Virginia, just as your manifest destiny is to tell the Mormon story. Most writers, do you notice, get country places. Chares Finger has done mighty well as a country laird and as a writer.

In pursuit of *West by God Virginia*, he and Anna detoured down near the Kentucky line to a quintessential West Virginia farm, with a field accessible only by an eighteen-foot ladder. The plow horse was hoisted in by a derrick. The farm, at the "fur end" of Tick Ridge, was owned by Fillmore Copley. "I've raised fifteen children first and last," he told them. "Been married three times. But my feet's give out on me now." From that visit came chapter two of *West by God Virginia*, "The Fur End of Tick Ridge."

The book had the interest of Hastings House, which published some of the Guides. Darel got as far as submitting "Tick Ridge" along with chapter one, about his grandfather's gas well, "McConkey No. 1,"—the world's biggest when drilled in 1900, which caught fire in 1902 and how it was put out. He planned to submit chapter three on the Hatfield and McCoy feud. No finished copy of that chapter survives. He left us a whole-book outline, tortuously wrought with Anna's prodding, and a plethora of preliminary material, but no evidence of further submissions.

He had gotten the *West by God Virginia* idea reading Carl Carmer's *Stars Fell on Alabama* while in Topeka in 1937. West Virginians had inserted "by God" between "West" and "Virginia" to punctuate their not being Tidewater flatlanders. The two states had been one until the Civil War, when West Virginia stayed with the Union while Virginia went south.

It was also during this latter part of 1940 that he worked up "Footnotes for First Parents." "Writing on the baby book," he told Dale, "Is going on with about the same facility as my liking for visits to the dentist and barber. It has got to, and will, be done, but old man McConkey is mighty lethargic about it."

Near the end of September, Doc Barrows, with whom Darel had worked at the Project's cities division before going to Utah, moved in with Anna and Darel while researching two books for which he had contracts. "Doc is a great good guy, and we will be mightily glad to see him again. If you don't hear too much from us in that time, you may console yourself with a picture of evenings around the fireplace, with tall drinks, settling the universe, and occasionally stooping to take in the international situation." Barrow's research turned to writing, and he was still with Anna and Darel shortly before Christmas, when he had a stroke and died. "We haven't recovered from the shock nor the fatigue yet," he told Dale.

Chapter Forty-One

Lincolnia

First real-property purchase.

I N THE SUMMER of 1941, Anna and Darel decamped to a log "cabin in the country," Silver Spring, Maryland, a D.C. suburb. The place had "a lawn to keep down and a garden to encourage upward." Darel tore down the old privy and built a new one. Drought that year held their garden to a third of its expected yield, and Dale took Darel to task for having spent five months in Utah without seeing how gardening was done in irrigation country.

By September, they had moved again, to Lincolnia, Virginia, just west of Alexandria. "We are living on our new-old 4-acre farm in Virginia." No longer renting, this was their first real-property purchase. "Right now, I keep so busy chopping wood I have no time for writing letters. We are otherwise snugging up for the winter, and fixing to add a new member to the family about New Year's." "We haven't 'decided' whether to have a boy or a girl."

In 1941, you could buy four acres in Lincolnia, today a mere jot in a megalopolis of incalculable extent. Dale once told me Darel would have farmed in a window box, and it seems that he would have. He was thirty-six,

Free-standing oil stove

Anna was thirty-three, and they were making their first real stab at returning to the land. The house was a roof overhead, adequate to their pioneering needs and possibly the best they could do on WPA money. They planned to replace the well's hand pump with an electric one, and the outside privy with an inside bathroom.

The kitchen was a lean-to tacked to the outside of the house; they would punch a door through from the inside. They cooked on a free-standing oil stove. The living room had a wood/coal stove for heat. Darel knew his tools, but fixer-upping's scale never fails to surprise novice expectations. Puttying a window, he declared, was "a pesky unworthy job no grown man should let himself be lured into." The following summer, however, after an intense freak hailstorm shattered many window panes, Darel boasted, "I was an expert glazier by the time all the glass was replaced." Lincolnia was their third address in the year since returning from Utah, and he promised Dale, "We're going to live here from now on. Please hang our *permanent* address on the tree."

Around 2:20 in the afternoon on Sunday, December 7, radio stations interrupted their broadcasts for a message from the White House:

The Japanese have attacked Pearl Harbor from the air and all naval and military activities on the island of Oahu, principal American base in the Hawaiian Islands.

The nation was stunned. Outrage was instantaneous. There'd been no warning, no declaration of war. The Japanese submitted their declaration an hour after the attack began. The next day, Roosevelt angrily declared

December 7, 1941, "a date which will live in infamy," and reciprocated with his own declaration.

If Japan meant to demoralize America, it badly miscalculated. Overnight, we burst the bonds of isolationism into a nation where mothers would send their sons to war and sons were champing to go. Though all males between the ages of eighteen and forty had been required to register for the draft, Darel, at age 36, was a year past the age at which they were being taken. He tried volunteering anyway, but was diagnosed with the most mundane of all disqualifiers—flat feet. So, he volunteered as a civil defense warden—plane spotter and blackout enforcer.

Pearl Harbor, December 7, 1941

Many scrambled to learn what and where Pearl Harbor was, but half of Americans had, in fact, been expecting war with Japan, just not from a sneak attack in the Pacific while we were watching Hitler shred his non-aggression pact with Stalin. In June, having been fought to a standstill by the Royal Air

Force, unable to mount a cross-channel invasion against Britain's superior navy, Hitler invaded the Soviet Union. He had expected to be in Moscow by September but failed to reckon on the poorly equipped Soviet army's ferocity.

Now it was December and, like Napoleon's before him, his invasion ground to a halt in the Russian winter, his army freezing, his supply lines stretched to breaking. And then Japan bombed Pearl Harbor.

Civil Defense warden

The attack meant to disable US meddling with Japan's efforts to replace Western power in the Pacific with her own—the British in Malaya, Singapore, and Hong Kong; the Dutch in the East Indies; the French in Indochina; America in the Philippines, Guam, and Wake Island. Four days after Pearl Harbor, Japan's Axis allies, Germany and Italy, submitted their own declarations of war, and America returned the favor. Before Pearl Harbor, Roosevelt couldn't have choked a declaration from the Senate. Now it fell all over itself giving him just that. Charles Lindbergh, the arch-isolationist, went on to serve with distinction in the Pacific.

Pat had arrived the same day Hitler invaded Poland, Helen a month after Pearl Harbor, January 9, 1942. Darel and Pat had gone to Anna's parents' to await the birth. "Poor little Pat," Darel wrote to Dale, "who is now a quarter past two, is so upset and apprehensive that he pulled up lame with a fever. On the way out—having been told that he and I were going to 'Mom's' (his grandmother's) while Anna went away for a new little baby—he asked Anna a series of leading questions:

"'We go out to Mom's in our tar. Me (you) get out?'

"'Yes.'

"'Darel get out and go in?'

"'Yes.'

"'Pat get out and go in?'

"'Yes.'

"'Little teeny new baby get out and go in?'

"He was so afraid Anna would go away any minute that he didn't even want her to go to the bathroom. Well, that was yesterday, and maybe he'll get settled in shortly." Presumably they dropped Anna at the hospital on the way to "Mom's." (We kids called our grandmother "Mom" to the end of her days.)

Helen was born in a snowstorm. Anna brought her home in a taxi. Pat, waiting with Darel, got the very grown-up job of paying the driver. Second children do not, unfortunately, rate 10,000-word essays, so we know less of Helen's arrival than of Pat's.

Almost overnight, D.C. was a boomtown. The White House was ablaze with lights as people collected across Pennsylvania Avenue in Lafayette Square to watch hurried comings and goings. By morning, the city was an armed camp, soldiers with fixed bayonets guarding bridges and strategic buildings.

Fighter planes buzzed the city's skies while civil defense wardens scanned for enemy aircraft. New workers invaded the precincts by the thousands. Prices rose, tires and fuel were rationed. There was a sugar shortage. Housing became nearly impossible to get, some people living four and five to a room.

"WPA is now being 'streamlined' for the war effort," Darel told Dale. Among Utah's works in progress was a guide to Fort Douglas, close enough to Salt Lake City for it to use the municipal airport as a B-17 bomber base. The Fort Douglas book now became *A Service Men's Guide to Salt Lake City and Vicinity*, a mainly recreational directory with the fort as a mere point of interest, stripped of anything interesting to enemy eyes. In every state, writers' programs set to work on comparable guides, with plans to sell them to the Army.

"Between us girls," Darel said, "I'm bored with the dam things, and must very soon get into 'em up to my neck or else get another job. I hope, frankly, for the latter."

Dale wrote Darel requesting details. Not hearing back, he wrote again, "You haven't answered my last letter, with its special inquiry about servicemen's guides!"

Darel responded, "You *demand* a letter, and I can't give you any very good answer, account of I haven't been to the office since March 23."

An *Atlantic* publisher had "blown into the office" expressing interest in the servicemen's guides, probably the whole series, but starting with one for the

Camp Blanding, Florida, area. Darel immediately hatched a plan to go to Florida, contact the military people, meet the publisher, and take the family along for a week at the beach.

"The third consideration blew up first. Pat fell victim to 'chitchin pots,' and the family angle was out. Before reaching the beach, I got my nastiest sore throat ever. The publisher didn't turn up. By the day of my armed forces visit, I felt too rotten to go anywhere, and the next day came home. The doctor ordered me to bed, my chief nutriment a series of large white pills all named sulfathiazole. Yep, strep. This evening was my first even to pump a bucket of water."

Most of the D.C. staff had been "redirected—out." Project Director Newsom was resigning to join the Army at age 49. "Merle Colby is the new 'director' of the sub-sub-sub-unit, which we now become, under the Cultural Services Section. Ruth Crawford and I are to remain till June 1, to 'mop up.'

"As I look at the bookcase of guides, I feel there is justice in our demise. We set out to do a job and we have done it. Now I feel it would be best if WPA were wiped out. Many of those in command seem mainly interested in widening their bottoms on government chairs for the duration, so when the next crackup comes, they will be important again. I say this with full realization that I am one of the bureaucrats, or will be until June 1."

He was not the sort to sit out the war. "It is time to move on. We did a good job, we gave people work when they needed it, and now there is another job to do. It will not be easy to find one's niche, where one can be happy and interested, and do one's country the most good, but I believe it possible."

West by God Virginia reached an inflection point. Through his contact with the Utah Guide's publisher, Hastings House, Dale maintained a dialogue regarding the book. He was also in conversation with Farrar and Rinehart, which was publishing his Humboldt book, and he broached *West by God* there. In mid-January, he had written Darel, "I hope you took seriously the letter from John Farrar. The more I thought it over, the more I thought Hastings was not the logical publisher for WbGVa. At the worst, if Farrar was interested, his interest would give you a needle to stick in Hastings and make them appreciate the property they have been kicking around so indecisively. If you let John Farrar see the book and if he likes it, I think he will get back of it. He is a perfectly swell guy. Anyway, there's the ball, and you can run with it or boot it right back, whatever you want."

Then, on April 9, Darel wrote: "I have been notified that I am fired as of April 23. This leaves only Merle Colby and a secretary as 'The Writers Program' in Washington. What good such an 'organization' will be to people in the states is not clear. There will be no national publisher for anything, and no editorial approval in Washington. You're on your own, boy, from here on out.

"Personally, I am doing no more work except seeing the [revised] Washington DC Guide through galleys and pages and index. It's my last job. The rest of my time will be devoted to job-hunting. I have until June 1 to find something, and hope by that time to break into some field that is exciting and in line with 'the war effort'—a weak phrase; wish people would stop using it.

"My agent (Darel referred often to his agent but never named him) whom I saw just before the doctor put me to bed, is going to see John Farrar about *W.b.G.Va.*, on the chance that he may finance me for the summer to write the thing. That would be nice, to stay here and work the 'farm' while writing, but I hesitate somewhat because of Selective Service. The word is that one's job (in war service) is to be more important than one's dependents, and I'd be hard put to justify doing a book."

Children are great levelers. Darel was no longer just a writer; he was a family man. Anna did her best to make writing possible for him, but he had to feed them, and insisted on being part of his kids' lives. Family began leveling him as it does all but the half percent of writers who *really* succeed. It leveled Anna, too. Gone was the Island. Gone were her carefree days at the Library of Congress. You can deprive yourself, but you can't deprive your children.

A month's leave from the Writers' Program carried Darel nearly to the end of May. Then he began writing pamphlets—*Children in War Time*—for the Office of Civilian Defense. He ghost wrote an article, 'What Can I Do to Help?' that appeared in the New York *Times* magazine over the byline of James M. Landis, director of the civil defense office.

In June, Dale heard from Farrar. "He told me that 'after fasting and prayer', they had decided not to take on *West by God Virginia*, feeling that the *Rivers of America* series was all the Americana they could do justice to at present, though you had fine material and handled it well. This is damned unlucky; I had hoped they would take on WBGV, since he is a swell guy to work with."

Darel replied, "Please don't feel badly about Farrar. It might have been a good thing for me to be required to write a book, but circumstances would have changed the picture considerably. Parts of it need more traveling, and the fuel and tire situation being what it is, such a thing would be out of the question. I have very little time, and it would have worn down the old man considerably to take on that book now. I'm going to do it sometime, but would just as leave not go into it at the moment. Even the genre-picture is undergoing rapid change in this war situation, and I have a feeling that such a book should not be written till after the war, when the socio-economic picture is different."

Dale, with the Utah guide behind him, moved to D.C. where there was greater promise of employment and better research facilities than in Salt Lake City. He stayed a week at the McConkeys' ramshackle Lincolnia house, then spent a week with the Howes before Maurice's employer, the Social Security Administration, transferred him to Denver. He found a studio apartment with a Pullman kitchen and a Murphy bed on Key Boulevard in Arlington, Virginia, in a neighborhood overlooking the Potomac that had been cow pastures before the wartime building boom.

Darel and Maurice offered comments on his Humboldt manuscript before Dale mailed it to Farrar and Rinehart, which sent it back for drastic cuts in mid-November. Dale interrupted his job hunt for that task.

He applied for a Civil Service rating, knocked on doors at the Office of Defense Health and Welfare, the news division of the Social Security Administration, the Office of War Information, the War Information Service. He briefly tried a freelancing gig, which netted him a paltry $35 for one week. An opening at the Library of Congress looked promising, until the draft board rejected the employee whose position he might have taken.

He celebrated Christmas with Anna, Darel, Pat, and Helen, all the while pursuing researches at National Archives and the Library of Congress on his next project, a history of the Mormons. By January, his money was nearly exhausted. He finally found a job at the Office of Price Administration, a wartime board that directed rationing, price controls, and production quotas. It was a demotion, from directorship of a Writers' Project to a lower-echelon editorial position, but he reckoned many others had been demoted to Pfc in Uncle's Army. He was serving his country in comparable style.

In the summer of 1942, German U-boats were being seen off the Atlantic coast. One landed four saboteurs on Long Island and another landed four in Florida. Within two weeks, the FBI had caught all eight. Darel offered his woodworking skills to the arms manufacturing effort, but here's no record of a response.

Chapter Forty-Two

Cartels

IN 1941, West Virginia Senator Harley M. Kilgore had been assigned to Senator Truman's committee investigating waste and fraud in military procurement. A year later, he was made chair of the Subcommittee on War Mobilization, formed to investigate technology in mobilization. Darel found a place on his staff as speech-writer and researcher. The job placed him "within the United States National Defense organization." In February, 1943, because Anna was from a country under Nazi occupation, Darel signed an affidavit promising not to divulge information which "could be deemed of value" to the Axis.

He wrote speeches mostly for Kilgore but also for a few others. He campaigned with Kilgore in 1944 and was with the committee until 1946. In addition to speeches, he ghost wrote articles for Kilgore's byline. In August, 1943, a Kilgore article entitled "The Science Mobilization Bill" appeared in *Science* magazine. In 1944, Kilgore's "Post-War Jobs for All" showed up in an undated little magazine called *Reader's Scope*. In November, an article appeared in *We, The People's Picture Magazine*, entitled "How *You* Can Have a Post-War Job!" also bylined Kilgore.

The December issue of *Flying* magazine ran an article, "The Administration's Air Policy," bylined Senator Harry Truman (who was by then Vice President-elect), but which Darel had ghost-written. In July 1945, Kilgore's "We Owe Aviation a Boost" appeared in *Skyways* magazine, and "The Axis Criminals" appeared in *The Independent*.

The hearings started with the committee's asking whether wartime patents would be open for general use after peace returned, or whether, as after World War I, they would be awarded to major corporations, as the Navy's radio patents had been awarded to RCA.

As the nation mobilized, mysterious shortages of critical materials began showing up. Zinc—alloyed with copper, it made brass for cartridge casings. Aluminum for airplanes was in short supply. The Aluminum Company of America, Alcoa, swore it could supply all military and civilian needs, but only succeeded in supplying half. Rubber for tires was short. Aircraft fuel.

These shortages bedeviled mobilization and were largely responsible for civilian-sector rationing—tires from Pearl Harbor on, joined by cars, sugar, typewriters, and gasoline. People were exhorted to donate aluminum pots and pans, recycle their tin cans, and plant "victory" gardens. By war's end, rationing extended to coffee, shoes, meats, stoves, processed foods, and bicycles.

Witnesses before the Kilgore and other committees disclosed a link between the shortages and the patents Kilgore was investigating. Standard Oil owned patents on synthetic rubber, but contracts with manufacturers overseas limited its production. Such international agreements worked as dodges to evade America's anti-trust laws.

Major industries in different countries—many without anti-trust limits— teamed up to share technologies among themselves, and the agreements enabled American industries to claim that their production limits were bound by contracts with overseas companies.

In those industrial pools, patents became communal property, so advances in technology couldn't advantage one member of the pool over the others. Normally, patents would be licensed to other manufacturers who would pay royalties for their use. Now, however, outsiders to the pools were simply frozen out.

The insiders established territories, set quotas, fixed prices, and agreed not to compete with each other. "You don't poach in my backyard, and I won't poach in yours." The pool set production quotas low so scarcity would drive up demand and, with demand, prices. Standard Oil, with perhaps an extra partner or so, got exclusive rights to America. But the agreement required it to pay the pool royalties on its own patents!

Those pools are known as cartels. The effects they had on our mobilization shocked investigators. Under one agreement, Henry Ford, as far back as the Battle of Britain, before Pearl Harbor, had refused to make aircraft engines unless they were guaranteed *not* to go to Britain. Remington Arms—owned by I. E. du Pont—couldn't sell Britain military-grade ammunition. Alcoa owned the patents on aluminum manufacture but, like Standard Oil with its rubber, was forbidden to make enough for wartime needs. As investigators dug, the trail led repeatedly back to one, enormous, sprawling German conglomerate, Interessengemeinschaft Farbenindustrie Aktiengesellschaft of Frankfort-am-Main—I. G. Farben for short.

Farben was a 1925 merger of six German chemical and pharmaceutical companies that made it Europe's single largest company. Individually, those six and a couple more had dominated 90 percent of the world market in dyestuffs. Originally allied with the liberal German People's Party, the Nazis accused Farben of being an "international capitalist Jewish company."

After Hitler took power in 1933, Farben switched loyalties, purged its Jewish employees, and became a major player in rebuilding Germany's war machine.

In the late 1920s and through the 1930s, Farben lured in major American concerns—Alcoa, Du Pont, Standard Oil—on promise of padded bottom lines. Those industries mostly signed on before the war, believing they were acting in their businesses' best interests. Once war broke out, they still felt compelled to honor their contracts. Senator Harry Truman called it treason. The only cartel member that didn't feel honor-bound was I. G. Farben, which had rigged the cartel to cripple Allied preparedness. Those royalty payments? They ended up in Hitler's pocket. A report stated, "Without I.G.'s immense productive facilities, its far-reaching research, varied technical expertise and overall concentration of economic power, Germany would not have been in a position to start its aggressive war in September 1939."

Roosevelt flexed his own muscle, seizing the patents under the war-powers act and putting the industries to work making armaments. Even there, impediments existed. In reducing output, many industries had decommissioned plants and now had to tool back up. However, given the handicaps we started with, it's all the more remarkable that we mobilized as fast as we did. When Roosevelt first asked for 50,000 planes a year for Lend-Lease, Congress swore it couldn't be done. But it was. The first 100,000 took just over two years, the second 100,000 but one year.

In mid-December, 1942, Edward R. Murrow first gave America the news of Hitler's "final solution."

Though a cross-channel invasion of Europe from England was the ultimate goal, the Allies were not yet strong enough to undertake so massive a land-based operation. The European war continued being fought mostly from the air. The first American planes arrived in England in mid-1942 but wouldn't become a significant part of the assault until March 1943. Except for Germany's Russian front, the war's main land-based theater was the see-saw conflict in North Africa. In May the US, still revving up, sent the Allies in Tunisia 200 tanks. We finally got boots on the ground eleven months after Pearl Harbor, joining the Allies invading Morocco, Oran, and French Algeria.

In response, Hitler reinforced his own troops by diverting men and material from Russia, but the Allies emerged victorious in May 1943. In July they invaded Sicily under heavy resistance, and from there began their struggle up Italy's spine. Mussolini's government surrendered, and on September 8 its replacement signed an armistice.

German paratroopers rescued Mussolini, who administered a puppet government from a German-held sector. The Axis, under German command, battled the Allies' Italian advance until war's end in May 1945. In the Atlantic, merchant convoys under armed escort dueled German U-boats to supply Great Britain. It was a battle of tactics and technology—advances in radar, SONAR, and decryption—in which the Allies managed to gain the upper hand by mid-1943. Darel's nephew, Bob—his brother Wendell's firstborn son—served in the Atlantic as an Army medic aboard a hospital ship, the converted ocean liner Queen Elizabeth.

In the Pacific, the Japanese had made a clean sweep. After Pearl Harbor, they kicked us off Wake Island and Guam and out of the Philippines. They kicked the British out of Hong Kong, Burma, Malaya, and Singapore, the Dutch out of Java, the French out of Indochina. They bombed Australia. They took prisoners in the tens of thousands. By US policy, Europe had priority, but the Allies began regrouping in the Pacific. In April 1942, Jimmy Doolittle flew a B-17 bombing raid over Tokyo from the decks of the aircraft carrier Hornet, boosting American morale and demonstrating the Japanese homeland's vulnerability.

We thwarted Japanese designs on Midway Atoll, preserving a strategic outpost. By mid-1943, though Japan battled fiercely and smartly, her comparatively modest industrial base was working against her as the Allies hopped, island-by-island, closer to her home. Darel's nephew Leon—Bob's brother—was a naval radio operator in the Pacific. Clyde's son Richard joined the Army Air Corps in 1943 and served in Europe and Africa.

The war was four years old when I was born, September 15, 1943. About mid-August, Anna left Helen with a babysitter and went to a doctor's appointment. Picking her up, she fell down the porch stairs, breaking her ankle and landing on top of Helen. Ankle, at any rate, was the official story. Helen said Anna wore a full-leg cast and thought she may have broken more.

Either way, it's no exaggeration to say that my birth did Helen more damage than it did our mother. Anna was in the hospital a month, partly because of her fracture and partly because of me. "Mom" Schuddeboom filled in at home. Helen spent the entire month missing her mother, and when her mother came home, she had me—Helen's replacement—with her. Without warning, Helen went from center of attention to outlier and it was my fault. She regressed. Anna and Darel let her revert to the bottle. To make matters worse, it was me that Anna finally decided to breast-feed. Helen registered her displeasure during feedings by bopping me on the head with her bottle, which in that period was glass, not plastic. On her second birthday, she marched around the table insisting, "I'm *not* two years old. I'm *not* two years old." That childhood trauma wounded her deeply. I never had a clue to the grudge she bore until she openly forgave me at age forty-five.

On June 6, 1944, the Allies were finally ready, and launched their European campaign on the beaches of Normandy, the biggest invasion in human history.

On April 12, 1945, an exhausted President Roosevelt died of a cerebral hemorrhage at Warm Springs, Georgia, shocking the nation and plunging it into deep mourning. Harry Truman, having graduated from senator to vice president just three months earlier, was suddenly in the driver's seat of a nation at war, which mercifully ended in Europe a month later. The full horror of Hitler's "final solution" was revealed to the world at large. Earth's only two hostile atomic blasts ended the Pacific war in August.

Chapter Forty-Three

Out of Your Pocket

O N MARCH 6, Darel's mother had died, prompting his essay, "The High Cost of Dying," an indictment of the funeral industry with the declaration of his personal wish to be cremated.

In June, we left our 4-acre Lincolnia farm ("we're going to live here from now on," he'd told Dale). The metropolitan area was in its wartime building boom, and it's easy to picture a developer making Anna and Darel an offer they couldn't refuse for those four prime acres. I haven't found a record of such a transaction, but knowing my family's talent for finance, I'd say the developer made out better than they did. The exchange did enable my parents to acquire the more modern dwelling at 509 Fontaine Street in Alexandria. Perhaps a growing family had rendered the fixer-upper lifestyle untenable.

The September 22 issue of the *Christian Science Monitor* magazine ran Darel's "One Man's Fight for Everybody's Freedom," about an Afton, Tennessee, storekeeper who went to court over the poll tax. His case was pending in the state supreme court as the magazine went to press.

Anna and Darel's fourth child, Tommy, had been born that August. He was hospitalized in February 1946 with an enlarged thymus that was pressing on a lung, making breathing difficult. Radiation was shrinking the thymus, but an X-ray revealed a hole in his heart. In May, Helen discovered him dead in his crib, after Anna had struggled unsuccessfully for twenty-four hours to get a measured quantity of liquid into him.

Darel's work with the Kilgore Committee ended in 1946, but thanks to wartime rationing, cartels were a national cause célèbre. Darel's one published book, *Out of Your Pocket, the story of cartels*, emerged from the committee's investigations.

Getting a book out is no simple process. Cartels had thousands of details needing checking and double and triple checking—just one, the question of revealing the salary of E. H. Bobst of Hoffman-La Roche. For Bobst's efforts on behalf of cartels, Hoffman-La Roche awarded him $300,000, the fifth highest salary in America. Darel obtained the figure legally from the Treasury Department, but it came with a caveat. Information derived from tax returns could not be "sold" or circulated "for consideration."

Periodicals using second-class mail were exempt, but including the figure in *Out of Your Pocket* would be circulating it "for consideration." Violating the provision was worth a $1,000 fine and/or a year in jail. Darel told the publisher he thought keeping the figure was worth the risk. If Bobst took them to court, there would be free publicity for the book and bad publicity for Bobst. Darel didn't think Bobst would take the chance. We don't have the publisher's reply, but the figure is in the book.

Tommy's health was a major distraction as Darel strove to create the manuscript. "My baby was in the hospital under oxygen," he told the publisher in February, "and we were very unsure from day to day whether we would ever bring him home again. It is only in the last two days that we felt sure we would. His case was finally diagnosed as an oversize thymus instead of an oversize heart, which so crowded one lung that that his condition was complicated by pneumonia.

"The X-ray treatments are already shrinking the thymus, he is out of oxygen and seems definitely on the mend. Not only do we feel better as a short-haul proposition, but his condition now seems curable and he has a chance for normal development. (Daily trips to the hospital also cut my writing time at least in half.)" On March 11: "My baby has been back in the hospital, but is home now, this time with diarrhoea [*sic*]. The poor little guy has been through the wringer, and so have the rest of us. I hope what I have written doesn't show it too badly, but I suspect it does."

Other offspring jeopardized progress as well. "Dear Leo, your letter of June 18 was apparently received by small son Jimmy, age 2. I have been piecing it together."

The book appeared on February 3, 1947, to good reviews when reviews there were. It had sold 12,000 copies by July and moved into a second printing. Ultimately there were three printings with sales of 17,000. There were talks of basing a documentary film on the book, though the idea didn't get very far. Warren Bower of WNYC's "Readers Almanac," read *Out of Your Pocket* and asked Darel to an interview for broadcast on March 3. Darel gave that and another interview to broadcaster Raymond Walsh.

A twelve-inch, 78-rpm disc of "a radio interview" survived into our childhood, but it didn't sound anything like our father and we were too young to understand it anyway. It undoubtedly met the same fate as most of those highly breakable 78-rmp discs. The book was published by a division of Reynal and Hitchcock called Pamphlet Press, founded by none other than Joseph Gaer, lately of the Federal Writer's Project.

Pamphlet Press sold its books for a dollar. Reynal and Hitchcock tried to arrange an interview with radio host Mary Margaret McBride, whose nationally syndicated program reached millions of housewives who might have been interested in cartels' effects on household budgets. The interview never happened because, apparently, the show's producers feared the subject would offend sponsors. Darel did get on a local D.C. women's show, and he spoke at Mary Washington College in Fredericksburg, Virginia. He tried getting hugely popular Walter Winchell involved, but there's no evidence that that effort panned out.

A book needs promotion to make money. Rare is the author who can make it happen on his own. A ten percent royalty on 17,000 copies at a dollar each would have netted but $1,700. Leo Huberman, Darel's main contact at Reynal and Hitchcock, apologized to Darel in October for the publisher's poor job on publicity. With a proper campaign, he felt, the book could have sold 100,000 copies. Darel himself had lamented the sluggish sales. "I hear my book sold 7600 copies in the first three weeks," he told Huberman in March.

"That isn't too bad, considering it has had no promotion. And apparently no advertising is budgeted for it. I'm still plugging away as I can, getting it mentioned here and there, but I'm beginning to get a little discouraged as the first month passes with only a scattering of reviews. Darel personally sent thirty copies to various outlets, including popular columnist Drew Pearson, and requested fifty more. He contacted publishers in Sweden (one of the book's personalities was Swedish) and Australia, ultimately unsuccessfully, and tried getting Anna's uncle in Holland, Jaap Mandersloot, involved in a Dutch edition, also without success."

Chapter Forty-Four

FAO

THE FIRST OF 1947 found Darel with a six-month assignment at the National Housing Agency, which was placing returned veterans in prefabricated homes. He was engaged, "in addition to other assignments," to collect information and materials for a movie on the Uniform Plumbing Code test at the National Bureau of Standards. Materials and designs were being tested with a goal, ultimately, of supplying 1 to 1.5 million housing units per year, where traditional methods had been limited to less than 500,000. (The real-estate lobby, naturally, considered the effort an intrusion on its domain, protesting that "we were not suffering from too little housing but from "overconsumption of space.") The job's more prosaic side included preparing fact sheets of specifications offered by the various manufacturers. He was allowed a certain amount of hooky, and spent it promoting *Out of Your Pocket*.

In May, the agency put in for a ninety-day extension of his appointment. It may or may not have gone through; by September, he was with the U.N.'s Food and Agriculture Organization, FAO, the first of his jobs that I remember. It involved editing, proofreading, and marking up other people's writings for publication—many of them book length. It was a month-to-month appointment. He was moonlighting for *Consumers on the March*, a two- to 4-page monthly bulletin of the National Association of Consumers. His "schedule" reminded him of February to June, 1942, when he was finishing up with the Writers' Project.

"I have a piece for *Survey Graphic* to finish, and requests for articles from Andy for the *Arizona Stockman* and the *Southwestern Social Science Quarterly*. Otherwise, I have scarcely a thing to do." The piece for *Survey Graphic* was apparently his *West-by-God* chapter on strip-mining, though I haven't found a copy of the publication, with or without the article. After nearly a year, FAO promised him a permanent, five-year appointment and a pay raise.

Anna's "surprise" birthday present that year was a baby boy named Jerry. He sprang his surprise a day ahead of Anna's actual birthday, on the 13th, dodging March's infamous Ides by a slim two-day margin. We're still not sure that was enough.

On June 15, Darel and Dale bundled Pat into the back seat of "new Dale car," as we kids called his circa 1946 Hudson, and drove to the land of Darel's nativity, in part to glean further material for the strip-mining chapter. Wartime demand for coal had brought strip-miners to West Virginia with a vengeance, and Darel's home county, Harrison, had been the hardest hit of all. The people who bought Dixie, where Darel grew up, had sold out to strip-mining. Pat told of the despoilment, stripping right up to the house's back door. Dale took a series of pictures, but none to a usably illustrative effect.

Emory Stout, whom Darel had played football with in high school, had a farm nearby and knew the bite of the strip-miner's shovel. One method was to "girdle" a hill to get at the underlying coal. The operators would slice downward into the hillside and level out a horizontal bench at the bottom of the cut, going all the way around. At Emory Stout's place, they left his cows marooned on top of the hill. Asked to create a ramp so he could get them down, they tore up 40 more acres of pasture.

The farmers themselves entered these agreements, which brought quick money, but they often failed to think of the environmental effects. The strip-miners said "scenery and industry don't mix."

Darel rejoined, "These hills are not just scenery. They are something to live by. There is something about them that puts you in tune with the Psalmist, where he says, 'I will lift up mine eyes to the hills, from whence cometh my help.' But hills supposed to be smooth and molded and well-buttressed and green can give the native son little strength if they are flayed open and their substance flows out as if from a charnel house. Subtly but strongly, some of the living values of a countryside have been stripped away."

In October, Dale climbed into his Hudson and embarked on a snaking odyssey to various American libraries and state historical societies, collecting material for his Mormon history, building a bibliography of Mormon source materials, and scoping the history of the fur trade. From Dixie he drove straight to New York for a weeks-long assault on that city's public library. (Approaching the city, something had gone "blooey with my gas pedal so it would only accelerate when shoved to the floor.…I had the car fixed the next morning;…the throttle linkage was badly worn.")

He was leaving D.C. for good. "It didn't make sense," Darel wrote him in New Haven, Connecticut, "till that night you came over with the bookcases and the odds and ends, and seeming yourself so utterly weary with a job not yet done.

"Then I knew you were leaving, and Anna knew, and we felt a real sense of loss as 'new Dale car' drove away.

"Since then, I have felt an aversion to any road leading to Rosslyn [Dale's Arlington neighborhood], as if the damn place had no right to be there with Dale gone."

From New Haven, Dale visited Canadaigua, New York, where Church of Latter Day Saints founder Joseph Smith had served 30 days for indebtedness and dictated the Book of Mormon. The town held a repository of much early Church material.

His automotive travails stand testament to motoring in the 1940s. He had his first flat at Canadaigua and had to buy an inner tube. AAA gave him a jump start. The same tire that went flat in Canadaigua "blew itself to hell…at 50 miles an hour the day I left Chicago."

His route from Chicago to his sister and brother-in-law at Fort Leavenworth would have taken him through Carthage, where Jospeh Smith, ordered to stand trial for polygamy, was shot and killed at age 38. He arrived at Leavenworth by Christmas, "with just 71 cents in my pocket and an overdraft of about 91 cents on my checking." He bunked with his in-laws and drove 42 miles each day to the Reorganized Church Library at Independence.

Not, however, before buying yet another tire. "And," he said, "the clutch has been misbehaving. And the brakes have been misbehaving. AND in the last week on three occasions the goddam car has refused to start at all….I had the car gone over pretty thoroughly in Leavenworth, and now, by heaven, it had better behave itself."

After a couple weeks' backtracking through Columbia, Jefferson City, St. Louis, and Springfield, he struck out for an uncle's house at San Marino, California, four blocks from the Huntington Library with its rich collection of rare historialia.

"A few miles south of Hot Springs, N. M.," however, "my right front tire blew out, something that has been an imminent possibility with both my front tires for 5,000 miles. To make matters worse, I had already discarded my spare because of a fearsome blister that developed west of Detroit—a case of ply separation about which nothing could be done except to open the blister with a razor. On those two reassuring tires, one with a serious crack in it, the other my reconverted spare, I drove the last 900 miles. The tires held up, but I shall certainly put at least one new tire on the car before I go north from here." All this by a man who couldn't hear a whisper of sound.

He drove north, visiting the Bancroft Library in Berkeley, before turning east for Salt Lake City, arriving there at the end of March 1948.

Chapter Forty-Five

Wisconsin

University of Wisconsin School for Workers, July 11-24, 1948

AROUND THE TIME Dale's Hudson delivered him home, a 1939 Studebaker replaced our 1934 Plymouth. It "runs well but eats 3 quarts of oil a week," Darel told Dale, and the first order was a ring job. "We had decided to give up the old jalopy and do without, but Easter shopping by bus and taxi broke us down. A friend drove by to pick up a kitten and we bought his old car for $450. A couple of hundred dollars will make it like new (almost). We might even go to Wisconsin in it."

"Wisconsin" was the course Darel taught at the University of Wisconsin's School for Workers. "The car gallantly enough carried us to our destination," he wrote Dale, "which we reached on a Saturday. The next day she shuddered and gave up to a rheumatic ailment in her universal joints. I had a rebuilding done on the front springs, bushings, etc. Except for two flat tires (the same one twice) we had no other trouble, and the car, with new Vitamin B in her joints, came home handily enough. Few cars have been so considerate in timing their breakdowns.

Pat, Jimmy, two unidentified kids, and Helen at the Blackhawk Cabins, Madison

"The two weeks in Madison was [*sic*] busy, even hectic, what with a class to bone up for every day and an evening meeting every day which management hoped I would attend. It did me good personally, for, though I was as frightened as a female valedictorian, I had to get up there every day for 11 days, and by the end I felt like I was pretty well over my stage fright. I presented the material I would like to put in a sequel to my book, found I had perfect freedom of expression, and nobody called me a C-- ------t [Communist]. Apparently, all I need for that is to wait around Washington a little longer. The U. asked me back. I hope this means I gave them fair return for their money.

"We pulled out of Madison Saturday morning the 24th, went east to

Jimmy, Anna holding Buster, Pat, Gladys holding Helen at Niagara Falls

Milwaukee and down the west shore of Lake Michigan through Chicago to Gary, Indiana." In Lakeshore Drive traffic, Helen exclaimed, "We're in a parade!" In Gary, we browsed the beach at Lake Michigan where I saw, or thought I saw, just the upper part of a ship out on the horizon.

The next day was Sunday, and there wasn't a drugstore open in Ann Arbor to buy a milkshake. Farther on, the Detroit River had a bridge and a

Buster, Anna, Gladys, Jimmy, Pat, and Helen at Lake Michigan

tunnel into Canada. We kids voted for the tunnel—who ever knew you could go *under* a river? One more day fetched us up at Niagara Falls, where we crossed back into the United States and the falls made me feel I was racing upstream while standing still. "The falls made the small fry so excited that we had to take them away."

Two days later, we were home.

"So, we had two hitches of life on the road—one going and one coming—which as you know is a separate existence from any other. Hectic, tiring, but often exhilarating. We had another hitch as 'permanent' (two-week) residents in a tourist camp and I as a 'perfessor.' That was hectic too, for I hadn't a minute to prepare before I left. It all came out of the briefcase in daily doses. It was the first real vacation this family—as now constituted—ever had. Now back to editing and publishing for FAO. Steps are being taken to promote me a grade, make me a section chief in charge of preplanning publications, and make me a permanent staff member. At least part of this seems to stand a fair chance of going through, but as of now I'm still temporary."

It had been just mid-June that we'd moved again. "The place," Darel wrote, "is in the little village of Burke. It's a 9-room house on an acre of ground, and I won't begin to catalog its livability. The place has the feel of home, and we all, down to and including Jimmy, fell head over heels in love with it."

In 1948, it was still possible to regard moving the 18 miles from D.C. to Burke as "leaving the Washington area." But, as with Lincolnia, Burke today is just part of the sprawling megalopolis. That acre of land, however, and the house (now dressed in aluminum siding) were still intact a half century later. Dale was "amazed and amused," at the move, "since it is hardly a year since Darel told me he no longer had ambitions to live in the country."

The house had faults, notably the roof, replaced with the help of Willy "Uncle Bill" Harlow, who topped up the job literally fiddling on our roof—"Turkey in the Straw" and other classics. That only came after the new furnace and sewage system. The furnace had expired at mid-winter, $250 thank you please. And an initial repair to the old sewage system ("our $200 hole in the ground") having diverted sewage into the road, a new $350 filtration field tore up the front yard for the summer, 1949. Phil, our "Man Who Came to Dinner," who had shown up earlier that season, helped get it back in trim.

On September 17, they finished sowing grass seed just in time for a torrential thunderstorm to wash most of it back out again. "Ah me! The joys of farming."

Pressures were beginning to tell on Darel. At age 44, "I don't take to treadmills as well as I once did. Two evenings last week I came home so tuckered that I went to bed at 8:30 and 9:30. My damned old bowels tie themselves in knots when the pressure is on, and I've threatened to turn them in on a new set, but you know how prices are on new equipment, and the trade-in on used guts is 16 degrees south of nadir. I suppose I'll have to live with them, but the partnership is not satisfactory.…Reading 184 foolscap pages for last-minute corrections, pressmarking same and getting them off to the printer, leaves little time for anything else until done, including such strictly personal matters as having lunch."

Two years after its release, *Out of Your Pocket* was still selling 100 copies a month. Two years after returning to Utah, Dale, frustrated by the lack of job opportunities and the shortcomings of Utah's research facilities, returned to D.C., arriving in October, 1950. He settled into an apartment in far Southeast D.C. We drove out to see him, crossing South Capitol Street Bridge. A midair turnoff right on the bridge amazed me. I hadn't known bridges could do that.

Off to the right was Bolling Air Base, arrayed on whose tarmac were formations of leftover WWII Grumman F4F Hellcat fighter planes, with wings that folded up. Darel made phone calls for Dale, which deafness prevented him from doing himself, but a year later Dale still hadn't found a position, and was sustaining himself freelancing, writing and editing for the Utah Historical Society, writing book reviews (which, he said, just about kept him in shoelaces) and even an encyclopedia entry, and by occasional loans from family and friends. On October 14, 1950, he wrote to Darel. His typewriter's "s" had broken and he substituted the "z" in its place.

Juzt like the mozt thrilling horze opera, when I got home lazt night, there under my door waz a telegram from Eberztadt zaying the check waz on the way. Zo thiz morning here came the check, the whole of it, zpecial delivery airmail. In conzequence, when the bank openz Monday morning I will be zolvent again and can even get my car out of hock. Accordingly, I return herewith the check your zo generouzly wrote for me, and zuggest that you zpend it on righteouz living of zome dezcription.

Howdya like my charming new accent?

He also copied the 1788 New York law under which Joseph Smith had been jailed for indebtedness, substituting the "f" for the archaic "long s," to equally comic effect.

He borrowed money on his car. He translated a German-speaking Swiss pioneer's memoir—hand-written in an archaic script—into English relying solely on a German-English dictionary, as he knew not a word of German. The professor who commissioned the translation offered to certify him to Civil Service as an expert translator! He declined. When he wasn't job-hunting, he was busy at his Library of Congress study shelf.

"One of these days my luck will turn," he said, "and when it does, I bet that in one mail I will be offered a historian's job by one agency, and information specialist's job by another, six magazine articles, and the revision of the Utah guide, all requiring to be done at one and the same time. But I would rather have experiences of that kind than this hellish barrel-scraping."

Darel had fared better. As of New Year's Day, 1949, FAO had locked in his appointment through the end of 1952. "I never had that much security in my life," he told Dale. "Guess I'll have to quit in the middle of it for lack of economic excitement." And as things turned out, he did. When FAO moved its headquarters to Rome in May, 1951, it offered Darel a 15-year appointment to go with them. After due consideration, he decided not to and resigned without immediate prospects.

In the employment lull, he turned back to his typewriter. In April 1949, he'd pulled his novel, *The Earth-Speaking*, that he'd tried to peddle in New York in 1934, out of mothballs. He told to Dale, "I got to reading and went right through till I'd finished. It is still fresh and still holds, at least the author's interest. Maybe when you come in the fall, I'll have it in shape to show you."

A year and a half later, Dale read the manuscript and commented, possibly in person, as we only have Darel's written response. "I could see," Darel said, "that the first part was altogether too saccharine. It needed uglifying."

The hero's name, Svastika, would have to be changed. "The supernatural closing, as you have observed, will have to come out. Obviously, the fishermen and the hunter are going to smell trouble. Just as obviously they are going to rescue our hero after he is dumped in the drink. The volcanic eruption can erupt as before, but only for atmosphere.

"The big question remains, of course, whether it is worth doing after all. Does it *say* something? Is it in tune with the anguished cries beginning to be heard from Africa, from Indo-China, etc.? If not, then let's consign it again to the archives and get back to really real things. I don't want it to be called a watered-down *Cry the Beloved Country*."

At the end of 1950, he set to work turning the Father April material into a story, and we hear no more of *Earth-Speaking*. But the two men launched unsparing critiques of each other's writings, Darel now casting his eye over Dale's Mormon history, the first installment of which had been due at Farrar and Rinehart the previous September.

In February, our family reached its full complement with the arrival of Mary on the 22nd, George Washington's birthday.

Darel continued refining *Father April*, and he drafted a letter for Senator Kilgore's signature recommending to the *Charleston Gazette* that they serialize *West by God Virginia*. "It was a good letter," he said. "I wrote it myself." That effort fizzled, but he plotted further sorties.

Chapter Forty-Six

Aftosa

SCARCELY A MONTH after FAO, a prospect opened at the Department of Agriculture. They were looking for someone to write the history of a 1947 foot-and-mouth outbreak in Mexico that was still ongoing.

It was three months between FAO's final paycheck and Agriculture's first, and the bank account was depleted. At the Hotel Monte Cassino in Mexico City, where we first stayed, Darel complained that we couldn't afford to stay and couldn't afford to leave. We could run up the tab but couldn't pay it. Until, at last, his first check came through.

Collecting and drafting the material extended the project's Mexico phase to a year and a half.

Dale had begun work on his signature opus, *Jedediah Smith and the Opening of the West*, and Darel, with Carlos Bosch as interpreter and cultural safari guide, combed Mexican archives looking for Smith's diary, unfortunately without success. Much of Smith's sojourn had been in California which, in his day, belonged to Mexico. The name, "Jedidiah Smith," echoed through our childhood.

Once back home—back in Burke—Darel cut the aftosa draft nearly in half. There were few at the Department of Agriculture inclined or qualified to take on the book's prepublication phase, so Darel, as he had done for FAO, undertook the process. The finished work ran 371 printed pages, including 77 illustrations.

But, at the page-proof stage, the project was suspended over objections by two Mexican officials and was not resurrected after their deaths. It had been a monumental effort. Darel persuaded them to give him an author's credit, rare for government publications. The credit is buried in the book's "Letter of Transmittal." In 2019, the family donated its personal, deteriorating set of page proofs to the National Agricultural Library.

After foot-and-mouth, Agriculture assigned him to screw-worm eradication.

We sold Burke—possibly in part because the Federal Aeronautics Administration was considering Burke as a site for Dulles International Airport—and moved to the farm. (Dulles ultimately landed in Chantilly, Virginia, displacing classmates at our high school in Leesburg.)

Chapter Forty-Seven

Are You Now, or Have You Ever Been.
A Member of the Communist Party?

A 1948 Herblock Cartoon © The Herb Block Foundation.

ONE TALE REMAINS. Darel told Arthur Schlesinger, Jr., that *Out of Your Pocket* had caused him "a good deal of harassment during the Joe McCarthy period." This was "The Second Red Scare," a reprise of the 1920s Scare. You minded your words lest some stray phrase mark you a Communist. It was a time of loyalty oaths, the House Un-American Activities

Committee, of Alger Hiss and Whittaker Chambers, of Julius and Ethel Rosenberg, of "McCarthyism."

It's helpful to review the Communist hysteria of the 1940s and '50's, spurred to warp speed by Russia's getting nuclear weapons. Anticommunists hadn't prospered in the Depression. And in WWII Stalin had been an American ally. But now war and depression were over, and Stalin was still up to his tricks. At the Yalta Conference in February 1945, that planned for post-war Europe, he promised free elections in the countries held by the Red Army, provided Churchill and Roosevelt guaranteed him free rein. The ink was hardly dry before Stalin was imposing communism. Barely a year after Yalta, Churchill declared, "An iron curtain has descended across the Continent." Miles of border fencing, and shoot-to-kill guards, frustrated but didn't stop escapes to the West.

In 1924, twenty-three-year-old Whittaker Chambers had read Vladimir Lenin's *Soviets at Work* and projected his own dysfunctional childhood onto America's middle-class malaise. A year later, he joined the Communist Party. In the mid-1930s, while opponents were struggling vainly to tar the New Deal with communism, Chambers was couriering secrets from spies in the American government to Soviet intelligence agents.

When Stalin's Great Purge began in 1936, however, Chambers lost faith. A friend and fellow spy was "disappeared" on a trip to Moscow. Chambers, fearing a similar fate, refused orders to appear in Moscow and left the Party. Taking some documents and microfilm as insurance, he went into hiding. He never meant to rat his fellow spies, many of them friends, but when the Soviet Union signed its non-aggression pact with Nazi Germany in 1939, he changed his mind and leveled his sights on Alger Hiss.

Overweight and slovenly, Chambers was the opposite of Hiss, who was tall, patrician, a graduate of Johns Hopkins and Harvard Law, had clerked for Oliver Wendell Holmes and served as Assistant to Assistant Secretary of State Francis B. Sayer, Woodrow Wilson's son-in-law. In 1939, Chambers's accusation that Hiss was a Communist went nowhere. In 1944, Hiss served as executive secretary to the Dumbarton Oaks Conference, which planned the United Nations. In 1945, he was part of the US delegation at Yalta.

But in 1948, Chambers's renewed accusation pricked the ears of freshman Representative Richard Nixon of the House Un-American Activities Committee (HUAC), who pegged his career on the anticommunist star and sped off after Hiss. Hiss denied that he had ever been a Communist or that he had ever met Chambers. Charges and countercharges flew. Chambers upped the ante from Party membership to espionage. Hiss sued Chambers for defamation.

The affair exploded in the media. Chambers's purloined documents convinced HUAC that Hiss had lied both about his Party membership and about not knowing Chambers. The statute of limitations had expired on his spying, but Nixon had Hiss tried for perjury. The first trial ended in a hung jury. On January 21, 1950, the second jury convicted. Hiss went to jail and Richard Nixon advanced to the Senate.

President Truman had no patience with the "Communist bugaboo," but the Republicans had used it in the 1946 midterms to gain their first congressional majorities since 1932. Ahead of the 1948 presidential campaign, to stave off Republican "soft on communism" charges, Truman signed an Executive Order requiring all federal employees—Darel McConkey included—to sign loyalty oaths, and created loyalty boards to investigate answers.

The Hiss/Chambers hearings stoked public anti-Communist jitters. When Truman insisted that the hearings were a "red-herring" designed to smear his administration, public positions hardened. It didn't help his case when he refused to give HUAC the results of the loyalty investigations. But in early 1948, FBI director J. Edgar Hoover sent Truman's Attorney General a 1,350-page brief and seventeen likely suspects to use against the Communist Party under the Smith Act, which made it illegal to advocate or belong to an organization advocating overthrow of the government. The act had passed in 1940 but, the Soviets being our wartime ally, hadn't been used. A successful prosecution now, Hoover calculated, would establish communism's illegality. Though the Justice Department, not the White House, owned the case, it helped Truman eke out his win.

It also bankrupted America's Communist Party, whose only defense had been to try winning public support. To buy time to develop its PR, it swamped the court with frivolous motions. As soon as the judge denied one motion, it filed another. Demonstrations around the courthouse swelled and got rowdier. Inside, the defense lawyers and their clients repeatedly interrupted the proceedings. The judge began sending uncooperative defendants to jail for contempt until just six remained.

It was the longest criminal trial in US history to that time, November 1948 to October 1949. In the end, the Communist attempt to win over the public just made the public sick of the attempt. The defendants were found guilty, their appeals were futile, their funds were exhausted. The Communist Party USA was no longer a force worth reckoning with.

The Hiss trial escalated anti-Communist hysteria, but in substance it couldn't compare to Julius and Ethel Rosenberg. The FBI had begun by tracking the wrong man, J. Robert Oppenheimer, head of the hyper-secret "Manhattan Project" that created America's atom bomb, but ended with the Rosenbergs.

Under the influence of women in his life, one he didn't marry and one he did, Oppenheimer had like many others joined the Communist Party in the 1930s. But he understood physics better than Marxist theory, and by the time he took over the bomb project, he was no longer a member. That fact did not spare him intense FBI scrutiny. In its zeal for Oppenheimer, the FBI neglected a far bigger fish, Klaus Fuchs.

Fuchs was a brilliant German physicist who had gone Communist in 1932 in reaction to Nazism, from whose blandishments he fled to England in 1933. In May 1940, England, by then at war with Germany, declared Fuchs an enemy alien and sent him to a Canadian internment camp. They took him back in December, however, forgave him his politics, and put his brain to work on Britain's own atomic bomb. He swore loyalty and took British citizenship.

In late 1943, he came to America with a team of British scientists, settled in New York, and began funneling secrets to the Soviet Union. In July 1944, the Manhattan Project whisked him off to its headquarters at Los Alamos, New Mexico, smack in the middle of the action. Arguably, he helped the Soviets develop their bomb two or three years sooner than they otherwise would have. The FBI finally fingered him in 1949, four years *after* the war, when he was back in England. It tipped off British Intelligence, which tried him for violating the Official Secrets Act, and on March 1, 1950, gave him fourteen years.

Decrypted transmissions from the Soviet embassy in D.C. to Moscow put the FBI on the scent of Fuch's courier, Harry Gold. Under questioning, Gold verified his collaboration with Fuchs, and named a draftsman at Los Alamos named David Greenglass…Ethel Rosenberg's brother. And that is how, five years after the war, the FBI landed on the Rosenberg spy ring. They had passed thousands of top-secret documents on radar, sonar, and jet propulsion to the

Soviets, few of them, however, pertaining meaningfully to nuclear bomb-making. Julius was the ringmaster. Ethel's role was sympathy with the cause and the transcribing of documents that Julius passed along. The two were nevertheless found equally guilty and sentenced to death. They were electrocuted at Sing Sing on June 19, 1953.

The execution, as much as the crimes for which the Rosenbergs were executed, sent American public debate freewheeling into the stratosphere. This was the climate Joe McCarthy rang into.

The American Communist Party was comatose, but what counted was perception. Joe was Michigan's unremarkable junior Senator in need of an issue when he gave an assigned, lower-echelon, Lincoln Day speech in Wheeling, West Virginia, February 9, 1950. "I have in my hand," he intoned, "a list of 205…a list of names that were known to the Secretary of State as being members of the Communist Party and who, nevertheless, are still working and shaping policy in the State Department."

Two hundred five was the number of cases the State Department had been looking at as of August 1946, three and a half years earlier. The next day in Salt Lake City, Joe changed it to 57, the number of cases still pending as of a 1948 House committee hearing. There were, in fact, no significant threats left at the State Department, but when Joe spoke, the public had just had Klaus Fuchs's confession, Alger Hiss had been convicted the previous month, Mao Tse-tung had turned China red the previous October, and the Soviets had exploded their atomic bomb the previous August, leading Robert Oppenheimer to equate the US and the USS.R. to "scorpions in a bottle."

Four months after Wheeling, North Korea invaded South Korea. That war spawned reports of mysterious oriental methods of mind control called brainwashing, and fears spread that Americans could be turned Communist without even knowing it. The public was primed for McCarthy, and he lost no time clambering onto the wagon and stepping to the driver's seat.

It was called the McCarthy era, but outside the 1953–54 Army-McCarthy hearings (which ultimately torpedoed McCarthy's reign of terror), the senator did little investigating himself. Instead, he became the megaphone for imaginary dangers, railing mainly from his Senate seat, which shielded him from libel.

The Hollywood blacklist was already a going concern when McCarthy showed up. Since 1947 HUAC, working hand-in-glove with the conservative

Motion Picture Alliance for the Preservation of American Ideals, had been hauling people up, grilling them, demanding they name names, jailing them for pleading the Fifth—tactics Martin Dies had pioneered back while smearing Federal One. The studios blacklisted those who ran afoul of HUAC, refusing to employ them. McCarthy invented none of it but got credit for it all.

The threat to government workers came not from McCarthy but from Harry Truman's loyalty boards. Truman gave no credence to "the bugaboo of communism." He'd created the loyalty boards during the 1948 election campaign solely to fend off charges that he was "soft on communism." He didn't expect the boards to find much, and they didn't. By mid-1949, of more than 2.5 million employees, just over 10,000 got full-field investigations; 5,450 got hearings, in which 5,118 were cleared, 102 were fired and 320 were under appeal.

As early as August 1948, after teaching in Wisconsin, Darel had couched his language in a letter to Dale: "I had perfect freedom of expression," he said of the course, "and nobody called me a C-------t. Apparently all I need for that is to wait around Washington a little longer." His own tête-à-tête with the red hunters didn't happen until 1952. Darel had been one of the 5,450 who warranted hearings, though owing to his being in Mexico, his interview was conducted by mail rather than in person. No subject of investigation, Darel included, was told where the FBI got its information.

Q. It has been reported that on April 18, 1947, you were a speaker on the topic, "The Cartel System," at a membership meeting of the Washington Cooperative Bookshop (Washington Bookshop Association), Washington, D.C.

Inasmuch as the Washington Bookshop Association has been declared by the Attorney General to be within the purview of Executive Order 9835 [Truman's loyalty boards], please explain in detail the reason for your attendance at a membership meeting of that organization, the nature and purpose of the meeting and the substance of your remarks on that occasion.

A. I spoke before the Washington Bookshop as a new author whose book on the subject of cartels had been recently published. I was under the impression that they were inviting various authors to address different meetings. I had no other reason for going than that of stimulating sales of my book; I made a number of other talks for the same purpose at about that same time. I spoke on the subject matter of my book. I am puzzled at the reference to a 'membership meeting.' I have no memory of membership business transacted on that occasion.

Q. Are you now or have you ever been a member of the Washington Bookshop Association? If so, please furnish full particulars, including the dates of your membership and the extent of your activities therein.

A. Never.

Q. Have you ever made any contributions in money or services to the Washington Bookshop Association? If so, please give details.

A. Never.

Q. It has also been reported that on June 10, 1947, you took the part of a witness in a "mock trial" entitled "the People vs. High Prices," which was held at the Hotel Pennsylvania at New York City under the auspices of the New York City Consumers Council and the New York Chapter of the National Association of Consumers. It has also been reported that the New York City Consumers Council was controlled by Communist Party members. Please state in detail the nature of your participation in the above affair and whether you knew that it was either directly or indirectly under Communist influence or control.

A. I was invited to attend the "mock trial" in much the same way I was invited to the Washington Bookshop—as a new author, and I accepted for the same reason as given above. I "testified" in much the same way as I had in the book. I had no indication that the New York Consumers Council was controlled by Communists.

Q. Are you acquainted with Chares Kramer [a known Communist]? If so, what has been the extent of your association with him?

A. Charles Kramer was on the staff of the Kilgore Committee at the same time as I was. I had no association with him outside the office and no great amount there, since I was employed as a writer, working under other people.

Q. Are you acquainted with Henry Hill Collins? If so, what has been the extent of your association with him?

A. Henry Collins was head of the staff of the Kilgore Committee when I went to work there. Because I was working under a chief of information, I had little to do with him directly in the office and no social contacts outside the office. Such work as he had for me to do, I assume, he passed on to me through the information chief. This line of command was observed pretty strictly, and that is why I had little contact with either Collins or Kramer.

Q. Are you acquainted with George F. Willison? If so, what has been the extent of your association with him?

A. George Willison was an employee of the WPA Writers Program during a good part of the time that I was. Our work was not in the same department and our contacts were semioccasional. I believe my wife and I saw the Willisons socially on two or three occasions but we have been out of touch with them for years.

Q. Are you acquainted with Jeanette Turner? If so, what has been the extent of your association with her?

A. I am not acquainted with Jeanette Turner unless she is a rather tubby lady introduced to me as Mrs. Turner at the "mock trial" in New York. If this is the person you mean, I have had no association with her except an introduction.

Q. Are you acquainted with Merle Colby? If so, what has been the extent of your association?

A. I have known Merle Colby since the days of the WPA Writers Program. We had no work in common during that program. I have met with him socially on a few occasions but not more than twice in the last five years.

Q. Did you during your association with any of the foregoing persons attend any meetings with them or any of them or at the request or invitation of any of them? If so, please furnish details.

A. To the best of my recollection, a true answer is no. I have never attended many meetings and have never been a "joiner."

Q. Have you ever subscribed to or regularly read the "Daily Worker" newspaper? If so, please furnish dates and reasons for your interest in this publication.

A. No.

Q. If your answer to Question 11 is in the negative, can you account for the fact that your name, telephone number, and address were contained in the desk telephone directory of the "Daily Worker" in Washington, D.C.?

A. I cannot account for this astonishing fact. In the absence of any date connected with this entry, I can only make a supposition which may or may not be true. During my time on the Kilgore Committee, we furnished press releases and statements at various times to all Washington newspapers and to many Washington correspondents. They may have put my name down as a news contact on the Committee, but I don't really know. I don't recall having ever given any news to them.

Q. Have you ever been a member of the Communist Political Association, the Communist Party, or any of their affiliated organizations? If so, please furnish particulars, including names of organizations and dates of membership.

A. Never.

Q. Have you ever attended any meetings of the Communist Political Association, the Communist Party or any of their affiliated organizations? If so, please furnish details.

A. Never to my knowledge. If the Washington Bookshop is considered an "affiliated organization," the answer is yes in this one instance.

Q. Have you ever made any contributions in money or services to the Communist Political Association, the Communist Party, or any of their affiliated organizations? If so, please furnish details.

A. Never.

Q. Have you ever advocated or been a member of an organization that advocated the overthrow of the United States Government by unconstitutional means? Please answer fully.

A. No.

Q. Are you a member of any organization that has been designated by the Attorney General as within the purview of Executive Order 9835? (For listing, see Title VIII, Paragraph 2398, Administrative Regulations, attached.) If so, name the organization and state the date your membership began.

A. I have read this list carefully. Most of these organizations I never heard of. I never belonged to any of them.

Q. If you are now a member of any such organization, please state your intention with respect to continuing such membership, in view of the fact that it has now been called to your attention that the organization has been cited by the Attorney General.

A. ----

Q. Please give in your own words any amplification of your answers to the foregoing questions that will explain or tend to explain your answers, or, particularly if your answers are in the negative, any implications in either the questions or the answers that you feel warrant explanation.

A. I do not understand the intent of this question. I have answered these questions as honestly as I know how, and there are no reservations to unqualified negatives where used. It is awkward to deal with these matters at this distance and in writing, but I am ready to answer any further questions you may have, either in writing or verbally to any designated representative who might be in this vicinity. I am more anxious than anyone to establish the fact that I am not, have never been, and never expect to be a Communist.

I, Darel McConkey, hereby swear (or affirm) that the foregoing answers to the respective questions are true and correct to the best of my knowledge and belief, and are given without any mental reservations whatsoever.

Darel McConkey
4 April 1952.

He was given a clean bill of ideological health. On July 18, 1957, Agriculture gave him a career appointment—$8,645 a year. Eight months later, he had a heart attack.